KU-687-336

FATHERHOOD AND FAMILY POLICY

Edited by

MICHAEL E. LAMB
University of Utah

ABRAHAM SAGI
University of Haifa
Israel

1983

LAWRENCE ERLBAUM ASSOCIATES, PUBLISHERS
Hillsdale, New Jersey   London

710 043078-4

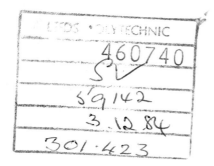

LEEDS POLYTECHNIC

460740

SV

5'9 142

3.12 84

301·423

Copyright ©1983 by Lawrence Erlbaum Associates, Inc.
All rights reserved. No part of this book may be reproduced in
any form, by photostat, microform, retrieval system, or any other
means, without the prior written permission of the publisher.

Lawrence Erlbaum Associates, Inc., Publishers
365 Broadway
Hillsdale, New Jersey 07642

Library of Congress Cataloging in Publication Data
Main entry under title:

Fatherhood and family policy.

Bibliography: p.
Includes index.
1. Fathers—Addresses, essays, lectures. 2. Father
and child—Addresses, essays, lectures. 3. Family
policy—Addresses, essays, lectures. 4. Child rearing
—Addresses, essays, lectures. 5. Custody of
children—Addresses, essays, lectures. I. Lamb,
Michael E., 1953–   . II. Sagi, Abraham.
HQ756.F38   1983   306.8'742   82-18282
ISBN 0-89859-190-2

Printed in the United States of America
10 9 8 7 6 5 4 3 2 1

Contents

£ 17.50

Quarter Library

must return this item on or before the date on
receipt.
ɹ return this item late you will be charged a fine
may be able to renew this item by using the
'v?' Hotline (0113 283 6161), or the Library

71 0043078 4
LEEDS BECKETT UNIVERSITY

FATHERHOOD AND FAMILY POLICY

Preface

In the last two decades, countries throughout the Western world have witnessed dramatic changes in social attitudes concerning sex roles. Traditional assumptions that women should devote themselves to their roles as wives and mothers while men should assume primary responsibility for economic support of the family have been widely reexamined. Spurred by the Women's Liberation Movement and by economic pressures, an increasing number of women have assumed permanent and personally important roles in the work force. Although many barriers remain, many of the industrial countries have passed legislation designed to ensure equal employment and legal opportunities for women.

Despite these efforts, many inequities remain. One reason for the slow progress appears to be that in their single-minded focus on equal opportunities for women, reformers have ignored the need to change attitudes regarding men's roles as well. As long as women have to fulfill the demands of two roles (family and employment) while men are responsible only for employment, inequities will remain, and women's advancement will be constrained. Apparently, then, further improvement in the status of women seems to depend on the increased involvement of men in their family roles. Child care seems to be a critical area; the extensive and enduring burdens of child care are traditionally borne nearly exclusively by women. Even when men wish to assume increased parental responsibilities, however, there exist many institutional, economic, legal, and attitudinal barriers. The goal of this book is to review the evidence concerning: a) the factors that limit or constrain male involvement in child care; b) the ways in which some of these factors are being or might be changed; and c) the effects of traditional and increased paternal involvement on men, women, and children. The book thus involves bringing together the scholarly literature and contemporary social policy concerns and should thus be of interest to professionals in fields as diverse as psychology, law, women's studies, social work, journalism, and sociology.

The attempt to examine fatherhood from this novel perspective began in a study group that was organized by Dr. Sagi and was held in Haifa, Israel in the summer of 1980. The book was written over the next two years by the participants and other invited contributors. The resulting volume represents the first attempt to address the issues surrounding social policies that affect fatherhood and men's involvement with their children.

Neither the study group nor this volume would have been possible without the support of the Foundation for Child Development (through the Society for Research in Child Development's Committee on Study Groups) and the Crossman Chair at the University of Haifa, School of Social Work. The Foundation for Child Development is a private foundation that makes grants to educational and charitable institutions. Its main interests are in research, social and economic indicators of children's lives, advocacy and public information projects, and service experiments that help translate theoretical knowledge about children into policies and practices that affect their daily lives. The Richard Crossman Chair at the University of Haifa School of Social Work is committed to the development and dissemination of knowledge in the area of social policy and planning. The Chair sponsors research in all areas of social and welfare policy, and attempts to mediate between scholars and policy makers, to the benefit of both. We are grateful to the School of Social Work at the University of Haifa, the Society for Research in Child Development, and the Foundation for Child Development for their support, as well as to Dr. Gabriel Lanyi at the University of Haifa for superbly handling all administrative details; to Prof. Naomi Golan, Dean of the School of Social Work at the University of Haifa for both financial and emotional support; and to Ms. Karen Boswell at the University of Utah who prepared the subject index after Dr. Lamb assumed partial editorial responsibilities.

Michael E. Lamb
Abraham Sagi

List of Contributors

Rivka Eisikovits, *Schools of Education and Social Work, University of Haifa, Haifa, Israel*

Eliezer D. Jaffe, *School of Social Work, Hebrew University of Jerusalem, Jerusalem, Israel*

Lois W. Hoffman, *Department of Psychology, University of Michigan, Ann Arbor, Michigan*

Sheila B. Kamerman, *School of Social Work, Columbia University, New York City*

Michael E. Lamb, *Departments of Psychology, Psychiatry, and Pediatrics, University of Utah, Salt Lake City, Utah*

James A. Levine, *Office of Program Development, Bank Street College of Education, New York City*

Joseph H. Pleck, *Center for Research on Women, Wellesley College, Wellesley, Massachusetts*

Norma Radin, *School of Social Work, University of Michigan, Ann Arbor, Michigan*

Graeme Russell, *School of Behavioural Sciences, Macquarie University, North Ryde, New South Wales, Australia*

Abraham Sagi, *School of Social Work, University of Haifa, Haifa, Israel*

Nachman Sharon, *School of Social Work, University of Haifa, Haifa, Israel*

Ross A. Thompson, *Department of Psychology, University of Nebraska, Lincoln, Nebraska*

Martin Wolins, *School of Social Welfare, University of California, Berkeley, California*

1 Fatherhood and Social Policy in International Perspective: An Introduction

Michael E. Lamb
University of Utah

Social policy is not a novel concept, for societies have implemented one or another form of family policy since before the introduction of income tax. Systematic family policies, however, were first developed by some European countries during the first half of the present century; less systematic policies designed in haphazard fashion to address specific problems as they arose were introduced by governments in other Western industrialized countries during the same period. Regardless of their comprehensiveness and systematic nature, however, family policies have (with a few notable exceptions) been concerned primarily with women and children. True, many legislative and administrative mandates assumed that males should take primary responsibility for the economic support of women and dependent children, but women and children were generally considered the groups to be protected. As a result, family policy is typically viewed as a "women's issue." The Conference on Fatherhood, Social Policy, and the Law took issue with this basic assumption. The participants in that conference, and the contributors to this volume, propose that effective family policies must consider the family and parental roles of men as well as women if these policies are to be equitable and if they are to achieve the goals intended by their architects. The purpose of this volume is to: a) discuss the ways in which official family policies in Western industrialized countries have dealt with fathers and male roles in the family in general; and b) articulate the likely consequences of changes in family policies designed to accord greater significance to male roles within the family. The present chapter reviews the principal issues that must be addressed in analyzing male roles in the family and sociopolitical supports for them.

The conference participants and the contributors to this volume adopted an unusually broad definition of family social policy. Whereas the term social policy commonly refers to legislatively derived policies, we are concerned here with all policies and practices relating to family responsibilities, opportunities, and rights, whether they result from legislative action or inaction, patterns of judicial implementation and interpretation, or institutional practices in both the private and public sectors. In other words, we are concerned with all practices, whatever their basis, that limit or enhance paternal involvement in the care, supervision, support, and socialization of children.

Why, the reader may ask, devote such single-minded attention to fatherhood and social policies pertaining to male roles in child care? Are not the rights of women, of children, and of society at large worthy of attention? Indeed they are, and although our focus is on fathers, readers will repeatedly find us referring to the responsibilities and rights of these other groups too. We believe, however, that one particularly crucial issue in the area of contemporary social and family policy concerns the rights, opportunities, and responsibilities of fathers.

The rationale for our focus is perhaps best illustrated by an examination of historical trends in the family social sciences. Although under common law, fathers were considered the heads of their households and thus the proprietors of all property and individuals in the household, social scientists have usually viewed fathers as nominal heads of their families only—authoritative, to be sure, but somewhat distantly involved in family relationships and household tasks. The primary role accorded to fathers was that of economic provider (Parsons & Bales, 1955). Over the last century, the assumptions of social scientists and their popular correlates have seen expression in the development of a variety of family policies. In the legal arena, for example, fathers' rights as the owners of wives and children were superceded around the turn of the century. It was argued that young children need the tender care of their mothers, and hence that they should be placed in the custody of their mothers rather than their fathers in the case of divorce. Only recently has this "tender years doctrine" been challenged successfully in the courts. In the vast majority of cases, however, judicial decisions, which ostensibly consider the "best interests of the child" without regard for the parent's gender, actually follow the dictates of the tender years doctrine in fact, if not by law.

Similar presumptions regarding the preeminence of mothers pervade other areas of social policy. The welfare system in the United States, for example, pays special attention to the needs of mothers with dependent children. One consequence of this concern is the well-known fact that it is financially advantageous to mothers and children for unemployed fathers to leave home, rather than remain with their families while searching for employment. Underlying practices like this lies the assumption that women and children are entitled to support by men, and that when men fail (for whatever reason) to provide this support, the state accepts responsibility in their stead. This assumption has translated into legislative edict and administrative policy the notion that men's family roles are primarily economic, and that (by implication) their roles as socializing agents and as emotional supports for mothers and children are either insignificant or not in the state's interest to defend.

In another arena, consider the attitudes of employers (in both the private and public sector) when the demands of family and employment roles conflict. As far as women are concerned, this is an area in which considerable progress has been achieved. Over the last few years, for example, employed women have fought for and in many cases won the right to *maternity* leave. The need for supplementary out-of-home care for young children has led to the development and subsidization of various forms of day care for the children of employed *mothers*. Many employers have come to recognize the responsibilities of parenthood by allowing *female employees* to use their sick leave to stay home with sick children. Other employers have increased the flexibility of work roles by introducing practices such as flexitime and shared jobs. In each case, however, the concern, either explicit or implicit, has been with female employees. With few exceptions, employers have consistently assumed that work and family role conflicts are salient only in the case of wives and mothers; rarely is there concern for what employment demands may be doing to the family involvement and responsibilities of husbands and fathers. Preoccupations of this sort have thus dominated the analysis of ''women's issues'' such as child care, support in the form of Aid for Families with Dependent Children, maternity leave, and equal employment opportunities in most of the Western industrialized nations.

The popular presumptions underlying these trends in the social policy arena also had an impact on the theorizing and research endeavors of social scientists. Like policy makers, they constructed theories of family function and socialization that defined men as the instrumental and economic leaders of the family; expressive emotional roles, including those deemed essential to child rearing and socialization, were accorded to women. So thoroughgoing were these assumptions that social scientists came to use the terms ''parents'' and ''mothers'' interchangeably. A vast body of literature on socialization focused nearly exclusively on maternal influences (Lamb, 1975). Maternal deprivation was viewed as potentially the most disruptive event in child development; that most studies involved paternal deprivation as well went unremarked for decades (Rutter, 1972). When fathers and paternal influences were considered, they were either deemed trivial or were viewed as important only by virtue of the hostile, competitive, distant characteristics of father-child relationships.

It was only a little over a decade ago that these assumptions began to be questioned by researchers. Earlier studies of father absence or paternal deprivation were undertaken as a means of exploring the significance of paternal influences. Dissatisfied with this strategy, researchers began in the early 1970s to explore directly the formation of father-child relationships, the distinction characteristics of mother- and father-child relationships, and the various ways in which fathers directly and indirectly contribute to their children's development (Lamb, 1976, 1981). Consideration of these diverse issues pointed toward a common conclusion, namely that whereas theorists had correctly identified mothers as the major sources of direct influence in traditional families, they had mistakenly assumed that they were exclusively important, and had thus ignored the many important ways in which fathers too affected both family functioning and child development.

The acknowledgement and recognition of paternal influences on child development occurred—probably not coincidentally—at a critical point in the lives of the civil rights and women's rights movements. For all the legislative and economic progress that had been made in the 1960s, equality had certainly not been achieved by the beginning of the 1970s. More importantly, an increasing number of the movements' leaders had come to realize that further progress toward the attainment of women's rights was dependent on changes in men's roles. First in Scandinavia and later in other countries, reformers came to realize that social and gender roles are intimately interrelated, because male and female roles are largely defined in relation to one another. Consequently, it is impossible to bring about major changes in either without complementary changes in the other. More specifically, it was recognized that women were not going to achieve equal opportunity in the employment sector, or become full participants in this sector, unless and until men assumed an increasing responsibility for family or home work. Equitable solutions were impossible so long as women who were weighed by both family and employment responsibilities had to compete with men whose primary—if not sole—responsibilities were in the workplace. To the extent that maternal and female employment were of value to women, their families, and the society at large, therefore, changing male roles—particularly changes that involved increased male participation in home and child care—were viewed as desirable from the perspectives of both women and society.

Changing male roles, however, potentially affect two other groups whose interests have to be considered—children and men. Because the raising and socialization of children is viewed as a primary responsibility of families, it is important to demonstrate that changing male roles will have beneficial effects, or at least not have harmful effects, on children. In fact, this has been a controversial issue, although the limited empirical evidence (most of which is reviewed by Hoffman in Chapter 10 and by Russell and Radin in Chapter 11) largely shows that children are not necessarily harmed either by the involvement of their mothers in the employment sector or by the unusually great involvement of their fathers in child care.

However great our collective commitment to the rights and interests of children, it is probably the case that men would not willingly choose nontraditional male roles simply because these would benefit children, women, or even society at large. Realistically, men are unlikely to relinquish social roles that accord them power and free them of time-consuming family responsibilities unless they believe that changes in these roles are likely to be advantageous to them. However, some recent surveys show that at least some young men would welcome a role change that allowed them to pursue emotional fulfillment in close family relationships (Sheehy, 1979), which would be one likely consequence of increased paternal involvement in child care. The costs and benefits of paternal participation as we know them today are evaluated in Chapter 9.

In sum, our focus on Fatherhood and Social Policy does not derive from a belief that paternal roles alone are worthy of close scrutiny. Rather, it emerges from the realization that gender roles, and social roles in general, are intimately interrelated such that any effort to equalize the lot of women cannot ignore the roles and responsibilities of men. More specifically, it is our belief that at this point in the evolution of modern, industrial, democratic societies, the major stumbling block to equal opportunity and egalitarianism are popular, legislative, administrative, and judicial attitudes and assumptions regarding male roles in the family. Hence our focus on fatherhood and social policy.

Equal employment opportunity and equal rights for men and women represent policy goals that are shared by many but by no means all citizens of the industrialized nations. For many others, the commitment to equal rights represents a frontal assault on the family and on society as they wish to preserve it. Both of these beliefs reflect controversial and deeply internalized values that democracies are bound to defend. These values are intimately related to the issues with which this volume is concerned. Although all the contributors are committed, to a greater or lesser extent, to equal opportunity and rights for men and women, these are not universal values. We need to emphasize, therefore, that ours is not an appeal for a new ideological orthodoxy or a new set of social/family policies designed to replace the traditional family with a role-sharing ideal. Because such an attempt would create new hardships for "traditional" men and women while serving the needs of the reformist nontraditionals, it would be difficult to predict a net improvement in the collective happiness.

Just as it would be unfair and undemocratic to impose nontraditional social roles on all individuals, regardless of their own values, however, it seems to us unfair and shortsighted to impose traditional social roles on those who would prefer to organize their lives and responsibilities differently. Consequently, our goal is to advocate social policies that are flexible enough to permit both traditional and nontraditional forms to exist side by side. The only reasonable and fair goal in a pluralistic democratic society is to increase the options available to men and women so that individual families can decide for themselves how best to allocate economic, household, and childcare responsibilities in accordance with their own values and preferences. One could thus improve the collective satisfaction by allowing those who are comfortable with the status quo to continue organizing their lives in accordance with traditional and well-tried roles while simultaneously increasing the satisfaction of those who are presently dissatisfied because current social policies impose a particular ideology and way of life on all men and women, regardless of their preferences and values.

By explicitly recognizing that we are dealing here with value-laden issues, the contributors hope they can keep distinct their dual roles as scientists and politically minded citizens. We try throughout to distinguish between the objective findings of social science research and our interpretation of their bearing on social policy. It is, of course, never possible to keep values out of science—any science, as either Albert Einstein or Robert Oppenheimer could attest—for scientists too are people with values and opinions. However, we hope that by explicitly acknowledging our dual roles and perspectives—scientific and political—we enhance the value and credibility of our analysis.

Besides the somewhat unusual marriage of science and public policy analysis, there are two other characteristics of this endeavor that are unusual enough to merit explicit attention. First, ours is a multicultural analysis, with a focus on the policies and practices of the Western industrialized nations. Although much of the research has been conducted in the United States, the contributors have attempted to consider the situations existing in other countries wherever possible. Even when the available evidence pertains to the U.S., therefore, the lesson learned is of broader relevance. This goal is also served by including among the contributors individuals with an expert knowledge of social policy in countries as different as Australia, Austria, Czeckoslovakia, France, Germany, Israel, Sweden, the United Kingdom, and the United States. The issues of interest to the contributors demonstrated that there are major similarities among the problems facing these countries, even if the differences often serve to obscure them. Multicultural analyses are valuable even when one is interested only in the policies of an individual country because they force one to attend to issues that are so often ignored, such as the effects of economic, cultural, and ecological characteristics on societal practices and aspirations. Unfortunately, the heterogeneity *within* countries is often obscured by the homogenizing assumption that the dominant subculture exemplifies the entire culture.

Second, ours is an interdisciplinary focus. When one is analyzing the goals and effects of diverse social policies, a comprehensive and sensitive understanding is impossible unless one benefits from the perspectives and knowledge bases of many disciplines. Among the contributors to this volume, therefore, we find persons whose training lies in anthropology, developmental psychology, journalism, social and clinical psychology, social welfare, social work, and sociology. Although each chapter is written by people representing only one or two of these disciplines, all benefited from the exchange of views that took place in the study group from which the volume derived. Indeed, readers may have difficulty identifying the disciplinary background of many of the contributors without looking at their affiliations!

These, then, are the issues with which the contributors grapple. Our goal is to analyze contemporary family policies and evaluate the extent to which societies (as well as the men, women, and children within them) would benefit from the development of alternative policies that made it possible for some men to become more involved in child care and family responsibilities. Because ours is a multidisciplinary analysis of the interface between social science and public policy, the volume includes several comparisons of different societies' responses to common problems, as well as cautionary statements about the need to appreciate inter- and intracultural diversity.

OUTLINE OF THE VOLUME

The chapters in this volume together provide the most systematic and thorough attempt yet made to address the issues outlined above. In the chapter that follows this introduction, Rivka Eisikovits summarizes the potential conflicts between values and objective research in issues pertaining to paternal participation. An anthropologist by training, Eisikovits reminds us that values figure into the analysis of paternal participation in a number of ways: as lenses that shape the type of research conducted and the interpretations drawn and as filters that lead us to selectively respond to and ignore empirical observations depending on their compatibility with contemporary ideology. It is important that scholars, like those contributing to the volume, recognize that their commitment to paternal participation represents a value, rather than a conclusion based on the evaluation of absolute, empirical evidence. It would be inappropriate for us to impose a new ideology on legislative, judicial, and executive bodies throughout the world, for in the final analysis, increased paternal participation must be viewed as something that is desirable to some and anathema to others. In this, as in other cases, the goal should be to work toward the broadening of options, such that families and groups who want greater participation by fathers can achieve this without facing institutional barriers and cultural disapprobation. These considerations are especially important when we attempt to view paternal participation in international perspective, for one has to allow for vast variability in cultural systems, family and economic roles, values, etc.

Issues in the conduct of cross-cultural analyses and in the translation of research findings obtained in one culture to applications in another come to the fore in Chapters 2 and 13. In these chapters, Rivka Eisikovits and Martin Wolins describe the appropriate and inappropriate uses of cross-cultural data. Their reviews emphasize the need to recognize the distinctive values and ecological demands of each society because these serve to define when lessons can be drawn legitimately from other societies and when cross-cultural generalization would be invalid and misleading. It is especially important to remember this point when discussing an issue as value-laden as paternal participation in child care. Since the circumstances making increased paternal participation desirable for some families are unique to a relatively small number of modern, secular, industrialized countries, it would be foolish to export this ideology to countries where circumstances and values are markedly different.

In Chapter 2, Rivka Eisikovits also focuses on a topic around which cross-cultural issues may readily be overlooked. Her analysis is concerned with countries in which immigration has brought together people with vastly different backgrounds, values, and practices. Because they now live in a single country, it is tempting—but misleading and counterproductive—to treat these diverse groups as parts of one homogeneous society or culture. In the United States, for example, large subgroups such as Hispanic Americans and Black Americans require separate and special consideration, as do smaller groups such as Arab Americans. In Israel, waves of immigration in the last half century have brought together, as citizens of one small country, Jews from modern Western countries, Jews from North African and Middle Eastern countries, Palestinian pastoralists, nomadic and industrial Arabs, and so on. Each of these groups has its own set of values and practices; social policies must be sensitive to the differing needs and desires of these diverse groups. These same considerations apply to many of the other Western countries, in which distinct subgroups (often the consequences of immigration) belie the homogeneous consistency of interests and ideology we tend to assume. In sum, diversity is as much a concern *within* pluralistic cultures as it is when different nations or cultures are compared.

Contemporary Family Policies

Before arguing that opportunities for increased paternal participation are desirable in modern industrialized countries, it is necessary to demonstrate that the policies implemented by most countries today neither encourage nor permit widespread male involvement in child care. This analysis is the focus of Chapters 3 through 8. In Chapter 3, Sheila Kamerman first reviews major aspects of family policy in several Western countries, emphasizing the extent to which national policies explicitly consider paternal interests and either encourage or inhibit paternal participation in child care. Michael Lamb and James Levine then focus in Chapter 4 on the parental insurance policy introduced by the Swedish government in 1974. This specific national policy comes in for close attention because it is the only policy specifically designed to increase paternal participation in child care, on the grounds that the equalization of male and female roles and opportunities in other aspects of the society (e.g., the employment sector) would never occur unless male and female responsibilities within the family were equalized too. Thus the Swedish government made it possible for either mothers or fathers to take paid leave when a child was born and launched an advertising campaign designed to encourage men to take advantage of this provision. In fact, as Lamb and Levine point out, the response of Swedish men has been rather disappointing relative to the policy makers' goals. Nevertheless, the availability of paid leave has permitted some Swedish men—about 5% of those eligible—to be much more involved than their peers elsewhere. In their chapter, Lamb and Levine suggest why Swedish men have and have not taken advantage of the paternal leave policy.

The focus then shifts to the ways in which the legal system has sought to define paternal rights, particularly in the context of divorce and child custody decisions. As Thompson points out in Chapter 5, there have been several shifts in judicial presumptions over the past two centuries. Initially, in accordance with the common law, wives and children were considered the legal property of men, and hence in the case of divorce, children were placed in the custody of their fathers. Towards the end of the last century, however, this practice gave way in the face of assumptions that the welfare of young children would be best served if they were placed in the custody of their mothers who, because they were primary caretakers, were most important to their children's mental health and future development. More recently, courts and legislatures have begun to recognize increased paternal involvement in the family. Most states now prohibit courts from considering the parents' gender in adjudicating custody petitions, and this has, in theory at least, increased the possibility that fathers may be awarded custody in contested cases.

Assuming that both parents petition for custody in an increasing number of cases, however, on what grounds should decisions be based? This is Thompson's focus in Chapter 5. Thompson appraises the available evidence concerning parental influences and the effects of divorce on child development in an attempt to identify well-established facts that could serve as the basis of judicial decision rules. Unfortunately, he concludes, the evidence is slim, although theoretical and empirical decisions do permit us to frame some general rules that should be helpful in adjudication. Thompson also includes suggestions for future research efforts that might help us frame clearer and more empirically-based decision rules.

One large scale empirical attempt to assess the opportunities available to men who desire a greater involvement in family roles is described by James Levine, Joseph Pleck, and Michael Lamb in Chapter 6. These three authors are codirectors of The Fatherhood Project, an attempt to explore: a) what attempts have been made to increase opportunities for paternal participation in the employment sector, legal and religious arenas, health sciences, psychological and social services, and education; b) which strategies have been successful, which have been less successful, and why; and c) how employees and employers evaluate the efforts that have been made. The goal of the project is to suggest to interested organizations and employers policies that would be useful to at least some of their employees and members. The strategy, scope, and goals of this project are described in Chapter 6.

In the final chapters in this section on social policy, Martin Wolins (Chapter 7) and Eliezer Jaffe (Chapter 8) examine the extent to which the literature, legislation, and social welfare institutions concerned with the provision of services directly to children have virtually ignored both fathers and male caretakers. Wolins and Jaffe identify two implicit and seldom-questioned assumptions: That children in institutional settings are best cared for by women and that they are not adversely affected by the exclusion of male figures from their lives. As some of the other chapters suggest, these assumptions are at best questionable and at worst dangerously incorrect.

Cost-Benefit Analyses

The contributors believe that we can identify circumstances—particularly those now characteristic of modern industrialized countries—in which substantial benefits might be achieved by broadening the degree of paternal participation in family functions and child care. The costs and benefits of increased paternal participation are analyzed and compared in Chapters 9 through 12. The authors examine in turn the effects of increased paternal participation on each of the groups likely to be influenced most directly: fathers themselves (Chapter 9), their spouses or partners (Chapter 10), their children (Chapter 11), and the society at large (Chapter 12).

In the first of these chapters (Chapter 9), Graeme Russell and Norma Radin argue that increased paternal participation offers men a chance to obtain personal fulfillment by becoming close to and helping shape the development of their children. This permits fathers a more broadly based sense of fulfillment than that obtained by traditional men pursuing occupational goals at the expense of all others. The cost in many cases is diminished occupational success and (at least until employers become more tolerant) the likelihood that promotional advancement will be denied to employees who clearly are not ''properly committed'' to their jobs.

When fathers are more involved, argues Lois Hoffman (Chapter 10), women are relieved of the dual burdens of family and economic work that employed women now have to shoulder. Their life satisfaction also increases when their responsibilities are eased, and this raises the possibility of increased fulfillment in both arenas. Not insignificantly, relief from complete responsibility for home and child care may make possible career advancement and success that were previously inconceivable. The cost, of course, is the loss of domination over the one arena in which women's superiority has never been challenged. In addition, dual-worker families with children may find that the demands of two taxing roles per adult make their lives hectic and chaotic (Russell, 1982).

Because there have been so few highly involved fathers available for study, the effects of increased paternal involvement on children have not been explored very thoroughly. However, in Chapter 11, Norma Radin and Graeme Russell evaluate what little evidence is available and introduce a number of other issues and considerations that bear on our understanding of this topic. The existing evidence suggests that children seem more likely to benefit than suffer from paternal involvement, but that the effects have to be viewed in the context of the dominant social values and the circumstances of specific families.

An evaluation of the costs and benefits accruing to society at large is provided by Abraham Sagi and Nachman Sharon in Chapter 12. These authors show that when individuals are able to allocate home, family, and economic responsibilities in accord with their personal values and desires, society as a whole benefits from the increased satisfaction of men and women. In addition, society may benefit from the increased labor force participation of skilled female employees whose involvement would otherwise be limited by family responsibilities. Finally, society benefits to the extent that paternal participation in families may help limit some of the social ills—crime, poverty, undereducation, alcoholism, drug abuse—that are more common in families and segments of society in which father have abrogated their responsibilities.

Integration

What, then, can we say about legislative, judicial, and administrative policies pertaining to fathers? Michael Lamb, Graeme Russell, and Abraham Sagi attempt in the volume's final chapter to lay out an agenda for future policy and research. Consistent with the cautions emphasized throughout the volume, these authors stress the need for policies that make increased paternal participation by fathers possible rather than mandatory. They point out the need to acknowledge cultural diversity in planning policy and research. They also point out the need for individuals to be aware of the potential advantages and disadvantages of paternal involvement, so that they can make an informed decision about the practices that would be of greatest value to families like their own. Our hope is that this book serves to inform and to facilitate the implementation of policies that would increase the options available to the mothers and fathers of the future.

REFERENCES

Lamb, M. E. Fathers: Forgotten contributors to child development. *Human Development,* 1975, *18,* 245–266.

Lamb, M. E. (Ed.). *The role of the father in child development.* New York: Wiley, 1976.

Lamb, M. E. (Ed.). *The role of the father in child development* (Rev. ed.). New York: Wiley, 1981.

Parsons, T., & Bales, R. F. *Family, socialization, and society.* Glencoe, Ill.: Free Press, 1955.

Russell, G. Shared-caregiving families: An Australian study. In M. E. Lamb (Ed.), *Nontraditional families: Parenting and child development.* Hillsdale, N.J.: Lawrence Erlbaum Associates, 1982.

Rutter, M. *Maternal deprivation: Reassessed.* Hardmonsworth, England: Penguin, 1972.

Sheehy, G. Introducing the postponing generation. *Esquire,* 1979, *92,* (4), 25–33.

2 Paternal Child Care as a Policy Relevant Social Phenomenon and Research Topic: The Question of Values

Rivka Eisikovits
University of Haifa

INTRODUCTION

In *The aims of education,* Alfred North Whitehead (1929) states: "It is the kind of questions asked, the nature of the problem brought forward, rather than what these are about that differs from age to age and assigns it to one age and not another [p. 7]."

In this sense the very concern with the issue of active paternal involvement in childcare in a social policy context is indicative of a climate of ideas that points towards change. It implies that certain groups think such participation beneficial. Some of the questions that immediately arise are: Who are the members of these groups? Who are considered the beneficiaries of change? Are fathers themselves among the beneficiaries? Put differently, do fathers agree with the proposition that they should take a more active part in raising their children? On what premises is this line of action advocated? These are all value-based questions, very much "of our age in nature and kind," that this chapter will attempt to address.

What are values? Values, according to Clyde Kluckhohn's classical statement in *Mirror for Man* (1959), are "the idealized goals set by a culture [p. 195.]" When we talk about culture change, what is actually meant is a shift in the idealized goals that constitute the building blocks of any cultural system. Thus, observed behavioral alterations can be considered of cultural significance only when demonstrated to stem from a change in values. Whereas in a monolithic, small scale tribal society a consensus on values can be quite safely assumed, it is an unrealistic expectation in pluralistic, complex societies. Although considerable intergroup and interpersonal variations in value configurations do occur, they

13

can still be regarded as an individual's or, more commonly, a group's interpretations of idealized cultural goals.

This chapter deals with three different themes:

1. A cultural analysis of paternal child care as an emerging social phenomenon of a certain magnitude and visibility.
2. Social science research—its approach to various aspects of paternal child care.
3. Social policy—deciding whose function it is to create the necessary conditions that allow paternal child care to be practiced by those individuals or groups that consider it beneficial.

Values form the link that ties these themes together; values also underlie all rational decision-making processes stemming from these themes. This is why values are such a crucial part of any discussion on the subject of active paternal involvement in child rearing. Paternal child care is a basic departure from traditional child care patterns; it is in itself an expression of a shift in values (to be discussed later), and thus a topic worth researching. Its presentation as a favorable future scenario, enjoying a certain grassroots support, turned it into a subject of policy interest. Social research, broadly conceptualized, carries the potential to serve as a mediator between phenomenon and policy.

This chapter examines both the value context of the issue and the value considerations pertaining to the research process. The policy-value link, although touched upon as relevant to the discussion, is not explored in depth here. First, the interplay between paternal child care and such current phenomena as the rising trend of women's participation in the labor force, economic impact on the family, and ensuing division of labor in the dual career/breadwinner family are considered. This is followed by a cultural analysis of the two barriers to a wide scale social acceptance of this new child-rearing pattern. An examination of how the dynamics of culture transmission, change, and adaptation affect the integration of such an "innovation" in traditional parenting styles is undertaken for both its theoretical and practical or policy-relevant implications. Finally the value-research link is explored to highlight both pitfalls and potential of social science research to enhance enlightened policy making related to our topic.

THE SOCIAL CONTEXT OF PATERNAL CHILD CARE: IMPLICATIONS FOR VALUES

Active paternal involvement in child care can be analyzed in terms of larger societal, family, and individual values. On the macrosocial level, changing trends in women's employment expressed in a massive increase in women's representation in the labor force have entailed major transformations in the traditional sex-role division of labor in the home (Hoffman, 1977; Hoffman, 1979). More intensive paternal participation in child rearing is one of these emerging changes.

Women's gainful employment outside the home becomes the most adaptive arrangement when looked at from a family economy perspective. Inflation and constantly rising living expenses make it impractical to forgo the wife's potential contribution to family income, particularly if she is educated. Thus, for a professional woman to devote all her time to child care would be wasteful.

On the individual level, higher education for women toward a professional career is regarded as an avenue for self-realization. It takes on the meaning of an intrinsically valued step in the direction of self-determination through the exercise of free choice (Dubois, 1955; Henry, 1963). While the increased participation of women in the labor market and various domains of public life is a social trend that carries intrinsic rewards for its adherents, paternal child care is most often treated as a by-product of these changes, or as a convenient arrangement. Until its underlying value bases and attitudinal dimensions are explored, it cannot be regarded as a culturally significant childrearing pattern.

THE TRANSMISSION OF CHANGING CULTURAL NORMS: IMPLICATIONS FOR PATERNAL CHILD CARE AS AN EMERGENT PATTERN

One of the central problems related to active paternal participation in child care is that most modern societies do not provide clear behavioral guidelines for intensely involved fathers. Neither role models nor culturally approved ways of treating the role incumbents are available. Yet as Spindler (1974) contends, "Cultures as systems really change only when they are transmitted differently to new members or within the peer group [p. 4]." Thus both the cultural acceptance and perpetuation of a changed pattern is contingent upon its mode of transmission.

Culture as a system of ideas transmits itself to neophytes as a "cognitive map" (Spradley, 1972) or a "cultural grammar" (Goodenough, 1963) that regulates social interaction. To accede to fully participatory membership in any given culture, neophytes have to familiarize themselves with these rules. According to Spindler (1974), societies alternate the use of such mechanisms as "cultural compression" and "cultural decompression" to socialize new members to their core values. "Cultural compression" refers to the application of strict limitations on the neophyte's socially approved behavioral alternatives until he has exhibited mastery over these rules of proper conduct. "Decompression," accordingly, means an ensuing broadening of such alternatives along with the allocation of social rights and responsibilities.

Culture transmission theory can be applied not only to explain the experience of the young being recruited to memebership in their society but also to conceptualize the individual's progression through a succession of social roles in a lifespan context. Simultaneous periods of compression may be experienced by initiates in several role sets. Thus, males as neophyte husbands, fathers, in-laws, not to mention on-the-job compressions, would constitute such a case.

This theory helps us visualize the basic discrepancy between nonexistent models for transmission on the one hand, and the very fundamental part transmission itself pays in bringing about culture change. The implications of this, more than conceptual, are that obstacles have to be assessed before any culturally significant changes in paternal child-rearing patterns can be expected to take place. On a more pragmatic level, the application of the concepts of "cultural compression and decompression" to individual lifespans, as well as family systems, underscores the importance of looking at parenthood in the context of the totality of the spouses' role sets.

Margaret Mead's (1970) classification of societies into postfigurative, cofigurative and prefigurative, based on *who* transmits *what* (culture content) *to whom* in societies characterized by different rates of change, offers a more optimistic framework for conceptualizing the problem of cultural models for paternal childcare. In post figurative or quasi-static isolated societies, events occur in accordance with tradition. Social norms and canons of behavior are well established. The elders serve as live models for the various social roles. The life of the young is premapped; behavioral options are clear and limited. All there is for the young to do is watch closely and listen carefully to emulate the models and absorb the great traditions (Beals, 1962; Lessa, 1966; Pierce, 1964; Williams, 1965). In such cultures, fathers play a central role as moral and social educators, especially for boys, in line with the Parsonian theory of sex-differentiated parental socialization functions (Parsons & Bales, 1955). Fathers are in charge of initiation rites and mystico-religious instruction in general, whereby adherence to the values of the larger community are inculcated. In addition to moral and social education, fathers are responsible for the "professional" or career instruction of young males as well. Eskimo boys join their fathers on hunting trips as early as the age of 6–7 (Chance, 1966); the Kwakiutl take their sons along on fishing expeditions around the same age (Wolcott, 1967). The Kpelle of Liberia take their 5–6–year–olds with them to the fields (Gay & Cole, 1967). Although the children occasionally help their fathers with some minor tasks, the bulk of the instruction consists of observing the adult role models at their work.

In cofigurative societies, the rate of change is considerable, a fact that makes the above described unidirectional style of culture transmission untenable. Tradition still provides partial guidelines for behavior but not in all domains. In the econo-technical sphere, changes are so rapid that peers become the only sources of knowledge. The old have to appeal to the young for advice in their area of expertise if they want to keep up, or even partially stay in touch with the "new times." In the realm of family roles, where behavior is considerably slower to change, the traditional models still largely uphold and the intrafamily division of responsibilities can be quite safely seen to fall into the instrumental-expressive Parsonian normative categories.

In prefigurative societies, because of the accelerated rate of change in all domains, tradition cannot serve as a source of knowledge, nor can present role models be relied upon as guides for the future. No subject matter transmission is relevant because of the imminent danger of obsolescence. Curriculum planners are busy devising programs that foster creativity and adaptive skills for life-long independent learning.

The integration of the above two conceptualizations of the process of norm transmission adds a significant heuristic dimension to our discussion at this point. Spindler's "compression-decompression" model presupposes a high degree of certainty and knowledge on behalf of the transmitters, which gives them the legitimation to manipulate both neophytes and social conditions throughout the socialization process. Applying Mead's paradigm to this model reveals that it is wholly feasible only in postfigurative societies and partially in the cofigurative types. At the prefigurative stage, learner-monitored culture acquisition is likely to replace traditional, instructor-centered culture transmission. The problem raised earlier concerning the unavailability of sanctioned cultural models for active paternal child care no longer exists. In this scenario all are neophytes, daily readjusting their adaptive formulae to a constantly emerging culture.

In "Effects of Conscious Purpose on Human Adaptation", Gregory Bateson (1972) states that "faced with a changing variable within itself, which it should control, the organism may make changes either within itself or in the external environment [p. 447]." He maintains that man naturally leans toward changing the external environment rather than himself in the process of evolutionary adaptation. At the prefigurative stage, the option to choose one or the other is not available. Man's ability to shape himself and his primary groups in accordance with external shifts becomes a measure of his adaptability, indeed a condition for his survival.

As far as attitudes are concerned, the area in which it is hardest to apply such canons of insecurity is the realm of family, our traditional hearth of stability. Family roles constitute a core concern in any cultural system. Increased paternal involvement in child care means a basic departure from previously sanctioned agents as well as styles of primary socialization.

Cultural lag theory (Beals, 1967; Goodenough, 1963; Harris, 1968; Herskovits, 1950) has been applied to explain the different pace at which various subsystems within any given society change. The economic subsystem is considered the fastest to change; the ideological and social subsystems are held to be much more reluctant to change. Within the latter, the family, and the values that support it, are regarded as the last to yield. Cultural lag theory is perceived as a functional explanation from a macrosocial perspective. It is interpreted to serve as a buffer against too rapid, chaos-inducing social change. Yet from the point of view of the family, this theory, by sanctioning the family-as-we-know-it status quo, hampers the emergence and social acceptance of alternative family life styles.

Cultural transmission and change and adaptation theories point toward long-range educational action aimed at changing values and basic attitudes through a slow but thorough process. The mass media portraying both men and women in a variety of nontraditional roles, books and movies devoted to successful personal records (Corman, 1978; Daley, 1978; Levine, 1976; Miner, 1978; Stafford, 1978) may serve as educationally potent channels for favorably predisposing public opinions and attitudes. The schools can, and many actually do, play a central part. By developing innovative curricula to replace former narrowly sex-role stereotyed programs, they allow and encourage boys and girls to experiment with nonconventional roles.

We are at a point where the emergence of alternative family and parenting styles, especially paternal child care, has become a social phenomenon of considerable visibility. Yet the lack of an explicit policy framework in many industrialized Western countries (Kamerman & Kahn, 1978) to accommodate the involvement of those men who wish to actively participate in child rearing, hinders them from doing so.[1]

The common argument against adopting such a policy, as Fred Barbaro claims in his "Case Against Family Policy" (1979), is that it ehances stereotyping and presents certain family styles as preferable to others. One could always counterargue that the lack of an explicit social policy is in itself a statement of policy. The danger of policy-induced favoritism or forcible norm-compliance is inconceivable in the context of liberal social policy that only serves to make a number of alternatives available for those who choose to make use of them.

Concluding their discussion of "Family policy as field and perspective," Kamerman and Kahn (1978) contend that "the policy, if adopted, should encourage diversity, or at least be neutral among a variety of acceptable alternatives in style, roles and direction [p. 503]." In my opinion it can do more than that. A comprehensive, responsibly conceptualized body of social policy maximizes rather than restricts available options. In this way it can, in effect, become a most powerful device of long-range pluralistic education.

VALUE CONSIDERATIONS IN RESEARCH ON FATHERS: IMPLICATIONS FOR POLICY

Researching any aspect of intrafamily roles and relations is a complex undertaking because the topic is so heavily value-laden. Competing ideologies translated into political and economic interests come into play. Research findings that sup-

---

[1]For the contrary, see Lamb & Levine's chapter in this volume on the impact of Swedish parental insurance on paternal involvement in child care.

port paternal involvement in child care as beneficial for the child's development are likely to raise opposition among conservative or orthodox religious groups interested in perpetuating the ideology of maternal child care as "established by the laws of nature," or "preordained." These groups often consider research an iconoclastic endeavor that threatens the status quo. Hence, researchers' objectivity often comes under attack, and accusations of partisanship are leveled at them. Although research interest in paternal child care was stimulated by the growing trends of women's employment and the liberation movement, this does not denigrate the researchers' ethics nor detract from the quality of their scientific work.

In effect, one of the major limitations of this research literature is that it has neglected the value-related aspects of the topic—a common omission in much of behavioral science research "practiced" under the banner of scientism. Clyde Kluckhohn (1959) cogently sums up this widespread fallacy:

> No tenet of intellectual folklore has been so damaging to our life and time as the cliché that "science has nothing to do with values." If the consideration of values is to be the exclusive property of religion and the humanities, a scientific understanding of human experience is impossible [p. 217].

Indeed, a review of the scientific literature on the father's role in child development shows that many of the studies stress the overt behavioral manifestations or "objectifiable" variables related to paternal inputs into child rearing. Some of the main topics are: characteristics of father-infant relationships with babies three, five, eight, and fifteen months old; controlled experiments that compare mothers' and fathers' accomplishments of certain infant-related tasks; differential infant reactions to mothers and fathers in various activities; effects of quantitative versus qualitative time investment in child care by mothers and fathers.

Yet, as stated earlier, changes on the behavioral level cannot be regarded as culturally significant unless it can be demonstrated that they originate from the value infrastructure of a given society. Martin Rein (1976) reiterates Kluckhohn's admonition from a policy perspective. He reminds us that all information becomes meaningful only within a certain value context. Studies that do not provide such a context are not usable for policy making purposes. Their findings remain unintelligible for all practical purposes until the value orientations that lead the researcher throughout the investigation are made explicit. It is values that determine both what is studied and how results are interpreted.

If influencing the course of social action via research is a desideratum, we do, indeed, need "better rather than more" studies, as Lamb points out in concluding his overview chapter on the role of the father in child development (Lamb, 1981). In order to be able to answer the question of how fathers from various walks of pluralistic modern societies value this role, extensive naturalistic exploratory studies should be undertaken.

Prior to investigating the specifics of paternal functioning in various intrafamily situations, research efforts should be directed to a phenomenological understanding of basic value orientations towards fatherhood. In other words, the focus should be on meanings of fatherhood as part of a holistic consideration of modern male worlds, roles sets, and social networks.

Although a few observational, longitudinal studies in natural settings are said to be in process (Russell, 1979, 1982), their reliability is questioned, often by the authors themselves, who may feel that this type of research has not reached "full fledged" status yet. Hence the apologetic tone about limitations of the sample and further need for replication, etc. The weaknesses rather than the uniqueness of the data are highlighted. In addition, the bulk of the research that has been done is highly fragmented. Many investigators continue to use traditional methodologies even though they themselves recognize the limitations of the traditional approaches. Taking an interdisciplinary approach as this book does constitutes a step in the right direction. It recognizes that conventional unidisciplinary approaches do not yield viable solutions.

In much of the research literature, paternal involvement is analyzed primarily with regard to the child's development and welfare. The same conceptual fallacy that underlay the advocation of maternal childcare—that it was for the child's benefit; that is, taking an instrumental approach to the mother's role—is largely being reenacted in the prevailing attitude to the father's role in child care. The "do it for your child, wife, or society" rhetoric may have little chance of success unless the intrinsic rewards for the involved fathers are understood and demonstrated.

Research findings have an important educational significance as well. Exposing the inherent fallacy underlying the biological determinist view that mothers "by nature" are and therefore should be childcare givers, is a major contribution. By presenting parenthood as a learned role that fathers are just as competent to master, given the opportunity, it underscored the tautologous nature of this explanatory scheme that has for so long served to justify the status quo of maternal child rearing. Such data carry the potential to influence prevailing value orientations towards the traditional parenting styles. Mothers have had more experience and a more thorough socialization in parenting and so became more skilled at it. Findings from shared care-giving families (Russell, 1979, 1982) indicate that fathers are not less efficient when in the care-giver role.

However, the fact that many of the families in the sample of shared-role or father-as-major-caregiver group either belong to the lower income brackets and engage in child rearing out of economic necessity (Russell, 1979) or are college students who reverse roles on a rotating basis or as a temporary arrangement (Radin, 1982), means that research on them is unlikely to influence public opinion to any considerable degree. It can be easily written off as something eccentrics do but no "normal middle class family" would consider. Therefore, more research is needed to investigate the extent to which parental child care is practiced among informants belonging to the more established economic and social strata.

To counter the argument that men are usually driven to active involvement in child care under the force of circumstances or as a temporary arrangement, research should focus on the question of why men wish to engage in this practice, given a free choice. Do they experience any lasting transformations in attitudes towards parenting as a result of their involvement? How do other significant males in their social network relate to this activity? (Russell, 1982). Do they see themselves as potential advocates for policy level action to enable more intensive male participation in child rearing for those interested in such an option? All these are important issues research can clarify and thereby possibly influence prevailing social attitudes and values.

SUMMARY

Both Merton & Lerner (1951) and Rein (1976) point out that the social sciences have a record of offering functional interpretations to prevailing phenomena because their findings are more readily accepted when they do not rock the boat. On the contrary, when they tackle touchy social issues the validity of their undertakings is often questioned. Yet functionalist explanations become decreasingly applicable in a context of rapid change.

Social science research has to spell out its underlying value assumptions to be useful. Researchers' values cannot be ignored. They are operant throughout the process from the very choice of topic, through the aspects of the problem tackled, the style of investigation undertaken, to the analysis and interpretation of findings. If properly acknowledged, this fact, however, does not discredit either the credibility or the scientific quality of the work. Only in this way can research make an impact on social action through either policy making or educational channels.

Through the concerted effort of research, policy action, and the various educational vehicles, paternal child rearing has the potential to acquire the status of a socially acceptable alternative. Thus decisions concerning the degree and style of paternal and maternal participation in child care do not need to be regulated by peer pressure or norm compliance but can, instead, take place on the level of individual or family choice.

REFERENCES

Barbaro, F. The case against family policy. *Social Work*, 1979, *24*, 455–458.

Bateson, G. Effects of conscious purpose on human adaptation. In G. Bateson, *Steps to an ecology of mind*. New York: Ballantine Books, 1972.

Beals, A. R. *Gopalpur: A south Indian village.* New York: Holt, Rinehart, & Winston, 1962.

Beals, A. R. *Culture in process*. New York: Holt, Rinehart, & Winston, 1967.

Chance, N. A. *The Eskimo of north Alaska*. New York: Holt, Rinehart, & Winston, 1966.

Corman, A. *Kramer versus Kramer*. New York: Random House, 1978.

Daley, E. A. *Father feelings*. New York: Morrow, 1978.

DuBois, C. The dominant value profile of American culture. *American Anthropologist*, 1955, *57*, 1232–1239.

Gay, S, & Cole, M. *The new mathematics and an old culture*. New York: Holt, Rinehart, & Winston, 1967.

Goodenough, W. H. *Cooperation in change: an anthropological approach to community change*. New York: Wiley, 1963.

Harris, M. *The rise of anthropological theory*. New York: Thomas Y. Crowell Company, 1968.

Henry, J. *Culture against man*. New York: Vintage Books, 1963.

Herskovits, M. J. *Man and his works*. New York: Knopf, 1950.

Hoffman, L. W. Changes in family roles, socialization and sex differences. *American Psychologist*, 1977, *34*, 644–657.

Hoffman, L. W. Maternal employment: 1979. *American Psychologist*, 1979, *34*, 859–865.

Kamerman, S. B., & Kahn, A. Family policy as field and perspective. In S. B. Kamerman & A. Kahn (Eds.). *Family policy*. New York: Columbia University Press, 1978.

Kluckhohn, C. *Mirror for man*. New York: Premier Books, 1959.

Lamb, M. E. (Ed.). *The role of the father in child development*. New York: Wiley, 1981.

Lessa, W. *Ulithi: a Micronesian design for living*. New York: Holt, Rinehart, & Winston, 1966.

Levine, J. *Who will raise the children: New options for fathers (and mothers)*. Philadelphia: Lippincott, 1976.

Mead, M. *Culture and commitment, a study of the generation gap*. New York: Garden City, 1970.

Merton, R., & Lerner, D. Social scientists and research policy, In D. Lerner & H. D. Lasswell (Eds.), *The policy sciences*. Stanford, Calif.: Stanford University Press, 1951.

Miner, R. *Mother's day*. New York: Richard Marek, 1978.

Parsons, T., & Bales, R. F. *Family, socialization and interaction process*. Glencoe, Ill.: Free Press, 1955.

Pierce, J. E. *Life in a Turkish village*. New York: Holt, Rinehart, & Winston, 1964.

Radin, N. Role sharing fathers and preschoolers. In: M. E. Lamb (Ed.), *Nontraditional families: parenting and child development*. Hillsdale, N.J.: Lawrence Erlbaum Associates, 1982.

Rein, M. *Social science and public policy*. New York: Penguin Books, 1976.

Russell, G. Fathers as caregivers: "they could if they had to." Paper presented at the Australia and New Zealand Association for the Advancement of Science Congress, Aukland, January 1979.

Russell, G. Shared caregiving families: an Australian study. In: M. E. Lamb (Ed.), *Nontraditional families: parenting and child development*. Hillsdale, N.J.: Lawrence Erlbaum Asociates, 1982.

Spindler, G. D. From omnibus to linkages—a model for culture transmission. *Council on Anthropology and Education Newsletter*, 1974.

Spradley, J. P. (ed.) *Culture and Cognition: Rules, maps and plans*. New York, Chandler Publishing Co., 1972.

Stafford, L. M. *One man's family: a single father and his children*. New York: Random House, 1978.

Whitehead, A. N. *The aims of education*. New York: Macmillan Company, 1929.

Williams, T. R. *The Dusun: A north Borneo society*. New York: Holt, Rinehart, & Winston, 1965.

Wolcott, H. *A Kwakiuth village and school*. New York: Holt, Rinehart, & Winston, 1967.

3 Fatherhood and Social Policy: Some Insights From a Comparative Perspective

Sheila B. Kamerman
Columbia University School of Social Work

INTRODUCTION

Social policy is often viewed as a field of governmental activity in which policies are designed and implemented by men to benefit a dependent population constituted largely of women and children. That the policies are in fact male-determined can be readily documented; policy makers are largely male in all countries. That the policies are targeted primarily at women and children is an assumption that warrants closer examination.

The extent to which men are the beneficiaries of social policies and the functions that such policies support—in particular, the role of fatherhood—is the focus of this book. My intention in this chapter is to show how knowledge of the social and family policies in advanced industrialized countries sheds new light on: (a) the meaning of fatherhood in these societies; (b) the value placed on fatherhood; and (c) the issues and implications that emerge for future policy discussion.

I shall begin with a brief definition of social policy, continue with a definition and overview of family policy as a component of social policy, and then explore how fatherhood is or is not treated in the family and social policies of different countries. The thesis I will develop is that fatherhood has been a target of social policy, implicitly or explicitly, but that the fatherhood function has been viewed largely as that of breadwinner. In contrast, motherhood has been addressed primarily as a nurturant and caretaking role. The economic role of mothers has been ignored until the last decade or so in Europe, and until the present in the United States. Social policies in the past have been heavily biased towards support of traditional gender roles. In recent years, however, especially in several European countries, there has been a significant move in family policy towards a more androgynous view of parenting roles and responsibilities, acknowledging the importance of both economic and nurturant/caretaking roles for men as well as women, fathers as well as mothers. I am convinced that ultimately, for children to be well reared and to develop well it is the parenting role and function that needs support–neither fathering nor mothering alone. At present, this may mean more deliberate attention to providing support for fathers in their nurturant and caretaking roles and for mothers in their economic roles. To what extent family and social policies reinforce traditional roles, and to what extent these policies, in some countries at least, are moving towards a more androgynous view of parenting as including multiple roles for both men and women, is the focus of this chapter.

SOCIAL POLICY AND FAMILY POLICY: DEFINING THE TERMS

By social policy I mean those societal activities (governmental and nongovernmental) concerned with the distribution of goods and services by other than market criteria and directed at assuring individuals a minimum standard of living and a decent quality of life (however the latter is defined) (Kahn & Kamerman, 1981). Governmental social policies include both what governments provide directly (cash and in-kind transfers) and what they provide indirectly through tax benefits (to individuals, employees, organizations, communities), subsidies (vouchers, contracts, grants), purchase, and regulation. In addition to this field of activities, social policy also involves a particular perspective. An ideology underlies these actions, influencing other governmental activity, the marketplace, the society at large, and thus facilitating the achievement of desired social goals. It is in this context that we see increasing intermingling of nonmarket concerns with market objectives in economic policy, in the labor market, in urban planning, in the development of a social infrastructure, and in government generally.

Family policy, a component of social policy, can be viewed similarly: as field and as perspective (Kamerman & Kahn, 1978). In many countries, family policy is viewed as that field of social policy that has as its manifest purpose improving the well being of children and families with children. Other goals may supplement this expressed concern, or may be superimposed on it, or may be latent. Thus, population replacement has been a major concern in France for almost 50 years and certainly plays a role in the continued strong and broad support for family policy in France. Population concerns are far more recent in Hungary and East Germany, emerging in force only in the 1970s. Yet such concerns have clearly influenced policy development in these countries too, and are now beginning to be a factor in the policies of West Germany.

Similarly, labor market objectives have played a significant role in policy development in several countries, in particular, Hungary, East Germany, and Sweden. Specific incentives have been incorporated into policies designed to influence women to enter the labor market or to withdraw from it. Certainly, in the sense that old age and retirement pensions include labor market as well as equity, adequacy, and social justice objectives, family policy includes labor market concerns, too.

In recent years, still another goal has been added to the three already mentioned, and that is achieving equity in the relationship between men and women. Only Sweden has announced this as an explicit objective of its family policy thus far. However, several countries have addressed the issue, and it is emerging as a more central concern in the current debate.

The extent to which family policy is used as a rationale—or an instrument—to achieve any of these last three goals (or any other goal) is difficult to discern. Regardless, those who view family policies as a way to improve the conditions of families with children—the economic as well as the social conditions—constitute a significant group everywhere, even when other goals are present.

In contrast, family policy as perspective is only beginning to be addressed as a holistic approach to policy making; and it has yet to emerge as such in popular discussion. By this, I refer to the need to consider ''family and child well-being'' as criteria in policy debate and development in a variety of areas, not just those directly affecting families with children (e.g. economic and urban development; immigration; transportation). In effect, those who are interested in policy coherence and harmonization and those who are concerned with children and families are experimenting with the concept of family policy used in this way. Others may follow. In Sweden, France, and to a lesser extent Hungary, there seems to be some indication of a growing use of family policy as an organizing principle for a segment of social policy generally. This use, clearly, is part of the cutting edge of the debate. In this chapter my focus will be on family and social policies as both policy field and perspective.

GENDER IN SOCIAL AND FAMILY POLICIES

The present-day field of social policy emerged from the confluence of three streams: religious/humanitarian concerns for those in difficulty and need; labor market concerns regarding who should (and who should not) be employed and how to assure this; and concern with social or societal solidarity. All these have contributed to the development of a gender ''dichotomy'' in social policy.

Very young children and their mothers (and the very old and the handicapped) were viewed historically as unable to work, and therefore, in need, if there was no male breadwinner in the family. This is part of the ''poor law'' history in

Western countries. These laws incorporated traditional distinctions regarding male/female roles as well as the distinction between the "deserving" and the "undeserving" poor. Those single mothers who could be defined as deserving have been a target of social policy, be it the early special—if limited—protection given widows and dependent children or the current protected status and benefits provided sole mothers in all industrialized countries.

Thus, women have always predominated among social (public) assistance recipients, either as widows or as other types of single mothers, even though European assistance benefits are available to two-parent as well as sole-mother families in contrast to the U.S. pattern under Aid to Families With Dependent Children (AFDC). Men (except, in more recent times, those with severe disabilities) have always been expected to work. No special provision has been made for men to rear children even when left as sole parents, e.g., widowers; it was assumed they would remarry and so gain a caretaker for the children, or would give the children to some other female family member for care. On the other hand, since the late 19th century men—fathers—have received increasing social policy support for their breadwinning role while women were ignored or qualified for far less. Thus, social insurance began in the 1880s in Germany as protection for the employed, largely men, against such socially defined risks as old age, retirement, accidents at work, unemployment. For many years, women received social insurance benefits only as dependents of male workers. Protection for working women against loss of income as a consequence of childbirth or child rearing is a much more recent development in almost all countries. In some, unemployment insurance for married women is still viewed as something of a social policy extravagance and old age insurance benefits continue to leave women at a disadvantage as compared with men in most countries. Added to this is the extensive social provision that now exists in many countries in the form of employer-provided benefits and services, once again far more likely to be available to men than to women (Kamerman & Kingston, 1982).

Family allowances, the cash benefits provided by government in 67 countries, including all industrial countries except the U.S., on the basis of presence and number of children in a family, are the first major income maintenance policy reflecting a more androgynous view of parenting roles. However, these are part of a later policy development. Moreover, they too began as a cash-benefit for fathers, rather than mothers, even though they are clearly a family or child benefit (Kamerman & Kahn, 1981).

The first policies to be explicitly labeled "family policy" date from the 1930s and 1940s in France and Sweden and responded rather to demographic and economic concerns regarding all families, not just a specific group of families with problems. Initially, family policy meant government action to supplement the income of families with children, to compensate for the fact that wages were not related to need and thus parents with many children—large families—would find it difficult to survive economically. The consequences for children could well be disastrous. Defining population replacement as a societal as well as an individual concern, countries provided cash benefits to encourage childbearing and to compensate working men for their low wages as well as the economic costs of rearing children. Only in 1978 was employment eliminated as a criterion for eligibility for family allowances in France and only in the 1970s was the bias in the French family allowance system towards the at-home mother reduced. (The French view their family allowance system as neutral towards male and female roles although the issue is debated on both sides.)

The second major stage in the development of family policy in Europe began in the 1960s. In the context of the highest rate of economic growth in history, the Western countries experienced a dramatic increase in social provision in all areas during this decade: income transfers, health care, education, housing, employment, and personal social services. Social provision for the aged—cash benefits and services—burgeoned in much of Europe; a similar development began in the U.S. too in these years and flourished in the early 1970s. One could argue that while the U.S. fought a small war against poverty in the 1960s, the continental Europeans launched a broad-based family policy initiative, universalist in principle but placing a high priority on meeting the needs of low income families. Family allowances were increased and the number of families and children covered grew. Cash allowances for housing were introduced in several countries and child care services and personal social services generally were expanded.

If population replacement and poverty were the focus of the first family policy wave, income inequality and income redistribution from those with no children to those with children were clearly the focus of the second. Gender issues were still present, however.

In Britain, one of the obstacles to introducing family allowances was concern that such benefits—paid to the child's mother—might lead to women being less dependent on their husbands (Land, 1977). Indeed, the effort in the mid 1970s to increase child benefits (family allowances in Britain) and to eliminate the tax allowances for children (a benefit that favors high income families over low income families) was unsuccessful initially because it involved taking money "from the wallet" and transferring it "to the purse"—thereby redistributing from fathers to mothers.

In most countries, payment of the child benefit to the mother represented the first policy acknowledgment of mothers' economic burden and of their economic dependency. In a growing number of countries, the benefit can now be assigned either parent, whoever carries more responsibility for the child.

The third family policy stage emerged in the 1970s, although beginnings could be discerned in at least one country, Sweden, a little earlier. Here, the focus seemed to be on policies responding to family change, both structural and role changes, as well as changes in the labor market and in society at large. Socialization, and the social and emotional support of children, became an important component of service provision as children were more likely to experience living in a one-parent family, in a reconstituted family, in a family with working parents. Childcare programs expanded very rapidly during these years. Contributing to this unprecedented development throughout Europe is a complicated attempt at: providing optimum experiences for children now being reared in smaller families, with fewer adults, often only one parent; compensating children coming from deprived backgrounds, often from migrant families from other cultures and with different languages; caring for the children of the growing number of working mothers or of two working parents.

The growth in female labor force participation—a consequence of the desire for women to earn wages and the need for their labor—led to family policy developments other than the increase in provision of child care services. Major changes in family law regarding marriage, divorce, abortion, child custody, and so forth occurred in the 1960s and 1970s as part of this development. Nor were the earlier threads lost; they were merely modified. Concern with family income now included special attention to the different needs of families with one earner or two earners and with one parent or two parents. And population concerns seemed less focused on whether large families could be encouraged than whether families might have two children instead of one or none! It is only in this context, in the need for women in the labor force and the growing significance of women's contribution to family income that policy support for the economic role of women as mothers has begun to emerge.

Now, in the 1980s, family policy development seems to be coalescing around a new formulation of issues. The focus is on a different family and lifestyle pattern than we have known before and on still a new concern, the relationship between work and family life. It is this focus that is at the forefront of the current debate and that is beginning to influence the nature of family and related policies in all industrialized countries (Kamerman & Kahn, 1981).

More specifically, work and family life are the two central domains in the daily lives of most adults in the developed world. A major change in the relationship between the two has occurred in recent years. As a consequence, many industrialized countries are now beginning to take account of this change and to initiate activities in response. The nature of the development and the kinds of responses now emerging in several European countries represent the core of family policy in Europe in the 1980s.

It is becoming increasingly clear that the central new family policy question is or will be: What is to be the nature of the relationship between work and family life, when most adults, regardless of gender, are increasingly likely to be in the labor force during the same years that they are at the peak of their childbearing and child-rearing responsibilities? What should be the role of government, and of the private sector, in addressing this issue?

Clearly, we are only just beginning to realize the significance of this major change and its ultimate implications for industrialized societies. The major phenomenon of the 1970s, which has been described as generating a social revolution in the industrialized world, is the growth in the labor force participation rates of women, especially married women with children. A concomitant development is a very significant decline in the birth rate in all these countries, serving as a reminder that if women who work are also expected to have children, there will have to be some diminution of the tension between the two domains. A separate but parallel development is the increase in the divorce rate and in the numbers of single-parent, sole-wage-earner families. Adequacy of family income has not been eliminated as a family policy concern, only placed in a different context; and other concerns have been added.

In summarizing the historical development of social and family policies it seems clear that the father's economic role has been a central concern. The absence of a husband meant women could receive some minimum financial support in order to carry out maternal responsibilities. When fathers cannot fulfill their prime role, because of age, disability, or loss of employment, some protection may be available. Only in more recent years has social insurance even begun to address concerns of equity for women. On the other hand, family policies have recently begun to acknowledge women's economic contribution to family life and to provide some support for it.

When we turn to the extent to which social policies have supported, or even permitted, men to take a more active caretaking or nurturant role, we see the reverse bias played out. Thus, sole fathers may qualify for social (public) assistance in some countries but rarely do so; they are expected to make childcare arrangements, and to work. Men have been able to qualify for dependent's benefits under their wives' social insurance entitlement in the U.S. only since the Supreme Court decision in 1972. A few countries are now beginning to provide special child support benefits as an alternative to the more stigmatized (and often less generous) benefits provided under social assistance; however, Sweden comes closest among the countries in permitting fathers with custody of their children to qualify as fully as mothers (Kamerman & Kahn, 1982). Although very few countries permit fathers to qualify for any portion of the paid leave permitted working mothers at the time of childbirth, some are beginning to expand the right of fathers to qualify for the unpaid but job-protected leave that may be available to supplement an initial paid maternity leave (see below).

Social policy in the U.S. has primarily addressed individual needs, with particular attention to assuring a minimum allowance to those with the least. In contrast, in those countries that claim to have a family policy, there has been greater attention to primary group relationships and to the quality of life for families with children. Because it has taken a more universal approach, it is family policy (or family-oriented social policy) that seems to offer the more likely policy perspective for greater attention to fatherhood. I would argue that for fatherhood in its broadest sense to be a concern of social policy, family concerns and benefits have to be a major policy component. There must be concern with the family as a major social institution—all families, not just one particular type, be it single-parent families, inadequate families, poor or deprived families. Different types of families may have different needs, but all warrant attention. There must be concern with the roles and responsibilities of average, normal parents, not just those with problems, or who are absent. There must be concern with parenting regardless of gender, not just motherhood or fatherhood, and not with conventional assumptions about segregated parenting roles. To explore how this is beginning to emerge in countries that have family policies, I turn now to a brief review of developments in some countries and an exploration of the implications for future policy development.

FAMILY POLICY IN THE 1980s

Although not every item is on each country's family policy agenda, the following is a listing of the major policy developments now emerging. Taken as a whole, this agenda provides the basis for an androgynous family policy, one addressing family needs and roles including parenting rather than specific concerns for fathers or mothers. The agenda includes a threefold focus:

1. *Supporting the economic roles of parents by:*
    (a) contributing to the economic costs of children and providing some financial compensation for those adults who contribute to the society's future—in addition to satisfying their own values—by rearing children; and
    (b) providing directly or indirectly (through subsidies) for the care of children while parents are away from home at work, thus assuring children and parents maximum opportunity for development both in and out of the home, without an undue economic burden on parents.
2. *Supporting the nuturing and care-taking roles of parents by:*[1]
    (a) expanding service provision for average families who now have less time and fewer resources to cope with complicated daily lives and diverse family and life cycle problems;
    (b) encouraging and supporting intrafamilial role adaptation to make possible a more equitable sharing between men and women of home and family tasks and responsibilities.
3. *Supporting both roles of parents by* developing employment policies, including adaptation in and at the work place, to facilitate a better balance between work and home so that adults can fulfill their roles as parents without either gender suffering penalties in the labor market.

---

[1]One could argue that child care services are relevant here too and I would agree. The conventional view, however, is that either they are a child policy, or a policy designed to permit parents to work.

The specifics are summarized below.

Supporting the Economic Roles of Parents

Family allowances continue to play a central role in compensating for the conomic costs of rearing children. In both east and west Europe as well as Canada and Israel these benefits represent a significant percentage of median wages, usually between 5 and 10 percent, and an even higher percentage for families with several children. They are an important income supplement for single parents.

In some countries such as Canada, Britain, the Netherlands, West Germany, Denmark, and Sweden, these benefits are available for all children beginning with the first. In other countries such as France and Hungary, the benefits begin only with the second child. Some countries provide a higher benefit for second and third children. Still others increase the amount according to the age of the child. Regardless of the specifics, these benefits provide a significant contribution to family income, in particular for low and median wage earners, for whom the cost of rearing even two children can be a particular burden.

France provides an additional, special supplement to low and middle income families with very young children (under the age of 3) or three or more children. The assumption here is that young children—or many children—make it increasingly unlikely that a woman could be in the labor force, and therefore such families may suffer an extra financial hardship in trying to manage, even for a short time, on the wages of the father. About three-quarters of the families who qualify for this benefit on the basis of children's age or family size meet the income eligibility level, which is set fairly generously.

An alternative approach to providing income supplementation to families with children is the provision of a similar child benefit through the tax system rather than as the direct cash benefit described above. In contrast to the tax allowance for dependents that exists in several countries, which is of value if you pay taxes (and of more value to those with higher incomes), the child benefit tax credit, where provided, is a fixed amount, benefiting equally those at all income levels. Furthermore, it may be refundable to those whose incomes are so low as to preclude any tax obligations. Family allowances (direct transfers or tax benefits) may also be provided to the children of migrant or "guest" workers, usually men, offering another illustration of policy supporting the economic role of fathers.

Housing allowances—direct cash benefits to pay for housing—are becoming an increasingly important component of family income supplementation. In one country, Sweden, more than one-third (until recently, one-half) of all families with children receive this benefit, which clearly plays the role in that country of a generous family allowance for low and middle income families with children. France has recently expanded its housing allowance benefit also, again on an income-tested basis. Many countries do, of course, subsidize housing, but the trend towards provision of cash benefits for housing as a consumption subsidy is relatively new and an extremely important income supplement in these times when the cost of housing represents a growing burden on family income.

These income supplements are important for the economic support provided parenting and suggest the emergence of a new androgynous view of the economic roles of mothers and fathers. Permitting a job-protected leave including protection of seniority and fringe benefits at the time of childbirth and providing a cash benefit to cover all or some portions of wages foregone at that time is another element (Kamerman, 1980). Thus far, however, this policy has been directed almost completely towards women on the assumption that it is only women who carry the biological and physiological burden of maternity. In Europe, paid maternity leaves range from a minimum of 3 months (Denmark and several other countries) to a maximum of 3 years (Hungary), albeit with a more limited cash benefit. The average is 6 months, with West Germany providing 7½ months and Sweden 1 year (with the last 3 months at a minimum benefit level only). The cash benefit is usually tax free (but taxable in Sweden) and usually covers the full wage up to the maximum wage covered under social security or a significant portion of it (or some combination of full wage followed by a smaller flat rate benefit). Only in Sweden is this benefit available to fathers and mothers on almost equal terms. (Only the mother can use the benefit to cover up to 6 weeks before anticipated childbirth; and at least 1 month after birth must be taken by the mother for health reasons). Indeed, parental equity is considered to be so important that the benefit is called "Parent Insurance" rather than maternity insurance as it was before the 1974 legislation. Norway and Finland permit partial use of "maternity leave" by fathers, but not full sharing.

Given the development of maternity policies over the past 15 years, I would expect many more countries to be moving towards a parental benefit rather than the more narrowly defined maternity benefit. Initially, these benefits were all viewed, as they still are in the U.S. today, as a way to protect the mother's health without imposing an undue financial penalty. (Even then such benefits are far from prevalent in the U.S. today.) By the early 1970s, in many countries, the function of the policy was extended beyond maternal protection to include some protection of the mother-child relationship and of child development. It is this concern that led to the extension of the leave and the benefit duration from 8 weeks after childbirth (the standard convalescent post-childbirth period) to 4, 6 or 9 months, depending on the country. Clearly, the policy has expanded from a maternal policy to include a child development component. With that in place, it will be increasingly hard to argue that it should not be available to fathers also. The problem, unfortunately, is the benefit level. As long as the benefit is limited to the maximum wage covered under social security, women, the lower wage earners, are more likely to use it than men. When full wage replacement is available, as it is for civil servants in Sweden, for example, men are more likly to take advantage of the benefit. Perhaps as women's wages compare more favorably with men's and the penalty of income loss falls equally on men and women, the choice may not be subject to such clear economic incentives. The improbability of men using such benefits even if eligible is even greater where the benefit is provided at a flat rate, as in Hungary's childcare grant, rather than as a wage-related benefit. Thus, although we may criticize such benefits for limiting eligibility to women, the reality is that if the benefit level is low, even if men qualified, few would be likely to use it, if only because of economic reasons.

In contrast to supplementing or replacing family income, the provision of childcare services is an obvious family policy that benefits fathers, mothers, and children alike (Kamerman & Kahn, 1981). What is important is that such services be available, accessible, of good quality, and at affordable prices if parents are to work and children to be well cared for. Although fully adequate provision exists nowhere, the continental European countries provide far more in the way of public (free, voluntary) preschools for 2- or 3-year-olds and older than Canada, Australia, Britain or the U.S. Infant and toddler care is scarce everywhere, but the need is attenuated when a parent can be at home (or both parents can share home care) until a child is 1 or 1½, as in Sweden. Regardless, although such provision emerged as more and more women—mothers—went to work, fathers clearly benefited too. Indeed, where childcare provision is inadequate, as in the Anglo-American countries, all family members suffer, father, mother, and children.

Supporting the Nuturing/Caretaking Roles of Parents

Family Support Services.   Apart from childcare services, there is little that has emerged among the personal services to respond to the changes occurring in families generally and in their daily life experiences as roles and family structures change. Various kinds of supportive services are available in the market place in the U.S. as consumer services: housekeeping and homemaker services; repair services, shopping services (including the growth in catalogue shopping), fast food, and catered services (Kahn & Kamerman, 1982). Inevitably, use of these services is limited to those with adequate access to the market place, i.e., the more affluent. There is growing provision of personal services by employers, at or through the work place, including: family counseling, recreational facilities, cafeterias and dining rooms, shopping. Extensive family benefits may also be provided by employers, including pensions, life insurance, holiday and vacation entitlements, and so forth. In the U.S. and several other countries, men are more likely to qualify for the more generous work-related benefits and services than women, because of the types of jobs they hold and industries they work in. However, because governments mandate employers to provide more benefits in some countries, for example, West Germany, the Netherlands, Sweden, Denmark, France, than in the U.S., provision is somewhat more equitable there, but still biased towards men. Housing amenities (communal recreation/social facilities) are an important source of family support provided by the market in the U.S. but through public subsidy in much of Europe. As with regard to childcare services, these family support services benefit the family unit and family members regardless of gender. Public subsidy for such services, as personal *social* services, reflects a growing awareness of family needs in a time of social change without reinforcing traditional gender roles.

Intrafamilial Adaptations.   This is not an arena in which direct government intervention is appropriate. As I pointed out earlier, existing social policies in many countries have supported—or been predicated on—traditional role assignments within the family. Such policies certainly need modification if equity in the family is to be supported.

Of particular importance in Europe in this regard is the beginning trend towards providing parental rather than only maternity benefits at the time of childbirth. Sweden, of course, has taken the initiative here. If women and men are to fulfill home and parenting roles satisfactorily, there have to be equal opportunities for each to do so. Family policies may be needed that support such options. However, such a development is likely to occur only in tandem with high female labor force participation, and under circumstances in which women contribute equally, or almost equally with men, to family income.

Obviously, most adaptation in the home will reflect the values and behavioral changes of the adults living there. There is some evidence in particular among the younger cohorts that as women enter the labor market, men do participate more actively in home and family responsibilities. I would assume that such changes accrue also to children who then may begin to get more attention from their fathers than they have heretofore.

Supporting Both Roles

Employment Policies: Jobs and the Workplace.   This is an essential arena for attention. Thus far it has not been a central focus of family policy, except with regard to the growing trend to statutory provision of the right for women—and in some cases for men as well as women—to take a leave from their jobs to concentrate on child rearing, with the assurance that their jobs will be kept for them and that their seniority and pension rights will be protected. In most countries in Europe the right to such leaves extends well beyond the period of time covered by childbirth-related paid leaves, and therefore becomes simply a right to an unpaid but job-protected leave, often for 1 or 2 years following the end of the paid leave.

Among the countries making such provision: France provides a 2–year leave for either parent under certain circumstances. Norway provides a parental leave of up to 1 year, as does Finland. Sweden provides an unpaid leave after the conclusion of the parent insurance benefit until a child is 18 months old of age, and guarantees parents the right to work part time (a 6–hour day) until their child is 8 years old. Assuring workers a right to take a specified number of days off from work to care for an ill child at home, or to visit a child in school, is also receiving attention in Europe. Working parents in Sweden are entitled to up to 60 days paid sick leave, the same as their own personal sickness benefits. West German workers are entitled to up to 5 days a year.

A variety of other developments are occurring, such as experimentation with flexitime, parttime jobs, alternative work schedules, and so forth as part of industry's response to social change, not as part of government policy. Consideration of employment policies as part of family policy is only beginning to be discussed as an issue.

CONCLUSION

There is little in the way of systematic assessment of the impact of family policies on families and children even in those countries stressing the importance of those policies.

Several countries, including Denmark, Sweden, and France, have concluded that families with children do benefit from the income transfers designed to favor them. The greatest effect seems to occur when tax and transfer policies are harmonized and when the benefit is significant. Certainly, these countries are supporting the economic role of fathers and, equally important, are moving towards a greater recognition of women's contribution to the family's economic well being. Central to this and not sufficiently attended to as yet are employment and labor market policies. Clearly, the economic role of parents cannot be sustained without adequate jobs for all. Income transfers cannot substitute for jobs and adequate wages.

The availability of childcare services may facilitate women's economic role but no evidence exists to support this. Such services may be a necessary but not a sufficient factor, alone. More important, such services can, however, assure children good care and optimal opportunities for development whether or not parents work.

Efforts to attentuate the time and work overload in carrying out parenting and job responsibilities and supporting the nurturing/care-taking roles of both parents is only a very recent policy objective, even in those countries most concerned with gender equity and family and labor market consequences. Thus far most attention has been paid to satisfying the labor market needs of the society by: (a) facilitating labor market participation by women; and (b) protecting children against undue harm as a consequence. As part of this, public policy has begun to pay more attention to the economic contribution women make to family well being and to the caretaking component they must partially relinquish—and share—if they are to work. The potential fathers have to nurture and share in care-taking has received little policy attention; most interest has been with fathers' economic role, but there are a few straws in the wind that suggest change. In contrast, U.S. policy has yet to move in this direction of supporting women's economic role in the family; nor, of course, has it addressed the nurturing component of the paternal role. Fatherhood has received more limited and circumscribed attention in the U.S. than in most other advanced industrialized countries.

Efforts to assess the consequences of these policies for family life, for husbands and wives, for parenting and child development, for the quality of life in general, seem to be largely a matter of faith where most countries are concerned. There is little evidence that parents spend more time with their children (or one another!) if their workday is shorter, and some evidence that highly educated fulltime employed women spend more time with their children than poorly educated fulltime at-home mothers. There is no evidence that more flexible work schedules reduce family stress or that working different shifts, which may permit greater participation in child rearing by fathers, leads to greater equity in parenting roles. This is a problem both of inadequate measurement techniques and a complicated analysis of factors that are difficult to disentangle. Finally, despite the conviction that such policies should have positive consequences, we are nowhere near understanding how different income levels, different patterns of employment and unemployment, and differing amounts of time availability affect parental behavior, family life, and child development.

Family policies—direct and indirect governmental actions designed to support fatherhood—have been the focus of this chapter. The thesis presented is that family policy is the one part of social policy broadly defined that is concerned with ordinary families and normal parenting roles. Only when ''parenting'' is a policy concern will a broad view of fatherhood be supported; and only when family and child well being is a policy objective will parenting be addressed in a broader framework. Otherwise, social policy attention is likely to focus on fathers as the economic mainstay of the family and on husbands as the means for women to avoid excessive dependency on social benefits. Family policies can incorporate an androgynous perspective on parenting, supporting economic roles for women as well as men and nurturing/caretaking roles for both. Only then will fatherhood be awarded more attention and support. Some countries have begun to move in this direction, first by supporting women's economic role, and second by acknowledging a potential care-taking role for fathers. U.S. policies have barely begun to acknowledge either the contribution all parents make to society by rearing children or the growing economic contribution of women to family income. No attention has been paid to a broader view of parenting for either mothers or fathers.

I would hope that researchers will improve their measurment skills and increase their knowledge base. Only then will we be able to provide evidence supporting the positive consequences of expanded roles for fathers, mothers, and children. For such evidence to be found, however, policies must first be established to permit and facilitate opportunities to ''parent'' by both men and women.

REFERENCES

Kahn, A.J., & Kamerman, S. B. From social security to societal policy: The changing domains of social policy in the welfare state. In E. B. Andersen, P. Milhøj, & J. Vedel-Petersen (Eds.), *Social policy and social sciences since the Second World War*. Copenhagen: Teknisk Forlag a-s, 1981.

Kahn, A. J., and Kamerman, S. B., *Helping America's Families,* Philadelphia: Temple University Press, 1982.

Kamerman, S. B. *Maternity and parental benefits and leaves: An international review*. New York: Columbia University Center for the Social Sciences, 1980.

Kamerman, S. B., & Kahn, A. J. (Eds.). *Family policy: government and families in fourteen countries*. New York: Columbia University Press, 1978.

Kamerman, S. B., & Kahn, A. J. *Child care, family benefits and working parents*. New York: Columbia University Press, 1981.

Kamerman, S. B., & Kahn, A. J. Child support programs. Some international developments. In J. Cassetty (Ed.), *Parental Support Obligations,* Lexington, Mass.: D. C. Heath, 1982.

Kamerman, S. B., & Kingston, P. Employer responses to the family responsibilities of employees. In S. B. Kamerman, & C. D. Hayes (Eds.), *Families that work: Children in a changing world*. Washington, DC: NAS/NRC, 1982.

Land, H. The child benefit fiasco. In K. Jones (Ed.), *Yearbook of social policy*. London: Routledge & Kegan Paul, 1977.

4

The Swedish Parental Insurance Policy: An Experiment in Social Engineering

Michael E. Lamb
University of Utah

James A. Levine
Bank Street College of Education

During the 20th century, and especially since the last world war, most of the industrialized countries of Eastern and Western Europe have developed comprehensive social welfare systems that include increasingly explicit "family policies" (Kamerman & Kahn, 1978, 1981). Each of these countries has adopted a set of policies designed to address its own special circumstances and problems. In the present chapter, we focus exclusively on Sweden because the policy pursued by the Swedish government in the last decade comprises an explicit commitment to equalizing the family involvement of mothers and fathers. Sweden is the only nation to have officially attempted to increase paternal involvement in child care by means of government planning. An analysis of Swedish policies and their effectiveness may have important implications not only for those concerned with Swedish social policy but also for policy makers around the world who wish to understand the factors affecting the extent of involvement by males in child care. Unfortunately, although much has been written and said about the "Swedish experiment" in both the popular and semiprofessional media, we know of no systematic attempt to evaluate the impact of the Swedish parental insurance (leave) policy on male involvement. In the first section of this chapter, we briefly outline the multiple goals of Swedish family policy in general and the parental leave policy in particular. Then we describe the parental insurance policy itself—as originally promulgated in 1974 and as it currently exists after several modifications. In the third section, we consider the extent to which the parental leave entitlement has been utilized by fathers. Finally, in the fourth section we discuss factors affecting the willingness of men to take advantage of the parental leave to which they are eligible.

THE GOALS OF FAMILY POLICY

In Sweden, as in most industrialized countries, the initial impetus behind the development of family support policies came from the declining birthrate: In general, those countries that have the most comprehensive family policies (e.g., Sweden, France, East Germany) tend to be those countries with the lowest birthrates. In each of these countries, concern developed about the ability of a diminishing work force to fuel continued economic expansion and to support (by way of contributions to national welfare and retirement plans) the growing number of old, unemployed, and retired citizens. Increasing the natural birthrate—at least to replacement levels—became an important goal of social policy. The earliest systematic family support programs provided economic incentives to parents in order to encourage them to have more children. These incentives involved either direct cash payments to families with children or income tax credits and deductions for wage earners with dependents. Both are still available in many countries, but nowhere do these appear to have had a major impact on the birthrate, although it is, of course, impossible to know what the birthrate would have been had these incentives not been made available.

A second phase in the evolution of social planning and family policy was initiated by the realization that roughly one-half of the potential work force is female. Thus every time a woman withdraws from the labor force in order to raise a child (and thus enhance the size of the future work force), the present labor force is diminished. Realizing this, several countries have sought to maximize the size of the current work force and to encourage childbearing by making it easier for women to have children and remain employed, or to withdraw from the labor force for as short a time as possible. These goals have been pursued in a variety of ways. First, efforts have been made to encourage employers, beginning with those in the public sector, to increase the number of parttime jobs available because these are preferred by women seeking to combine motherhood with paid employment (Gustafsson, 1979). Second, countries like Sweden, Denmark, and France have required employers to offer liberal maternity benefits, which often include medical costs at the time of delivery, extended paid leave before and after birth, the opportunity to take additional unpaid leave, and a guarantee of reemployment without loss of seniority at the end of the parental leave period. Third, governments have urged and financially underwritten the construction and staffing of vast numbers of childcare facilities designed to provide high quality out-of-home care when both parents are working outside the home. These policies have, of course, occurred alongside a social revolution, 'the woman's movement,' which popularized the belief that women and men should have equivalent opportunities for employment. The women's movement further accelerated the rate of involvement by women in the paid labor force. This social evolution, supplemented by explicit social policies, inflationary pressures that have made it difficult for most families to live comfortably on only one income, and a spiraling escalation in the incidence of divorce and single motherhood, have drastically increased the labor force participation of women. In most industrialized countries, more than two-thirds of adult women are in paid employment, and the proportion of mothers who are employed is not much lower. In Sweden, 71% of married women were employed in 1977 as were 53% of those with children under 7 (the age at which school begins in Sweden).

Unfortunately for social planners, however, the increased labor force participation of women had not significantly increased the birthrate, for despite the best efforts of government planners, women have increasingly chosen paid employment *rather than* motherhood. In most Western countries, in other words, couples are having fewer children and they are having them later. The situation in Sweden is representative, if a little extreme. Between 1973 and 1978, the annual increase in population was only 0.3%, and in 1979 this fell to 0.2% (Skandinaviska Enskilda Banken, 1980). Of the families with children, one-half currently have only one child and one-third have only two (Swedish Institute, 1979). Clearly, despite several decades of intensive efforts, the birthrate is still below replacement levels.

THE PARENTAL INSURANCE SCHEME

Concerns about the birthrate and the size of the labor force (present and future) have motivated Swedish family policy throughout most of the 20th century, and they remain important considerations (Liljestrom, 1978). However, a wave of concern with sexism, sex discrimination, and the unequal opportunities available to men and women swept the country in the 1960s with an intensity exceeding that manifest elsewhere in the world. Appreciation of these inequities led Swedish social scientists, reformers, and politicians to the recognition that Sweden's family policies were predicated upon the existence of traditional family patterns and were destined to perpetuate these patterns (e.g., Dahlström, 1971). As long as official policy assumed that mothers were housekeepers and primary childbearers and that fathers were breadwinners, they argued, women would never achieve equal employment opportunities. Existing family policies were designed to make it easier for *mothers* to combine parenthood and employment responsibilities, but employment practices made it impossible for men to do the same. It was increasingly evident, however, that the ability of women to fill the competing demands of the work force and the family depended in large part on the willingness and ability of men to relieve them of some family responsibilities. Clearly, institutional restrictions of men's ability to participate in the family needed to be eliminated. Finally, considerations of equity suggested that couples should decide for themselves how to divide childcare responsibilities: Public and private institutional practices should not mandate (albeit unwillingly) that mothers must assume the bulk of the responsibilities.

For these reasons, the Social Democratic government of Prime Minister Olaf Palme introduced a radical new policy in 1974. Under the terms of this policy, each couple was entitled to 7 months of leave around the time of a child's birth. The parents were free to decide for themselves how to divide the leave. During the leave period, the parent who took the leave was to be paid out of a national insurance fund at a rate that was, on average, equivalent to 90% of the parent's regular salary. The minimum payment under the scheme was set at 25 crowns per day (roughly $6); the maximum was set at 150 crowns per day (roughly $33). (Benefits have since been raised to offset increases in the cost of living since 1974. See below).

In addition to making substantial financial contributions to the parental insurance fund, employers were also required to allow fathers 10 days of paid sick leave when a new child was born, and they were forbidden to penalize any parent (male or female) who chose to take parental leave. Employees who took parental leave were legally guaranteed the right to return to work without loss of seniority or benefits at the end of their leave period. All of the provisions of the parental leave policy were explicitly neutral with respect to the parent's sex: The leave could be taken by either parent or could be divided between the two at their discretion. Roughly one quarter of the children in Sweden are born out of wedlock (Linnér, 1977), and the law states that the parents do not have to be legally married to take or share parental leave benefits.

The parental insurance scheme is funded primarily (85%) by employer contributions (1.329 billion crowns in 1976), and only minimally (15%) by general state revenues (234 million crowns in 1976). According to statistics released by the Unit of Judicial and Social Welfare Statistics (1978), the total cost of parental insurance payments in 1976 was 1.564 billion crowns, which was equivalent to 1.8% of the total expenditure on social welfare programs (87.85 billion crowns) and 11.6% of the total amount spent in social welfare payments for families and children.

Since the policy was introduced in 1974, several modifications of the program have been introduced in an attempt to maximize its usefulness. Over the years, the trend has been to increase the amount of paid leave available and to maximize parents' freedom to use the leave when it would be most useful to them. Interestingly, although the policy was introduced by the Social Democratic government, which lost power in 1976, the more conservative coalition that succeeded them has supported and extended the program.

As of early 1979, new parents are entitled to 6 months of paid leave at 90% of their salary, up to the stipulated maximum. This must be taken within the first 9 months of the child's life, and can be divided between the parents at their discretion. Each parent is then entitled to another six weeks of leave that can be taken immediately, transferred to the other parent, or taken at any time in the first 7 years of the child's life. This "special leave" can be used to reduce the employee's workday from 8 to 6 hours per day for some portion of the child's life, but the reimbursement is only at the minimum rate, regardless of the parent's normal income. In addition, parents are entitled to 12 days of paid sick leave per year to attend to a sick child (15 days per family if there are two children; 18 days per family with three or more children). The latest policy also requires employers to make certain benefits available without pay to their employees of either sex. Parents are entitled to fulltime leave until their infants are 18 months old, and to a reduced workday (6 hours per day instead of 8) until their children are 8 years old. As in the case of employees taking paid leave under the parental insurance scheme, employers are required to allow parents to keep their former jobs and their former rate of pay. The unpaid leave provisions are available to both parents, regardless of whether or not they previously took paid parental leave. (See Svenska Arbetsgivareforeningen, 1978, for further details about the new provisions.)

These extended leave provisions are designed to facilitate shared caretaking and so permit much of the child's care to be provided by family members. There is a serious shortage of childcare facilities in Sweden, and priority is given to the children of single parents. As a result, it is extremely difficult for two-parent families to obtain fulltime day care for their children, and well-nigh impossible for them to obtain places in publicly supported facilities. There are only enough of the latter facilities to serve less than 30% of the children needing care (Kamerman, 1980).

Swedish family policy thus has multiple goals. It aims to add women to the current labor force, to augment the size of the future labor force by increasing the birthrate, to effect social reforms by encouraging men and women to share employment and family/child-rearing responsibilities, and to alleviate the shortage of places in childcare facilities by making it possible to have some care provided within the family. Our focus in this chapter is on the extent to which the parental leave policy has been successful in increasing paternal involvement in childrearing.

UTILIZATION OF PARENTAL LEAVE BY FATHERS

When paid parental leave was made available to fathers in 1974, its advocates expected a positive response from men, since they obviously anticipated widespread support for the goals of equal opportunity and sexual equality. In fact, the response was disappointing. In the first year in which parental leave was available, only 2% of the eligible fathers claimed parental leave, and the majority of these took only a small amount of parental leave. Furthermore, these fathers often took leave at a time when the mothers were also at home, making it difficult to determine how much responsibility for child care the fathers actually assumed. Rates of paternal participation did not increase dramatically in succeeding years either. The disappointing experience of the first few years led the proponents of paternal leave to propose reforms designed to increase paternal participation.

First, a nationwide advertising campaign was launched. Wrestlers, soccer players, and other decidedly "masculine" men were pictured holding, feeding, and strolling with babies, exhorting other men to share the joys of parenthood (see Figure 4.1). Booklets describing the parental leave policy included illustrations and textual material designed to emphasize that fathers too were entitled to parental leave. The campaign was so extensive that few Swedes today can remain unaware that parental leave benefits are available to fathers as well as mothers.

FIG. 4.1.

Second, when they recommended that the amount of paid leave available to couples be increased, the Social Democrats proposed limiting availability of part of the leave period to fathers only. Perhaps because the present (conservative) government is less committed to social reform than were the Social Democrats, this restriction was not included in the revised regulations passed by the Riksdag, and the 45 days of leave that are earmarked for fathers can readily be transferred to mothers, as they usually are.

Despite the best efforts of the government and the program administrators, the number of fathers requesting parental leave has remained low. In 1977, 14% of the fathers of newborns in families containing two adults who worked fulltime (7800 out of 70,000 families) claimed one *day* or more of leave (Sidenbladh, 1979). Of the fathers involved, 50% took less than 1 month of leave, and most of the rest took 2 months of leave. Of those who took leave, the average request was for 42 days. Early trends suggest that the rate of involvement by fathers in two-earner families fell to 10.5% in 1979, despite some program reforms. Rates of paternal participation appear slightly lower when all eligible fathers are considered, rather than only those whose partners were employed fulltime. Thus Table 4.1 shows that, in 1977, less than 10% of the eligible fathers took one day or more of paid parental leave.[1]

Table 4.1 indicates how much leave was taken by fathers in 1974 through 1977. Evidently it is the rare father who takes any paid parental leave, and it is rarer still for fathers to take any substantial amount of parental leave. The latter fact is evident from an inspection of Table 4.2, which indicates how much leave was taken by fathers within each of several income/benefit categories. (In 1977, 198 crowns per day was the maximum benefit possible). Across all income categories, most of the fathers who claimed any parental leave took a month or less of leave, and only 24% of those taking leave took 2 months or more. The table reveals no relationship between income level and the likelihood of taking parental leave. Table 4.3, presenting data for all users, regardless of sex, shows that as income (i.e., level of insurance benefits) increases, the amount of parental leave claimed decreases significantly, but this reflects a confound between sex and income level (see below). The Swedish government has recently commissioned a study designed to relate utilization rates to various demographic indices (such as maternal and paternal education and occupation), but there is no reason to believe that the situation has changed since the 1977 report by the Familjestödsutredningen was completed. (See also Statens Offentliga Utredningar, 1978). Their examination of the relationship between parental occupation and the utilization of parental leave by fathers revealed that fathers who

---

[1]Many more fathers take paid sick leave (to be distinguished from parental leave) around the time of the child's birth. In 1976, 64% of the eligible fathers took at least 1 day, and 40% took the maximum (10 days). The mean for those taking parental leave was 7.5 days (Familjestödsutredningen, 1977).

TABLE 4.1

Number and Proportion of Eligible Fathers Who Took Paid Parental
Leave in the Years for Which Complete Statistics Are Available

	1974	1975	1976	1977[1]
Number of fathers who took at least one day of leave	715	3169	5357	2855
Proportion of the number of eligible fathers	2.4%	5.2%	7.7%	9.7%
Average amount of parental leave taken by participating fathers (days)	26	33	40	42

[1]Estimates based on preliminary data for the first half of the year only.
Data from Familjestödsutredningen, 1977.

TABLE 4.2

Number of Fathers Taking Parental Leave in the Third Quarter of 1977,[1]
and the Size of the Benefit They Received

Number of Days that Fathers Took Parental Leave[2]	Size of the Father's Benefit in Skr Per Day					Total
	25	26–49	50–99	100–197	198	
1–9	9	1	11	250	24	295
10–19	6	6	21	247	29	309
20–29	7	1	18	332	48	406
30–39	4	1	6	243	30	284
40–49	2	—	12	130	21	165
50–59	1	—	9	155	14	179
60–69	2	—	5	112	16	135
70–79	3	—	2	52	3	60
80–89	2	—	4	66	5	77
90–99	2	1	2	46	5	56
100–109	2	—	3	34	5	44
110–119	2	—	3	19	3	27
120–129	—	1	1	16	1	19
130–139	—	1	1	12	1	15
140–149	1	—	—	10	—	11
150–159	1	—	—	9	—	10
160–169	—	—	—	8	3	11
170–179	1	—	1	8	—	10
180–210	2	—	2	26	2	32
Totals	47	12	101	1775	210	2143

[1]This is the latest period for which detailed statistics are available.
[2]Not all of this leave was claimed during the relevant quarter year.
Data from Familjestödsutredningen, 1977.

TABLE 4.3
Who Uses the Parental Insurance and How Much do They Get?
Statistics for the Third Quarter of 1974 in Percentages

No. of Days of Parental Leave	Size of Parental Insurance Benefit (in Skr/Day)[1]					Prop. of Total
	25	26–49	50–99	100–149	150–	
0	29.7	21.6	22.1	26.9	36.2	25.6
1–4	2.1	5.0	6.2	7.8	10.5	4.3
5–14	4.7	10.8	15.5	19.1	24.8	10.3
15–29	8.1	18.6	23.5	19.1	15.2	16.0
30–49	13.2	20.1	18.2	15.0	9.5	16.1
50–59	13.6	9.8	6.6	6.0	—	10.1
60–	20.6	14.1	7.9	6.1	3.8	17.6
Prop. of total (column)	100	100	100	100	100	100
Prop. taking 30 days or more of leave	55.4	44.0	32.7	27.1	13.3	43.8
Total number of persons involved	13617	4121	12391	1066	105	31300

[1]A benefit of 25 skr/day was paid to those who earned less than 10300 skr/annum; 26–49 skr/day to those who earned between 10400 and 20000 skr/year; 50–99 skr/day to those who earned between 20100 and 40300 skr/annum; 100–149 skr/day to those who earned between 40400 and 60600 skr/annum; and 150 skr/day to those who earned more than 60700 skr/annum; benefits were computed at 90% of the individual's regular gross income.
Data from Statens Offentliga Utredningar, 1975.

had more education and higher status jobs were more likely to take paid parental leave. When they did so, furthermore, they were likely to take somewhat longer periods of paid leave than were fathers who had lower status jobs. These data are presented in Table 4.4. Unfortunately, we do not know how many Swedish fathers take an increased role in later child care as a result of increased involvement during the first year, or how many choose to work only 6 hours per day so as to care for their toddlers and preschoolers. However, it seems clear that despite the availability of paid paternal leave, the bulk of child-rearing responsibilities are still assumed by mothers.

FACTORS LIMITING UTILIZATION OF PAID PARENTAL LEAVE BY FATHERS

Why do so few fathers take parental leave, even for a few days? Unfortunately, the answer to this question remains largely unknown; few attempts have been made to determine what distinguishes those fathers who do take parental leave

TABLE 4.4

Proportion of Eligible Fathers Choosing Various Amounts
of Paid Parental Leave Broken Down
by Paternal Occupation (1976 data)[1]

Fathers' Occupation	0	1.29	30–	31	Total
Unskilled workers	95.6%	2.5%	1.9%	4.4%	2863
Semi-skilled	94.5	3.1	2.4	5.5	7564
Skilled trades	92.1	4.3	3.6	7.9	8729
Clerical, janitorial	93.4	3.8	2.8	6.6	1272
White collar, supervisory	91.8	4.3	3.9	8.2	3209
Engineering	91.4	4.5	4.1	8.6	11084
Professional	89.2	5.1	5.7	10.8	7010
Agricultural	98.2	0.8	1.0	1.8	2658
Total	92.2	4.1	3.7	7.8	43525

[1]This is the latest period for which detailed statistics are available.
Data from Familjestödsutredningen, 1977.

from those who do not. At present, we can only speculate why more men do not request parental leave, and why those who do take so few days of leave.

First, immediate financial costs do not seem to be critical. The minimum benefit as of January 1981 was 32 crowns per day (11,520 Skr per annum or $2560 per annum), and the maximum 298 crowns per day (107,280 Skr per annum or $23,840 per annum). Both figures are now index linked, and thus increase as the cost of living increases. Within the 32 to 298 Skr range, parents are paid 90% of their regular wage. (Since tax rates are high, this means that take-home pay is only marginally less during parental leave than during times of employment.) According to statistics supplied by the Skandinaviska Enskilda Banken (1980), the average wage of industrial workers ("wage earners") in 1979 was 64,000 Skr per annum ($16,222) and of salaried workers (mainly white collar workers) 90,000 Skr per annum ($20,022); relatively few people earned more than the ceiling ($26,489) above which the parental leave benefit would amount to less than 90% of the normal wage.

Nevertheless, official statistics indicate that the likelihood of taking paid parental leave does not change as income rises. Representative statistics illustrating this tendency were presented in Table 4.2. Table 4.3, which presents data concerning all users (male or female), shows that utilization decreases as income rises, but this is probably because men are likely to be overrepresented at the high income levels and women at the lower income levels. Even as recently as 1974, the average Swedish woman working fulltime earned 42% less than the average man, mainly because women tended to have less prestigious and pecunious occupations (Gustafsson, 1979). Furthermore, 45% of the employed women and 55% of employed mothers were employed parttime and thus earned much less than their partners did.

The nature of the person's employment responsibilities may also affect h is or her willingness to take paid leave. Those earning high incomes are likely to have professional occupations in which substitutes cannot easily replace individuals who are on leave. Thus work is likely to mount up during the period of absence. In addition, future prospects as an academic or as a trial lawyer, for example, may depend on continued visibility and professional activity. Thus although there may be little immediate financial cost for these people, the long-term costs may be substantial. The self-employed likewise cannot afford (in the long run) to take much time away from their jobs, even if they are paid during this period, because their reputation and clientele are at stake. Even today, men are more likely to be constrained in this way than women are because they are more likely to hold professional occupations.

It is also important to recognize the economic significance of the "black market" structure in Sweden. There are, of course, no official statistics available on the size of the black market, but this sector is obviously large and growing exponentially. Many services are supplied unofficially or in exchange for other services in a barter system, so as to avoid taxes. Thus even when individuals are paid 90% of their official (declared) income while enjoying parental leave, they have to forego the undeclared income, which may have accounted for a significant—even a major—portion of their total income. This is likely to have a greater impact on men than women because men predominate in those occupations (construction, engineering, plumbing, painting, car repairs, etc.) in which the black market has become especially important.

Although men seeking parental leave are legally protected against discrimination by employers, many men reportedly fear that their employers would disapprove and that sanctions would be imposed if they pursued this option. Such concerns are especially prevalent among those who are employed in the private sector: Interestingly, men employed in the public sector are more likely to take parental leave than are men employed in the private sector (Familjestödsutredningen, 1977; Sidenbladh, 1979). The relevant statistics for 1976 (see Table 4.5) indicate that men who are employed in the private sector, especially those who hold lower-status jobs, are much less likely to take parental leave than are their peers employed in the public sector. Presumably, men in the private sector feel vulnerable to punitive reactions by employers, and this concern appears to increase as the employee's status lessens and their replaceability increases. Financial considerations may also be involved: Public employees are entitled to leave at full salary, even if this is higher than the maximum benefits level.

The attitudes of major employers toward men taking parental leave was illustrated (perhaps unrepresentatively) by a recent highly publicized case. The head of the postal service took several weeks of parental leave to care for his young son and thus elicited a fair amount of attention in the press. A p rominent

TABLE 4.5

Proportion of Eligible Fathers in Each Occupational
Category Who Took Parental Leave Broken Down by
Type of Employer (1976)

Father's Employer	Fathers' Occupation[1]			
	1	2	3	Overall
National Government	10.4	10.7	12.2	11.0
Municipal Government	9.6	10.8	11.4	10.8
County Government	12.0	15.5	11.8	12.9
Private Sector	5.8	7.7	9.7	6.8
Overall	6.4	8.9	10.8	8.0

[1]Occupational code: 1 = unskilled, semiskilled and skilled workers;
2 = clerical, white collar and engineering workers; 3 = major professionals. Agricultural workers excluded.
Data from Familjestödsutredningen, 1977.

industrialist was thereupon moved to comment that if every father followed this example, the economy would suffer; he expressed the hope that most fathers would show a greater sense of responsibility to their employers and to the national interests! Attitudes like this are understandably likely to limit the number of fathers seeking parental leave.

The sex-role stereotypes that motivate employers like this industrialist must also affect the employees' behavior directly. Many men have been taught little about childrearing while growing up, and have been socialized to perceive themselves as economic providers rather than childminders. As a result, few men aspire to become primary caretakers, regardless of the efforts made by employers and legislators to facilitate their involvement in such activities. Furthermore, many women may be uneasy about becoming secondary parents, since they have been socialized to perceive themselves as primary caretakers. The importance of these factors, and the extent to which their influence is changing, remain to be investigated.

In collaboration with Joseph Pleck and Philip Hwang, we are currently initiating research designed to determine why more Swedish fathers do not take paid parental leave. Our goal is to interview fathers who did take parental leave and those who did not in order to determine what factors affected their decisions. We also plan to interview the partners of these men. In our interviews we will focus on individual attitudes and values, as well as the presumed attitudes of workmates and employers. When fathers have taken parental leave, we will question them closely about the reactions of their supervisors, as we wish to assess the frequency with which employees are punished for behaving "irresponsibly." Similar data will be obtained from those who did not take parental leave because of a fear of retribution. It is, of course, difficult to determine just how likely adverse reactions really would be, but we hope to gain some insight by interviewing employers as well as employees in various locations around the country. Unfortunately, sex-role prescriptions and attitudes currently constitute an emotion-laden issue, and so it will not be easy to assess the extent to which individual inhibitions and employment-related concerns affect the utilization of parental leave by fathers. Nevertheless, the topic is important enough to merit extensive research.

REFERENCES

Dahlström, E. (Ed.). *The changing roles of men and women* (1962). New York: Beacon Press, 1971.

Familjestödsutredningen. *Sa anvärides Föräldraförsäkringen ar 1976.* Stockholm: Riksforsakringsverket; Matematisk-statistiska byran, 1977.

Gustafsson, S. Women and work in Sweden. *Working life in Sweden,* December 1979 (Whole No. 15).

Kamerman, S. B. Child care and family benefits: Policies of six industrialized countries. *Monthly Labor Review,* November 1980.

Kamerman, S. B., & Kahn, A. J. (Eds.). *Family Policy: Government and families in fourteen countries.* New York: Columbia University Press, 1978.

Kamerman, S. B., & Kahn, A. J. *Child care, family benefits, and working parents.* New York: Columbia University Press, 1981.

Liljeström, R. Explicit and comprehensive family policy: Sweden. In S. B. Kamerman, & A. J. Kahn (Eds.), *Family Policy: Government and families in fourteen countries.* New York: Columbia University Press, 1978.

Linnér, B. No illegitimate children in Sweden. *Current Sweden,* April 1977 (Whole No., 157).

Sidenbladh, E. Usage of paternal leave. *Svenska Dagbladet,* April 23, 1979.

Skandinaviska Enskilda Banken. *Basic Facts about Sweden—1980.* Stockholm: Skandinaviska Enskilda Banken, 1980.

Statens Offentliga Utredningar (SOU). *Förkortad arbetstid för småbarnsföräldrar.* Stockholm: Betänhande au Familjestödsutredningen, 1975.

Statens Offentliga Utredningar (SOU). *Föräldraförsäkring.* Stockholm: Betanhande au Familjestödsutredningen, 1978.

Svenska Arbetsgivareföreningen. *Leave for the care of a child and parental allowance—New provisions in 1979.* Stockholm: Svenska Arbetsgivareföreningen, Circular letter number 6, 1978.

Swedish Institute. Equality between women and men in Sweden. *Swedish Institute Fact Sheet on Sweden,* Number FS 82 e Ohjs 1979.

Unit for Judicial and Social Welfare Statistics. *The cost and financing of the social services in Sweden in 1976.* Stockholm: National Central Bureau of Statistics, 1978.

5

The Father's Case in Child Custody Disputes: The Contributions of Psychological Research

Ross A. Thompson
University of Nebraska

INTRODUCTION

The past few decades have witnessed a dramatic increase in the divorce rate in the United States and elsewhere, a phenomenon that reflects and influences changing social attitudes toward marriage and the family. When offspring are involved, the divorce process becomes further complicated by considerations over custody and visitation rights. And when the parents themselves cannot resolve these issues, the courts are faced with the difficult task of making a custody decision.

The adjudication of child custody disputes raises important and interesting questions, among them the role of fathers as caregivers. For many years, courts have assumed a preference for the mother, contending that a mother's nurturance and love constitute irreplaceable components of early sociopersonality development, particularly during the "tender years." More recently, however, judges have been using a more egalitarian "best interests of the child" guideline, in which mother and father can compete on a more equal footing for the custody of offspring. Yet this new guideline is a mixed blessing. Although it opens the door to fathers, its conceptual ambiguity permits a wider latitude of subjective judgment on the part of judges, which often results in an implicit maternal preference. The question of what *are* the child's "best interests," and how these may be served by a custody decision, is crucial if this decision-rule is to play a useful role in the custody adjudication process.

During the last decade, students of child development have devoted a good deal of attention to early sociopersonality development and how it is influenced by family conditions. In contrast to earlier work that tended to focus on the maternal role in the traditional nuclear family, recent research has become more broadly based and more socially relevant. Topics of research have included, for example, the father's contributions to early development, the experience of growing up within a single-parent family headed by the father or the mother, and the impact of divorce on the child. As such, research of this kind, combined with empirical and theoretical contributions from other areas in psychology, may contribute to clarifying a child's "best interests" in ways that are relevant to the resolution of custody disputes.

The purpose of this review is to consider the relevance of this research to the best interests guideline, particularly concerning the strength of the father's claim to custody. My focus is on offspring who are infants or young children because these are the ages for which jurists' maternal preferences are the strongest. Of course, a range of other factors enter into any specific custody dispute, including the nature of the temporary custody arrangement, specific family history, economic considerations, and other factors.[1] The research literature may be valuable, however, in helping to develop a broader perspective within which these and other considerations may be put into perspective, especially with respect to a child's changing developmental needs and capacities. My primary goal, therefore, is to provide a review of recent research concerning fathers as caregivers for legal scholars, lawyers, judges, and others involved in making custody decisions. At the same time, I hope to alert research psychologists to important areas in which future study is needed.

The discussion opens with a consideration of the best interests guideline: its historical development, and the ambiguities inherent in how it is conceptually defined and assessed in the courtroom. After a short aside about the general relevance of psychological research to legal issues, we then consider the research evidence relevant to the father's case in custody disputes. We consider, in turn, the role of fathers in the intact family, the experience of divorce and its effects on the child in the more typical case of maternal custody, and research concerning fathers as single parents. From this review, I offer several conclusions concerning the relevance of this work to custody disputes.

THE DEVELOPMENT OF THE BEST INTERESTS GUIDELINE

In hearing a custody dispute, a judge is faced with an unusual and difficult decision. Most legal disputes focus on the documentation of facts relevant to a case; child custody decisions entail more subjective judgments of parental caregiving

---

[1]Another important consideration relates to siblings: Courts have preferred to keep siblings together in awarding custody to a parent, even though considerations related to each child alone may suggest a different decision. In this discussion, I focus upon the individual mother-child/father-child relationship, as have most researchers, even though many custody decisions pertain to several children within the family unit.

competence. Furthermore, custody disputes cannot be resolved on the basis of judicial precedent. Rather, they must be addressed on a case-by-case basis, taking into consideration the unique history and circumstances of the family in question. The judge's decision-making is further complicated by the predictive nature of the custody award. That is, he or she must consider the long-term ramifications of the decision, including the future economic and living conditions of each parent, the developmental needs of the child, and the potential availability of extrafamilial support systems. Finally, custody decisions rely heavily upon a judge's discretionary powers in applying legislative guidelines to the particular family in question. For all these reasons, the resolution of child custody disputes entails decision-making considerations that most jurists are poorly trained to address. Thus they find these cases excruciatingly difficult to resolve (Mnookin, 1975).

To be sure, most parents who divorce can agree on custody of the children without seeking judicial help. Despite the dramatic increase in the rate of divorce over the past two decades (Glick, 1979) and the broadening of legislative guidelines to put parents on a more equal footing in seeking custody, fewer than 15% of the couples who divorce will proceed with a fully contested custody battle. And, of course, the overwhelming majority of custody awards are to the mother: Fewer than 10% of divorce decrees award children to the father (Weitzman & Dixon, 1979). In many cases, fathers who receive custody do so with the consent of the noncustodial mother.

But although the proportion of disputed custody cases seems to be stable, the absolute number of disputes is increasing sharply due to the rising divorce rate. Coupled with the gradual changes in parental roles evoked, in part, by the increasing number of working mothers (Hoffman, 1979), it is reasonable to expect that the number of divorce petitions in which both parents want custody will continue to increase in the years to come. Therefore, it is important to clarify the guidelines by which judges resolve these disputes.

The legislative guideline that currently prevails in most states—that is, awarding custody according to the "best interests of the child"—is historically the least explicit. Interestingly, English legal tradition long asserted a paternal preference, reflecting a time in which offspring were regarded as heirs to privilege and wealth and as parental property (Mnookin, 1975; Roth, 1977). Thus the father was viewed as the primary guardian of his legitimate children and, in the event of a dissolution of the marital bond, he assumed exclusive custodial rights. With the changes in social structure wrought by the Industrial Revolution and changes in social philosophy provoked by writers like Locke and Rousseau, this common law assumption gradually broke down. Instead, by the 19th century, both English and American law put the wife on an equal footing with her husband: Both were to receive equal consideration in a custody decision. In practice, however, this usually resulted in an implicit maternal preference, because custody decisions were based on evaluations of parental fitness and wives, as the customy initiators of divorce action, were in a better position to argue against their husbands (Mnookin, 1975). Concurrently, an explicit maternal preference when the children were in their "tender years" (generally speaking, under the age of seven) helped to consolidate this implicit bias for the mother in the courts (Roth, 1977). In short, changing judicial guidelines were reflecting changing social values. Childhood was increasingly viewed as a period of nurturance and education, and mothers typically assumed a major role for both.

Early in the 20th century the maternal presumption became consolidated in judicial decision-making, sometimes by explicit statute but more often in the form of case law. Jurists assumed that, except in instances when the mother was clearly unfit, it was consistently best for the child to benefit from the love and nurturance provided by the mother (Roth, 1977; Weitzman & Dixon, 1979). They were supported in this assumption by contemporary psychoanalytic theory, which stressed the unique role of a mother's love to early psychological development (cf. Freud, 1938).

More recently, however, the maternal presumption has been increasingly questioned in favor of a more egalitarian guideline. Much of the impetus for this reconsideration has come from social critics who regard the maternal preference as inherently sexist and a perpetuation of traditional gender roles. The dramatic rise in the number of working mothers in recent years and the concurrent increase in demand for infant and preschool childcare services are particularly salient manifestations of the changing American family. Thus the traditional family system in which mother is a fulltime caregiver is no longer the norm, and this has undermined the rationale for an explicit preference for mother in custody disputes. In addition, of course, there are a number of instances in which an explicit maternal presumption is clearly inappropriate, such as when the father or another person has assumed sole caregiving responsibilities, or when the mother is abusive or neglectful. Finally, many critics contend that the maternal presumption focused attention on judicial evaluations of parental fitness rather than on child-centered concerns. Thus the purpose of the best interests guideline is to encourage an appraisal of the custody dispute in light of the contributions (actual and potential) of each parent to the child's present and future needs.

Problems with the Best Interests Guideline

This legislative intent may be significantly undermined, however, by the ambiguity concerning how the child's "best interests" are to be determined. Judges are provided few explicit decision-rules to determine what a child's best interests are, much less rules that take into account a child's changing developmental needs. Even when statutes provide broad guidelines defining the child's best interests, these guidelines are seldom very explicit and judges are offered no guidance concerning which of these interests are most important in determining custody. This leaves judges broad discretion in defining these interests, with the result that custody awards can be determined on the basis of highly subjective criteria that may vary widely on a case-by-case basis. Alternatively, many judges simply adhere to a maternal presumption despite the changed mandate (Roth, 1977; Weitzman & Dixon, 1979). In short, one of the greatest problems with the best interests guideline is the current lack of certainty concerning how this expression should be interpreted (see Whobrey, Sales, & Lou, 1982).

A fundamental question, for example, concerns which of the child's many "interests" should predominate in a judge's deliberations over a custody award. Fundamentally, of course, children require the basic necessities that promote physical well being: adequate nourishment, a warm, safe home environment, sufficient health care, clothing, and an interpersonal environment that is not overtly abusive or oppressive. Beyond these basic necessities, however, there is considerable controversy concerning which of the child's other needs merit primary consideration. Is it important that the child be with the parent who has provided the most care in the past (i.e., ensure continuity of care)? What of the child's future educational or religious training? Should jurists be concerned with the child's "character development"? Is continuity in living circumstances important? Should the child be with the same-sex parent? To put it simply, should the child's best interests be strictly construed to mean only the basic requirements of adequate caregiving, or should the courts be more interested in the child's optimal development?

There is no easy answer to this question, and opinions vary widely. Some legal scholars, such as Mnookin (1973, 1975) and Wald (1975, 1980), advocate a more limited interpretation of the child's interests in order to curtail the court's discretionary powers in deciding child placement cases (e.g., custody, foster care, etc.). On the other hand, writers like Goldstein, Freud, and Solnit (1973), in a widely publicized volume, argue that "psychological parenting" should be the primary consideration in determining child placement; that is, to whom has the child developed a lasting emotional bond? There is, in short, no clear consensus concerning what constitute the child's primary interests in determining a custody award.

Assuming that the best interests guideline is meant to include factors other than physical well being alone, a second question concerns the limits of this construction. That is, how do we evaluate the parental caregiving practices that promote the child's best interests? Is one parent's warm but permissive approach preferable to another's less affectionate limit-setting? Should judges prefer a custody arrangement that is likely to foster a strong traditional gender identity in the child? These and a range of similar questions surround most custody decisions and concern the implicit goals and values that underly a court's preference for one parent over the other.

It is doubtful that there is much broad consensus within most Western societies concerning these child-rearing goals and practices. As with differences in lifestyle, parents vary greatly concerning the traits and characteristics they seek to develop in their children, and they employ a range of practices for achieving these goals. This diversity contributes to the heterogeneity of a society, in fact, and courts have traditionally hesitated to infringe upon parental freedom to raise their children as they prefer. Indeed, apart from those instances in which state intervention is mandated by manifest child abuse or neglect, greater concern has been voiced over the state's overregulation of parental decision-making in areas such as education, religious training, and medical care. In short, society encourages a great deal of freedom and diversity in child-rearing goals and practices and, by and large, the courts have insured this freedom.

In the adjudication of child custody disputes, however, judges frequently rely on subjective judgments of a parent's caretaking style that are often based on personal values and beliefs. Sometimes these judgments concern the "moral climate" of the home. In some cases, a judgment is based on a parent's occupational commitments, political affiliations, expectation of remarriage, or economic circumstances rather than his or her relationship with the child. In short, these judgments of caretaking often involve intuitive, usually unarticulated value judgments that are relative to the values and beliefs of the judge determining a custody settlement. These values are likely to reflect sociocultural and social class biases as well as religious beliefs and moral attitudes. Importantly, they usually entail judgments of parental fitness, with secondary regard for their actual or potential effects upon the child (see Lowery, 1981). Thus a second difficulty with the best interests guideline concerns judging the parental practices that contribute to a child's best interests. In the absence of a prevailing social consensus, judges tend to use their own intuitive value judgments that may or may not reflect child-centered concerns (Mnookin, 1975).

It is important to note, however, that intuitive judgments of parental practices are not limited to jurists. Indeed, "expert testimony" from various sources, including psychiatric witnesses and social workers, has been criticized as being largely subjective and value based, and thus unreliable (Ennis & Litwack, 1974; Mnookin, 1975; Okpaku, 1976).

In other words, *any* subjective assessment of a family is likely to result in speculative and unreliable judgments. Furthermore, this unreliability is especially likely when the family is under stress (as in a custody battle), when normal patterns of interaction are affected by emotional turmoil. Thus it is doubtful whether assessments of family interaction at the time of a custody dispute—by a judge or an "expert witness"—yield meaningful information about parent–child relationships.

A third ambiguity in the best interests guideline concerns the time frame within which a child's interests are appraised. Divorce presents parents and children with immediate and difficult adjustments (see below). Should judges seek a custody arrangement that helps the child to negotiate these short-term transitions? Or should longer–term concerns take precedence if they conflict with more immediate needs? These, too, are questions of judgment about which legislative guidelines or judicial precedent offer little guidance.

Taken together, the major difficulty with the best interests guideline is the broad interpretational latitude permitted judges in deciding custody disputes. Disagreement exists concerning which of the child's many interests should be included in a judge's deliberations, how these interests are translated into judgments of parental child-rearing practices (and how these practices should be assessed), and whether short-term or long-term concerns should take precedence. These conceptual ambiguities thus delegate a good deal of discretionary power to judges, with the result that custody decisions may be based on implicit value judgments that are relative and thus inappropriate to legal decision-making. Of course, these interpretational problems are most acute when the child's best interests are broadly construed, but to some extent they are inherent within any such inclusive formulation.

In view of this, some legal scholars have called the process of child custody adjudication ''indeterminate''—that is, there are often no reliable, objective and legally satisfying ways of awarding custody to a parent according to the child's best interests (Mnookin, 1975; Okpaku, 1976). Whereas some custody cases are always relatively easy to resolve (such as when one parent is abusive, or has abandoned the family, and the other parent has not), for the majority of cases there exist no generally accepted, easily applied decision-rules by which the child's best interests may be determined fairly and objectively. The same case presented to two judges may be decided in very different ways. The indeterminacy of child custody adjudication also has important implications outside the courtroom. Legal guidelines usually serve as negotiating parameters by which the parties to a dispute can assess their relative chances of success in adjudication and modify their demands and expectations accordingly. Under the best interests rule, fathers and mothers are provided little information of this kind (Mnookin & Kornhauser, 1979). Thus articulate and consistent custody guidelines are necessary both for the adjudication process and for the interpersonal bargaining that precedes it.

What is the solution to judicial indeterminacy in custody cases? Some have suggested a return to more specific, all-encompassing legislative decision-rules (e.g., custody awarded to the mother if the child is age 5 or younger; custody awarded to the same-sex parent with older children). This would limit judicial discretion, but a proportion of disputes would certainly be resolved unfairly. Another proposal is for a greater emphasis on predivorce mediation to encourage parents to seek their own solution to the custody dispute short of a court battle. A third—and more radical—alternative is to decide custody disputes by some random process: in essence, a judicial coin-flip (Mnookin, 1975). Such an approach would acknowledge the inherent inability of the court to make an objective, reliable custody award, and would prevent the noncustodial parent from feeling that he or she was judged to be a less adequate parent than the spouse with custody.

Short of these alternatives, it is clear that judicial decision-making in custody disputes entails highly idiosyncratic considerations that must be addressed on a case-by-case basis. The history of the family in question, the wishes of the child, the nature of the temporary custody arrangements, the quality and quantity of predivorce parental caregiving involvement, and prospective living conditions for the child with either parent are all considerations (to name a few) that should figure prominently in a custody award and that are likely to vary from one family to another. The important question, however, is whether there exists a valid overall framework within which these factors can be considered and by which further information may be requested and evaluated. In other words, judges and lawyers require some general understanding of the nature of family functioning in intact and divorced homes in order to properly interpret and weigh these considerations relevant to the child's best interests. Operating within such a framework, jurists may be less likely to base custody decisions upon idiosyncratic and value-laden considerations. It is in providing such an overall knowledge base that psychological research may have a limited but important role in the adjudication of child custody disputes. This is particularly true concerning the role of fathers as caregivers, which is the topic of this review.

THE RELEVANCE OF PSYCHOLOGICAL RESEARCH TO JUDICIAL ISSUES

There are many reasons why judges, lawyers, and other legal experts are often hesitant to use psychological research in arguing legal issues (Collins, 1978). A fundamental problem is the different orientation to human behavior adopted by the jurist and the behavioral scientist. The former gathers information relevant to a set of circumstances to make a decision in a particular case; the latter seeks to understand broad, normative trends in behavior. The difference between the ideographic and nomothetic approaches often makes it difficult to translate ideas and questions from one discipline to the other.

For example, the behavioral scientist approaches the issue of behavioral prediction on a probabilistic basis: Given a set of conditions, research studies may indicate that one outcome is more likely to occur than several alternative outcomes in the general population. Although this is informative, such a conclusion is of limited value to the jurist, who seeks greater certainty concerning specific predictions relevant to a unique set of circumstances. It is unlikely, however, that psychological research will be able to attain this kind of specific predictive efficiency in the foreseeable future. Indeed, the results of several longitudinal developmental studies have shown how poorly antecedent variables can predict later outcomes in specific cases (e.g., Bayley, 1970; Kagan, 1971; Kagan & Moss, 1962; see review by Beckwith, 1979). Nevertheless, psychological research can be very helpful in identifying normative trends in behavior and development that are generally characteristic of the population as a whole, within certain boundaries of statistical certainty. This information can be heuristically valuable in appraising individual cases, even though prediction on this basis is probablistic rather than definitive.

A second issue limiting the perceived usefulness of psychological research to judicial issues concerns its relevance to the kinds of questions that concern lawyers and judges. In exploring the research literature, jurists quite often find it focused on issues that are too remote from the specific questions for which they seek answers. In particular, behavioral research is usually oriented to questions concerning normative behavioral processes in the isolated individual. On the other hand, jurists are looking for information on the individual in a sociocultural and environmental milieu, and for information that addresses issues of practical import.

This shortcoming has been noted within the psychological community itself (e.g., Bronfenbrenner, 1974, 1977). Behavioral scientists are often guilty of focusing their attention on the individual or the family unit without consideration of broader economic conditions, extrafamilial support systems, and other relevant factors. Researchers also tend to be more interested in normative social conditions (such as the traditional nuclear family unit) than in nonnormative conditions. Unfortunately, when they do address applied issues, behavioral researchers often define their variables of interest with excessive generality, limiting the applications of their findings.

These problems in applying existing psychological research to judicial concerns are well illustrated in previous reviews of research relevant to child custody issues. Ellsworth and Levy (1969), for example, drew heavily upon studies of father absence in considering the effects of maternal custody. As they and others (e.g., Herzog & Sudia, 1973; Levitin, 1979; Pedersen, 1976) recognized, however, these studies are limited in their relevance to custody issues because of deficiencies in sampling and method. "Father absence" was treated as a homogeneous condition in most studies, for example, even though it resulted not only from divorce, but also from death of the father, occupational exigencies (e.g., military service), abandonment, imprisonment, or other factors. Social class was an important mediating variable that was not explored in most of the studies. Nor were interpersonal variables considered, such as the quality of the child's relationship with the noncustodial father. As problematic as they were, however, these studies were included in research reviews largely because they constituted the bulk of scientific knowledge concerned with nontraditional family circumstances relevant to divorce.

Similarly, other divorce-related research included in these reviews drew upon clinical populations in which researchers examined the occurrence of parental divorce as a factor in the life experiences of children later referred for psychiatric disorder. This method of investigation exaggerates the maladaptive effects of divorce on children, especially since few of these studies employed appropriate comparison groups. In short, the legal researcher surveying the psychological research literature is likely to be impressed with the small number of studies that directly address issues relevant to legal questions. It is little surprise that, in 1969, Ellsworth and Levy concluded: "As must be painfully clear, the psychological research that can be considered both relevant and useful to the problems of custody adjudication is minimal [p. 198]."

Fortunately, however, this situation is beginning to change. Motivated in part by the need to justify new research expenditures, behavioral scientists are increasingly asking more socially relevant questions that can be more easily applied to contemporary social problems. Some of the current shift in research interests also reflects changing social conditions. For example, the nuclear family unit, long the focus of research on early socialization influences, is no longer the normative experience for a growing number of children. As a result, developmental psychologists are beginning to look at children growing up in nontraditional homes in which parental caregiving roles are modified or reversed. Some of this research is reviewed in a subsequent section of this review. In addition, the results of several highly detailed longitudinal studies of children's experience with the divorce process are also described, all of which were conducted during the last decade. Thus, for various reasons, one of the more encouraging trends within psychological research in recent years has been an increasing interest in applied social problems, and this is likely to have a salutary effect on the relevance of this work to judicial concerns.

At the same time, it is important to acknowledge the limits of behavioral research—in particular, that certain questions are not amenable to well-designed psychological inquiry for ethical reasons. Okpaku (1976) has identified a range of questions entailed in judicial decision-making during custody disputes for which research findings would be highly useful. Does it matter at what age a child is separated from a "marginally adequate" mother? How and under what circumstances do alternative custody arrangements cause emotional difficulties in children? What family factors either exacerbate or mitigate the difficulties? Are children more vulnerable to separation trauma at some ages than others?

These are indeed important questions, yet ethical considerations prohibit researchers from conducting well-designed experimental interventions that would provide relevant data. Children simply cannot be assigned to potentially maladative custody arrangements so researchers can study their effects. Similarly, society would not permit researchers to manipulate family circumstances to observe their effects on children's divorce adjustment. Information pertaining to questions such as these must be derived from pre-existing social and family conditions that are investigated on a post–hoc basis, and this is a much less satisfying manner of obtaining valid data. In short, research studies are a valuable information-gathering tool, but they are limited in the kinds of questions that can be investigated.

This leads to a third area of conflict between jurists and behavioral researchers: the proper place of psychological theory. Legal scholars (e.g., Mnookin, 1975; Okpaku, 1976) have commented on the range of theories of human behavior, each with a set of unique assumptions about human beings that conflict with those of other theories. No theory has been demonstrated to be clearly superior to the others, especially with respect to accurately predicting the behavior of individuals on a long-term basis. Apart from the research they generate, then, of what value are psychological theories to the custody adjudication process?

In light of the number of questions that research studies cannot ethically address, psychological theories are important by helping to fill in gaps in our knowledge by providing meaningful linkages between existing bodies of research. In providing a broader frame of reference, theories thus help researchers make responsible applications of current findings to under–researched or impossible-to-research areas, as well as indicating other potential topics for additional study. Theories also posit explanatory constructs that can help us to better understand research findings (e.g., attachment bond, ego defenses, etc.). To be sure, behavioral observations can be explained in various ways by different theories; the evaluation of competing theoretical explanations always entails a critical evaluation of their explanatory sophistication and comprehensiveness. But this diversity in perspective is a sign of a healthy scientific discipline and surely does not argue against the usefulness of psychological theories as heuristic aids. In other words, theories are not simply speculative explanations of human behavior. When supported by a body of research, they permit responsible applications of existing knowledge to other areas.

Taken together, there is reason to believe that psychological research and psychological theory can have a limited but important place in the adjudication of child custody disputes. Although research findings may not always provide the kind of answers jurists require, they do provide some important information that merits consideration. Litwack, Gerber, and Fenster (1980) have offered a similar argument.

> It must be noted, however, that unless custody disputes are to be determined by fixed and unbending rules—i.e., as long as custody decisions require consideration of which custody alternative is likely to serve the "best interests" of the child—some prediction must be made in custody cases. That being the case, the issue is not whether psychologists or psychiatrists can predict the outcome of alternative custody arrangements with anything approaching absolute accuracy, but whether psychological testimony can provide the court with information, *not otherwise readily available to the court,* which will increase, however slightly, the accuracy of the prediction the court must make [pp. 282–283; italics in original].

In particular, psychological research can contribute to an improvement in judicial decision-making by providing an overall frame of reference within which the idiosyncratic considerations relating to particular custody disputes can be appraised.

This review of research focuses on one important aspect of a judge's considerations—the strengths of a father's claim to custody under the best interests guideline. As the foregoing discussion of legal issues indicates, mothers are typically awarded custody because of the perceived importance of a mother's love and nurturance to the child, especially during the early years. Is this a valid claim? What do we know of the nature of mother-child and father-child relationships, and how they compare? What is the infant or young child likely to lose relationally if custody is awarded to the mother or the father? These questions guide the first part of the research review, which concerns studies of family relationships during the child's infancy. We focus on this developmental period because of the greater sophistication of the research in this area, and also because it permits a more rigorous evaluation of the validity of the "tender years" doctrine that often directs judicial decision-making.

Custody adjudication also entails consideration of the child's adjustment to the parents' divorce, and its short-term and long-term effects upon both parents and child. The second part of the review describes two major longitudinal investigations that have examined children's and parents' divorce adjustment over the months and years following the marital break-up. These studies highlight some of the factors that foster both successful and unsuccessful coping in children of various ages.

Both of these studies, however, concerned mother-custody families. What is the child's experience in a father-custody home? Are single fathers adequate caregivers? What are some of the characteristics of their caregiving? Although studies in this area are limited, these questions are discussed and evaluated in the third and final part of the research review. Following this, I conclude with a brief summary of research findings and a discussion of their implications for child custody adjudication.

FATHERS IN THE INTACT FAMILY

What do we know of the kinds of relationships shared by fathers and their children? During the last decaade, research on father-infant and father-child relationships has mushroomed, such that we can now make more confident assertions concerning the nature of the father's contributions to child development in the intact family.

Quantity and Quality of Paternal Involvement

One very important factor differentiating mother-child from father-child relationships is the *quantity* of caretaking. In traditional homes, of course, the mother is usually relegated childcare as well as other domestic chores while fathers spend most of their day away from the home. With the reappraisal of gender roles during the last decade, one might anticipate a softening of these traditional childcare assignments wihin the home. Several recent studies of time use suggest, however, that fathers are still largely uninvolved in routine caretaking tasks (e.g., Ban & Lewis, 1974; Kotelchuck, 1976; Pedersen & Robson, 1969; Pleck, 1979; Pleck & Lang, 1978; Pleck & Rustad, 1980; Robinson, 1977; Walker & Woods, 1976). Kotelchuck (1976) found, for example, that less than 8% of his 144 middle-class Boston fathers shared infant care responsibilities equally with their wives, and only 25% had any regular daily caretaking responsibilities at all. Similarly, according to Ban and Lewis (1974), fathers reported that they averaged only 15–20 minutes of daily contact with their infants.

When the mother also works outside the home, the situation improves somewhat, but not markedly so. Pleck (1979; Pleck & Lang, 1978) reported that fathers spend less than two-thirds of the amount of time in childcare activities that working mothers do. Although this appears to be a dramatic increase in involvement compared to 15 or 20 minutes daily, this difference is due largely to a comparative decrease in the amount of time working mothers are devoting to caregiving activities compared to nonworking mothers, rather than to an increase in the father's involvement (Pleck & Rustad, 1980). Other studies have reported similar findings (e.g., Robinson, 1977; Walker & Woods, 1976), and these gender differences in caregiving responsibilities are apparent cross-culturally as well (Szalai, Converse, Feldheim, Scheuch, & Stone, 1972). In short, whether or not their spouses are working, fathers do not spend a great deal of time caring for their infants and young children.

What *do* fathers do with their children? Consistently, researchers studying two-parent families have found that fathers spend proportionately more time playing with their infant sons and daughters than do mothers (Belsky, 1979; Clarke-Stewart, 1978; Kotelchuck, 1976; Lamb, 1976b, 1977c). For example, in his home observational study of 8–month–olds with their parents, Lamb (1976b) reported that fathers held their infants more than 30% of the time for the purposes of play, whereas the same was true of mothers less than 10% of the time. Mothers, in turn, more frequently picked up their infants for caregiving purposes and discipline (e.g., removing the baby from a forbidden object). Thus fathers are not only less involved in general, but they also distribute their time differently. To put it another way, infants are more likely to interact with their fathers in the context of play than in the more perfunctory manner typical of routine caretaking activities.

Futhermore, when they play with their babies, mothers and fathers play in qualitatively different ways. Lamb (1976b, 1977c), for example, coded the kinds of play interactions he observed at home between infants and their parents. He reported that fathers played more physically active, rough-and-tumble games with their infants. Mothers, in contrast, used more low-key conventional games (e.g., peek-a-boo, pat-a-cake) and toy-mediated games. Similar differences in father-infant and mother-infant play behaviors have been noted by several other investigators (Belsky, 1979; Clarke-Stewart, 1978; Yogman, 1977; Yogman, Dixon, Tronick, Adamson, Als, & Brazelton, 1976).

Taken together, these differences in the quality and contexts of mother-infant and father-infant interaction reflect a basic difference in each parent's role vis-à-vis the baby. In most instances, the mother is the infant's *primary caretaker,* even when she is employed outside of the home. That is, she more typically provides for the baby's basic needs—feeding, bathing, diaper-changing, soothing of distress, preventative protection from harm, and similar ministrations—as well as being a salient social partner in low-key play. In contrast, the father's typical role as a *secondary caretaker* is less focused around specific caregiving activities and more focused on vigorous, physically stimulating play with the baby. Play is thus a more basic interactive context for infants with their fathers than with their mothers; in addition, different kinds of play activities also distinguish each parent. In short, infants begin to know and develop expectations for each parent in somewhat different social contexts.

Does this division of roles mean that fathers are less competent than mothers in basic caretaking tasks? Evidently not, according to a series of studies conducted by Parke and his colleagues (Parke, 1979; Parke & O'Leary, 1976; Parke & Sawin, 1976; Parke & Tinsley, 1981; Sawin & Parke, 1979). In these investigations, they observed fathers as they interacted with their young infants and compared the quality of these interactions with those of the mothers and their infants. In an initial study (Parke and O'Leary, 1976), for example, fathers were given their newborn infants both alone and in the presence of the mother while an observer scored a variety of interactive behaviors over a 10-minute period. Compared to mothers and their babies, fathers were also active and competent caregivers: They held, rocked, kissed, looked at, explored, and vocalized to the neonate as much as or more than the mothers did, whether or not mother was also present. In fact, only one reliable difference between parents emerged from these analyses: Mothers tended to smile more at their infants than did the fathers. These findings were robust. In repeated studies with lower income as well as middle-class families, fathers were found to be interactively competent with their newborn infants.

Another way of viewing caretaking competence is in terms of each parent's responsiveness to the baby's signals. In a feeding situation, for example, the infant provides a variety of visual and auditory cues—coughing, spitting up, burping, turning away—that should influence the subsequent behavior of the parent in reliable ways. Statistically, this responsiveness can be appraised in terms of conditional probabilities of certain kinds of parental responses: Is the probability of a parent stopping a feeding, for example, increased immediately following (i.e., conditional upon) an infant cough, compared to its occurrence during the rest of the feeding? Using such an analytical strategy, Parke and Sawin (1976; Sawin & Parke, 1979) compared the conditional probabilities of critical maternal and paternal responses to infant cues when mothers and fathers were observed feeding their newborn infant. They reported few differences between the responsiveness of each parent; that is, fathers responded in a comparably prompt and appropriate manner to the baby's signals, even though they typically fed their infants less frequently than did the mothers. Fathers were, if anything, somewhat more cautious than mothers in their feeding interactions, often hesitating to physically disturb the baby. Yet they were just as successful: The infants ingested the same amount of milk with each partner.

This observational account dovetails with laboratory investigations of parental responsiveness to infant smiles and cries conducted by Frodi and her colleagues (Frodi, Lamb, Leavitt & Donovan, 1978; Frodi, Lamb, Leavitt, Donovan, Neff, & Sherry, 1978; see review by Thompson & Frodi, in press). Using psychophysiological measures such as blood pressure and heart rate, Frodi and her colleagues found few differences in maternal and paternal reactions to videotapes of smiling and crying infants. Although self-report and mood measures revealed some sex differences, both parents exhibited heightened arousal to the sight and sound of an infant crying, and both gave indications of increased attention and interest in the smiling baby. These findings are similar to those of other investigators using a variety of psychophysiological and self-report measures (see Berman, 1980).

Thus fathers are competent and responsive caretakers, whether their competence is appraised in terms of the occurrence of certain caretaking behaviors or their responsiveness to infant cues. Similarities in mother-infant and father-infant nurturant and caretaking activities have been noted for parents in other cultures as well (see Parke & Tinsley, 1981). Such findings are ironic in view of the strong tendency of fathers to eschew caretaking roles at home. In other words, fathers can be highly competent caretakers when called upon to do so, even though they seldom assume such responsibilities spontaneously. Instead, they spend a greater proportion of their time engaged in vigorous, physically active play with their infants. This competence-performance distinction is, of course, pertinent to any evaluation of the capabilities of fathers as single parents, to which we shall turn later.

The Development of Social Expectations in Infants

What is the impact of this distinction in caregiving involvement on the baby? Are the infant's responses to each parent influenced by these differences in interactive context and style, and if so, in what ways? In posing such questions, researchers interested in early social development are seeking to understand the development of the baby's earliest expectations for interaction with each parent. These expectations presumably grow out of the history of interactions shared by the baby with each partner and, in turn, shape the baby's behaviors toward them. These expectations thus figure prominently in the development of mother-child and father-child relationships during the early years.

It is clear that infants respond differently to their fathers than to unfamiliar adults, and prefer their fathers from an early age. In an impressive series of investigations, Kotelchuck and his colleagues (Kotelchuck, 1976; Lester, Kotelchuck, Spelke, Sellers, & Klein, 1974; Ross, Kagan, Zelazo, & Kotelchuck, 1975; Spelke, Zelazo, Kagan & Kotelchuck, 1973) examined infant responses to father, mother, and stranger in a variety of social contexts and cultural settings. The procedure consisted of a series of 13 3-minute episodes. Each episode entailed a significant change in the social setting of an unfamiliar playroom while the infant played with toys. At times, for example, a stranger entered the room and later withdrew; on other occasions, one parent left and then returned. Kotelchuck and his colleagues scored a range of social and emotional responses observed in the infants, age 6 to 24 months.

They reported that on a variety of measures, responses of infants to their fathers differed significantly from those directed to the stranger and, in fact, more closely resembled mother-directed behaviors. Infants stopped playing when fathers as well as mothers left the room (versus increasing play behavior when the stranger left), cried during separations from either parent (in contrast to decreased crying during stranger separations), and sought proximity to fathers as well as mothers during reunions (which was not observed with the stranger). In short, infants of a variety of ages directed social behaviors toward their fathers in a manner resembling their mother-directed responses, and in clear contrast to their reactions to the stranger. Similar findings have been obtained at home for an American sample (Ross et al., 1975), and in Guatemala as well (Lester et al., 1974).

Thus infants form emotional attachments to their fathers as well as to their mothers, a conclusion that has been replicated by other researchers. Cohen and Campos (1974), for example, found that all of their measures of proximity-seeking in 10- to 16-month-old infants yielded preferences for the father over the stranger. Yogman and colleagues (1976) found that infants under 6 months of age displayed significantly more negative emotion toward strangers than toward fathers. Finally, Lamb (1978) tested infants with both their mothers and fathers in the "Strange Situation" paradigm, a semsistandardized procedure designed to assess the "security" of an infant's attachment to a caregiver (see Ainsworth, Blehar, Waters, & Wall, 1978). Of the 32 1-year-olds he tested, 20 were rated as securely attached to their fathers, and 21 were secure with their mothers, with 16 of these securely attached to both parents. (See also Main and Weston, 1981.) In short, infants form attachments to both parents.

The more critical question, however, is how father-infant and mother-infant relationships compare, both in their interactive quality and their emotional salience to the baby. In a series of investigations, Lamb (1976a, 1976d, 1977a, 1977c) has provided useful information pertaining to this question. Lamb observed a group of infants with their fathers and mothers throughout the first 2 years, examining developmental changes in social responsiveness as well as differences in responding to each parent. His observations were conducted both at home and in a laboratory playroom in order to take advantage of the strengths of each observational context. Most important, Lamb differentiated among two kinds of social responses in these infants. The first—*attachment behaviors*—included approaching, seeking to be held, touching, reaching, proximity-seeking and fussing to an adult. These behaviors were interpreted as reflections of a baby's emotional attachment to an adult partner because they indicate a desire for close proximity and contact. The second group—*affiliative behaviors*—included smiling, vocalizing, looking, laughing, and proffering a toy to an adult. These sociable responses were taken to indicate a baby's friendly, positive responsiveness to a partner, whether or not an attachment relationship existed, because they are primarily distal in quality.

In his first series of home observations, Lamb (1977c) observed 20 infants with their parents on four occasions: twice when the infants were 7 to 8 months old, and again at the end of the first year. Each observation lasted about 1½ hours, and was designed to tap natural interactions among family members at home. An unfamiliar "visitor" was also present in addition to the observer. With respect to the baby's attachment behaviors, Lamb found that both parents were preferred over the visitor at each age and there was no evidence for a preference for one parent over the other. On the affiliative measures, however, infants were more responsive to their fathers than to either their mothers or the visitor. Thus infants were clearly attached to both parents during the first year, although fathers also received more friendly, sociable overtures from their infant sons and daughters. Developmental changes were also evident: As infants grew older, they became increasingly restrictive in their attachment behaviors, directing them exclusively to their parents.

The increased salience of the father in the infant's social world was reflected in the second series of observations during the infant's second year. At 15, 18, 21, and 24 months of age, Lamb (1977a) observed 20 infants (including 14 from the earlier study) with their parents and the visitor at home in a manner similar to that described above. This time the father was the recipient of a greater number of affiliative *and* attachment behaviors by the baby compared to the other two partners (the mother was preferred to the visitor on the attachment measures, but the reverse was true on the affiliative indices). In the comfortable home environment, fathers seem to be highly attractive social partners to their infants, especially during the second year.

Similar findings have been obtained by other researchers who have also conducted home-observational studies of father-infant and mother-infant interaction. Belsky (1979), for example, found that 15-month-old infants were more likely to vocalize to, move toward, and show things to their fathers than their mothers. And Clarke-Stewart (1978) noted that 30-month-old toddlers were rated as more involved, interested and cooperative with their fathers than with their mothers in a set of specific play initiatives. Toddlers also expressed a preference to play with their fathers.

In explaining these findings, Lamb, Belsky, and Clarke-Stewart have each suggested that the infant's affiliative preference may be largely a derivative of the father's more active, vigorous, stimulating play style. In other words, because play is such a salient feature of early father-infant interaction, and because fathers regularly play in more exciting and engaging ways than mothers, babies respond with a range of sociable behaviors when their fathers are near, and respond more positively to him. In other words, fathers are fun to play with, and babies have learned this by the second year.

Lamb (1976a, 1976d) also conducted a series of observations in a laboratory playroom as well—a context that not only affords greater environmental control over the observations, but also permits an examination of mother-infant and father-infant interactions in a less familiar, and thus more stressful, social context. His laboratory procedure consisted of four 9-min episodes: An initial episode in which both parents were present; and then two episodes in which one parent (either mother or father) was alone with the baby first, followed by the other parent; and a final episode in which both mother and father were with the baby together with an adult stranger. Parents were instructed to remain responsive to the infant but to refrain from initiating interaction. From behind one-way windows, an observer scored the baby's attachment and affiliative behaviors as in the home studies.

Observing the sample of 20 12-month-olds from his longitudinal study, Lamb (1976d) found patterns of infant responsiveness that generally replicated the findings of the home observational studies. That is, during the first three episodes, infants directed a greater proportion of their affiliative behaviors toward their fathers than their mothers. There were no parental preferences on the attachment measures during the first three episodes. However, during the fourth episode—when a stranger was also present—infant social responses changed markedly. Affiliative behaviors were no longer preferentially directed to the father. The attachment measures showed a clear bias for the mother. Infants touched, fussed toward, sought to be held by, reached toward, and remained closer to their mothers than their fathers throughout this final episode.

Lamb suggested that this change may have resulted from the increased stress of the fourth episode. By this time, the 1-year-olds had been in the unfamiliar playroom for nearly ½ hour, and further had to negotiate the additional presence of an unfamiliar adult. In fact, Lamb noted a general increase in attachment behaviors to both parents during this period, which may also reflect increasing fatigue or stress. Lamb interpreted the increase in mother-directed attachment behaviors to reflect an infant preference for one attachment figure over another in a stressful situation—that is, the figure who has regularly provided soothing and comforting in similar situations in the past. This preference was not evident at home, he suggested, because home is a nonstressful environment for babies, even with strangers present.

Very similar findings were obtained when Lamb (1976a) tested 18-month-old infants in this laboratory procedure. During the early episodes there were more father-directed affiliative behaviors but no attachment preference; in the fourth episode, infants displayed more mother-directed attachment behaviors. However, Lamb (1977a; see also Lamb, 1976c) failed to replicate this finding using a somewhat different laboratory procedure in which infants were observed at 24 months of age. Whether this was due to procedural differences or developmental factors is unclear at present.

Other researchers have, however, also found that infant preferences for the mother exhibited in stressful laboratory contexts. Cohen and Campos (1974), for example, employed a 6-min laboratory procedure that entailed frequent disruptions of the infant's behavior and recurrent encounters with unfamiliar adults. They found that on nearly all of their measures of proximity-seeking, 10- to 16-month-old infants were oriented toward the mother. For example, infants spent twice as much time in proximity to their mothers as to their fathers. Kotelchuck (1976) also reported that a maternal preference in proximity-maintaining behaviors emerged at 12 months of age in his laboratory procedure.

Taken together, the research on mother-infant and father-infant relationships indicates that fathers are preferred as play partners from a relatively early age, and mothers are preferentially sought when infants are fatigued, alarmed, or stressed. As earlier indicated, the paternal preference is unsurprising in view of the contexts in which infants typically encounter their fathers and the kinds of exciting, physically active games fathers play. Infants seem to learn that fathers are fun to play with during the second year. Similarly, infants' preferences for their mothers under stress are also unsurprising in view of the maternal caretaking role in most families. Mothers typically feed, bathe, clothe and, importantly, comfort their babies when the infants are distressed; infants seem to learn early on that their mothers are a source of soothing.

Theorists concerned with the development of infant-parent attachments (e.g., Ainsworth, 1973; Ainsworth et al., 1978; Bowlby, 1969) have been especially interested in this stress-related parental preference in view of the adaptive functions of attachment relationships to infant development. Drawing on evolutionary concepts, they suggest that the development of an emotional bond between infant and caretaker primarily served to protect the infant from predation by fostering proximity to a mature adult in dangerous or stressful circumstances. This preadapted tendency in human young in the environment of evolutionary development promoted species survival, they contend, and is currently manifested in the kinds of proximity- and contact-seeking activities (Lamb's "attachment behaviors") evinced by infants from an early age. To attachment theorists, then, parental preferences exhibited under stressful circumstances reveal important differences in the psychological salience of each parent that may not be apparent in nonstressful conditions.

Lamb (1981a, 1981b) has argued that stressful circumstances may also constitute one of the earliest conditions for the development of infant expectations for the parent. When infant distress is followed by the soothing ministrations of a caretaker (typically picking up and holding the baby), infants characteristically enter into a state of "quiet alertness" (Korner and Thoman, 1970, 1972) that may foster the association of the caregiver's cues (e.g., sound of voice, body odor, sight, feeling of being held, etc.) with the experience of being comforted. According to Lamb, these "distress-relief sequences" provide the earliest opportunities for the baby to learn about the caregiver's physical attributes and, more important, behavioral propensities. Insofar as mothers are likely to be the comforting agent in these situations, it seems likely that the baby is learning about the reliability of mother as a source of soothing under stress as early as the first ½-year of life.

Thus mothers and fathers differ importantly both in their caretaking roles and, it seems, in how they are perceived by the baby from an early age. Mothers as primary caregivers in most families spend a greater amount of time with their infant sons and daughters and assume greater responsibility for routine caretaking tasks, even when they also work outside of the home. Fathers as secondary caregivers spend less time with infants overall but devote a greater proportion of their time to physically vigorous, arousing play. These differences in parental involvement are manifested early in differences in infant responsiveness. Infants prefer their fathers as play partners and respond more positively to them in these situations. Under conditions of stress, however, they turn to mothers, reflecting different expectations for each parent that develop during the first year. In short, infants learn about their mothers and fathers in different contexts, and develop different expectations for them as a result.

Other Paternal Influences

Recent research concerned with fathers and their young children has indicated important paternal influences in specific areas, most notably the development of gender identity and intellectual development. We turn to a brief discussion of these contributions.

A variety of research studies have demonstrated that there are important sex differences in parental responsiveness to infants, with fathers taking a much greater interest in their male offspring. This difference is evident virtually from birth. Parke and O'Leary (1976) reported that fathers touched and vocalized to their firstborn sons more than to their firstborn daughters, and other research conducted by Parke and his colleagues indicated other early differences in paternal responses to infant sons and daughters.

This differential responsiveness is also evident later in the first year. Kotelchuck (1976) reported, for example, that the fathers he questioned reported playing about half an hour a day longer with their firstborn sons than with their firstborn daughters. Similarly, Lamb (1976b) reported that the fathers he observed held their sons longer than their daughters. By the infant's second year these differences are even more apparent. Belsky (1979), for example, reported that fathers interacted more and displayed more affection toward their 15-month-old sons than to daughters. Lamb (1977a) and Weinraub and Frankel (1977) noted that fathers were more active with sons. In addition, according to Clarke-

Stewart (1978), the father's role as a playmate with both sons and daughters increased significantly from 15–30 months of age, thus increasing his salience as a social partner. In general, then, fathers have been found to respond preferentially to infant sons from an early age. Although some researchers (e.g., Belsky, 1979) have found a maternal preference for daughters, this influence seems to be more muted during the early years compared to that of fathers (see, for example, Lamb, 1977a, 1977b).

What influence does the father's responsiveness have upon his children? By and large, researchers have not found strong sex differences in infant responsiveness to parents during the first year. During the second year, however, sex differences in infant responsiveness are more apparent. Kotelchuck (1976) reported that at 21 months of age, boys played more and interacted more with their fathers than with their mothers. Belsky (1979) also noted that sons were more likely to move toward and vocalize to their fathers at home. And Lamb (1977b), in a reanalysis of the longitudinal home observational data, noted that by the end of the second year sex differences in infant responding to fathers and mothers were strong, even using conservative criteria. By the 24–month observation, eight of the nine boys showed greater responsiveness to their fathers; five of the six infants preferring their mothers were female. Furthermore, these parental preferences were reasonably stable during the second year observations, in contrast to the marked changes in parental responsiveness more characteristic of the first year observations.

Taken together, these findings indicate that male infants receive increased attention from their fathers from a young age, and respond preferentially to them in a reliable manner by the end of the second year. These conclusions are consistent with a large body of studies indicating the father's important role in the acquisition of a gender identity in children (e.g., Bronfenbrenner, 1961; Brown, 1956, 1958; Fagot, 1974; Goodenough, 1957; Lansky, 1967; Sears, Maccoby, & Levin, 1957; Tasch, 1952; see Biller, 1971, 1974, 1976 for reviews). In sum, fathers play a significant role in the development of gender differentiation in young children.

A growing research literature also indicates the importance of fathers to the child's intellectual development, and this influence begins to appear during infancy. Clarke-Stewart (1978) found, for example, that a cluster of variables concerned with the father's positive involvement with his child (including measures of his ability to engage the infant in play, his positive attitude toward his children, and the duration of his interactions with the child in home observations) were strongly and positively related to assessments of the infant's intellectual competence. With older children, research by Radin (1981) and others indicates that paternal contributions to intellectual development become more sex-differentiated, with fathers positively contributing to the achievement of their sons more than their daughters (see review by Radin, 1981). This may, of course, be related to the paternal encouragement of sex-typed behaviors in young children described above.

Fathers in Nontraditional Families

Thus far, most of the research we have reviewed has been concerned with family relationships in traditional family contexts—that is, in single-wage-earner families in which the father works and the mother remains home with domestic responsibilities. However, this kind of family organization is becoming decreasingly typical of Western industrialized nations as rising inflation and redefined sex-roles are moving more and more mothers into the job market. This important social change also influences the ecology of child development, as parents increasingly share their caretaking responsibilities with members of the extended family and childcare workers. And within the family, fathers may be assuming more of the responsibilities—and satisfactions (Russell, 1982)—of a major caretaking role. Although the family remains the most important socialization context for young children, it is reasonable to expect that these changes in caretaking roles and responsibilities would influence the nature of mother-infant and father-infant relationships. In short, how do these relationships compare in traditional and nontraditional families?

Pedersen, Cain, Zaslow, and Anderson (1982) sought to address this question by observing single- and dual-wage-earner couples in their interactions at home with their firstborn 5-month-old infants. In 13 of the families they observed, the mother was employed outside the home on a full- or part-time basis; in the remaining 28 families mother was a fulltime caretaker at home. In all families the father worked. They were observed for two 1-hour visits during the early evening (when both parents could be present) by an observer who recorded specified parent and infant behaviors.

Pedersen and his colleagues found that for certain behaviors this nontraditional family arrangement appeared to modify a parent's style of interacting with the baby; for other behaviors, however, gender differences in caretaking were similar to those observed in more traditional homes. For example, mothers talked to, smiled, fed, and gazed at their infants more than did fathers in both family contexts, which is concordant with earlier research concerning traditional families. On the other hand, parents in dual-wage-earner families touched their infants more than did parents in more traditional homes. There were also some informative interactions between family context and sex of the parent in caretaking behaviors. That is, employed mothers talked to their infants much more than did the other parent groups. In addition, whereas fathers in traditional families engage in more social play than do mothers, the pattern was reversed for dual-wage-earner families: Employed mothers played with babies much more than did fathers.

Indeed, Pedersen and his coworkers noticed that in most behaviors, employed mothers were more active with their infants than were the other parent groups. Their husbands, in turn, seemed to recede into the background, typically showing fewer interactive behaviors than other parents. In view of the early evening period in which these observations were conducted, these researchers suggested that the working mothers were using this time to reestablish contact with their babies after having been away for the day. The fathers, also returning from work, appeared to be giving precedence to their wives at this time. In general, then, the dual-wage-earner families were characterized by a greater bifurcation of involvement with the infant, with employed mothers increasing their interactions, and their husbands playing a less active role. At the same time, maternal and paternal interactive styles were, on the whole, consistent with those observed in more traditional homes, with mothers displaying more vocal, affectionate behaviors toward their babies.

Exploratory research of this kind, of course, raises questions as well as resolving them. For example, would similar differences in parental interactions be evident with older infants who can take greater initiative of their own? Fathers do, in fact, become more actively involved with their infants as they grow older, and this might modify the low levels of interaction noted in the fathers of dual-wage-earner families with their 5-month-olds. In addition, the employed mothers in this study had returned to work shortly before these observations took place, and were probably still negotiating the transition from fulltime to part-time caregiver. Would they be less active social partners with their older infants, once home and work activities had become more routine? Questions such as these remain for future research inquiry.

When mothers are employed outside the home, an even more extreme departure from traditional family arrangements may occur when fathers remain at home as the baby's primary caretaker. How does this arrangement influence the quality of mother-infant and father-infant interactions? Field (1978) observed three parent groups—12 primary caretaker mothers, 12 primary caretaker fathers, and 12 secondary caretaker fathers—as they interacted with their 4-month-old infants during three 3-min episodes. Specific parental behaviors were coded from these videotaped observations. Field reported that on some behaviors fathers differed from mothers regardless of their caretaking status: Fathers played more games and "poked" their infants more than did mothers. On other behaviors, primary caretaker fathers more closely resembled primary caretaker mothers: Primary caretakers displayed more smiling, imitative facial expressions, and high-pitched imitative vocalizations than did secondary caretaker fathers. (Unfortunately, Field did not assess secondary caretaker mothers to provide a fourth comparison group.) In short, primary caretaker fathers resembled traditional fathers in certain ways, and traditional mothers in other ways.

A third investigation of parental caretaking roles in nontraditional family contexts consists of a series of investigations conducted in Sweden by Lamb, Frodi, Hwang, Frodi, and Steinberg (1982a,b; Lamb, Frodi, Frodi, and Hwang, 1982). Since 1974, Swedish parents have been entitled to 9 months of paid parental leave following the birth of the baby, to be divided between the two parents at their discretion. Although a very small proportion of fathers have taken advantage of this policy to assume a primary caretaking role with their infants, a sufficient number have done so to permit an investigtion of their caretaking behaviors compared with those of more traditional fathers.

Lamb and his colleagues contacted couples prenatally through childbirth preparation classes and observed them interacting with their 8–month–old infants. The sample was divided into two groups based on the extent of the father's caretaking involvement during the preceding 3 months. Fourteen fathers had spent one or more months as the baby's primary caretaker (the average was three months); 34 of the fathers had never assumed exclusive responsibility for child care. Observations were conducted during the early evening hours when both parents were present. Parental behaviors—including holding the baby, play, affectionate, and caretaking behaviors—were coded by an observer, as in Lamb's earlier investigations.

Somewhat surprisingly, Lamb and his colleagues found that parental gender was a more significant determinant of parental behavior than was caretaking role. Regardless of their caregiving role, mothers vocalized, smiled, tended, held, and displayed more affection toward their infants than did the fathers. They were also more likely to hold their babies for soothing or discipline (e.g., removing the infant from a forbidden activity). These differences accord, of course, with parental differences in caregiving described earlier for traditional American homes, although Lamb and colleagues did not observe the expected sex differences in play behavior. In contrast to these gender differences there was only one behavior by which parents varied significantly according to caretaking role: Secondary caretaker fathers played more with their infants than did primary caretaker fathers, while the reverse was true of the mothers.

Very similar findings were obtained when these families were observed again when the infants were 16 months old (Lamb, Frodi, Frodi, & Hwang, 1982). Although the differences were not as strong, mothers were again observed to vocalize, tend, soothe, hold, touch, and display affection toward their babies more than fathers, regardless of the caretaking role of either parent. There were no significant differences according to caretaking role alone.

Thus in this Swedish sample, sex differences in parent-infant interaction were remarkably robust, even in nontraditional homes. To be sure, it is important to note that the paternal commitment to primary caretaking in the Swedish families was an avowedly temporary one: Fathers were at home fulltime for a limited period and expected to return to work soon afterwards. Thus behavioral changes in caretaking activities owing to the parental role changes may have been diminished by both parents' awareness that this was a temporary arrangement. In contrast, in Field's families, for whom the paternal commitment to primary caretaking was (perhaps) a more enduring one, these fathers more strongly resembled primary caretaking mothers in their interactions with the baby. One may conclude that, to a certain extent, the behaviors of fathers with their infants may change depending on their caretaking role and their expectation that this role will be an enduring one. Although these fathers maintain their characteristic paternal interactive modes (e.g., vigorous, stimulating play), these are complemented by the more low-key vocal and affectionate behaviors that are more commonly observed in mothers in traditional homes. Clearly, however, further research is required to elaborate and clarify the findings reported thus far.

Another important question is how these parental differences influence the infant and young child. Do children treat their primary caretaker fathers in ways similar to mother-child interactions in more traditional family arrangements? Although informal anecdotes abound of children from nontraditional homes calling for their fathers after a skinned knee, there has been no systematic research inquiry concerning this issue. The only relevant research comes from a study by Spelke, Zelazo, Kagan, and Kotelchuck (1973), who reported that infants whose fathers were highly involved in caretaking evinced significantly less fear of an adult stranger than did infants whose fathers were little involved. More generally, research findings from Israel (Sagi, 1982) and the U.S. (Radin, 1982) indicate that children thrive in homes in which fathers assume major caretaking responsibilities (see also Radin and Sagi, 1982). This is a domain of research in which more information is needed, although these initial findings are encouraging.

Taken together, it appears that the father's behaviors with his infant are influenced by his caretaking role, particularly if his role as a primary caretaker is an enduring one. As primary caretakers, fathers seem to develop a synthesis of characteristically "paternal" interactive behaviors with the gentler verbal and affectionate activities more often noted in mothers. This adaptive synthesis does not appear, however, if fathers are temporarily involved as primary caretakers, or in homes in which fathers as well as mothers are employed outside the home.

THE EFFECTS OF DIVORCE ON CHILDREN AND THEIR PARENTS

One of the most important research contributions to the adjudication of child custody disputes has been the recent exploration of divorce and its effects on the child. Whereas earlier investigations of divorce relied on parental reports of child adjustment or divorce as an antecedent to child psychiatric disorder, these recent efforts have entailed more direct observational and interview measures of child behavior at various points in time as well as parental assessments. Such studies have permitted researchers to examine divorce as a multistage phenomenon that changes over time. In this section, some of the major findings from two important longitudinal investigations of parental divorce and child adjustment are discussed.

The first study—the Virginia Longitudinal Study of Divorce (Hetherington, Cox, & Cox, 1976, 1978, 1979a, 1979b, 1982)—was a longitudinal investigation of 72 white, middle-class boys and girls and their divorced parents together with a matched, nondivorced control sample. Divorced families were identified and contacted through court records and lawyers. All the divorce settlements awarded custody to the mother. The target children were preschool-age. A battery of observations and interviews were administered to these families on three occasions: two months, one year, and two years following the divorce. The measures included parent interviews, observations of parents and children interacting in the laboratory and at home, school observations of the children, teacher and peer ratings, and semistandardized assessments of the child's gender identity, cognitive performance, and social development. An additional series of assessments was also conducted six years after the divorce, but results from this later series have not yet been reported.

The second study was called the California Children of Divorce Project (Kelly & Wallerstein, 1976; Wallerstein & Kelly, 1974, 1975, 1976, 1980). In this investigation, 60 families who volunteered to participate in a short-term counseling-research project were studied initially for a 6-week period immediately following the parents' separation and filing for divorce. The families were primarily white, middle-class families living in the San Francisco Bay Area. Families learned of the service through attorneys, social agencies, ministers, and newspaper articles, and some were referred through the courts. In contrast to Hetherington's subjects, these families participated in order to obtain supportive assistance during the separation period as well as to assist the research endeavor. The initial 6-week study consisted of multiple in-depth parent interviews and interview, play, and drawing sessions with the children. A total of 131 children participated, ranging in age from 3 to 18. Parents and children were later contacted for 1-year and 5-year follow-up studies entailing a similar array of interview and observational measures. Most of the eventual custody awards were to the mothers in these families.

The assessment tools varied in these two longitudinal investigations, as did the research samples and the theoretical orientations of the investigators. In view of this, there is a striking consistency in the principal findings of these studies pertaining to the developmental course of the divorce process and its short-term and long-term effects on boys and girls.

Both studies characterized divorce as a crisis for all family members, with the most acute adjustments required during the weeks and months immediately following the break-up of the family. During this period, multiple stresses impinged upon parents and children: Mothers renegotiating their new roles as heads of the household and breadwinners, changes in childcare arrangements necessitated by the mother's occupational responsibilities, changes in residence in many cases, negotiating visitation arrangements with the father, and similar adjustments were faced immediately after the parents' separation. In addition to these practical problems of changed living conditions, family relationships had to be renegotiated: Mothers assumed the role of primary disciplinary agent; fathers often adopted an "every day is Christmas" demeanor during visits with their children; and, of course, stressful interactions occurred between ex-spouses. The children, meanwhile, acutely felt the loss of the noncustodial parent and other losses deriving from the break-up of the family; nearly all viewed the parents' divorce as a mistake, and many hoped for and actively encouraged a reunion. In short, for all family members, the immediate postdivorce period was one of extreme stress and emotional upheaval.

For mothers, these stresses were especially acute. In addition to their changed occupational and family roles, these newly separated women also experienced dramatic changes in their self-concept—both studies reported that women felt a loss of self-esteem, competence, and worthiness coupled with intense anger and depression stemming from the failed marriage. Although expanded social contacts with other adults and, in particular, new heterosexual relationships greatly improved their emotional state, pursuit of these supports was limited because of the children at home. Many mothers, in fact, reported feeling "walled in" or "trapped" by their children. Apart from their diminished attractiveness to single males, they faced the logistical problems of negotiating child care during evenings or nights away from home.

In view of this, it is not surprising to find that home life was disorganized and, at times, scattered—a condition that was still strongly evident at the 1-year follow-up in both studies. Mealtimes and bedtimes were erratic, children arrived at school late and were often unsupervised during afterschool hours, and household tasks were left undone. Although there is no indication that these conditions posed any serious risk to the children, the disorganization of the home environment reflects the extent to which the newly divorced mothers felt stressed and overtaxed by their new roles and responsibilities.

This stress influenced the mother-child relationship. Divorced mothers tended to become more authoritarian disciplinary agents (perhaps in attempting to compensate for the loss of a strong paternal influence) but were inconsistently so, sometimes rigidly enforcing household rules but acting in a lax and ineffective manner at other times. On the whole, divorced mothers were less affectionate to their children, communicated more poorly with them, and made fewer maturity demands compared to mothers of nondivorced families. Their children, in turn, were often demanding, dependent, and oppositional, directing a greater proportion of negative behaviors toward their mothers than children from nondivorced homes. The result was a vicious cycle of mother-child conflict fostered, in large measure, by the unsatisfied emotional needs of each partner. Wallerstein and Kelly (1980) commented that "many women felt severely threatened by their children's rebelliousness and were reduced to tears, nagging, or screeching [p. 112]." Similarly, at the 1-year postdivorce interview, some of the mothers in Hetherington, Cox, and Cox's (1982) study described their relationships with their children as "declared war," "a struggle for survival," or "like getting bitten to death by ducks."

Both groups of researchers noted that conflict was especially characteristic of mother-son relationships in divorced families. Sons were more aggressive, resistant, and negative than were daughters, and mothers directed more negative sanctions and fewer positive behaviors toward sons than daughters. And in general, by the time of the 1-year follow-up, both studies reported that boys were coping much less adaptively with the divorce than were girls in these mother-custody families. Boys showed more depression and fewer indications of accepting the divorce than did girls. And these differences were evident outside the home environment. Hetherington and her colleagues (1979a,b, 1982) reported, for example, that boys were gradually becoming more socially isolated from their male peers even at the 2-year assessment, preferring instead to play with younger children and girls. This may have been due, in part, to the fact that these boys exhibited more negative, coercive, and dependent behaviors in their social interactions than did boys from nondivorced homes. Their play behaviors were more severely and persistently disrupted than were those of girls from divorced families. Boys displayed more solitary and onlooker play and less cooperative, constructive, imaginative or game-type play than did boys from nondivorced homes. Finally, these boys also received more negative treatment from their teachers. In contrast, girls from divorced families had more positive interactions with their teachers and more positive, supportive peer relationships.

Both groups of investigators strongly implicated the boys' continued longing for the noncustodial father in these behaviors. Although both sons and daughters missed their fathers very much, boys felt this loss more acutely and experienced greater adjustment difficulties in the mother-custody homes. In addition, differences in mother-child interaction at home may have also contributed to the boys' difficulty in coping. Both studies indicated that daughters were, in general, treated better by custodial mothers than were sons, due perhaps to the greater rebelliousness of the boys, their similarity to the divorced spouse, their dependent behaviors (a gender-inappropriate trait in boys) and other factors. In short, sons had a more difficult experience at home than did daughters.

What of relationships between children and the noncustodial parent? Interestingly, the fathers in these longitudinal studies varied in the extent to which the frequency of their visits during the immediate postdivorce period was maintained long after the divorce. Hetherington, Cox, and Cox (1982) reported, as have others, that paternal contacts with the children declined dramatically during the two years following parental separation. In contrast, Wallerstein and Kelly (1980) indicated that postdivorce visits by fathers did not decline precipitously over time. Importantly, both groups found little relationship between the quality of the predivorce father-child relationship and the quality of that relationship after the parents had separated. That is, some fathers who were unusually close to their children before the divorce visited infrequently and irregularly, but other fathers improved dramatically in the frequency and quality of their contacts with the children. It was difficult to predict the quality of the visiting relationship on the basis of predivorce father-child interaction.

Just as mothers faced an array of practical problems relevant to their changed living conditions, fathers faced considerable adjustment to the role of noncustodial parent and to interacting with their children in a visiting relationship. What to do with the children during visits, what role to play in discipline and moral training, how to handle their own heterosexual contacts in relation to the children, and how to involve the children in their own changing lifestyles were some of the questions faced by fathers during the immediate postseparation period. This was an uncomfortable and difficult time for both fathers and children.

Even in the best of these relationships, however, the father's influence on his children gradually declined following the divorce and, compared with intact families, divorced fathers had a different and reduced influence on the child's development. This declining impact was particularly evident in intellectual development and the acquisition of gender identity, especially for male offspring (Hetherington, Cox, & Cox, 1982). On a sex-role preference test, for example, boys from divorced homes scored lower on male preferences and higher on female preferences than did boys from intact homes at the 2-year assessment. At the same time, only one paternal variable ("paternal availability") was statistically related to children's sex typing at this time, in contrast to a range of significant paternal influences at earlier assessments. In short, the father's role was changing over time, both qualitatively and quantitatively. By the time of the 5-year follow-up, according to Wallerstein and Kelly (1980), "the great majority of the father-child relationships had become emotionally limited over time [p. 238]," with less than a third of the children sharing an "emotionally nurturant" relationship with their noncustodial fathers.

Taken together, it is clear that the experience of divorce has significant and far-reaching influences on all family members and the relationships they share. In addition to changes in parental roles and responsibilities, interactions between parents and children are impaired by the crisis of the postdivorce family environment. In the mother-custody families examined by these investigators, boys seemed to be more profoundly and negatively influenced than girls. In light of these findings, it is hard to conceive of "victimless divorces" in a large number of cases.

Wallerstein and Kelly (1980) reported that children varied in their reactions to divorce depending on their age at the time of the marital break-up. Preschool children, lacking the cognitive capacities to understand the complex motivational factors underlying the divorce, tended to be self-blaming in interpreting the causes of divorce, and were unrealistic in their perceptions of parental needs and the prospects of reconciliation. School-age children understood better the causes of the marital break-up and its personal implications, but were also highly vulnerable to feelings of abandoment and deprivation. In contrast, older school-age children and adolescents were buffered, to some extent, by their peer relationshps and other extrafamilial support systems and were more capable of coping with parent loyalty conflicts and the economic and social ramifications of the divorce.

Generally speaking, the difficulties and adjustments necessitated by the parents' separation persisted through the first year after the divorce. Indeed, some difficulties (particularly the adjustment problems of sons) reached a peak at this time. Parent-child interactions continued to be problematic and, although the parents themselves were showing some signs of adaptive adjustment to their postdivorce lives, family life as a whole had not significantly restabilized.

By the time of the 2-year follow-up reported by Hetherington and her colleagues (1982), however, there was considerable improvement in both parents and children. Mothers and fathers experienced a greater sense of psychological well being and adaptive adjustment to the divorce, owing to more stable occupational circumstances, increased social contacts and, for some, remarriage. Mothers also were less negative and more consistent in their child-rearing practices, although there remained consistent differences in the interaction patterns characteristic of divorced and nondivorced families. Similarly, the children—particularly daughters—exhibited less negative, dependent behaviors and more positive adjustment to the postdivorce family situation. Considerable concern remained for the boys, however, who continued to exhibit impaired peer relationships and social behaviors at the 2-year assessment.

Similarly, by five years after their separation, according to Wallerstein and Kelly (1980), most of the parents were happier and were experiencing greater personal satisfaction, typically viewing the divorce as ultimately a beneficial experience. Their children had, by and large, accepted the divorce and adapted to it, although an important proportion of the children still exhibited lingering indications of loneliness and anger. In another recent interview study, Kurdek, Blisk, and Siesky (1981) also reported high degrees of adjustment in 8- to 17-year-old children interviewed four and six years after their parents' divorce. There was also strong consistency in adjustment scores over the two assessments. In their long-term follow-up, Wallerstein and Kelly also noted some continuity in children's postdivorce adjustment. That is, children whose initial adjustment was good were found to have successfully coped with the divorce five years later; children who were initially highly vulnerable to stress improved dramatically during the succeeding years (due to the termination of the unhappy predivorce family environment, they suggested). Children whose initial adjustment was in the middle range, however, were most difficult to predict at five years.

Within these general trends, however, both Hetherington and Wallerstein and Kelly reported great individual differences in the long-term adjustment of children to the divorce. A variety of factors were associated with these differences, the most important including the eventual postdivorce adjustment of both parents (especially the custodial parent), the occurrence of frequent or persistent stresses in the family (including economic difficulties or continuing conflict between ex-spouses), the commitment of both parents to the children and its effect upon parent-child relationships, the ongoing relationship with the noncustodial father (see also Hess and Camara, 1979), the availability of extrafamilial support systems, and, in some cases, the readjustment of the family network with the remarriage of one or both parents.

To summarize, these investigations characterize divorce as a multistage process with multiple influences on family members. During the period immediately following the divorce, the family is in crisis, characterized by emotional turmoil in parents and children and impaired parent-child relationships. Most of these stresses were still evident one year following the divorce, with boys in mother-custody families displaying more acute difficulties in adjusting to divorce than girls. Following this, however, was a period of restabilization for the family and its individual members. Parents achieved greater personal stability and happiness, and this fostered improved interactions with their children. The children themselves also showed signs of growing adjustment to new family conditions, although persisting difficulties remained even at five years, especially for boys. Children's long-term divorce adjustment was a function of both their earlier success at coping and the growing stability and support of the home environment. But even long after the parents had separated, children and their families were still adjusting to the effects of this critical event on their lives. Divorce is, in short, a difficult transition for all concerned, and long-term outcomes vary considerably for parents and children.

FATHERS AS SINGLE PARENTS

Adjudication of child custody disputes inevitably entails making predictive judgments: Are the child's best interests better insured in the home environment of one parent or the other? In considering this question, we turned first to research concerning mother-infant and father-infant interaction in the intact family, in order to understand the child's developing conceptions of and expectations for each parent. What does the child lose relationally in different custody arrangements? Next we considered research concerning the divorce process and its impact on the child in mother-custody homes. What is the child's experience during the months and years following the parents' separation in the typical mother-custody situation? In this final section of the research review, we turn to studies examining fathers as single parents, and the experience of children being raised solely by their fathers.

Unfortunately, the research studies we have to draw upon in this area are scanty and somewhat qualified (see Bartz & Witcher, 1978; Gasser & Taylor, 1976; Gersick, 1975; Keshet & Rosenthal, 1978a, 1978b; Mendes, 1976a, 1976b; Orthner, Brown, & Ferguson, 1976; Santrock & Warshak, 1979; Santrock, Warshak, & Elliott, 1982; Warshak & Santrock, 1980—all studies conducted in the United States. For research conducted in other countries, see Katz, 1979 [Australia]; Schlesinger, 1979; Schlesinger & Todres, 1976; Todres, 1975 [Canada]; Ferri, 1973; George & Wilding, 1972; and Hipgrave, 1978

[Great Britain].) First, with only one exception, all of these studies rely upon interviews with single fathers without direct observation of father-child interaction. Their portrayal of family life is thus inherently subjective and, quite likely, positively skewed. Second, the fathers who were interviewed included widowed and abandoned fathers as well as those who were divorced, although the large majority were the latter. Among the divorced group, most fathers received custody by mutual consent of both spouses, but some fought for custody in the courts. Thus the causes of the marital break-up and custody decision were varied, and this undoubtedly had an effect on subsequent family interaction. Third, nearly all of these studies report on single fathers who were interviewed long after making the adjustment to being the sole caregiver. Their descriptions of the transition were thus retrospective rather than direct, and it is sometimes difficult to know how they should be interpreted. Finally, these fathers were contacted through informal, word-of-mouth sources, advertisements or, on occasion, single-parent support groups (such as Parents Without Partners), and thus probably reflect a select, highly motivated, and involved sample. This final concern over unrepresentative sampling may be excused, in part, due to the rarity of single fathers in most Western cultures.

For these reasons, we should be cautious in comparing these reports of fathers as single parents with the preceding description of the child's experience in mother-custody homes. These studies can be useful, however, in providing information concerning fathers' perceptions of their caretaking competence, as well as alerting us to the recurrent worries or concerns experienced by fathers in the single-parent household.

What are the characteristics that distinguish fathers who seek custody of their children from those who do not? The only information we have is provided by Gersick (1975), who interviewed 40 divorced fathers. Twenty of them had sought custody of their children; the remainder had not. The interview consisted of a range of structured questions concerning the fathers' childhood, marriage, and divorce, as well as some semiprojective questions. Perhaps most striking in Gersick's comparison of custody-seekers with noncustody-seekers was the absence of any difference in predivorce caretaking involvement, reported emotional tie to the child, sex-role orientation, and age of the father. That is, fathers who sought custody of their children did not participate more in child care (at least during the early years of the marriage), did not express more love for their children, were not more "feminine" in their overall sex-role orientation, and were only slightly older than the fathers who did not seek custody. There were, however, two variables that distinguished the two groups. First, custody-seekers reported enjoying closer relationships with their own mothers and feeling disappointment with their fathers' emotional distance. Fathers who sought custody may have been attempting to provide for their children a degree of paternal caretaking involvement that they missed as children.

The second factor distinguishing custody-seekers from noncustody-seekers was the hostility surrounding the marital break-up. Fathers who sought custody had more hostile divorces than did the other fathers. Gersick suggested that the decision to pursue a custody award may have been motivated, in part, by a desire to punish the mother for behavior leading to the divorce. Relevant to this point was Gersick's report that the majority of the 40 fathers he interviewed regarded the divorce as *completely* the fault of the mother, usually owing to extramarital affairs. In sum, the motives underlying a father's decision to seek custody of his children are likely to be complex, entailing issues relating to the marriage itself as well as child-centered concerns.

The transition to single parenting—especially after a divorce—entails many of the same stresses and difficulties for fathers as for mothers. The interview studies of single fathers characterize the first year after the marital break-up as particularly stressful, with fathers required to negotiate personal problems (e.g., loneliness, depression) as well as the reorganization of the household. Keshet and Rosenthal (1978a), for example, described this period as "a series of trial-and-error adjustments" in home management and childcare arrangements, with some of these responsibilities shared with older children. Fathers in this study and others reported feeling inadequate, overtaxed, and even somewhat frightened. Personal activities and social contacts with other adults were dramatically curtailed in the wake of new responsibilities and commitments. Although most fathers in these studies were financially well off, they experienced a decline in income after the separation, and some required public assistance. Many also reported difficulty obtaining and financing childcare arrangements.

In addition, single fathers faced several unique adjustments and difficulties during the first year. Juggling work and childcare responsibilities was especially difficult for many due to their longstanding job commitments. Some managed to modify their working hours and responsibilities; others reduced their hours or, in a few cases, quit work altogether to become fulltime caregivers. Many fathers reported feeling isolated or ostracized in the community because of their unique caretaking status. They felt there were few people who could offer understanding and helpful advice to them.

Following this initial period, however, these studies uniformly report that fathers felt increasingly competent and successful in their domestic responsibilities. Very few fathers employed housekeepers or babysitters; most assumed cooking, cleaning, and caregiving responsibilities by themselves. Fathers rapidly attained competence in domestic chores or discovered ways of reducing these responsibilities. Indeed, most fathers reported that their greatest difficulty in fulfilling domestic tasks was lack of time rather than incompetence—and most reported enjoying, to some extent, these new obligations. In short, the adjustment of single fathers to their new domestic responsibilities appears to have been reasonably rapid and successful.

And, according to their report, the same was true with child care. Indeed, single fathers reported feeling closer to their children in the years following the marital break-up, in marked contrast to the experience of fathers as noncustodial parents. Many reported having the capacity to give and receive affection more openly and seeking activities to enjoy together with the children. By and large, these fathers also reported that their children adjusted well to their new caretaking circumstances over time. For example, Bartz and Witcher (1978) reported that single fathers assessed their children's feelings of security, self-esteem, school performance, and responsibility as stable or improved several years after the divorce.

Mendes (1976a) found that paternal satisfaction with the caretaking role was strongly related to the conditions under which custody was obtained. Fathers who had actively sought to become single parents (Mendes called them ''seekers'') reported having excellent relationships with their children and strong, positive feelings about being fathers. In contrast, fathers who had not sought single parenthood but had acceded to circumstances or to the wishes of others (''assenters'') felt much less satisfaction with the parenting role. As one would expect, Mendes reported that all of the ''seekers'' were divorced fathers or were in the process of obtaining a divorce; a much higher proportion of the ''assenters'' were widowed. In short, the fathers who actively sought custody of their children were likely to be the ones who derived the most satisfaction from the role of single father.

To be sure, the areas of recurrent worry or concern for the single fathers interviewed in these studies were also child-centered. Many voiced concern over their adequacy in dealing with the child's ''emotional needs''—in particular, the child's needs for affection and nurturance. Underlying this worry one can discern, perhaps, broader cultural beliefs about the importance of a mother's love for the young child. Fathers also worried about their lack of time and patience with their children. Finally, the fathers of daughters—particularly daughters approaching adolescence—voiced concern over their child's sexuality and the lack of appropriate female role models. Many fathers enlisted the help of a trusted female friend (e.g., a favorite schoolteacher, relative or family friend) to provide advice and support for their daughters.

Taken together, these interview studies of single fathers characterize these parents as competent and resourceful primary caretakers. Although the transition to this kind of family structure was difficult and entailed multiple adjustments for all family members, fathers reported a good deal of success and satisfaction with their new roles after this period. These reports are especially important in view of the fact that, by and large, these fathers had had little prior preparation for homemaking and caretaking responsibilities. Prior to the divorce, mothers had usually been the primary caregivers and paternal involvement in domestic tasks had been minimal. In addition, the age and gender of the children in these single father families were diverse: Fathers assumed custody of infant as well as adolescent sons and daughters, and were thus faced with a range of caretaking responsibilities. In short, on the basis of these reports, there is little reason to doubt the competence or adequacy of fathers as single parents.

The major qualification to this conclusion is, of course, the data from which it is derived: Single fathers are likely to offer an optimistic portrayal of family life when interviewed about their experience as single parents. Similarly positive impressions are, in fact, derived from interview studies of single mothers as well (e.g., Kurdek & Siesky, 1978, 1979). In view of this, it is surprising how few researchers have directly observed parent-child interaction in single-father, single-mother, and intact families.

In one study, Lowenstein and Koopman (1978) used a standardized questionnaire to measure the self-esteem of boys (age 9 to 14) from single-mother and single-father divorced homes. They found no significant differences in the self-esteem scores of boys from the two groups; nor were self-esteem scores correlated with the length of time they lived in a single-parent home or the self-esteem of the custodial parent. Lowenstein and Koopman did find, however, that the self-esteem of boys who saw the noncustodial parent less than once a month was significantly lower than that of boys who saw the noncustodial parent more frequently. Thus the quality of the ongoing relationship with the noncustodial parent was an important factor in the postdivorce adjustment of these boys. Unfortunately, Lowenstein and Koopman did not further assess whether there were differences between boys living with their mothers or their fathers in this factor. Nor did they directly observe parents interacting with their children.

Fortunately, there is one research project that has done so, conducted by Santrock, Warshak, and their colleagues (Santrock & Warshak, 1979; Santrock, Warshak, & Elliot, 1982; Warshak & Santrock, 1980). In this study, 64 white, predominantly middle-class families were interviewed and observed both at home and in the laboratory. Approximately one-third of the families were single-father families; one-third were single-mother families; the remaining third were intact, two-parent families. The children in these families were boys and girls ranging in age from 6 to 11 years at the time of the assessment. Families in all three groups were matched for the age of the children, family size, and socioeconomic status. At the time of the assessments, parents in divorced families had been separated an average of three years; the portrayal of family interaction thus reflects the adjustment of both children and parents following the immediate postdivorce period.

A multimethod approach to studying family interaction was used by these investigators. First, the parent and child were invited to the laboratory to participate in two structured interactional sessions that were videotaped. (Children from intact families were observed on separate occasions with each parent). Following this, children were independently interviewed concerning their feelings and perceptions of their parents and, when pertinent, the divorce experience. At the same time, parents completed a battery of personality and self-report scales concerning the child and their child-rearing practices. Finally, on a later date, the interviewer talked with the parent at home while the child was given a battery of self-report scales. Thus the major data sources for this study consisted of scores from standardized scales and ratings derived from the laboratory observation session and the interviews.

Parental reports of the family's divorce adjustment were consistent with the findings reported earlier and varied little in mother-custody and father-custody families (Warshak & Santrock, 1980). For both children and their parents, the weeks and months immediately following the parents' separation were reported to be emotionally draining. Most parents, however, perceived improvement in the parent-child relationship since this period, and children tended to concur with their parents on this point. Interestingly, however, 85% of the children expressed a strong desire for their parents' reconciliation three years after the divorce, regardless of their custodial situation. Over two-thirds of the children preferred the intact, predivorce family over their current circumstances.

There were, however, some important differences in the living conditions of mother-custody and father-custody families. First, the annual income of single mothers was significantly lower than single fathers' income. Second, extrafamilial support systems—such as babysitters, friends, and childcare centers—were being used twice as frequently by single fathers as by single mothers. Third, and most important, these families varied significantly in the child's relationship with the noncustodial parent over time. Noncustodial mothers were significantly more assessible to their children than were noncustodial fathers. Mothers with custody reported a deterioration in the father-child relationship in the months following the divorce, but the reverse was not reported by single fathers (Warshak & Santrock, 1980).

Ratings of the parent-child laboratory interactions were analyzed to determine the effects of the different custody arrangements (Santrock & Warshak, 1979). The results were striking. In comparing the interactions of divorced families with intact families, Santrock and Warshak discovered that the effects of family structure were mediated by the gender of both parent and child. That is, boys in father-custody homes were rated as more mature, sociable, warm, and independent in their interactions with their fathers compared with the interactions of boys from intact families with their fathers. In contrast, girls in father-custody homes were rated as *less* mature, warm, and sociable and as more demanding than girls from intact families with their fathers. When boys and girls from mother-custody families were compared with children from intact families, however, there were few consistent differences. In short, single fathers appeared to get along better with their sons and more poorly with their daughters than fathers in traditional homes.

Similar findings were obtained when Santrock and Warshak compared parent-child interactions in father-custody and mother-custody families. On measures of maturity, sociability, and independence, boys in father-custody homes uniformly showed greater social competence than father-custody girls. In mother-custody homes the reverse was true: Girls were more socially competent than boys. Taken together, these results indicate that children interact better with the same-sex custodial parent. Similar findings were obtained from ratings derived from the child interviews (Santrock, Warshak, & Elliott, 1982; Warshak & Santrock, 1980), although these results were somewhat less reliable.

These researchers have suggested several reasons to account for the more positive interactions of children with the same-sex custodial parent. On one hand, children may benefit from the availability of a same-sex adult role model in the home, especially while negotiating the difficult transition to the postdivorce family. Conversely, parents may also be more adequate caretakers of same-sex children because they can draw upon their own childhood experiences and perhaps offer greater understanding of their child's difficulties. For example, divorced fathers may be more tolerant of dependent behaviors in their sons because they are having to cope with similar feelings themselves. On the other hand, there are reasons to expect greater difficulty when children live with the opposite-sex parent. For example, children are likely to exhibit many of the characteristics of the divorced spouse, and this may result in more negative encounters with a parent who is recovering from a difficult marriage and divorce. Clearly, these alternative explanations merit further exploration.

Taken together, the work of Santrock and Warshak and other investigators of single fathers suggests that fathers can be competent primary caretakers following a period of adjustment to this new role. As one ould expect, they face the same kinds of difficulties encountered by single mothers in juggling domestic, employment, and personal needs but, according to these reports, do not fare significantly more poorly than do mothers with custody. Single fathers evince appropriate concern for their children's needs and also report satisfaction with their caretaking role—especially if they actively sought this role. The children, in turn, seem to do well with single fathers, especially sons.

These conclusions must be regarded as tentative, however, because of our reliance on the interview studies of single fathers. More research is needed. Such research should include direct observation of single fathers, their children, and the interactions they share. Are the generally optimistic reports offered by the fathers in these interview studies verifiable? Longitudinal study of fathers and children during the years following the divorce is also needed. As the Hetherington, Cox, and Cox and the Wallerstein and Kelly studies have shown, repeated assessments of the postdivorce family can yield useful information concerning which sequelae of divorce are more enduring over time and therefore a greater cause for concern. In addition, longitudinal analyses can help us to identify "sleeper" effects of various custody arrangements that may not be immediately apparent in the postdivorce family but that gradually emerge over time as the developmental needs of children change.

Future research concerning single fathers should also pay more attention to the manner in which a custody award to the father was determined. In the studies reviewed, most of the fathers obtained custody of children with the consent of the mother. The reasons for this agreement are often unclear. Did both parents agree that the father was the better caregiver? Did the mothers seek a ''fresh start'' after the divorce? Did future occupational or geographical commitments for either parent necessitate this kind of arrangement? The nature of the child's relationship with each parent is likely to vary significantly if the custody award to the father was the outcome of a court dispute or of parental agreement. For example, to what extent could the greater conflict between single fathers and their daughters (noted by Santrock and Warshak, 1979) have been due to the daughter's perception of having been rejected or abandoned by a mother who did not seek custody? In view of our interest in the father's case when custody is disputed, these interpretational questions are significant ones, and mandate new investigations of single fatherhood in alternative kinds of custody determinations.

SUMMARY AND CONCLUSIONS

From this research review, several conclusions seem warranted.

First, despite important differences in the amount of time they spend with their infants and young children, *both* fathers and mothers are significant figures in the infant's world from a very early age. By the end of the first year, infants recognize both parents and prefer them to unfamiliar adults. By this time and increasingly during the second year, infants respond differently to each parent, reflecting the development of a rudimentary appreciation of each parent's unique role in their world. The research indicates that there are more similarities than differences in infant responsiveness to fathers and mothers: They protest separation from either parent, delight in being reunited with them, and play comfortably in the presence of either father or mother. By all accounts, it is apparent that infants develop emotionally salient attachment relationships with each parent by the end of the first year. In short, both mother and father are ''psychological parents'' to their young infants, even when the father does not assume major caregiving responsibilities. There is every reason to assume that the psychological salience of each parent persists as the child grows older.

Second, even though both parents are important figures in the infant's world, mothers and fathers differ significantly in their caretaking roles and responsibilities in most homes. Mothers typically assume basic caretaking tasks such as feeding, cleaning, dressing, soothing of distress, and preventative protection from harm. When they play with their babies, they use low-key verbally-oriented and toy-mediated games. In contrast, fathers are typically much less involved in routine caretaking tasks. Rather, they spend a greater proportion of their time engaged in play—specifically, a vigorous rough-and-tumble, physically stimulating kind of play. Earlier in this review, I suggested that these differences could be viewed in terms of the nature of the caretaking role: Mothers as primary caretakers, assuming major responsibility for routine but necessary tasks, and fathers as secondary caretakers with more limited involvement in this area.

Such a distinction was intended not only as a conceptual aid, but to show how these differences in parental roles are likely to be perceived by the infant. That is, who does the baby anticipate will feed or bathe her? From which parent does the infant expect exciting, arousing play? And, in fact, the research indicates that during the latter half of the first year, infants begin to form social expectations for each parent that influence their responsiveness to mothers and fathers. In comfortable settings, fathers receive the majority of the baby's affiliative gestures and are preferred as play partners. Infants get more aroused and excited during play with their fathers, reflecting the importance of play encounters as a context for father-infant interactions. In contrast, mothers are especially preferred by infants in situations of stress, fatigue, alarm or upset—situations, in other words, in which the baby seeks comfort and soothing. Because the mother has been a reliable source of relief from distress in the past, it is unsurprising that infants should seek her assistance in stressful situations even when the father is also present.

Are these differences in caregiving role gender-based, or are they amenable to change when family circumstances change? Our third conclusion from the research review is an endorsement of both: Fathers can be adequate and competent in the primary caretaking role, although they maintain a traditionally "paternal" interactive style. Such a conclusion derives from three lines of evidence. First, Parke and his colleagues (as well as other researchers) have found that fathers closely resemble mothers in their caretaking behaviors when observed with their young infants. Second, fathers who stay at home to care for their children seem to combine the gentler, verbally oriented interactive style characteristically observed in mothers with their more typical physically-stimulating approach—in other words, they resemble traditional mothers as well as traditional fathers (although the research evidence is somewhat mixed). Third, single fathers report feeling comfortable and adequate as sole caretakers; after a period of adjustment, these fathers seem to adapt well to the demands of single parenting. Taken together, the bulk of the evidence suggests that fathers can be adequate primary caregivers if they choose to do so.

This conclusion indicates that it may be more useful, in examining parenting in the family, to distinguish between the caretaking roles assumed by each parent than to distinguish on the basis of gender. That is, rather than arguing over whether mothers are more important to their infant sons and daughters than are fathers (a dispute that is increasingly complicated by changes in the nature of the American family over the past two decades), it may be more important to view parenting in terms of primary and secondary caretaking roles and responsibilities, at least concerning infants and young children. Such an approach takes into account the capacity of each parent to assume either role, and provides a more versatile way of appraising parental roles in nontraditional as well as traditional families. Such a distinction may also better characterize how parents are perceived by infants and young children.

The fourth conclusion from this research review concerns the effects of divorce on children. The longitudinal studies of Hetherington, Cox, and Cox and of Wallerstein and Kelly both indicate that the greatest upheaval resulting from the break-up of the family occurs during the first year after the divorce. During this period, family relationships are being renegotiated and children are required to cope with their changed relationships with both the custodial and noncustodial parents. Typically, for children as well as parents, this is the period of greatest emotional distress. There is some evidence, in addition, that children's initial postdivorce adjustment is predictive of their long-term coping with changed family conditions, although more research is needed. Therefore, in considering the various ramifications of a custody decision for children, it seems reasonable to give greater weight to those factors that promote the child's more immediate postdivorce adjustment.

Fifth, and finally, there is evidence from Santrock and Warshak's research that children fare better with the same-sex parent. The longitudinal studies of divorce also indicate particular difficulty in mother-son relationships, whereas single fathers reported feeling anxiety concerning the needs of their preadolescent daughters. Taken together, these studies indicate that the child's gender should be considered in determining a custody award.

There are thus a few general guidelines provided by research studies concerning the father's case in child custody disputes relevant to the child's best interests. They consistently support the importance of the father in the young child's social world and the competence of fathers as caretakers. They also affirm the special contributions of fathers to the development of sons, and indicate that this may also be true from a very early age. In short, there is no clear reason for a bias against fathers in the determination of a custody award, even when infants or young children are concerned. Instead, custody determinations should be based on factors other than parent gender.

These research studies also yield one other general conclusion pertaining to the child's "best interests." With respect to infants and young children—who have been the focus of this review—there is reason to prefer the child's primary caretaker, whether this role is assumed by mother or father. A bias toward the parent who assumes the range of basic caregiving ministrations derives primarily from the importance of these activities to the infant. The major theories of early social development stress the adequacy and consistency with which the baby's basic needs are satisfied and the importance of these caregiving ministrations to the baby's development of confidence in others and perception of self as a competent elicitor of satisfactions from his or her environment. Such a view realistically reflects the dependence of the infant and toddler on the social world and suggests that the one who provides for these needs is accorded special importance by the child during the early years. There is empirical evidence for this conclusion: Infants turn to the primary caregiver for comfort or soothing when they are in stressful or alarming circumstances. In considering a custody decision, these factors seem to justify maintaining consistency in these caretaking responsibilities with infants and toddlers. Placing the child with the parent who has been the primary caregiver (whether mother or father) is likely to result in a less difficult transition for the child than if another caretaker assumes these responsibilities, even though the other parent is likely to perform these tasks adequately. In other words, placing the child with the secondary caretaker requires a more significant renegotiation of relational expectations that may result in heightened stress for the cognitively unsophisticated infant or very young child. Of course, the break-up of the family is likely to be stressful with either parent; we are concerned here with the *degree* of stress engendered by this transition.

It is not clear at all whether similar considerations pertain to older children, for at least two reasons. First, the preschooler is less dependent and behaviorally and cognitively more sophisticated. The preschooler's social interactions focus less on the satisfaction of basic needs than the infant's. This means that the nature of the parenting role also changes, entailing a broader range of shared experiences in addition to basic caregiving ministrations (e.g., trips together, conversing about the day's experiences, instruction, discipline encounters, etc.). Both parents are likely to take an active part in these activities. Thus the broadening of parenting concerns with the child's development makes it much more difficult to define "primary" and "secondary" caretaking roles and responsibilities, even in the traditional family. Both parents are likely to be primary caregivers if they are more than minimally involved with the child, although, of course, the extent of each parent's involvement with the child is still an important consideration. The second reason for hesitancy in applying a preference for the primary caretaker to older children is a lack of research knowledge concerning how older children perceive and respond to differences in parental roles in traditional as well as nontraditional families. It is likely that older children have more sophisticated and differentiated conceptions of their parents and of the relationships they share with them, and this might facilitate their transition to alternative kinds of custody arrangements. This is an area in which future research inquiry is needed.

These conclusions pertaining to parent caretaking roles, the effects of divorce and alternative custody arrangements are, of course, framed very broadly, and inevitably must be viewed within the range of specific considerations and circumstances pertaining to a particular custody award. These applications of research findings to child custody adjudication are, in other words, framed in terms of a *ceteris paribus* (other things being equal) assumption. Obviously, this assumption is unjustified in individual cases, and therefore any recommendations must be viewed within the context of the interrelationships among multiple specific considerations.

In addition to noting applications of research findings to custody issues, this review has also highlighted areas in which new research is needed. We do not have a lot of information, for example, about the nature of parent-child relationships in dual-wage-earner families (who are becoming increasingly typical in Western industrialized nations). We need more direct observations of fathers in the role of single parents, and the experience of children growing up in these homes. We require more information about the nature of parental roles and responsibilities during the child's preschool years and, more important, how mothers and fathers are perceived and responded to by their preschool sons and daughters. And we need greater in-depth study of the transition from a dual-parent to a single-parent family and how this transition is experienced by children of various ages. These are, of course, difficult research tasks, but they constitute an important part of the agenda for further work in this area.

Throughout this review, we have considered custody issues from the standpoint of awarding custody to either one parent or the other. In view of the importance of both parents to the infant's social world, a joint custody arrangement would most likely foster the child's long-term best interests. But joint custody should not be viewed as a panacea for the agonizing decisions entailed in custody deliberations. Indeed, there are a variety of important considerations bearing on the advisability of a joint custody award for any family in divorce (see an excellent review of these issues by Clingempeel and Reppucci, 1982). Can both parents establish the kind of cooperative relationship necessary to make joint decisions concerning the child's present and future welfare? Will the child be protected from loyalty conflicts and other stresses that may be engendered by continuing disputes between ex-spouses? If the child alternates between two different home environments, how can consistency in basic caretaking activities be maintained? These and other considerations entail making certain predictive judgments, namely, whether joint custody is likely to provide the child with the benefits of sustained parental relationships that outweigh the potential stresses of shared decision-making by ex-spouses. Certainly joint custody should never be judicially imposed if it is not sought by both parents. When it is sought, however, and specific practical decisions can be successfully negotiated in the child's interests, there are reasons to support a joint custody award as reflecting a child's "best interests."

There is little hope, however, that the development of new custody options or the generation of new research data will be able to significantly reduce the difficult decisions faced by jurists in determining a custody award. Although research can provide an overall framework within which specific information pertaining to the family in question can be integrated and evaluated, there are limits to the kinds of knowledge that research studies can provide. Ultimately, the weighing of the many idiosyncratic factors entailed in any specific custody dispute depends, for better or worse, on the wisdom of lawyers and judges. Hopefully, that wisdom can be fostered by the work of behavioral scientists and others who are concerned with children and families.

ACKNOWLEDGMENTS

The preparation of this review was stimulated by a series of enormously valuable discussions with David Chambers, Mary Hendrikson (both of the University of Michigan Law School), and Michael Lamb, while I was at the University of Michigan. They offered perspectives and questions to the issues discussed in this review that often provoked agonizing—but fruitful—reappraisals of my thinking and writing. Although their contributions were substantive, the ultimate responsibility for this discussion is, of course, mine alone.

Work on this review was supported, in part, by a fellowship from the Bush Program in Child Development and Social Policy at the University of Michigan.

I am grateful to Gary Melton, David Chambers, and Michael Lamb for their thoughtful comments on an earlier version of this chapter.

REFERENCES

Ainsworth, M. D. S. The development of infant-mother attachment. In B. Caldwell and H. Ricciuti (Eds.), *Review of child development research* (Vol. 3). Chicago: University of Chicago Press, 1973.

Ainsworth, M. D. S., Blehar, M. C., Waters, E., & Wall, S. *Patterns of attachment.* Hillsdale, N.J.: Lawrence Erlbaum Associates, 1978.

Ban, P. L., & Lewis, M. Mothers and fathers, girls and boys: Attachment behavior in the one-year-old. *Merrill-Palmer Quarterly,* 1974, *20,* 195–204.

Bartz, K. W., & Witcher, W. C. When father gets custody. *Children Today,* 1978, *7,* 2–35.

Bayley, N. Development of mental abilities. In P. H. Mussen (Ed.), *Carmichael's manual of child psychology* (Vol. 1). New York: Wiley, 1970.

Beckwith, L. Prediction of emotional and social behavior. In J. D. Osofsky (Ed.), *Handbook of infant development.* New York: Wiley, 1979.

Belsky, J. Mother-father-infant interaction: A naturalistic observational study. *Developmental Psychology,* 1979, *15,* 601–607.

Berman, P. W. Are women more responsive than men to the young? A review of developmental and situational variables. *Psychological Bulletin,* 1980, *88,* 668–695.

Biller, H. B. *Father, child, and sex role.* Lexington, Mass.: D. C. Heath, 1971.

Biller, H. B. *Paternal deprivation.* Lexington, Mass.: D. C. Heath, 1974.

Biller, H. B. The father and personality development: Paternal deprivation and sex-role development. In M. E. Lamb (Ed.), *The role of the father in child development.* New York: Wiley, 1976.

Bowlby, J. *Attachment and loss* (Vol. 1). New York: Basic Books, 1969.

Bronfenbrenner, U. The changing American child. *Journal of Social Issues,* 1961, *17,* 6–18.

Bronfenbrenner, U. Developmental research, public policy, and the ecology of childhood. *Child Development,* 1974, *45,* 1–5.

Bronfenbrenner, U. Toward an experimental ecology of human development. *American Psychologist,* 1977, *32,* 513–531.

Brown, D. G. Sex role preference in young children. *Psychological Monographs,* 1956, *70,* 1–19.

Brown, D. G. Sex role development in a changing culture. *Psychological Bulletin,* 1958, *55,* 232–242.

Clarke-Stewart, K. A. And daddy makes three: The father's impact on mother and young child. *Child Development,* 1978, *49,* 466–478.

Clingempeel, W. G., & Reppucci, N. D. Joint custody after divorce: Major issues and goals for research. *Psychological Bulletin, 1982, 91,* 102–127.

Cohen, L. J., & Campos, J. J. Father, mother, and stranger as elicitors of attachment behaviors in infancy. *Developmental Psychology, 1974, 10,* 146–154.

Collins, S. M. The use of social research in the courts. In L. E. Lynn, Jr. (Ed.), *Knowledge and policy: The uncertain connection.* Washington, D.C.: National Academy of Sciences, 1978.

Ellsworth, P. C., & Levy, R. J. Legislative reform of child custody adjudication. *Law and Society Review, 1969, 4,* 167–233.

Ennis, D., & Litwack, T. R. Psychology and the presumption of expertise: Flipping coins in the courtroom. *California Law Review, 1974, 62,* 693–752.

Fagot, B. I. Sex differences in toddlers' behavior and parental reaction. *Developmental Psychology, 1974, 10,* 554–558.

Ferri, E. Characteristics of motherless families. *British Journal of Social Work, 1973, 3,* 91–100.

Field, T. Interaction behaviors of primary versus secondary caretaker fathers. *Developmental Psychology, 1978, 14,* 183–184.

Freud, S. *An outline of psychoanalysis.* London: Hogarth, 1938.

Frodi, A. M., Lamb, M. E., Leavitt, L. A., & Donovan, W. L. Fathers' and mothers' responses to infant smiles and cries. *Infant Behavior and Development, 1978, 1,* 187–198.

Frodi, A. M., Lamb, M. E., Leavitt, L. A., Donovan, W. L., Neff, C., & Sherry, D. Fathers' and mothers' responses to the faces and cries of normal and premature infants. *Developmental Psychology, 1978, 14,* 490–498.

Gasser, R. D., & Taylor, C. M. Role adjustment of single parent fathers with dependent children. *The Family Coordinator, 1976, 25,* 397–401.

George, V., & Wilding, P. *Motherless families.* London: Routledge and Kegan Paul, 1972.

Gersick, K. *Fathers by choice: Characteristics of men who do and do not seek custody of their children following divorce.* Unpublished doctoral dissertation, Harvard University, 1975.

Glick, P. C. Children of divorced parents in demographic perspective. *Journal of Social Issues, 1979, 35,* 170–182.

Goldstein, J., Freud, A., & Solnit, A. J. *Beyond the best interests of the child.* New York: The Free Press, 1973.

Goodenough, E. W. Interest in persons as an aspect of sex differences in the early years. *Genetic Psychology Monographs, 1957, 55,* 287–323.

Herzog, R., & Sudia, C. E. Children in fatherless families. In B. M. Caldwell and H. N. Ricciuti (Eds.), *Review of child development research* (Vol. 3). Chicago: University of Chicago Press, 1973.

Hess, R. K., & Camara, K. A. Post-divorce family relationships as mediating factors in the consequences of divorce for children. *Journal of Social Issues, 1979, 35,* 79–96.

Hetherington, E. M., Cox, M., & Cox, R. Divorced fathers. *The Family Coordinator, 1976, 25,* 417–428.

Hetherington, E. M., Cox, M., & Cox, R. The aftermath of divorce. In J. H. Stevens and M. Matthews (Eds.), *Mother/child father/child relationships.* Washington, D. C.: National Association for the Education of Young Children, 1978.

Hetherington, E. M., Cox, M., & Cox, R. Family interaction and the social, emotional, and cognitive development of children following divorce. In V. Vaughn and T. B. Brazelton (Eds.), *The family: Setting priorities.* New York: Science and Medicine Publishing Company, 1979. (a)

Hetherington, E. M., Cox, M., & Cox, R. Play and social interaction in children following divorce. *Journal of Social Issues, 1979, 35,* 26–49. (b)

Hetherington, E. M., Cox, M., & Cox, R. Effects of divorce on parents and children. In M. E. Lamb (Ed.), *Nontraditional families.* Hillsdale, N.J.: Lawrence Erlbaum Associates, 1982.

Hipgrave, T. J. *When the mother is gone: Profile studies of 16 lone fathers with preschool children.* Unpublished masters thesis, Child Development Research Unit, Nottingham University, England, 1978.

Hoffman, L. W. Maternal employment: 1979. *American Psychologist, 1979, 34,* 859–865.

Kagan, J. *Change and continuity in infancy.* New York: Wiley, 1971.

Kagan, J., & Moss. H. A. *Birth to maturity: A study of psychological development.* New York: Wiley, 1962.

Katz, A. J. Lone fathers: Perspectives and implications for family policy. *The Family Coordinator,* 1979, *28,* 521–528.

Kelly, J., & Wallerstein, J. The effects of parental divorce: Experiences of the child in early latency. *American Journal of Orthopsychiatry,* 1976, *46,* 20–32.

Keshet, H. F., & Rosenthal, K. M. Fathering after marital separation. Social Work, 1978, *23,* 11–18. (a)

Keshet, H. F., & Rosenthal, K. M. Single parent fathers: A new study. *Children Today,* 1978, *7,* 13–17. (b)

Korner, A. F., & Thoman, E. B. Visual alertness in neonates as evoked by maternal care. *Journal of Experimental Child Psychology,* 1970, *10,* 67–78.

Korner, A. F., & Thoman, E. B. The relative efficacy of contact and vestibular-proprioceptive stimulation in soothing neonates. *Child Development,* 1972, *43,* 443–453.

Kotelchuck, M. The infant's relationship to the father: Experimental evidence. In M. E. Lamb (Ed.), *The role of the father in child development.* New York: Wiley, 1976.

Kurdek, L. A., Blisk, D., & Siesky, A. E. Correlates of children's long-term adjustment to their parents' divorce. *Developmental Psyschology,* 1981, *17,* 565–579.

Kurdek, L. A., & Siesky, A. E. Divorced single parents' perceptions of child-related problems. *Journal of Divorce,* 1978, *1,* 361–370.

Kurdek, L. A., & Siesky, A. E. An interview study of parents' perceptions of their children's reactions and adjustments to divorce. *Journal of Divorce,* 1979, *3,* 5–17.

Lamb, M. E. Effects of stress and cohort on mother- and father-infant interaction. *Developmental Psychology,* 1976, *12,* 435–443. (a)

Lamb, M. E. Interactions between 8-month-old children and their fathers and mothers. In M. E. Lamb (Ed.), *The role of the father in child development.* New York: Wiley, 1976. (b)

Lamb, M. E. Interactions between two-year-olds and their mothers and fathers. *Psychological Reports,* 1976, *38,* 447–450. (c)

Lamb, M. E. Twelve-month-olds and their parents: Interaction in a laboratory playroom. *Developmental Psychology,* 1976, *12,* 237–244. (d)

Lamb, M. E. The development of mother-infant and father-infant attachments in the second year of life. *Developmental Psychology,* 1977, *13,* 637–648. (a)

Lamb, M. E. The development of parental preferences in the first two years of life. *Sex Roles,* 1977, *3,* 495–497. (b)

Lamb, M. E. Father-infant and mother-infant interaction in the first year of life. *Child Development,* 1977, *48,* 167–181. (c)

Lamb, M. E. Qualitative aspects of mother- and father-infant attachments. *Infant Behavior and Development,* 1978, *1,* 265–275.

Lamb, M. E. Developing trust and perceived effectance in infancy. In L. P. Lipsitt (Ed.), *Advances in infancy research* (Vol. 2). Norwood, N.J.: Ablex, 1981. (a)

Lamb, M. E. The development of social expectations in the first year of life. In M. E. Lamb, & L. R. Sherrod (Eds.), *Infant social cognition.* Hillsdale, N.J.: Lawrence Erlbaum Associates, 1981. (b)

Lamb, M. E., Frodi, A. M., Frodi, M., & Hwang, C.-P. Characteristics of maternal and paternal behavior in traditional and nontraditional Swedish families. *International Journal of Behavioral Development,* 1982, in press.

Lamb, M. E., Frodi, A. M., Hwang, C.-P., Frodi, M., & Steinberg, J. Attitudes and behavior of traditional and nontraditional parents in Sweden. In R. Emde & R. Harmon (Eds.), *The development of attachment and affiliative systems.* New York: Plenum, 1982.

Lamb, M. E., Frodi, A. M., Hwang, C.-P., Frodi, M., & Steinberg, J. Mother- and father-infant interaction involving play and holding in traditional and nontraditional Swedish families. *Developmental Psychology,* 1982, in press. (b).

Lansky, L. M. The family structure also affects the model: Sex-role attitudes in parents of preschool children. *Merrill-Palmer Quarterly*, 1967, *13*, 139–150.

Lester, B. M., Kotelchuck, M., Spelke, E., Sellers, J. J., & Klein, R. E. Separation protest in Guatemalan infants: Cross-cultural and cognitive findings. *Developmental Psychology*, 1974, *10*, 79–85.

Levitin, T. Children of divorce: An introduction. *Journal of Social Issues*, 1979, *35*, 1–25.

Litwack, T. R., Gerber, G. L., & Fenster, C. A. The proper role of psychology in child custody disputes. *Journal of Family Law*, 1980, *18*, 269–300.

Lowenstein, J. S., & Koopman, E. J. A comparison of the self-esteem between boys living with single-parent mothers and single-parent fathers. *Journal of Divorce*, 1978, *2*, 195–208.

Lowery, C. R. Child custody decisions in divorce proceedings: A survey of judges. *Professional Psychology*, 1981, *12*, 492–498.

Main, M., & Weston, D. R. The quality of the toddler's relationship to mother and to father: Related to conflict behavior and the readiness to establish new relationships. *Child Development*, 1981, *52*, 932–940.

Mendes, H. A. Single fatherhood. *Social Work*, 1976, *21*, 308–312. (a)

Mendes, H. A. Single fathers. *The Family Coordinator*, 1976, *25*, 439–444. (b)

Mnookin, R. H. Foster care–In whose best interest? *Harvard Educational Review*, 1973, *43*, 599–638.

Mnookin, R. H. Child-custody adjudication: Judicial functions in the face of indeterminacy. *Law and Contemporary Problems*, 1975, *39*, 226–293.

Mnookin, R. H., & Kornhauser, L. Bargaining in the shadow of the law: The case of divorce. *Yale Law Journal*, 1979, *88*, 950–997.

Okpaku, S. R. Psychology: Impediment or aid in child custody cases? *Rutgers Law Review*, 1976, *29*, 1117–1153.

Orthner, D. K., Brown, T., & Ferguson, D. Single-parent fatherhood: An emerging life style. *The Family Coordinator*, 1976, *25*, 429–437.

Parke, R. D. Perspectives on father-infant interaction. In J. D. Osofsky (Ed.), *Handbook of infant development*. New York: Wiley, 1979.

Parke, R. D., & O'Leary, S. E. Family interaction in the newborn period: Some findings, some observations, and some unresolved issues. In K. Riegel & J. Meacham (Eds.), *The developing individual in a changing world* (Vol. 2). The Hague: Mouton, 1976.

Parke, R. D., & Sawin, D. B. The father's role in infancy: A re-evaluation. *The Family Coordinator*, 1976, *25*, 365–371.

Parke, R. D., & Tinsley, B. R. The father's role in infancy: Determinants of involvement in caregiving and play. In M. E. Lamb (Ed.), *The role of the father in child development* (Rev. ed.). New York: Wiley, 1981.

Pedersen, F. A. Does research on children reared in father-absent families yield information on father influences? *The Family Coordinator*, 1976, *25*, 459–464.

Pedersen, F. A., Cain, R. L., Zaslow, M. J., & Anderson, B. J. Variation in infant experience associated with alternative family roles. In L. Laosa, & I. Sigel (Eds.), *Families as learning environments for children*. New York: Plenum, 1982.

Pedersen, F. A., & Robson, K. S. Father participation in infancy. *American Journal of Orthopsychiatry*, 1969, *39*, 466–472.

Pleck, J. H. Men's family work: Three perspectives and some new data. *The Family Coordinator*, 1979, *28*, 481–488.

Pleck, J. H., & Lang, L. *Men's family role: Its nature and consequences*. Wellesley College Center for Research on Women Working Paper #10, 1978.

Pleck, J. H., & Rustad, M. *Husbands' and wives' time in family work and paid work in the 1975–76 study of time use*. Wellesley College Center for Research on Women Working Paper #63, 1980.

Radin, N. The role of the father in cognitive/academic/intellectual development. In M. E. Lamb (Ed.), *The role of the father in child development* (Rev. ed.). New York: Wiley, 1981.

Radin, N. Primary caregiving and role-sharing fathers. In M. E. Lamb (Ed.), *Nontraditional families: Parenting and child development.* Hillsdale, N.J.: Lawrence Erlbaum Associates, 1982.

Radin, N., & Sagi, A. Childrearing fathers in Israel and the USA. *Merill Palmer Quarterly,* 1982, in press.

Robinson, J. P. *How Americans use time.* New York: Praeger, 1977.

Ross, G., Kagan, J., Zelazo, P., & Kotelchuck, M. Separation protest in infants in home and laboratory. *Developmental Psychology,* 1975, *11,* 256–257.

Roth, A. The tender years presumption in child custody disputes. *Journal of Family Law,* 1977, *15,* 423–462.

Russell, G. Shared-caregiving families. An Australian study. In M. E. Lamb (Ed.), *Nontraditional families: Parenting and child development.* Hillsdale, N.J.: Lawrence Erlbaum Associates, 1982.

Sagi, A. Antecedents and consequences of various degrees of paternal involvement in child rearing: The Israeli project. In M. E. Lamb (Ed.), *Nontraditional families parenting and child development.* Hillsdale, N.J.: Lawrence Erlbaum Associates, 1982.

Santrock, J. W., & Warshak, R. A. Father custody and social development in boys and girls. *Journal of Social Issues,* 1979, *35,* 112–125.

Santrock, J. W., Warshak, R. A., & Elliott, G. L. Social development and parent-child interaction in father-custody and stepmother families. In M. E. Lamb (Ed.), *Nontraditional families.* Hillsdale, N.J.: Lawrence Erlbaum Associates, 1982.

Sawin, D. B., & Parke, R. D. Fathers' affectionate stimulation and caregiving behaviors with newborn infants. *The Family Coordinator,* 1979, *28,* 509–513.

Schlesinger, B. Single parent fathers: A research review. *Children Today,* 1979, *7,* 12–39.

Schlesinger, B., & Todres, R. Motherless families: An increasing societal pattern. *Child Welfare,* 1976, *55,* 553–558.

Sears, R. R., Maccoby, E. E., & Levin, H. *Patterns of child rearing.* Stanford, Calif.: Stanford University Press, 1957.

Spelke, E., Zelazo, P., Kagan, J., and Kotelchuck, M. Father interaction and separation protest. *Developmental Psychology,* 1973, *9,* 83–90.

Szalai, A., Converse, P. E., Feldheim, P., Scheuch, E. K., & Stone, P. J. *The use of time.* The Hague: Mouton, 1972.

Tasch, R. J. The role of the father in the family. *Journal of Experimental Education,* 1952, *20,* 319–361.

Thompson, R. A., & Frodi, A. M. The sociophysiology of infants and their caregivers. In W. M. Waid (Ed.), *Sociophysiology.* New York: Springer-Verlag, in press.

Todres, R. Motherless families. *Canadian Welfare,* 1975, *51,* 11–13.

Wald, M. State intervention on behalf of "neglected" children: A search for realistic standards. *Stanford Law Review,* 1975, *27,* 985–1040.

Wald, M. Thinking about public policy toward abuse and neglect of children: A review of Before the best interests of the child. *Michigan Law Review,* 1980, *78,* 645–693.

Walker, K., & Woods, M. *Time use.* Washington, D.C.: American Home Economics Association, 1976.

Wallerstein, J., & Kelly, J. The effects of parental divorce: The adolescent experience. In E. J. Anthony and C. Koupernik (Eds.), *The child in his family: Children at psychiatric risk.* New York: Wiley, 1974.

Wallerstein, J., & Kelly, J. The effects of parental divorce: The experiences of the preschool child. *Journal of the American Academy of Child Psychiatry,* 1975, *14,* 600–616.

Wallerstein, J., & Kelly, J. The effects of parental divorce: Experiences of the child in later latency. *American Journal of Orthopsychiatry,* 1976, *46,* 256–269.

Wallerstein, J., & Kelly, J. *Surviving the breakup: How children and parents cope with divorce.* New York: Basic Books, 1980.

Warshak, R. A., & Santrock, J. W. Children of divorce: Impact of custody disposition on social development. In E. J. Callahan and K. A. McCluskey (Eds.), *Life-span developmental psychology: Non-normative life events.* New York: Academic Press, 1980.

Weinraub, M., & Frankel, J. Sex differences in parent-infant interaction during free play, departure, and separation. *Child Development,* 1977, *48,* 1240–1249.

Weitzman, L. J., & Dixon, R. B. Child custody awards: Legal standards and empirical patterns for child custody, support and visitation after divorce. *University of California Davis Law Review,* 1979, *12,* 472–521.

Whobrey, L., Sales, B., & Lou, M. Social science and the best interests standard: Another case for informed speculation. Unpublished manuscript, University of Nebraska, 1982.

Yogman, M. W. *The goals and structure of face-to-face interaction between infants and fathers.* Paper presented at the biennial meeting of the Society for Research in Child Development, New Orleans, March 1977.

Yogman, M. W., Dixon, S., Tronick, E., Adamson, L., Als, H., & Brazelton, T. B. *Development of infant social interaction with fathers.* Paper presented at the Eastern Psychological Association annual meeting, New York, April 1976.

6

The Fatherhood Project

James A. Levine
Bank Street College of Education
Joseph H. Pleck
Wellesley College
Michael E. Lamb
University of Utah

The contributors to this volume all agree that much more work is needed on the origins and implications of father-child relationships. Drawing upon the limited evidence now available, Russell and Radin (Chapter 11), Radin and Russell (Chapter 9), and Hoffman (Chapter 10) attempt to review the costs and benefits to individual men, women, and children of increased paternal involvement in child care. Sagi and Sharon (Chapter 12) evaluate the costs and benefits to society as a whole. Each of these authors, however, raises a common concern: Why is it that more men do not assume a major role in the care of their children? Are they disinterested, thanks to their biological heritage and psychological histories, or are they inhibited by employment practices and socioeconomic constraints that require them to choose between paternal involvement and secure employment rather than combine the two? At this stage, we really do not know.

To answer these questions, the three authors recently initiated The Fatherhood Project, a large scale effort designed to critically examine innovative policies and programs in the legal, employment, health, education, social service, and religious sectors that permit or encourage fathers to take a greater role in child care. It will also critically review the existing literature regarding paternal involvement and paternal influences. The goal of the project is not to embrace increased paternal involvement as a universal objective but to identify practices that would increase the potential for men and women to decide for themselves how to divide childcare responsibilities. The aim of the present chapter is to review the issues that promoted us to undertake The Fatherhood Project, and to describe the components of this research.

THE PROBLEM

As we enter the 1980s, there is a growing consensus that an increased male role in child rearing is desirable for children, for women, and for men themselves. This consensus derives from three different though related sources:

1. *A new awareness of the role of fathers in child development.* Developmental psychologists, having more or less "discovered" fatherhood during the past 15 years, now emphasize that mothers are not the only salient adults in children's lives. Research by scholars such as Lamb (e.g., 1976, 1981), Biller (e.g., 1971, 1974), Parke (1979), Pedersen (1980), Radin (1981), and Staples (1978), among others, points to the effects of fathers on children's cognitive, socioemotional, moral, and sex-role development.

2. *Recognition of the impact of men's low participation in child care on women's equal opportunity.* Virtually every major psychological, sociological, or historical analysis of the status of women in American society—including such diverse works as Dorothy Dinnerstein's *The mermaid and the minotaur* (1976), Adrienne Rich's *Of women born* (1976), Janet Giele's *Women and the future* (1978), Nancy Chodorow's *The reproduction of motherhood* (1978), William Chafe's *The American woman* (1974), Peter Filene's *Him/her/self* (1976), and Betty Friedan's reassessment of the women's movement, *The second stage* (1981)—points to increased father participation as essential in the realization of women's equal opportunity as well as to women's full psychological development.

3. *Recognition of the meaning of fatherhood in the lives of men themselves.* Some 15 years after the rebirth of the women's movement, and after scores of books about the meaning of motherhood in women's lives, a literature by and about fathers is now beginning to find its way into popular consciousness and college curricula. This diverse literature—including popular novels like *Kramer versus Kramer* (Corman, 1977), and *Mother's day* (Miner, 1978), first-person accounts like Eliot Daley's *Father feelings* (1974), sociological studies like Bittman and Salk's *Expectant fathers* (1978), and writings of the "men's liberation" movement, such as Herb Goldberg's *The new male* (1979)—calls for fathers to be more involved with their children because of the enriching effect such involvement will have on men's own lives.

Though they all recognize the importance of increasing the paternal role in childrearing, none of the current psychological, sociological, or historical analyses pays serious attention to how it can be achieved. Each identifies the problem—often eloquently—but stops short of addressing how any practical changes in social policy or institutional practices could be brought about. As National Book Award winner Adrienne Rich stated in *Of women born,* for example,

"Until men are ready to share the responsibilities of full-time universal child care as a social priority, their sons and ours will be without any coherent vision of what non-patriarchal manhood might be [p. 211]." Or, as psychologist Dorothy Dinnerstein puts it in *The mermaid and the minotaur* (1976): "So long as the hand that has rocked every cradle is female, psychoanalytic theorists and taxi drivers will go on, in their respective ways, complaining that the minimal, irreducible individualism of women is unwomanly, and pontificating about the masculine protest, and wondering angrily who wears the pants [p. 93]."

Sociologist Alice Rossi has gone the farthest, perhaps, towards making a specific recommendation for change. In her controversial 1977 article for *Daedalus*, "A Biosocial Perspective on Parenting," Rossi asserted that "a society that chooses to overcome the female's greater investment in children must institutionalize a program of compensatory education for boys and men that trains them in infant and child care." Doubting that it could ever be achieved, however, Rossi did not begin to explain how such compensatory education might be implemented.

The reluctance or inability to address the problem of male involvement in more practical or immediate terms is quite understandable. First, it is a problem that is just coming into focus. Second, it is a problem that some consider intractable; Rossi and some sociobiologists, for example, claim that biological factors set an upper limit on men's ability to nurture children. Third, it is a problem of enormous complexity that tends to prompt either of two diametrically opposed but equally passive responses: (1) it is an individual issue only, for men and women to work out in their families; or (2) an exhortation that "society must change," without any serious attempt to analyze where such change might begin. In either case, one is hardpressed to know where to begin. The question of how to increase male involvement in child rearing remains problematic for individual families and for our whole society, and nobody has tried to address it specifically and systematically.

The Fatherhood Project takes the position that the nurturing role of males can be increased and that, in spite of the enormity and complexity of the task, there does appear to be a way to begin. Although it is not widely recognized, a variety of efforts to increase father participation in child rearing exist. Scattered throughout the country, and geared to varying populations of men at different points in their lives, these efforts cover a broad range, including: educational programs for elementary and high school boys (prospective fathers); postpartum father support groups organized by hospitals; employer-sponsored parental leave policies; and divorce and custody mediation services for divorcing parents. To cite but a few examples:

• New York City: at the Collegiate School, 11- and 12-year old boys now vie for posts in a course on infant care, the school's second most popular elective, ranking just behind the course on computers; at the New York Council on

Adoptable Children, the former executive director, Jim Green, offered seminars for other single men—like himself—who wanted to adopt or who had adopted children.

• Boston: a community mental health group called COPE (Coping with the Overall Parenting Experience), which has representatives in over 20 Boston area communities, offers postpartum support groups for mothers *and* for fathers (it is just becoming well known that fathers as well as mothers may experience postpartum depression); in nearby Cambridge, the Divorce Resource and Mediation Center has been pioneering efforts to keep divorcing couples out of the courts and to help them work towards a new type of postdivorce parenting, in which both fathers and mothers remain actively involved in their children's lives.

• Washington, D.C.: Children's Hospital, which serves a heterogeneous population, has changed its visiting policies to encourage mothers *and* fathers to stay overnight with hospitalized children.

• Cleveland: the Program for Sexual Learning is developing a series of discussion groups in traditionally male forums—the Elks Club, Masons, etc.—to help fathers feel more comfortable in talking with their children about sexuality.

• Chicago: the Male Motivation and Education Program at Planned Parenthood is helping teenage fathers stay more involved with their children and to be more supportive of the children's mothers.

• Pittsburgh, California: at the Los Medanos Community College, child development specialist Bob Zavala is offering courses on early childhood education and parenting geared to men who, like himself, come from Mexican-American backgrounds.

Such scattered beginnings are not merely an American phenomenon. Several of the Western European countries—at least those in the European Economic Community—are also starting to see the formation of father groups or father programs. In Sweden, the government sponsors and subsidizes a Parental Insurance System, the most explicit policy initiative anywhere, to encourage or enable fathers to be more involved in child rearing. Initiated in 1974, the policy allows mothers *or* fathers to remain home for up to 9 months after the birth of a child and still receive up to 90 percent of their prebirth salary for 6 months and a minimal level thereafter (see Lamb & Levine, this volume).

There is no denying that the question of how to increase male involvement in child rearing is an enormously complex social issue. However, if we are going to do more than identify it as a contemporary problem, if we are going to think more constructively about social change, then we may have much to learn from the assortment of attempts—however few and far between—that are already being made to encourage men to participate more in child rearing. That is where the Fatherhood Project begins.

GOALS AND OBJECTIVES

The overall goal of the Fatherhood Project is to foster the development of institutional strategies that will enable men to become more involved in child rearing. To work towards this goal in the short term, the Project has three objectives:

Research: to provide a "state of the art" assessment of both the feasibility and desirability of increasing male involvement in child rearing. Project research will pay special attention to the particular concerns and needs of minority and low income populations, who have often been stereotyped in or excluded from examinations of fatherhood. Findings will be made available in *The future of fatherhood,* a publication that shifts us from a problem-oriented to a solution-oriented perspective. This major trade book will integrate and analyze as no one else has to date: (1) the data on the nature, extent, and current limits of father involvement; (2) the arguments for increased father involvement; (3) the evidence for the effects of father involvement on children, women, and men; (4) the evidence—both from Sweden and the United States—of both the possibilities and the limitations of institutional change; and (5) specific and practical recommendations for future change.

Demonstration: to establish, assess, and derive training materials from two innovative educational programs, one designed to help young boys become more comfortable in taking care of babies, and one designed to help fathers become more comfortable with their infants and toddlers.

Dissemination: to provide those who are interested in learning about, starting, or funding programs related to fatherhood—e.g., employers, educational institutions, foundations—with a reliable and comprehensive source of information about research and innovative programs.

In the long term, the Project has the following objectives:
- Through its activities and publications to make the male role in child rearing a significant topic of public discussion.
- To generate new programs or policies in support of fatherhood.
- To establish a process or processes for working towards longer term change.

The Fatherhood Project is not designed, it should be noted, to end up simplistically endorsing the notion that increased father involvement is a "good thing" or the same thing for all families, in all situations, offering universal remedies for social change. Rather, the Project is carefully designed to determine whether and under what circumstances increased male involvement is desirable, and then to find ways that changes in the level of male involvement can be brought about. The Project will not offer prescriptions with the idea that they can or should be taken by all; it will, on the other hand, specify changes that would broaden the option for greater male participation in those families that desire it.

DESCRIPTION OF ACTIVITIES

The Fatherhood Project is divided into three interrelated components—research, demonstration, and dissemination—each with subcomponents. This section describes the substance of activities to be carried out in each of these three areas.

Research

The research component has three subcomponents—field research in the United States, field research in Sweden, and a literature review. Taken together, these will yield a new perspective on a complicated social issue. Rather than providing yet another lament about the low level of paternal involvement, it will offer (1) a "social map" of fatherhood innovations underway throughout the United States; (2) a clear analysis of what we know and do not know about the determinants and effects of father involvement; and (3) an analysis of both the possibilities and constraints of institutional change.

Field Research: United States

The Project will make the first systematic effort to date to identify, describe, and analyze the implementation and consequences of institutional strategies designed, in whole or in part, to permit or promote increased male involvement in child rearing. At present, there is relatively little information available about such programs or policies, especially as they pertain to minority and low income populations. What does exist is not organized in any coherent or useful way. Who is starting them? Why? How? What conditions encourage or constrain their development? What do they really do? What are their effects, if any?

To provide a coherent framework for understanding the variety of existing programs, the Project will divide them into six institutional sectors: employment, law, education, health, social services, and religion.

Employment. In the past decade, a variety of alternative work schedules and practices have been implemented, in part to reduce the conflict between work and family life. Some, such as paternity leave, are specifically designed to increase male involvement in childrearing whereas others, such as flextime, job sharing, and permanent parttime work, may have that effect. This area of investigation will address the following questions: What changes, if any, are being made by employers to allow or encourage more male involvement in child rearing? Emphasis will be on identifying places of work with substantial numbers of minority employees. Who are the change agents and what strategies have they used to bring about change? What are the resistances and how might they be overcome? What are the characteristics of the populations to which such options are being offered? Where are they being used, how frequently, and by whom? Is there a differential in availability to and use by minority populations? If such policies are not being used, why not?

Law. The most widespread, albeit controversial, institutional changes being made with regard to father involvement appear to be in the legal arena. Recent years have seen the acceptance of joint custody by more and more courts, and by state legislatures. A number of divorce mediation and custody mediation services, designed in part to enable parents to work out more equitable postdivorce child-rearing plans, are now scattered throughout the country. This research will: (a) review the status and impact of joint custody legislation and other legislative changes as they affect men; and (b) identify the most promising efforts at divorce and custody mediation, with particular attention to those that are responding to minority and/or lower income populations, not just to white middle-class populations. How do these groups work, and with what effects? Which models are most effective in encouraging fathers to maintain their postdivorce involvement as parents?

Education. Any long-term changes in the male role will probably require, in part, a new type of education—or a reeducation—about sex roles across the life cycle. This research will identify the diversity, little acknowledged, of the efforts that are being made, including infant care curricula for elementary school boys, programs for teenage fathers, and contraceptive education programs for teenage males that include materials about being a parent. Parent education programs with an emphasis on fathers will also be researched. Of these programs, some are freestanding "father support" groups, and others are attached to institutions such as community colleges. We will examine how such programs have been initiated, to whom they are offered, by whom they are used, what impact they are having, and how other similar efforts might be established. Particular attention will be paid to the identification of programs made available to minority and low income populations.

Health. Some recent research suggests that the amount of father involvement during pregnancy, childbirth, and the postpartum period may have an impact on father participation in—and disposition towards—child rearing. This section will identify new hospital policies and programs that are designed to encourage father involvement around the time of childbirth, including childbirth education and postpartum support groups. It will also look at other hospital policies—visiting hours or rooming in, for example—that relate not just to neonates but more generally to the involvement of fathers with their children during times of illness. For both sets of policies and practices, the project will identify how and why changes are being made and with what resistances. Are these new programs and policies offered in institutions that are available and accessible to minority and/or low income populations? By whom are these new programs and policies being used?

Social services.   The social service sector is an important locus for programs promoting fathering. Many youth-oriented services such as the Boy Scouts and "Big Brother" programs foster relationships between adult and younger males. Social service agencies focusing on family life are beginning to offer groups and workshops for fathers. The nature, availability, and utilization of these programs will be analyzed.

Religion.   Religious organizations offer many social service and educational programs. The project will examine their efforts to support and encourage men in their fathering role. As in the other areas, the accessibility of these programs to low income and/or minority populations will be considered.

Field Research: Sweden

As an adjunct to its field research in the United States, the Project will conduct the first systematic inquiry into the reasons for use or nonuse by fathers of Sweden's parental insurance system (see Lamb & Levine, this volume).

Initiated in 1974, this government-sponsored and subsidized parental leave policy allows mothers or fathers to remain home for up to 9 months after the birth of a child and still receive up to 90 percent of prebirth salary for 6 months. Although it is most frequently used by mothers, Sweden's parental insurance system represents the most clearly articulated and most fervently promoted government program in the world designed to increase the male role in child rearing.

Despite government subsidy, promotion, and the apparent removal of institutional barriers, relatively few fathers take significant amounts of parental leave. The reasons for this are not clear. In this volume (Chapter 4) Lamb and Levine provide the most detailed analysis of the plan's usage by eligible Swedes and speculate about possible reasons for participation or nonparticipation of Swedish fathers. To date, however, nobody has gone beyond such speculation.

We propose to move beyond speculation by interviewing in depth a carefully selected sample of Swedish men who have used and who have chosen not to use the parental insurance program, as well as their wives and some employers. Who takes paternal leave? What problems do they face? Why do others prefer not to take advantage of what is available? Although the Swedish experiment is very culture specific, there is no better example available anywhere of social policy mechanisms being used to influence the male role. Analysis of the Swedish experience will add a significant dimension to our understanding of what is going on—or not going on—in the United States.

Literature Review

While it examines the feasibility of institutional approaches for encouraging father involvement, the Project will also comprehensively and critically analyze: (a) the existing literature on the nature, extent, determinants, and limits of father involvement; and (b) the variety of current arguments about the desirability of father involvement.

These arguments, which have considered a variety of effects on children, women, and men themselves, are considerably more complicated than they appear at first. The value judgments of researchers have greatly affected their interpretation of findings and it is often value-laden interpretations—rather than objective findings—that are promulgated (see Eisikovits, Chapter 2). Some psychologists, for example, argue that more fathering is a good thing because it will reinforce traditional sex roles. Others advocate the same goal for the opposite reason: More fathering is good because it increases androgyny in children and helps break down traditional sex-role stereotypes.

What do we *really* know about the effects of father involvement on children, women, and men? What are the areas of conflict in our evidence, what are their sources, and why are they important for future research and practice?

The Project's review of previous research will elucidate the value judgments and assumptions behind the principal popular arguments for father involvement and will explain how value assumptions conflict with one another. It will evaluate all arguments in relation to available data, both assessing the quality of existing data and specifically identifying areas where better data are needed.

Particular concern will be taken in the literature review to consider variations in father involvement and its effects in minority families—both Black and Hispanic—as well as in different ethnic, socioeconomic, and subcultural groups. Because most previous discussions of paternal involvement have focused on white middle-class America, it is especially important to elucidate the special concerns and needs experienced by minority groups as a result of their unique economic, legal, and social circumstances. Traditional social scientific research and theory has often viewed Black fathers as inadequate—in particular, as being poor sex-role models for their sons and poor family economic providers. Other research argues, to the contrary, that Black husband-fathers are superior to whites on criteria of sex-role flexibility and support for women's changing roles.

Demonstration

At the same time that it researches innovative practices throughout the country, the Project will implement and assess two innovative educational programs at Bank Street College of Education—one designed to help young boys become more comfortable in taking care of babies, and one designed to help fathers become more comfortable with their infants and toddlers. Aside from their intrinsic values, these demonstrations will serve, in effect, as local sites for the sort of field research we will be doing elsewhere in the country; they will allow us to test programs we develop ourselves, not just look at those implemented by others.

Infant Care will be offered as an elective to 10-, 11- and 12-year-olds at the Bank Street School for Children. The 10-week course will be designed and taught by a male teacher and will include hands-on experience with infants—holding, feeding, diapering, bathing, walking. Courses in infant care are currently being offered in two New York private elementary schools (Dalton and Collegiate), but several features of the Bank Street experiment will distinguish it for demonstration, research, and future training purposes. First, this will be the only such course taught by a man, thus setting a model for other courses. Second, it will be the only such course with a research component designed: (a) to identify and then work to overcome early socialized inhibitors of nurturance in young males; and (b) to assess change in attitudes among the participating boys and girls. Third, it will be the only such course to produce training materials—a combination of videotape and written text—that will enable it to be implemented or adapted elsewhere.

The courses for Fathers with Infants and Toddlers will have many of the same structural features as the courses on infant care for elementary school children: a male teacher, an emphasis on the hands-on caring for and being with very young children, a research component, and the production of training materials. The program for Fathers with Infants and Toddlers will be offered twice a year—fall and spring—for 10 consecutive sessions each time. Approximately 10 fathers and their infants will participate in each group, though there may be a need to offer several groups concurrently. Changes in attitudes and skills of participating fathers will be assessed, and the entire experience will be documented. Materials that can be used in father groups in other parts of the country will be developed. Concurrent with this course, we will begin planning one aimed at teenage fathers.

SUMMARY

In sum, The Fatherhood Project is the first attempt of which we are aware to review policies and programs made in the legal, employment, health, education, social service, and religious sectors to permit interested fathers to assume a major role in child care. By analyzing patterns of utilization and by interviewing actual or potential users as well as providers and policy makers about the problems, prospects, and successes of these efforts, we hope to come to a clearer understanding of the factors impeding and impelling paternal involvement in child care. We will also systematically examine past and current research on the determinants and consequences of paternal involvement in child care. By disseminating this information to interested employers, service agencies, and policy makers, finally, our goal is to increase the range of options available to mothers and fathers who wish to divide child-rearing and breadwinning responsibilities in accordance with their individual preferences and needs.

ACKNOWLEDGMENT

The three authors are codirectors of The Fatherhood Project, which is supported by the Ford Foundation, the Levi Strauss Foundation, the Ittleson Foundation, and the Rockefeller Family Foundation.

REFERENCES

Biller, H. B. *Father, child, and sex role.* Lexington, Mass.: D. C. Heath, 1971.

Biller, H. B. *Paternal deprivation.* Lexington, Mass.: D. C. Heath, 1974.

Bittman, S., & Salk, S. *Expectant fathers.* New York: Hawthorn, 1978.

Chafe, W. *The American woman: Her changing social, economic, and political roles, 1920–1970.* New York: Oxford, 1974.

Chodorow, N. *The reproduction of mothering: Psychoanalysis and the sociology of gender.* Berkeley, Calif.: University of California Press, 1978.

Corman, A. *Kramer versus Kramer.* New York: Random House, 1977.

Daley, E. A. *Father feelings.* New York: Morrow, 1974.

Dinnerstein, D. *The mermaid and the minotaur: Sexual arrangements and the human malaise.* New York: Harper and Row, 1976.

Filene, P. G. *Him/her/self: Sex roles in modern America.* New York: New American Library, 1976.

Friedan, B. *The second stage.* New York: Summit, 1981.

Giele, J. *Women and the future: Changing sex roles in modern America.* New York: Free Press, 1978.

Goldberg, H. *The new male: From self-destruction to self-care.* New York: Morrow, 1979.

Lamb, M. E. (Ed.). *The role of the father in child development.* New York: Wiley, 1976.

Lamb, M. E. (Ed.). *The role of the father in child development* (2nd ed.). New York: Wiley, 1981.

Miner, R. *Mother's day.* New York: Marek, 1978.

Parke, R. D. Perspectives on father-infant interaction. In J. D. Osofsky (Ed.), *Handbook of infant development.* New York: Wiley, 1979.

Pedersen, F. A. (Ed.). *The father-infant relationship: Observational studies in a family setting.* New York: Praeger, 1980.

Radin, N. The role of the father in cognitive, academic, and intellectual development. In M. E. Lamb (Ed.), *The role of the father in child development* (2nd ed.). New York: Wiley, 1981.

Rich, A. *Of woman born: Motherhood as experience and institution.* New York: Norton, 1976.

Rossi, A. A biosocial perspective on parenting. *Daedalus,* 1977, 106, 1–31.

Staples, R. (Ed.). *The Black family* (2nd ed.). Belmont, Calif.: Wadsworth, 1978.

7

The Gender Dilemma in Social Welfare: Who Cares for Children?

Martin Wolins
University of California, Berkeley

Aside from the procreational imperative, several millenia of human social existence should have been sufficient as evidence that fathers are worthwhile. Only in the 20th century have we begun to wonder whether it is possible to do without them and "get away" with it. The assumption, spread by changing mores and theories of human well being, first seems to have pervaded the psychosocial sphere through theories of psychiatry; then entered the economic, in doctrines of socialized economic support; and is now continuously encroaching on the biological, as homo sapiens are produced without fathers. These signposts of "human progress," as some would designate them, have not been confined solely to the paternal side. Mothers, too, can apparently be done without. As the sperm is planted in the uterus to produce a baby Louise, one is led to wonder how long it will be before the mother's body around the uterus will be necessary, or, for that matter, even the uterus itself.

This bit of rumination is a first reaction to a recent rediscovery of paternal importance. As Lamb (1981) and others in their many studies have shown, it is downright useful for most children to have fathers, even after the procreative act is passed. They have also shown that the data are partial, often inconclusive, at times contradictory, and usually ignored in the formation of social welfare policy and social work practice.

Social work in general and child welfare in particular have been maternally focused enterprises. In a society where fathers went off to their daily struggle with the market economy and mothers remained at home holding together the family, rearing the young, providing succor to offspring and mate, this social work attitude seemed natural. Social work literature and practice were in this regard much influenced by Bowlby's (1952) *Maternal care and mental health,*

Levy's (1943) *Maternal overprotection* and similar scholarly tracts in which the centrality of the mother was discussed in detail and the father's role in child caring was largely ignored. Yet a closer look at evidence developed over the past several decades shows the importance of fathers in the rearing process and, therefore, the need to modify social work practice in order to allot to fathers the full measure of significance they merit.

Fathers are important in the welfare enterprise in at least three ways: They tend to enhance the economic and psychosocial quality of life for their children; they, on occasion, present a burden—as occurs when public assistance law requires father absence to establish a family's eligibility for financial aid—or a danger—when the father is physically abusive; and they seem to be an enigma, or perhaps an insurmountable challenge, to social work and social welfare, where they are in large measure, ignored. The following discussion will focus on all three of these issues. First I will deal with the father as an asset. The focus will be mainly on certain social welfare issues where a father's presence is likely to obviate the need for social intervention and societal assistance to the family and child. Second to be considered is the father as a problem, both by virtue of his absence and, under certain circumstances, by his presence. Third to be discussed are social welfare orientations seemingly premised on the father's irrelevance in child welfare operations. Finally, there is a somewhat serendipitous attempt to test a series of hypotheses on the use of males and females in extrafamilial child-caring operations.

THE FATHER AS ASSET

There is considerable evidence that the presence of a father in the home has generally positive consequences for a child. The beneficial effects are of several kinds. Children whose fathers live at home enjoy better physical conditions, are less likely to be recipients of welfare, less likely to suffer neglect and, apparently, less likely to be abused. Moreover, fathers, as foster parents, on occasion, rear "other people's children." Generally they seem to do this with devotion and considerable success. Clearly, fathers constitute a decided asset. Social workers should bear this in mind both in clinical practice and in the formation of social welfare policy.

This welfare perspective on the father's role is supported by evidence on parental roles in general. It is refreshing to find in Lamb's (1981) paper that ". . . the best adjusted adults are those who in childhood, had warm relationships with effective mothers and fathers [p. 37]." Furthermore, we seem to know, though we must use this information with caution, that a father's masculinity and his status in the family are correlated with (and, since they antecede, may even cause) the masculinity of sons and femininity of daughters [Lamb, 1981]. Moroever, social competence and psychological adjustment also appear to be related to paternal presence and caring (Lamb, 1981). These are all obviously important contributions a good father makes to a family, but we must note with equal care some other dimensions that are more likely to surface in the social work literature as it concerns itself with various problem populations. First, families with fathers are better off financially. Even when the comparison is of families involved in the social welfare system, the difference is profound. A fatherless English family of the 1970s, for example, had one-third the mean weekly income of a two-parent family and about half the income of a father-only family (Hunt, Fox, & Morgan, 1973). In the six geographic study areas that these authors analyzed, between 53–78% of fatherless children resorted to free school meals as compared with 11–36% of motherless children and 3–10% of those from two-parent homes. Twenty-two percent of the fatherless white children shared beds, 18% of the motherless, 6% of those from two-parent homes. (Corresponding values for colored children were 41%, 33% and 25%.) Income data for the United States show a similar pattern. The median income for father-headed families is reported as double that of families headed by mothers (U.S. Bureau of Census, 1978).

Aside from providing income security for the family, fathers also serve an important social role by keeping families off welfare. Of the 1973 new applicants for Aid to Families of Dependent Children, half were the direct result of the father's leaving home or reducing financial support (U.S. Department HEW, 1975b). In 1975 only 10% of all AFDC families had a natural father, adoptive father, or legally responsible stepfather in the house. Second, among low income families, some of whom were referred to agencies for possible child neglect, the father's contribution to the quality of the child's surroundings was reflected in many ways. Using a childhood level of living scale (CLL), Polansky and his coworkers (1979) report more positive scores for children with fathers present on each of the following dimensions: general care of the child, state of repair of household, neglect, physical care. They conclude that the "absent father is missed for this financial contribution and for his direct work toward the child's physical care. His absence, therefore, makes neglect more likely [p. 169]." Interestingly, in these low income families, the research group did not find the variation in physical care explainable by income, nor did they find an association between father absence and psychological care variables such as the encouraging of competence or of superego development.

Third, the lesser likelihood of child neglect when father is present also appears to hold for child abuse. An extensive study of abused children in Birmingham, England (Hanson, McCulloch, & Hartley, 1978) yielded some 62 variables significantly correlated with documented child abuse. These fell into three clusters. The heaviest loading for the primary cluster was the absence of the natural father in the home. (It should perhaps be noted for later reference that of the 62 characteristics associated with abuse, 43 pertained specifically to the mother, 13 to neither or both parents and only 6 (!) to the father. Are we to conclude that fathers don't abuse, or that not many paternal characteristics are considered? The second conclusion seems more tenable.)

Fourth, fathers are an asset also when they rear other people's children. As stepfathers, adoptive, and foster fathers, they assume a parental role others have vacated or never filled. So far as can be deduced from the available evidence, fathers are doing rather well in all these roles. It has been estimated (Rallings, 1976) that in 1970 some 15% of all U.S. children under 18 years were living with a divorced parent and about 60% of these (i.e., some 9% of the total child population) were living with stepparents. (About half are stepfathers?) Children from stepfather families were not found to be significantly different from those with both natural parents present (Wilson, Zurcher, McAdams, & Curtis, 1975). Given the climbing divorce and remarriage rates, child rearing by stepfathers is a significant issue requiring attention.

Foster family care also affects hundreds of thousands of children in the United States (Kadushin, 1980). Although recently some children have been placed in single-parent, mainly female, homes (see below), most foster homes have fathers in them. In a detailed study, Fanshel (1966) has analyzed the role and attitudes of these fathers and found them to be positive. They were "quite strong and firm in the areas they perceive[d] to be within the proper area of functioning [p. 151]." A large majority believed they could adequately substitute for the natural parent, felt they had as important a role as their wives in rearing the foster child, found the role more satisfying than they had hoped, and expected the relationship to continue indefinitely.

Perhaps the most interesting development in father substitution, however, pertains to single-parent adoption. Although most single-parent adopters are female (the ratios reported by various agencies tend to be between 3 : 1 and 10 : 1), some single men do adopt children. The trend is still too new, only some 10-15 years, and the numbers still too small for serious conclusions other than the absence of grossly negative ones. On this score, both the single mothers and single fathers seem to pass (Feigelman & Silverman, 1977; Kadushin, 1970; Shireman & Johnson, 1976). One variable of interest (which will seriously hamper incisive evaluation) is that these single parents are often accepted only if they consent to adopt "hard-to-place" children. Even at the inception of this program, the Director of New York City's Adoption Services Division was quoted in *The New York Times,* (January 20, 1968) as saying: "qualified single persons would probably receive . . . those [children] over two years of age, the handicapped and those of mixed race." This is an interesting paradox that points to the divergence of goals as determinants of social policy. For lack of adequate placements, the most demanding children are placed with the most vulnerable adult units.

Finally, the child-rearing situation of the single father merits some brief attention. Their numbers alone are impressive. Some one million chidren were estimated (Keshet & Rosenthal, 1978; U. S. HEW, 1975a) to be living with single male parents. Although these represent only about one-tenth of the U.S. children living in single-parent households (Canadian data indicate a 1: 5 ratio—Schlesinger, 1978), their number is large enough to require serious social welfare policy attention. Financially, these families are generally doing quite well (Bartz & Witcher, 1978; Orthner, Brown, & Ferguson, 1976; Schlesinger, 1978). Fathers also seem to be attentive, affectionate caretakers (Bartz & Witcher, 1978; Fast, 1979; Keshet & Rosenthal, 1978; Mendes, 1976). However, Mendes (1976) Fast (1979) and others also find that single fathers have inadequate knowledge of child development and particular difficulty in relating to their daughters.

THE FATHER AS PROBLEM

Fathers may also be problematic. Their absence predisposes the family to economic privation and social stigma and often places unexpected burdens on those who seek to provide the child with a substitute family. An absent father, for example, may preclude or at least delay the adoption of his out-of-wedlock child. A father's presence may also have its problematic aspects, particularly when he physically abuses his children. Paradoxically, the father may be a problem to his family both in his absence and in his prescence. Absence essentially creates the obverse of the various contributory relationships detailed above. When the father is not there, his contribution to the economic, psychological, and social well being of the child is limited at best. This is clearly the case for nearly 90% of the over seven million children who received AFDC at any time in 1978 (Kadushin, 1980). For such children, paternal absence is always accompanied by an edge-of-poverty existence. If Elder's and Elder & Rockwell's findings as cited in Lamb (1981) apply here, then the father's absence should exaggerate the effects of economic deprivation and lead to low aspiration levels. Problems in the masculinity development of boys and difficulties in male interaction of girls should also be anticipated in aggravated form.

In the event that the children's mother is unmarried, the AFDC situation is complicated even further. Although the illegitimacy rate appears to be declining slightly (possibly due to better birth control and more readily available abortions), it is still estimated at some 25 per 1000 unwed women ages 15–44 (National Center for Health Statistics, 1978). In some age and racial groups it is over four times as high. A very large proportion of these children are kept by their single mothers with mother and child becoming AFDC recipients.

Some recent studies (Bracken, Klerman, & Bracken, 1978; Clapp & Raab, 1978; Festinger, 1971) find both a low inclination to give up the child for adoption and a readiness to accept a welfare recipient role. In such situations, contact with the father tends to wither away, particularly when the mother is an adolescent. Clapp and Raab (1978) found only 17% of the mothers had initiated court proceedings to establish paternity. And although a year after the child's birth 90% said they could rely on the father in an emergency, this dropped to 20% in the third year. Moreover, 60% of this sample were on AFDC at the time of the study. From this and other studies it would seem reasonable to agree with Chilman (1977) that "the availability of public assistance appears not to cause out-of-wedlock pregnancy, but it may affect what a young woman does about this pregnancy [p. 308]." That clearly happens in a preponderance of cases: If a woman opts to carry to term, she will keep the child and use public welfare as a means of full or partial support.

The triple burden of fatherlessness, poverty, and probable stigma appears to take its toll. In a massive English study by the National Children's Bureau, natural-mother-reared illegitimate children and an adopted control were followed up for 7 years. Summarizing their results, which showed that the adopted made better developmental progress than those in out-of-wedlock homes, Crellin, Kellmer-Pringle, and West (1971) wrote: "Illegitimately born children . . . continue in a very real and literal sense to suffer from the 'sins' of their fathers (and mothers)—at least in all aspects we were able to examine in our study [p. 112]." To be sure, mores change and so does social policy. The handicap such children bear in the U.S. of 1981 may be less than that of England in the 1960s. Yet, from what we do know about such populations, the signs are not favorable.

Nor is the adoptive route free of the father as a problem. For one thing, the unmarried mother may not wish to have contact with him. When a casework agency working with these mothers offered to contact and help the fathers, 27% rejected the offer and another 16% acceded only with reluctance (Pannor, Massarik, & Evans, 1971). Yet recent legal decisions require contact with the father in order to obtain his consent for relinquishment and adoption even in situations where he is not contributing to a child's support. Since many such fathers are difficult to locate and mother's cooperation is not always assured, the adoption agency is compelled to delay permanent placement of the child. Although court decisions have varied, some emphasizing the welfare of the child, others the rights of the unwed father, the mere possibility of such court action and a reversal of agency decision leads to caution and delay (Dukette & Stevenson, 1973). In the interim an infant may grow into a toddler, or even a preschooler, remaining, at best, in a temporary foster home or in a fatherless, group care environment such as a maternity home.

The pursuit of elusive fathers is by no means limited to the change of legal guardianship situations. In fact, these are numerically insignificant compared with those sought for child support. This, more than the adoption phenomenon, tends to set up an adversary relationship between the child's two natural parents. The situation is ripe with conflict and acrimony. Although most of the support battles are fought outside of the social welfare arena, millions are within it. For many years U.S. mothers applying for AFDC were required to name (and help locate) the child's father, and, under the Noleo Amendment, local jurisdications were obligated to institute a registry and pursuit. This public stance was embodied in considerable legislation coming before national and state bodies in the early 1970s. In the first session of the 93rd Congress, for example, there were eight bills collectively described as aiming to insure that every individual meets his "natural, moral, and social obligation to support the members of his immediate family." This rather broad language was aimed quite specifically at males whose children were among the millions of AFDC recipients. Hearings on the legislation pointed out that "there were some two million fathers who have left home and whose children are being supported under AFDC [U.S. Congress, 1974]." Criminal sanctions were proposed, including making it a Federal offense for a father to cross state lines in order to avoid paying child support.

Prodded by constant legislative and general public criticism, AFDC has been subjected to repeated reviews on the absent father issue. Attempts to establish paternity and obtain support are a regular feature of AFDC implementation. A 1975 report cites efforts to establish paternity or obtain support for 40% of the 3.4 million families on AFDC during May of that year (U.S. Department of HEW, 1975b). The success rate in such ventures is relatively low. Even when support obligations are established, the proportions of men who meet them are small and, most significantly, the fathers make reimbursements to public welfare agencies for funds already expended, rather than contributing directly to their children. In short, these fathers are remote from their children, their relationship is compelled, and what contributions they do make are so indirect as to have no relevance to the child.

Under such circumstances it is doubtful that the data from the usual father absence studies apply. Whether we accept their inconclusiveness (Herzog & Sudia, 1973) or their conclusiveness (Rosenfeld J. M., Rosenstein, E. & Raab, M., 1973) or the cautious conclusiveness (Lamb, 1981), the studies are likely to fall short of reflecting the consequences of father absence in AFDC. Conflicting objectives of public policy have resulted in a program where the well being of a child and the interest of the state are often pitted against each other. In fact, the pressures for support exerted (except in AFDC-U—unemployed) are such that father absence often leads to *increased* economic well being of the family unit, which may become eligible for public assistance only as a result of his actual or staged desertion. As Bradbury (1977) stated:

> By providing an alternative source of income to women with dependent children, the AFDC program has reduced the economic pressure for women either to remain married or to remarry. In addition, because AFDC benefits in some states are available only to single parent families, the benefits to be gained from splitting or the costs entailed in getting married may be as high as $6,200. AFDC incentives to split in the range of $600 to $1,600 per year are quite common [p. 2].

So another paradox: The fathers presence is disadvantageous, at least financially, for some children of poverty. His presence may be a problem in other ways as well. Although the evidence points rather weakly toward the possibility that single parents (mothers) are more likely to abuse their children than those in two-parent households, there is also considerable child abuse by fathers and "father figures." In a review of seven controlled studies in the etiology of child abuse, Allan (1978) found five with various variables of abusive mothers and two others with variables for abusive mothers *and* abusive fathers. It is not clear whether fathers were present in all these situations and whether their characteristics were taken fully into account. Hanson, McCulloch, and Hartley (1978) also found many more maternal than paternal characteristics associated with child abuse.

Recent reviews of U.S. nationwide child neglect and abuse reports also show single parent households to be considerably overrepresented (American Humane Association, 1979). However, neglectful families are more often single parent and abusive families are more often two-parent. Moreover, it is fathers, in this study, who are more frequently abusive. A more detailed analysis with a large sample and over a 5-year period (1968–1972) of abuse cases reported in seven U.S. southeastern states tends to support the father-as-abuser hypothesis. Fathers were perpetrators of child abuse in 49% of the cases, mothers in 43% (other individuals in those remaining). And of the fathers living in the home of an abused child, 57% were abusers. Also fathers or father surrogates were likely to be coperpetrators of abuse in 55% of the cases (Johnson, 1974).

Particularly distressing is the available evidence on sexual abuse. Although the numbers reported are subject to considerable error due to problems of definition, data collection, and sampling, the problem, though possibly exaggerated by recently reawakened professional interest, is nonetheless substantial. Annual estimates of sexual abuse in the U.S. range up to the two hundred thousand mark, with a ratio of ten girls to one boy among the victims. Most victimizers are fathers and the mean ages of victims are 11–14 years (U.S. Department of HEW, 1979; Sarafino, 1979).

Numerous explanations have been offered for this rather difficult to comprehend implementation of the paternal role. A review of the literature about abusive parents by Spinetta and Rigler (1972) advanced a number of assumptions, apparently more related to the theoretical orientation of the proponents than to the availability of supportive data. Among these were the following conditions of parents:

1. Feelings of inadequacy; inability to fulfill roles;
2. Immaturity, impulsiveness, self-centeredness;
3. Role-reversal as in the situation of an unemployed father;
4. Low intelligence;
5. History of abuse suffered by the current perpetrator.

Whatever the etiology, there is good reason to hold *some* fathers suspect. Protective service workers, while intent on preserving the child's natural family, must also keep a watchful eye for the possibility that the relationship is "patrogenic." A thin line separates appropriate intervention from grievous error in such cases.

THE FATHER AS AN IRRELEVANT FIGURE

Whether by virtue of these difficult distinctions, or possibly due to the general inclination in psychology and psychiatry to do so, social welfare also has, on occasion, opted to ignore the father. Some examples are in financial assistance, foster family care, single-parent adoption, and the child guidance movement.

Interestingly, none of these programs deliberately set out to separate the father from the household. On the contrary, the clinical and social policy literature is full of protestations on the importance of preserving a whole family or of involving fathers in the caring and therapeutic processes. For example, a well-known and highly respected child welfare expert (Kadushin, 1980) reports that "some warnings come frequently: More attention needs to be paid to foster fathers because they are more significant determinants of placement outcome than we had thought [p. 334]."

A brief look at the four programs—financial assistance, foster care, single-parent adoption, and child guidance—will illustrate the policy dilemma involved. First, AFDC. Assuming a low income family with relatively weak ties between the parental couple and a governmental program predicated on providing reasonable, decent support levels for children, yet not relieving fathers of their economic responsibility, the outcome is predictable. The burden of the father remaining in the AFDC home is simply too great for the father, the child, and the mother and the social worker. It has been suggested that at times, as an act of self-sacrifice, the father withdraws from the household—at least formally. Only a few years ago, when social welfare was less permissive, night raids to search for "the man in the house" were still a common occurrence.

There appears to be no detailed information that would shed light on the progression to fatherlessness of AFDC cases. The incontrovertible fact is, though, that except in AFDC-U, which has not been adopted by all states and which constitutes only some 10% of the caseload, the AFDC program has operated as though fathers were irrelevant at best, and debtors to the public till to be pursued under the Noleo Amendment at worst. Only the recent introduction of AFDC-U shows a change in approach.

Foster family care also suffers from an assumption of paternal irrelevance, or nearly so. A few pieces of evidence:

1. The professional literature pertaining to foster parenthood and how to cultivate it is quite plentiful. In an impromptu analysis, three well-known volumes

were selected and references to foster fathers and mothers were counted in the chapter each contains on the foster family.

    a. Glickman (1957), Chapter 5, "Foster families." Mother references 192, father, 19.
    b. Kline and Overstreet (1972), Chapter 5, "The foster family." Mother references 27, father, 8.
    c. Gruber (1978), Chapter 6, "Foster parents." Mother references 12, Father, 3.

  2. Training of foster parents is often oriented not to the parents, but, as the title of Mills R. B., Sandle, R. R. & Sher, M. A. (1967) paper suggests, is concerned with "Introducing Foster Mother [sic] Training Groups" into the program. Understandably, this article never mentions the father.

  3. Attempts at program evaluation are likely to be similarly short on the father side.

    a. In a survey of 118 foster homes reported by Rowe (1976), questionnaires were sent to each mother and father. Of the slightly over 50% return rate, only 7% included a father's questionnaire in the response.
    b. Using a questionnaire based on Fanshel's (1966) work, Cautley and Aldridge (1975) attempted to predict success for new foster parents. To do so, they requested social workers to describe (rate) the newly selected mothers and fathers. The social workers first rated the mothers. "A similar evaluation of the foster fathers was asked for but could not be used because many workers were not familiar with them [p. 49]."

In all fairness, it should be noted that some of these examples are dated and that the evidence is partial and selective, but the fact remains that it is there, though recently both the literature and clinical behavior have been more balanced.

  A similar approach to balance is to be seen in the perception of fathers when their children are in "treatment." Psychiatric clinic services of the 1950s to 1970s also tended to ignore the father. Expectations of family members to be seen (as expressed by the clients) in one comparative study of New York and California (Maas & Kahn, 1955) were reported as follows:

Mother and child	40.5%
Child only	27.7%
Mother, father and child	22.3%
Other combinations	9.5%

The authors went on to comment that "only two in every ten parents had expectations that coincide with the current expectations of most clinics—that mother and father and child be seen, at least initially [p. 57]." But were these really the professional expectations resisted by an uncomprehending public? We have something of a clue to the professional state of mind. After locating an article (Rosenthal, 1954) on exactly the same topic and for 1954, the same year the Maas and Kahn study was done, we counted the references to each parent. Result: mother, 44; father 3. The flavor of this approach, which was detailing "therapy with parents and child," is conveyed in a single sentence. "Therapy was oriented toward permitting the mother [sic] to express her marked ambivalence [p. 21]."

In a short span of some 20 years, professional and public expectations (what is the causal direction here?) have changed considerably. Minuchin's *Families and family therapy* (1975) provides better balance:

Chapter 6. The family in therapy. Mother references 32, father 16.
Chapter 8. Restructuring the family. Mother references 34, father 25.

On balance, looking at these three programs, matters appear to be improving. AFDC-U is a positive move and so is a book like Minuchin's. They reflect a trend. Yet, is it a trend with no retreats? What about the single-parent adoption phenomenon where as a matter of public policy fathers are nonexistent in most cases? Even more seriously, the children adopted under these circumstances are those requiring most care. Single-parent adoptions offer a lesson about the devious ways of public policy decisions that for reasons of expediency, are surely based on more than we know.

THE "PROPER" GENDER OF CARETAKERS

Whereas child welfare in substitute settings seems to be generally characterized by an omission of the male role, this does not hold for all extrafamilial or pseudofamilial settings. In fact, a cursory look at the full panoply of nonfamilial environments tends to suggest some pattern, some order, as to the "appropriate" gender of the primary caretaker. Three sets of variables appear to be involved: (1) characteristics of the care recipient (e.g., age, nature of the problem); (2) the kind of effect to be achieved (e.g., nurturance, change, protection of care recipient or of others); (3) the type of instrumentality used to provide care (e.g., a small, intimate unit or a large hierarchical organization).

A familiarity with a broad range of settings suggests a series of hypotheses that may then be subjected to test by a review of staffing statistics. Any layman walking into an American hospital will notice that caring is the role of (mainly) female nurses and modifying patients' conditions is mainly the task of male physicians. Similarly, the age of care recipients appears to relate to the gender of staff. Thus, for example, young school children are tended to by female teachers primarily, whereas male teachers are more often found instructing older children and college students.

Cursory observation seems to suggest that in the provision of extrafamilial care, tasks of caretakers have acquired gender specificity to a point of nearly unquestioned persistence. For example:

1. As early as the 19th century, institutional care of *deprived* children seems to have been primarily the task of females, but males staffed programs for the *depraved*. The former were thought to need nurturance, the latter to require changing.

2. Foster care as conceived by its earliest practitioner in America, Charles Loring Brace, was oriented to the farmer and his wife, because it was to instill skills. As it evolved—during the time of Birtwell, Folks, and others (see Wolins & Piliavin, 1964)—into a nurturing system, paternal roles became deemphasized.

3. Substitute care-taking structures that are intimate, governed by affective relationships, possessing few formal rules and a high order of voluntary reciprocity (Gemeinschaft) tend to have female caretakers (e.g., small group homes, foster homes). Large settings, organized hierarchically, governed by numerous rules, will have proportionately more male caretakers.

Combining the variables of children's characteristics, kind of effect, and type of residential instrumentality, it would be expected that on one end of the distribution (young, deprived children receiving succorance in a Gemeinschaft program, for example) the staff should be largely female. On the other end (older delinquents, subjected to change in a Gesellschaft-type setting) the staff would be mainly male. As an adendum to the present exploration of paternal roles in child welfare, it seemed appropriate to subject these and several similar hypotheses to an empirical test. The hypotheses could be tested, were statistics available by: (1) The child's characteristics; (2) the effect to be achieved; (3) the type of substitute instrumentality in use; and (4) a breakdown by gender of staff in these settings. It would be anticipated that the first three pose difficulties in definition and collection but the fourth variable—staff gender—is readily available. Surprisingly, this is not the case. A review of the best-known references to substitute child care, in particular referring to institutional environments, leaves us empty-handed. The desirable gender of caretakers (at times implying it should be female) is alluded to in a few studies, but statistical data are not provided.

A few examples will illustrate the problem:

1. The 11th census of the United States (conducted in 1890) yielded a volume on crime, pauperism, and benevolence. It described the inmate population of jails, almshouses, and benevolent institutions, but provided no mention of staff (U.S. Bureau of the Census, 1895).

2. Some 10 years later, a special U.S. Census report dealing with benevolent institutions listed inmate populations by age and sex but staff was aggregated without gender data (U.S. Bureau of the Census, 1905).

3. A decade later, the Census data became even more detailed. Employees of institutions were classified by profession, but still not by gender (U.S. Bureau of the Census, 1919).

4. In the meantime, there was an attempt to define "woman's influence in juvenile reformatories" (Sickels, 1894), which claimed the caretaker role for women. "In the case of children under public care it seems peculiarly fitting that motherly instincts should be permitted to reach the many unfortunate ones [p. 164]." But the article offered no data on the gender (presumably male) of caretakers functioning at the time.

5. A definitive book on *The child and the state* was published in the 1930s. It traced the development of special care for children in America, including life in children's institutions, but made no mention of staff gender (Abbott, 1938).

6. *Institutions serving children* (Hopkirk, 1944) contained a full section of three chapters on staff qualifications, training, living, and working conditions but alludes only to the housemother as the staff person in charge. The numbers and activities by gender (actual or desired) of other staff are left to the reader's imagination.

7. A severe critic of "child saving" as practiced in 19th and early 20th century America placed the whole effort squarely in the femininity domain but left the reader with no more than inference of a relationship between care-taking, nurturing, and femininity (Platt, 1969).

8. The latest comprehensive *Census of children's residential institutions in the United States, Puerto Rico, and the Virgin Islands, 1966,* (Pappenfort & Kilpatrick, 1970) continues the legacy of providing no data by gender. This seven volume compendium, which appears to address almost any question one may ask about residential care of children including staff categories, ratios, working patterns, qualifications, supervision, and turnover, is silent on such a simple variable as gender.

Two possible explanations come to mind for this rather curious omission: (1) the sex of caretakers is considered irrelevant; (2) the roles of caretakers are a sex-specific constant and no statistical reporting is in order as the relationships between gender and the variables of child, task, and setting type are generally known.

The first explanation does not seem to apply as the comments of Sickels (1894), Platt (1969) and many others (Nelson, 1980) demonstrate. The second is more plausible. Phrases like "the nurse . . . she," "the teacher . . . she," and "the guard or superintendent . . . he," convey the message. In short, the lack of statistics by gender implies a fixity of gender-related tasks that by virtue of public and professional acceptance requires no further evidence because it is not a subject of public policy disputes. But, we may ask, is this what should be? Are such fixed role-gender relationships that the data (or their absence) imply for the good of children? Some answers to these questions are in other chapters of this book.

SUMMARY AND CONCLUSION

A review of the child welfare literature indicates that fathers significantly affect the well-being of children whose lives are touched by social welfare programs. There are economic, social, psychological, and even physical consequences for the child whose father resides in the household or who is absent. Some of these are salutary, others are, regrettably, problematic, but all are significant. Fathers have a major role in financial assistance, foster care, adoption, child neglect and abuse—in short, in all child welfare programs. Inconceivably, though, until recently, fathers appear to have received little attention in the literature pertaining to these programs or in the clinical practice associated with them.

This was largely a woman's world insofar as the caring operations were concerned. So well fixed and accepted were the gender-related arrangements that statistics on child welfare operations do not include the sex of caretakers of various settings and populations. Although it seems we know that females have usually cared for young children in intimate environments, and males have staffed the larger, more formal settings where adolescents were subject to change, proof is not possible. One matter is reasonably clear: The gender issue has been ignored, probably because it was considered settled.

Considerable evidence exists that the fixity of roles in child caring that was presumed to exist, and, in some measure, did exist, is not in the best interests of the family or its adult and child members. A greater awareness of the male's contribution to child rearing and his capability in it seem in order. This should be reflected in future clinical practice, social welfare policy and even statistics on the gender of caretakers in various settings for children.

REFERENCES

Abbott, G. *The Child and the state* (Vols. 1 & 2). Chicago: University of Chicago Press, 1938.
Allan, L. J. Child abuse. A critical review of the research and theory, in J. P. Martin (Ed.), *Violence and the family*. New York: Wiley, 1978.
American Humane Association *Official child neglect and abuse reporting*. Englewood, Colo.: October, 1979.
Bartz, K. W. & Witcher, W. C. When father gets custody. *Children Today*, 1978, 1, 2–6.
Bowlby, J. *Maternal care and mental health* (2nd ed.), Monograph Series No. 2. Geneva: World Health Organization, 1952.
Bracken, M., Klerman, L., & Bracken, M. Coping with pregnancy resolution among never married women. *American Journal of Orthopsychiatry,1978 48*, 320–332.
Bradbury, L. The effects of welfare reform alternatives on the family. Madison, Wis.: Institute for Research on Poverty, 1977.
Cautley, P. W., & Aldridge, M. Predicting success for new foster parents. *Social Work*, 1975, *20*, 48–53.
Chilman, C. *Social and psychological aspects of adolescent sexuality—An analytic overview of research and theory*. Milwaukee: Center for Advanced Studies in Human Services, University of Wisconsin, Milwaukee, 1977.

Clapp, D. F., & Raab, R. S. Followup of unmarried adolescent mothers. *Social Work, 1978, 23,* 149–153.

Crellin, E., Kellmer-Pringle, M. L., & West, P. *Born illegitimate—Social and educational implications.* London: National Children's Bureau, 1971.

Dukette, R., & Stevenson, N. The legal rights of unmarried fathers: The impact of recent court decisions. *Social Service Review, 1973, 47,* 1–15.

Fanshel, D. *Foster Parenthood: A role analysis.* Minneapolis: University of Minnesota Press, 1966.

Fast, A. H. *The father-only family: An alternative family style.* Unpublished doctoral dissertation, Brandeis University, 1979.

Feigelman, W., & Silverman, A. R. Single parent adoptions. *Social Casework, 1977, 58,* 418–425.

Festinger, T. B. Unwed mothers and their decisions to keep or surrender children. *Child Welfare, 1971, 50,* 253–263.

Glickman, E. *Child placement through clinically oriented casework.* New York: Columbia University Press, 1957.

Gruber, A. R. *Children in foster care, destitute, neglected . . . betrayed.* New York: Human Sciences Press, 1978.

Hanson, R., MuCulloch, W., & Hartley, S. Key characteristics of child abuse. In A. W. Franklin (Ed.), *The challenge of child abuse.* New York: Grune and Stratton, 1978.

Herzog, E., & Sudia, C. Children in fatherless families. In Caldwell, B. M. & Ricciuti, H. N. (Eds.). *Review of child development research,* (Vol. 3). Chicago: University of Chicago Press, 1973.

Hopkirk, H. *Institutions serving children.* New York: Russell Sage Foundation, 1944.

Hunt, A., Fox, J., & Morgan, M. *Families and their needs: With particular reference to one parent families* (Vols. 1 and 2). London: Her Majesty's Stationary Office, 1973.

Johnson, C. L. *Child abuse in the southeast: Analysis of 1,172 reported cases.* Athens, Ga.: Regional Institute of Social Welfare Research, 1974.

Kadushin, A. Single parent adoptions: An overview and some relevant research. *Social Service Review, 1970, 44,* 263–274.

Kadushin, A. *Child welfare services* (3rd ed.). New York: Macmillan, 1980.

Keshet, H. F., & Rosenthal, K. M. Single parent fathers: A new study. *Children Today, 1978, 7(5),* 13–17.

Kline, D., & Overstreet, H. F. *Foster care of children, nurture and treatment.* New York: Columbia University Press, 1972.

Lamb, M. E. Fathers and child development: An integrative overview. In M. E. Lamb (Ed.), *The role of the father in child development.* (Rev. ed.). New York: Wiley, 1981.

Levy, D. M. *Maternal overprotection.* New York: Columbia University Press, 1943.

Maas, H. S., & Kahn, A. Sociocultural factors in psychiatric clinic services for children. *Smith College studies in social work,* 1955, 25, entire volume.

Mendes, H. A. Single fathers. *The Family Coordinator, 1976, 25,* 439–444.

Mills, R. B., Sandle, R. R. & Sher, M. A. Introducing foster mother training groups in a voluntary child welfare agency. *Child Welfare,* 1967, 46, 575–580.

Minuchin, S. *Families and family therapy.* Cambridge, Mass.: University Press, 1975.

Mrs. W. Metterman, divorcee, discusses adoption of girl 3, under new NYC policy of encouraging adoptions by suitable single people. *New York Times,* January 20, 1968, p. 18, col. 1.

National Center for Health Statistics, Public Health Service, Series 21, No. 30, September, 1978, p. 23.

Nelson, K. E. *The best asylum: Charles Loring Brace and foster family care.* Unpublished dissertation, University of California—Berkeley, 1980.

Orthner, D. K., Brown, T., & Ferguson, D. Single-parent fatherhood: An emerging family life style. *The Family Coordinator, 1976, 25,* 429–437.

Pappenfort, D., & Kilpatrick, D. *A census of children's residential institutions in the United States, Puerto Rico and the Virgin Islands, 1966.* Chicago: The University of Chicago, 1970.

Pannor, R., Massarik, F., & Evans, B. *The unmarried father.* New York: Springer, 1971.

Platt, A. M. *The child savers: The invention of delinquency.* Chicago: University of Chicago Press, 1969.

Polansky, N. A., Chalmers, M. A., Butterwieser, E., & Williams, D. P., The absent father in child neglect, *Social Service Review,* 1979, *53,* 163–174.

Rallings, E. M. The Special Role of Stepfather. *The Family Coordinator,* 1976, *25,* 445–450.

Rosenfeld, J. M, Rosenstein, E., & Raab, M. Sailor families: The nature and effects of one kind of father absence. *Child Welfare,* 1973, *52,* 33–43.

Rosenthal, M. J. Collaborative therapy with parents in child guidance clinics. *Social Casework,* 1954, *35,* 18–25.

Rowe, D. C. Attitudes, social class and the quality of foster care. *Social Service Review,* 1976, *50,* 506–514.

Sarafino, E. An estimate of nationwide incidence of sexual offenses against children. *Child Welfare,* 1979, *58,* 127–133.

Schlesinger, B. Single parent fathers: A research review. *Children Today.* 1978, *7,* 12; 18–19; 37–39.

Shireman, J. F., & Johnson, R. R. Single persons as adoptive parents. *Social Service Review,* 1976, *50,* 103–116.

Sickels, L. M. Woman's influence in juvenile reformatories. *Proceedings of the National Conference of Charities and Correction.* Boston: G. H. Ellis, 1894.

Spinetta, J. J., & Rigler, D. The child abusing parent—A psychological review. *Psychological Bulletin,* 1972, *77,* 296–304.

U.S. Bureau of the Census. *Report on crime, pauperism, and benevolence eleventh (1890) census.* Washington, D.C.: Government Printing Office, 1895.

U.S. Bureau of the Census. *Special reports—Benevolent institutions.* Washington, D.C.: Government Printing Office, 1905.

U.S. Bureau of the Census. *Money income and poverty status in 1975 (Spring, 1976, survey of income and education).* 1978.

U.S. Congress House Committee on the Judiciary. *Subcommittee on claims and government relations,* 93rd Congress Session 1, 1974.

U.S. Department of Commerce, Bureau of the Census. *Statistical directory of state institutions for defective, dependent and deliquent classes.* Washington, D.C.: Government Printing Office, 1919.

U.S. Department of HEW. *Child sexual abuse—Incest, assault and sexual exploitation.* Washington, D.C.: Government Printing Office, 1979.

U.S. Department of HEW. *The studies of children.* Washington, D.C.: Office of Child Development, 1975. (a)

U.S. Department of HEW. *AFDC 1975 recipient characteristics study, Part 1, demographic and program statistics. Part 2, child support enforcement.* Washington, D.C.: Government Printing Office, 1975. (b)

Wilson, K., Zurcher, L. A., McAdams, D. C., & Curtis, R. L. Stepfathers and Stepchildren: An Exploratory Analysis from Two National Surveys. *Journal of Marriage and the Family,* 1975, *37,* 526–536.

Wolock, I., & Horowitz, B. Child Maltreatment and Material Deprivation Among AFDC-Recipient Families. *Social Service Review* 1979, *538,* 175–195.

Wolins, M., & Piliavin, I. *Institution or foster family: A century of debate.* New York: Child Welfare League of America, 1964.

8 Fathers and Child Welfare Services: The Forgotten Clients?

Eliezer D. Jaffe
Hebrew University of Jerusalem

It is not our purpose here to make a case concerning the importance of fathers and their role in child care and family life. This task has been done by various writers (see Lamb, 1981) in different countries and we will not review their works. However, it is interesting to note how little has been published about fathers in social work and child welfare literature (Wolins, this volume). Apparently this is not specifically an American oversight but one common to other countries as well. Our own brief review of the international child welfare journals shows only occasional attention to fathers. Israel is no exception to this pattern. This author recently examined all articles published since the inception in 1957 of *Saad* (which was recently renamed *Society and Welfare*), the Israeli quarterly journal of social work. Not a single article was found dealing with fathers *per se* as welfare clients. Although one article discussed the subject of therapy for divorced fathers, this was a Hebrew translation of an article published earlier in *Social Casework* (Leader, 1973). Despite the lack of discussion about this subject, social workers claim to acknowledge and accept the importance of the father's role. When one looks closely at the organization of the social services, the background of the manpower that provides these services, and the nature of the services provided, a pattern emerges that verges on *de facto* discrimination in most countries concerning fathers as social service clients. Despite lip service, social services do not take the father's role seriously and are not geared to accommodate fathers. Unfortunately, a good deal of the social work literature on fathers focuses on crises around the absence of a father due to death (Alexandrovitz, 1969; Grossberg & Crandall, 1978), desertion and nonsupport (Snyder, 1975), and separation (Keshet, 1977); or on irresponsible, problematic fathers who have had incestual relations with daughters (Gentry, 1978; Spencer, 1978), are abusive

(David, 1974; Hindman, 1977) single (Fast, 1979; Mendes, 1976; Todres, 1975), or have asked for or taken custody of children (Bartz & Witcher, 1979; Russell, 1969). Although normative attitudes value the father as an important social service client, social work literature and actual practices tend to stereotype "welfare fathers" as problematic, hard-to-reach clients as compared to mothers and children who are usually the primary clients of child welfare workers.

Why have fathers, despite lip service to them and to their role in child rearing and family life, become "forgotten" clients? What are the implications of this oversight or neglect for social work practice? What do we mean when we talk about father's roles? Which aspects of fathering are we referring to? The following presentation will discuss some of the processes that have led to a devaluation of the father's role in welfare work, and explain the need to examine and understand the role of the father within different cultural contexts. Exploration of these topics, will, hopefully, open a broader discussion among child care workers, family counselors, and researchers in various countries concerning fathers and family welfare services.

DEVALUATION OF THE FATHER'S ROLE

Mothers and Children As Handy Clients

A large number of the selective, personal social services, unlike the more universal social insurances, were created specifically for the purpose of coming to the aid of mothers and children in distress. More important, however, is the fact that the clinically oriented treatment services, adopted by social work from the psychiatric and medical professions, gravitated towards assisting a relatively cooperative, motivated, and paying clientele. Outreach work with less available, less motivated and/or hostile clients has only developed in recent decades but, unfortunately, has not had a major impact on mainstream social work practice.

In the same tradition, the working hours of the majority of social workers, particularly civil service and welfare department employees, do not include evening or night shifts that could enable more fathers to take off from work to meet social workers. Home visits, when made, are daytime visits, planned to see the mother and children. Social workers rarely schedule visits to the father's place of employment to see him during his lunch break. When this author served as director of the Jerusalem Municipality's Department of Family and Community Services several years ago, the municipal welfare office branches were encouraged to institute evening reception hours (for appointments and walk-ins), and the number of male parents who showed up increased dramatically. It is surprising that more efforts have not been made to serve fathers, especially since community organization workers have been exceptionally successful in organizing fathers for social action. When proper conditions for father's involvement are created, fathers tend to respond. But barrring these outreach attempts, the father client is often unfairly labeled as "hard to reach." This is especially true of lower-class fathers, because of their work routine or apparent lack of interest. Welfare service organization, "normal" working hours, and father's employment tend to reinforce the subtle stigma concerning uncooperative fathers, or fathers as passive client partners, cooperating by proxy through their wives.

Fathers too, often have their own stereotypes about what their role should be in relation to social services and social workers. Many fathers delegate these contacts to the wife, who is considered more available for appointments and who is presumed to handle these matters. Sometimes father's roles are conditioned by the roles social workers "give" them. For example, an absence of efforts to involve fathers can be taken as a message not to get involved. If these social worker "messages" match the father's own stereotype of his wife's role as in charge of social worker contacts, there is little chance of obtaining the father's input and involvement. Unfortunately, these messages are often conveyed to fathers in foster care, school social work, and other services that cater instinctively to the major partner, the mother, who often is also usually the applicant for the service. Fathers are much less frequently *treated* as major clients in child welfare, even though good practice has implicitly tended to presume equal importance. By default or by design, fathers are the neglected partners in social work.

Women Treating Women

Social work, in most countries, is primarily a women's profession. In America, approximately 63% of the national membership of the National Association of Social Workers are females (Kadushin, 1975; Loavenbruck, 1973; Sheehan, 1976). One study by Fischer and others (1976) found that a strong profemale bias characterized the judgments of a sample of American social workers; however, this finding was not reconfirmed in a subsequent replication study (Dailey, 1980). In Israel, as well, nearly 80% of all social workers are women (Israel Association of Social Workers, 1980). Not only is the working day geared for women social workers raising their own children, but wage agreements for Israeli welfare workers have always included special benefits for working mothers, including shorter working hours and daycare subsidies. The Israeli public welfare scene is essentially one of women social workers helping female clients. There is strong evidence suggesting that this is true in the United States as well, where the majority of female social workers are employed in direct practice rather than administrative roles (Fanshel, 1976).

"Child welfare," too, as a field of social work practice, is predominantly a female profession, both factually and stereotypically. Teenage prostitutes in Israel, for example, were generally classified as a "child welfare" concern. Consequently, only women social workers work with them. Unfortunately, this arrangement never really allowed for or facilitated work with the girls' pimps located in unsavory hangouts in the various cities where women workers would not go. However, when the work with juvenile prostitutes was transferred from the Child Welfare Division in the Jerusalem municipality to the predominantly male-staffed Division of Rehabilitation, male social workers engaged in outreach work with both the pimps and the adolescent prostitutes, with very successful results. Moreover, for the first time, many young girls had access to a stable, helpful, father figure: the male social worker. For the first time, pimps were threatened by the male social worker who vied for the loyalty of "their" girls. In a very effective, planned way, the new father surrogates weaned the girls from dependency on the pimps to a more independent, satisfying lifestyle.

Caretaking and Father Figures

One particularly distressing area of social service where fathers, or the importance of the father figure, has been neglected, is that of institution or boarding school placement. This is especially true for most socialist countries of Europe, but also for many Western countries as well.

In Israel, child placement has been a major response to family disruption, mass immigration absorption, poverty, and overcrowded housing (Jaffe, 1982a). The Youth Aliyah organization alone cares for over 20,000 youths living away from home (Department of Children and Youth Aliyah, 1979) and the Ministry of Labor and Social Affairs is responsible for placing 12,000 children (Merari, 1978).

Although there is substantial literature on problems of separation and the need for mother figures in dormitory settings, less emphasis has been placed on the need for father figures and male role models. How much contact is provided with a consistent adult *male* figure? Is this possible in view of the relatively rapid turnover of institution counselors, cottage parents, and other male staff members? One variation of congregate care, the S.O.S. children's villages, originated in Austria by Herman Gemeiner (Dodge, 1972), rejects as a matter of principle the concept of cottage fathers, and insists on employing only unattached cottage *mothers* in order to guarantee long-term stability of the person in the mother surrogate role. Unfortunately, the childcare theory underpinning this policy has never been clearly explained or researched, despite the rapid expansion of S.O.S. villages around the world (S.O.S., 1977).

Congregate care generally tends to deemphasize the father role for either logistical or conceptual reasons, and this development is an important subject for further study. It is ironic that many of the dependent children in placement came from homes without healthy father relationships. They never really have an opportunity in placement to make up for that loss. Indeed, in a study of dependent institution children's attitudes towards their parents, Jaffe, (1982b) found that institution children had more positive feelings for their fathers than did children awaiting placement or children living in normal home situations.

In summary, despite the apparent importance attached to fathers as key partners in social work practice, other realities have resulted in a downgrading of this
partnership and a marked lack of accommodation for fathers.

FATHERS AS A SUBCULTURE

All too often, the term "fathers" is used to specify a presumably homogeneous
group of people who occupy a certain role in the family. But any discussion of
fathers must ask: *Which* fathers we are talking about? Is there a prototype? Do we
relate to "fathers" as some mythical, universal, Western father, or are we thinking about different fathers from various cultural groups? Are we talking about
disadvantaged or affluent fathers, about immigrant fathers or "old-timer" fathers? On second glance, everyone will acknowledge that beyond certain universal similarities there are vast differences in the role and status of the father in
different cultures, and that even within various cultures the father role can be
studied as part of a specific subculture. For social workers and child care professionals this information is crucial if one is to provide services and function properly. One excellent example of the importance of such information can be seen
from Riszk's (1977) advice to supervisors of social workers working with Arab
village families in Israel.

> The Arab family structure is avowedly patriarchal. The father is the authority; he is
> God-on-Earth. The way his children are raised, his relationship to his wife, are
> based on his teaching, his orders, and his use of physical punishment to resolve
> problems. Only infrequently is encouragement given to internal strengths and abili-
> ties of the family members, and rarely does he encourage them to express them-
> selves regarding their problems. There is no trace of the principle of equal rights in
> their relationship with him. . . . In essence, all these things show that the major
> factor in father-child relationships is the fact that the children and other family
> members must blindly obey and honor their elders, otherwise they will be called to
> order by physical force [p. 18].

Without the insights noted above, it would be folly to attempt childcare work
with the fathers described. Similar information has proven vital for work with
Jewish fathers who immigrated to Israel from Moslem countries and fathers from
ultraorthodox communities who came from Poland, Hungary, or Russia. How
many American social workers have studied the subculture of the Puerto Rican,
Cuban, Mexican, or Native American father? And how many British social
workers have studied the father's role in West Indian, West African, and Asian
migrant families who came to England in recent decades? These cultural, ethnic,
and social aspects of social work with immigrant fathers and families are matters
of concern today for most Western countries and in recent years have become
topics for regional and international meetings of social workers.

Because the issue of fathers in social work practice has been neglected in general, this situation hardly afforded grounds for studying fathers as part of a specific subculture. Much has yet to be learned about fathers in new cultures. What do we know about the changing role of fathers as a result of the clash between traditional and modern cultures among immigrant groups? What has the father's handling of his role change done to the self-image of his children, to their image of the father, and to their selection of male role models? How do second-generation sons of immigrants, torn between new and old cultures, relate to social services and social workers? Are their attitudes different from that of their fathers', and if so, in what ways?

In most countries, social welfare workers are drawn primarily from the dominant culture, whereas their clientele are drawn from ethnic minorities (Jaffe, 1977). This has provided a built-in strangeness between helpers and receivers of service and a need for both social workers and clients to learn about the other's culture. Affirmative admission policies at various schools of social work and the introduction of some courses on ethnic customs and cultural anthropology may have alleviated the problem somewhat. Nevertheless, within this larger picture, there is an urgent need for studying the subcultures of different groups of fathers in a systematic way. This can be done "in the field" after one's professional education, but universities today are also beginning to grapple with this problem. Perhaps one of the reasons for the delay in teaching about fathers in different subcultures (and perhaps about mothers, too) was a reluctance to acknowledge or legitimize the importance of ethnic issues in childcare practice. The goal in most Western countries for many decades has been towards rapid acculturation of immigrants within the melting pot, rather than encouraging diversity and cultural pluralism. Furthermore, early denial of the importance of ethnic issues in social work education in favor of "generic" principles and methods of intervention may have served to allay fears of middle-class, white social workers concerning their own competency to understand and treat problems of all clients regardless of ethnic background. In Israel, for example, until the early 1970s it was generally considered unacceptable and socially devisive to emphasize Sephardi-Ashkenazi (i.e., Middle-Eastern vs. Western) differences and ethnic background as correlates of social stratification and social problems. After all, they were all Jews, and the country had been founded on the principle of the Ingathering of the Exiles.

Fortunately, reality has caught up with social ideology in most countries, and professionals involved in social welfare and their social institutions are becoming more aware of ethnic issues and the need to accept and understand ethnic subcultures. Among the pioneering educators in this endeavor are Billingsley (1968), Billingsley and Giovannoni (1972), Montiel (1970, 1973), Kim (1973, 1976), Rothman (1977), Turner (1972), Jaffe (1981), and Jenkins and Morrison's (1978, 1980). For social work education, Jenkins latest (1981) work is of great importance because it attempts to develop a typology for incorporating ethnic factors into social welfare based on experiences with five ethnic groups in America. Jenkins also reviews ethnic issues in Britain and Israel. She is one of the few social work educators to present the ethnic dilemma in social services in international perspective, and her observations show quite clearly how all of us in different countries are struggling with very similar problems. Nevertheless, Jenkins' research did not deal with fathers in ethnic subcultures, although by sensitizing social workers to the general topic, she may provoke more specific research on fathers.

SUMMARY

It is ironic, perhaps, that the renewed interest in women's rights and women's roles in modern society has also led to a "rediscovery" of the role and problems of fathers as a distinct client group. As society begins to identify each parent as a separate entity and experimentation with family roles becomes more acceptable, the male, as well as the female parent role, is receiving more attention.

For social welfare and childcare workers, this development is very important because there has been, as this chapter shows, a tendency to overlook the father as a client. The reasons for this situation are varied, ranging from the organization and demographic make-up of the social work profession to stereotypes about fathers and a lack of knowledge about ethnic groups. Whatever the reasons, social work practice and research has not accommodated or appreciated the role of the fathers. He has been dealt with as a problematic figure rather than a full partner in social service delivery. In order to correct this situation, both conceptual and administrative changes may be necessary in child and family care practice. Above all, a greater sensitivity to the role of fathers as partners and clients is needed. If social work still includes outreach, if office hours do not dictate clientele, and if father subcultures are more sympathetically understood, then social work has a chance to help fathers.

Beyond the issue of father's rights to social services, it is important to emphasize that effective "child welfare" practice begins with parents, biological or psychological, and that inadvertent or conscious discrimination against either parent can result in poorer service to children.

REFERENCES

Alexandrovitz, D. Children's reactions to loss of a parent. *Saad*, 1969, *13*, 36–40 (Hebrew).
Bartz, K. W., & Witcher, W. C. When father gets custody. *Children Today*, 1979, *7*, 2–6.
Billingsley, A. *Black families in white America*. Englewood Cliffs: Prentice-Hall, 1968.
Billingsley, A., & Giovannoni, J. M. *Children of the storm: Black children and American child welfare*. New York: Harcourt Brace Jovanovich, 1972.
Dailey, D. M. Are social workers sexists?: A replication. *Social Work*, 1980, *25*, 46–50.

David, C. A. The use of the confrontation technique in the battered child syndrome. *American Journal of Psychotherapy*, 1974, *28*, 543–552.

Department of Children and Youth Aliyah. Statistical summary for April 1, 1979. *Annual Report of the Youth Aliyah Department*. Jerusalem: The Jewish Agency, 1979.

Dodge, J. SOS children's villages throughtout the world: Substitute or superior service. *Child welfare*, 1972, *5*, 344–353.

Fanshel, D. Status differentials: Men and women in social work. *Social Work*, 1976, *21*, 448–454.

Fast, A. *The father-only family: An alternative family style.* Unpublished doctoral dissertation, Brandeis University, 1979.

Fischer, J., Dulaney, D. D., Fazio, R. T., Hudak, M. T., & Zivotofsky, E. Are social workers sexists? *Social Work*, 1976, 428–433.

Gentry, C. E. Incestuous abuse of children: The need for an objective view. *Child Welfare*, 1978, *57*, 355–364.

Grossberg, S. H., & Crandall, L. Father loss and father absence in preschool children. *Clinical Social Work Journal*, 1978, *6*, 123–134.

Hindman, M. Child abuse and neglect: The alcohol connection. *Alcohol Health and Research World*, 1977, *1*, 2–7.

Israel Association of Social Workers. New data on social work manpower. *Meidos*, 1980, *18*, 5 (Hebrew).

Jaffe, E. D. Manpower supply and admissions policy in Israeli social work education. *Journal of Jewish Communal Service*, 1977, *3*, 242–249.

Jaffe, E. D. *Ethnic preferences of Israelis.* Tel Aviv: Tcherikover Press, 1981.

Jaffe, E. D. *Child Welfare in Israel.* New York: Praeger Publishers, 1982. (a)

Jaffe, E. D. Perceptions of family relationships. *Israelis in Institutions.* London: Gordon & Breach, 1982. (b)

Jenkins, S. B. The ethnic agency defined. *Social Service Review*, 1980, *54*, 249–261.

Jenkins, S. *The ethnic dilemma in social services.* New York: The Free Press, 1981.

Jenkins, S. & Morrison, B. Ethnicity and service delivery. *American Journal of Orthopsychiatry*, 1978, *48*, 160–165.

Kadushin, A. Men in a woman's profession. *Social Work*, 1975, *21*, 440–447.

Keshet, H. F. *Part-time fathers: A study of separated and divorced men.* Unpublished doctoral dissertation, University of Michigan, 1977.

Kim, Bok-Lim C. Asian-American: No model minority. *Social Work*, 1973, *18*, 44–53.

Kim, Bok-Lim C. An appraisal of Korean immigrant service needs. *Social Casework*, 1976, *57*, 139–148.

Lamb, M. E. (Ed.). *The role of the father in child development* (Rev. ed.). New York: Wiley, 1981.

Leader, A. Family therapy for divorced fathers and others out of the home. *Social Casework*, 1973, *54*, 13–18.

Loavenbruck, G. NASW manpower survey finds increases in pay for most members. *National Association of Social Workers News*, 1973, *18*, 10–11.

Mendes, H. A. Single fatherhood. *Social Work*, 1976, 21, 308–312.

Merari, T. Placement of children away from home. *Society and Welfare*, 1978, *1*, 490–497 (Hebrew).

Montiel, M. Recent changes among chicanos. *Sociology and Social Research*, 1970, *55*, 47–51.

Montiel, M. The Chicano family: A review of research. *Social Work*, 1973, *18*, 22–31.

Riszk, S. Social work supervision within the Arab culture. *Saad*, 1977, *21*, 17–26 (Hebrew).

Rothman, J. (Ed.). *Issues in race and ethnic relations: Theory, research and action.* Itasca, Ill: Peacock Publishers, 1977.

Russell, M. A father's role in the custody and rearing of his children (V. Jordan, Ed.). *Conference for the Advancement of Private Practice in Social Work*, 1969.

Sheehan, J. C. (Ed.). *Statistics on social work education in the United States.* New York: Council on Social Work Education, 1976.

Snyder, L. *The impact of the criminal justice system of Baltimore City on the deserting, non-supporting father in relation to his role as provider.* Unpublished Doctoral dissertation, Columbia University, 1975.

S.O.S, *S.O.S. News.* Vienna: S.O.S. Kinderdorf International, 1977.

Spencer, J. Father-daughter incest: A clinical view from the corrections field. *Child Welfare,* 1978, *57,* 581–590.

Todres, R. Motherless families. *Canadian Welfare,* 1975, *51,* 11–13.

Turner, J. B. Education for practice with minorities. *Social Work,* 1972, *17,* 112–118.

9 Increased Paternal Participation: The Fathers' Perspective

Graeme Russell
Macquarie University

Norma Radin
University of Michigan

Researchers and policy makers, for the most part, have concentrated on the effects that family changes might have on children. Little consideration has been given to possible consequences for mothers, and even less still, to consequences for fathers. Yet, it seems obvious that family changes are likely to have both direct effects on mothers and fathers, and, under many circumstances, as a consequence of these, indirect effects on children. Furthermore, it may very well be that parents place more importance on the actual or perceived effects on themselves (e.g., on their feelings of well being) or the family (e.g., on financial security), than on the possible effects on children. The present volume represents a marked divergence from previous analyses of family changes (e.g., analyses of the effects of maternal employment and paternal absence) by examining the likely consequences that a change in paternal participation will have on *all* family members. It is fathers themselves who are the subject of the present chapter; subsequent chapters focus on mothers, children, and society.

The aim of this chapter is to examine the issue of increased paternal participation in child care within the broad framework of three questions. First, what are current levels of paternal participation, and what potential is there for an increase? To answer this question, data are presented on paternal participation from studies in several cultures, focusing both on the consistent finding of low levels of participation, and more recent reports of highly participant fathers. The second question examined is: What are the likely benefits and costs for fathers themselves if they become more highly participant? Specifically, what impact is this likely to have on: fathers' relationships with their children and their wives; their own personal development; and on fathers' commitments to their jobs and careers. Findings from the very few studies of highly participant fathers provide the basis for this analysis. Finally, this chapter asks: What factors are likely to influence increased paternal participation? The possibilities discussed include: traditionally accepted beliefs about parental roles, and how they might inhibit participation; fathers' previous experiences and socialization, particularly in relation to the development of the male role; the experiences and socialization of mothers; and the constraints that might be placed on fathers by the work/employment structure.

It is readily acknowledged that there are huge gaps in the literature about paternal child rearing, particularly in relation to families that are nonwhite and non-middle class. There are also specific domains where empirically based knowledge is scarce even about Caucasian, well-to-do parents. The latter areas are highlighted throughout the paper when relevant topics are discussed. A statement that is applicable to the entire paper, however, is that research is needed on fathers from low income families, and from different cultural groups (e.g., fathers from black, Hispanic, and Asian homes in the United States). Further, because of the restricted nature of the samples used in most studies on fathering, generalizations beyond the groups investigated should be made with extreme care.

PATERNAL PARTICIPATION

There are many different ways in which paternal participation can be defined, ranging from: active participation during pregnancy, e.g., showing concern for the welfare of the fetus; sharing in the early day-to-day care of a child; helping with school work; responding sensitively to the needs of children; washing diapers and preparing meals. Radin (1978), in one of the early discussions of the problems of definition, delineated five possible areas of paternal participation: *involvement* (the extent of contribution to child rearing); responsibility taken for *physical care*; responsibility taken for *socialization; decision making* relating to the child; and *availability*. Sagi (1982), who used the same categorization in an Israeli study, stresses that the significance of paternal participation in each of these areas might not be constant across cultures. He points out, for example, that paternal availability during meal time is a much less significant indicator of participation for a father on a kibbutz than it is for a father in a city in Israel. Given these findings, it is necessary to discuss the various components of participation separately rather than combining them into one overall measure. This is the approach taken here.

Most of the studies on participation to date have been on families with very young children, and most have focused on either birth attendance, availability, or participation in physical care and play. Little study has been made of the degree of responsibility fathers take for discipline, socialization, or decision making, or of the nature of paternal participation with older children. Studies that have been conducted to date fall into two broad categories. First, there are studies of traditional families in which fathers are employed full time. These provide the basis for the description of modal patterns of paternal participation presented below. Second, there are several studies of a minority group of nontraditional families, and it is these families that form the basis of a discussion of the possibilities there are for increased paternal participation.

Modal Patterns

Major studies of paternal participation in traditional families have been conducted in the United States, the United Kingdom, Australia, and several European countries. Despite differences in samples and methods of data collection, a consistent pattern has begun to emerge. This pattern is that fathers, in comparison to mothers, generally have only a very minor commitment to the day-to-day responsibilities of child care, and that overall, the area in which fathers are most highly participant is play.

Attendance at Birth.   Recent reports from most Western industrialized nations indicate that it is now much more common for fathers to attend rather than not attend the births of their children. Data collected in 1981 from four major hospitals in Sydney, Australia, revealed that the attendance rate varied from 60–80%, and in a quasi-random sample of Australian families recruited for a study in 1978, approximately 50% of fathers reported they had attended the births of their children (Russell, 1982a). Richards (1981) also reported that the attendance rate in the United Kingdom is in the range of 60–80%.

The picture is somewhat different in the U.S. A nationwide study conducted in 1972 indicated that in only 27% of the 320,000 births reported were fathers admitted into the delivery room (Phillips & Anzalone, 1978). According to a 1978 book on fathers' participation in the birth of their children, not all delivery rooms are open to fathers (Phillips & Anzalone, 1978). However, American hospitals have been criticized for making childbirth more difficult for mothers by separating them from their families (Haire, 1975), and an increasing number of parents are expecting fathers to be present during the delivery as a result of their having attended childbirth training courses (Newman & Newman, 1978). Thus, conditions may change more quickly than anticipated.

Although the figures for actual presence at the birth can be considered reasonably high in some countries, and they have shown a dramatic increase in recent years in Australia (e.g., Alwyn [1977] reported that in one major Australian hospital only 0.7% of fathers attended births in 1962), it cannot be readily assumed that the same number of fathers are *active* participants in the birth process. Indeed, we know very little about the extent of paternal participation either before or during the birth. How many fathers, for example, are merely present at the very final stages of the birth and are simply spectators? For countries in which fathers are present but passive, active involvement is perhaps the next step in increasing paternal participation in child rearing. For countries where fathers are kept outside of the delivery room, permitting them to be present would be a step forward. Perhaps the ultimate in paternal participation is for the father to deliver the baby. A few doctors in the U.S. are succesfully training men to perform this task in a hospital, under the guidance of a doctor who stands nearby. The results appear to be very positive, with the fathers feeling closer to the child as a result (Block, 1981; Yarrow, 1981).

Availability.   What happens when the babies come home from hospital? How much time are fathers at home and available to their children during their waking hours? Studies of middle-class U.S. fathers with young infants report that fathers are at home when their children are awake for approximately 25 hours each weak (Kotelchuck, 1976; Pedersen & Robson, 1969), and Russell (1982a), in a study of a more diverse sample (in terms of social class characteristics and ages of children) of Australian families, reports that fathers are available for an average of 33 hours per week. In contrast, mothers have been found to be available for 63 hours per week in the U.S. (Kotelchuck, 1976) and 76 hours per week in Australia (Russell, 1982a). Given that the overwhelming majority of fathers are employed in the paid work force, their potential to be available more is obviously dependent on employment demands. This possible constraint is discussed in detail below.

Time Spent on Child Care.   Despite differences in methods employed, findings for the amount of time spent each week by fathers on basic childcare tasks (e.g., feeding, diaper changing) are remarkably consistent across several studies. Estimates for U.S. fathers have been reported to be 2.1 (Robinson, 1977; Walker & Woods, 1976), 1.7 (Pleck & Rustad, 1980) and 2.8 (Kotelchuck, 1976), and for Australian fathers, 2 hours per week (Russell, 1982a). A time budget study conducted in 13 countries (mainly in Eastern and Western Europe), estimated the figure to be 1.6 hours per week (Newland, 1980). Differences between mothers and fathers are again quite marked. Estimates of time spent by unemployed mothers on childcare tasks range from 9 hours per week (representing 85% of the total time spent by both mothers and fathers performing childcare tasks) in the 13–nation study (Newland, 1980), to 18 hours per week (89%) in the Australian study (Russell, 1982a). Moreover, it is abundantly clear that these differences are not simply explained by differences in the amount of time spent at home. In an analysis of Australian data, for example, it was reported that if mothers and fathers shared equally the childcare tasks *when they were both at home,* fathers would be performing 35% of them—a figure well above the actual figure of 11%.

Time Spent in Play.   Fathers have consistently been found to be more likely to spend time playing with their children than performing childcare tasks. This pattern has been found both in a home observational study of father-infant interaction (Lamb, 1976) and in interview studies (Kotelchuk, 1976; Russell, 1979b). The two interview studies both reported fathers spent approximately 9 hours per week playing with their children. Even though fathers spend more time on play than on performing childcare tasks, they still spend less time on play than mothers do. Estimates on time spent by mothers playing with their children range from 14 hours per week to 20 hours per week (Kotelchuk, 1976; Russell, 1982a).

Mother-father differences have also been found for types of play activities. Both Lamb (1976), in his observational study, and Russell (1979b), in his interview study, found that fathers were more likely to be involved in physical, rough and tumble, and idiosyncratic nonstereotyped play, and mothers were more likely to be involved in conventional, toy-oriented and creative-type play. Also, studies in both Australia (Russell, 1982a) and the U.K. (Jackson, 1980) have found that mothers are much more likely to read stories to their children.

Degree of Responsibility Taken for Children. Few studies have inquired about the degree of responsibility taken for the day-to-day care of children, or for specific childcare tasks; most have focused instead on time spent with children, or on the relative frequency of carrying out various tasks. However, there need not be a high correlation between task performance and the degree of responsibility taken.

Two recent studies have reported data on differences in responsibility taken by mothers and fathers. In one study it was found that only 7.5% of fathers shared childcare responsibilities equally with their wives, and 75% did not take *any* responsibility for the day-to-day care of their children (Kotelchuck, 1976). In another study (Russell, 1982a), parents were asked who had the major responsibility for child care. In over 90% of the families, both mothers and fathers responded that it was mothers. Another question in the same study inquired about the amount of time fathers spent taking the sole responsibility for their children. Sole responsibility was defined as that period of time when fathers were at home with their children and the mother was out and could not be called upon. Fathers were found to spend an average of only 1 hour per week taking sole responsibility, which contrasts quite markedly with the figure for mothers who reported spending an average of 40 hours per week taking sole responsibility for their children. Moreover, 80% of fathers did not have this type of responsibility each week, and 60% of fathers had never taken the sole responsibility for their children (Russell, 1982a).

Summary. The modal pattern of paternal participation appears to be one of fathers being much less likely than mothers to be available to, or interact with their children either in the context of play or child care, a pattern that has been reported in several different cultures. Another consistent finding reported is that overall, fathers' participation is much more play-oriented, and they engage in different types of play activities than mothers do. Finally, fathers were found to be significantly less likely than mothers to taken responsibility for the day-to-day care of their children, and at least one study reported that the majority of fathers had never take responsibility for their children when the mother was not at home and available.

As was discussed earlier, most studies on paternal participation have been on familiar with young children, and they have focused on the time spent on (or the frequency of doing) childcare tasks or playing with children. Studies are needed to supplement the available data by investigating families with older children and other areas of participation such as socialization, discipline, and decision making. Our understanding of the quality of the father's interaction with his children and his sensitivity to their needs over time would also benefit greatly from controlled, longitudinal investigations.

Possibilities for Increased Participation

The above discussion of modal patterns of paternal participation clearly shows that in comparison to mothers, there is plenty of scope for fathers to increase their levels of participation. The aim of this section is to discuss two major possibilities for fathers to participate more: one that assumes the retention of traditional divisions of labor for employment in the paid work force; and one that involves changes in divisions of labor for both child care and employment.

Increases Within a Traditional Nuclear Family. What is being discussed here are increases within families in which the mother is unemployed and at home and the father is employed in the paid work force. The possibility of fathers in traditional families increasing their levels of participation in child care, play and degree of responsibility taken, is supported by findings from three recent studies that have drawn attention to traditional fathers who are highly participant.

Kotelchuck (1976), in his U.S. study, as reported earlier, found that around 8% of his sample of fathers shared childcare responsibilities with their wives. From the figures presented by Kotelchuck it can be estimated that these fathers were spending approximately 11 hours per week performing childcare tasks—considerably more than the previously mentioned average, found across several different cultures, of approximately 2 hours per week.

In Russell's (1982a) Australian study of a heterogeneous sample of families, however, only 1% of fathers were found to spend 11 hours or more on childcare tasks. Nevertheless, 15% of fathers were found to be highly participant in *all* aspects of child care on a regular day-to-day basis, spending at least one hour a day on these tasks. These were fathers who did appear to share childcare tasks and responsibilities with their wives when they were both at home.

A group of highly participant fathers has also been reported recently by Jackson (1980) in a national sample study of nearly 12,000 U.K. families with a 5-year-old child. Jackson reports that these highly participant fathers played a substantial part in running the home and were likely to have regular close personal contacts with their children (e.g., putting them to bed; readiang stories to them).

The extent to which it is possible for fathers in traditional families to increase their levels of participation is, of course, severely constrained by the demands of employment. More radical changes in fathers' involvement in child care, therefore, are dependent on changes in traditional divisions of labor for paid work. It is this change that is considered next.

More Radical Changes in Family Patterns. The second possibility for increased paternal participation involves a major change in divisions of labor for both family and paid work; for fathers (or males) to take over a substantial portion of child care and for mothers (or females) to share or have the major responsibility for paid work. In support of this possibility, several recent publications have reported on families in which fathers were highly participant in daily care-giving. In many of these families, fathers either had equal or major responsibility for child care, and in most, breadwinning was shared or was the sole responsibility of the mother. This family pattern been noted in Norway (Gronseth, 1978), Sweden (Lamb, Frodi, Hwang, Frodi, & Steinberg, 1982; Lamb, Frodi, Hwang, Frodi, & Steinberg, 1982), Australia (Harper, 1980; Russell, 1982a, 1982b), in the U.S. (De Frain, 1979; Field, 1978; Levine, 1976; Radin, 1978, 1981, 1982), and Israel (Sagi, 1982).

Comparative analyses of these studies of highly participant fathers are difficult, as sample characteristics and methodologies have been quite varied. Nevertheless, one point is abundantly clear from all studies: The fathers described are indeed highly participant in comparison to the modal pattern described earlier. In Radin's (1978, 1981, 1982) U.S. study, samples of fathers were reported to perform 41% and 57% of childcare tasks, whereas in DeFrain's (1979) study, fathers were reported to perform 46% of tasks. Sagi (1982) does not provide specific data on levels of father participation in his Israeli study; however, he does state that in 15 families it was agreed that the father was more involved than the mother was, and there were 20 families in which mothers and fathers agreed they had equal responsibility for child rearing. In an Australian study (Russell, 1982a), fathers were reported to spend an average of 26 hours per week taking sole responsibility for their children (compared to 16 hours per week for mothers), and they performed 44% of childcare tasks (spending an average of 9 hours per week doing them). There is no indication as to how prevalent these types of families are within each of the cultures studied. One estimate has been that they constitute 1–2% of families in which there are young children (Russell, 1982a). Irrespective of the accuracy of this estimate, it is obvious that this type of family is indeed a minority.

Both of these possibilities for increased paternal participation involve a significant departure from the current modal, and widely accepted, pattern of paternal participation. Although both would be expected to have a major impact on fathers and families, it is the latter, more radical changes in both paid and family work responsibilities for which the impact would be expected to be the greatest. The question of the possible impact of increased paternal participation from the perspective of the father is considered next.

POSSIBLE IMPACT OF INCREASED PARTICIPATION ON FATHERS

What are the likely consequences for fathers if they significantly increased their participation levels? There are very little data available to answer this question as most studies have concentrated on traditional fathers and on the effects that fathers have on child development. What little data there are available comes from interview studies of families in which changes have been of the more radical type—in which fathers have either the major or equal responsibility for the day-to-day care of their children. These studies suggest that increased paternal participation is likely to have an impact on family relationships—specifically, father-child and mother-child relationships; fathers' personal development, e.g., on self-esteem; and on fathers' relative commitments to employment and family.

Family Relationship

Father-Child Relationship

There are several possible ways in which fathers' relationships with their children might change if fathers were to spend more time with their children, interact with them more, and take more responsibility for them. On the positive side, fathers might become closer to their children, and more sensitive to their needs and feelings. Alternatively, an increase in childcare responsibilities might lead to more tension and conflict between fathers and children.

Closer Father-Child Relationships.   The possibility that increased participation will affect a father's feelings about his children and his perceptions of the closeness of his relationship with them is supported by findings from several recent studies (Gronseth, 1978; Hood & Golden, 1979; Kelley, 1981; Radin, 1982; Russell, 1982a). One study (Russell, 1982a) investigated parents' perceptions of changes in father-child relationships associated with fathers either sharing or having the major responsbility for child care. Sixty-nine percent of the fathers and 64% of the mothers reported that fathers had become much closer to their children and were now more positive about their relationships with them. Furthermore, when asked an open-ended question about what they perceived to be the major advantages of their "shared-role" lifestyle, 64% of fathers said it was their improved relationships with their children. Fathers themselves, therefore, appeared to place high value on their changed and closer relationships with their children.

Three other studies offer additional support for this positive effect on fathers. In an investigation of families in which mothers had returned to school, fathers were found to increase their levels of participation, and as a consequence, 52% of the fathers and 60% of the mothers felt this had resulted in an improved father-child relationship (Kelley, 1981). A study of Norwegian shared-role families (shared for both work and child care) also reported that as a consequence of fathers having more time and experience with their children, they had better and more open contact with them (Gronseth, 1978). In an in-depth study (Hood & Golden, 1979) of the impact of work scheduling, high paternal participation was also reported to be associated with fathers feeling closer to their children. Finally, in another study, 20 middle-class fathers who were primary caregivers of preschoolers in two-parent families were asked about the disadvantages of this arrangement (Radin, 1982). All but one volunteered information about the advantages as well. Sixty percent of the 20 cited factors related to the children; that is, the fathers reported that they felt closer to their children, got to know their children well, and enjoyed being with them.

Findings from the five studies reviewed here suggest, therefore, that increased participation brings fathers closer to their children, and that this change has a positive effect on fathers themselves. Such a conclusion seems especially justified when it is considered that in two of the studies reported above, *both* fathers and mothers reported significant positive effects for the father-child relationship and fathers (Kelley, 1981; Russell, 1982a).

Enhanced Sensitivity to Children.   Increased participation is also likely to result in a change in paternal understanding of and sensitivity towards their children. In support of this proposition, Lamb and Easterbrooks (1981) have speculated that the degree of involvement fathers have with their infants will affect their sensitivity towards them. They argued that: "Interaction facilitates the growth of parental sensitivity by providing practice differentiating among, interpreting, and responding to infant signals. Fathers who have more interaction with young infants may be better prepared for sensitive responding later. [p. 142]."

The possibility that fathers' sensitivity towards and understanding of their children is enhanced by increased participation is given tentative support by two recent studies. Gronseth (1978) reported that 66% of his shared-role fathers (N = 16) felt they understood their children better after they began to spend more time with them. In another study of highly participant fathers (N = 71), 28% of the fathers and 26% of the mothers reported that fathers, because of their increased participation, had a better understanding of their children and their day-to-day needs (Russell, 1982a). Fathers in this study also reported that it was not just the increased time they spent with their children that affected their understanding, but the *way* in which the time was spent. Specifically, fathers argued the most important factor was spending time *alone* with their children, taking the sole responsibility for them on a continuing day-to-day basis. Fathers also reported that this increased understanding and sensitivity had produced a change in their views about their roles as parents; they felt more self-confident and more effective as parents. This change in fathers' feelings about and satisfaction with their parental roles are discussed in further detail below.

Although support was found for the hypothesis that increased paternal participation leads to enhanced sensitivity and understanding of children, the evidence to date is not very strong, and there are some contradictory findings. In the Radin study referred to previously (1982), audio tapes were made of fathers interacting with their preschoolers during the interview, and the tapes were subsequently coded for paternal nurturance (this included sensitivity to the child) and for restrictiveness. The coding system and categories developed in a previous study of paternal behavior were employed (Epstein & Radin, 1975; Radin & Epstein, 1975). No differences in either the nurturant or restrictive category were found between fathers who were primary caregivers and traditional fathers. These findings are in keeping with data obtained when fathers in the study were asked to rate their own nurturant behaviors with their children in a questionnaire; the correlations between indices of father involvement and amount of paternal nurturance for the most part were not significant (Radin & Sagi, 1982). However, for a comparable group of middle-class traditional and primary caregiving fathers in Israel, nurturance as assessed by questionnaire data and the amount of father involvement were highly related (Radin & Sagi, 1982). Clearly additional data are needed, particularly data from cross-cultural studies examining responses to infants' and children's cues and signals of fathers who are and who are not highly participant. Longitudinal data are also needed so it can be determined if it is the already sensitive father who becomes highly participant.

Increased Tension and Conflict.   In most families it is mothers who have the major responsibility for child care, and therefore, it is mothers who have to deal constantly with the day-to-day problems of bringing up children. Having this type of constant responsibility for children is also likely to have consequences for parent-child relationships, for parents' evaluations of their roles, and for their perceptions of themselves. This effect is well illustrated by a recent study of traditional families (Russell, 1982a). Parents in this study were asked how they could change their current behavior to improve their relationships with their children. Forty percent of the mothers, but only 9% of the fathers said they could be more tolerant or patient with their children. In contrast, the majority of fathers (50%) felt they could improve their relationships by spending more time with their children. It is mothers, therefore, who appear to be more affected by the pressures of the day-to-day problems and conflicts of child rearing, and it is *their* perception that their reactions to these problems has an effect on parent-child relationships.

It is not unreasonable to expect, therefore, that if fathers also had to deal constantly with day-to-day child-rearing problems, they would experience the same kinds of reactions as mothers in traditional families. Some data are available to support this hypothesis. Both Kelley (1981) and Russell (1982a) report that one of the consequences of fathers becoming more highly participant is that conflicts between fathers and children increase. Indirect support for these findings also emerged from the Radin study of primary care-giving fathers. It was found that children in families with high paternal participation perceive fathers as more punitive than children in traditional families (Radin, 1978; Radin & Sagi, 1982). Russell (1982a) also found that 18% of highly participant fathers (compared to 9% of traditional fathers) reported that parent-child relationships could improve if they were more patient. Despite there being higher levels of conflict reported, parents in both studies also felt that as a consequence of more paternal involvement, the father-child relationship was more realistic because children now saw more sides of the father (the patient and the impatient). Furthermore, mothers were more likely to view this as a positive change associated with high paternal participation (Russell, 1982a).

When fathers take on a major responsibility for care-giving, therefore, they appear to experience increased tension and conflict similar to that experienced by mothers in traditional families. These tensions and conflicts, however, are not as likely to increase markedly if father participation is increased only within the confines of the traditional family. Nevertheless, increased paternal participation could lead to a reduction in tension and conflict experienced by mothers in traditional families. Additional research is now needed that explores the likely positive and negative changes in both fathers' and mothers' relationships with their children as a function of the nature of paternal participation, and the effects that these changes have on parents and their self-images.

Father-Mother Relationships

There are at least two major possibilities for changes in father-mother relationships. First, if fathers become more highly participant in child care, this could lead to greater equality in the marital relationship, and thus both parents could be more satisfied with their relationship. Second, the quality of the relationship might suffer, either because of fathers' dissatisfactions with spending more time on child care, or because of increased conflicts over housework and child-rearing practices (tasks that are traditionally almost exclusively a mother's domain). Three recent studies report data on father-mother relationships in families in which fathers are highly participant.

Gronseth (1978) reports that sharing child care and paid work has a positive effect on relationships between mothers and fathers. Thirty percent of the families in his study reported there was less domination of one parent over the other, and approximately 50% said there was more equality between parents after they had changed family lifestyles. There was little evidence of increased tension and conflicts. Nearly 50% of the families reported, however, that their relationships were characterized by equality before they changed lifestyles.

In contrast to Gronseth's findings, Russell (1982a, 1982b) reports a mixed reaction to increased father participation. Approximately 40% of both mothers and fathers either reported there was greater equality or their relationship had improved because each parent was now more sensitive to the other. Nevertheless, approximately 50% of parents reported their relationships had suffered either because they spent less time together or because tension and conflict had increased. It is uncertain how much of this tension and conflict is attributable to fathers' increased participation and how much is attributable to other features of these parents' lifestyles. Unlike the families in Gronseth's study, parents did not share both child care and paid work, and in over 50% of the families, both parents were employed fulltime (cf. in Gronseth's study in which neither parent was employed fulltime). It is possible, therefore, that the increase in marital tension noted by Russell is associated with work overload.

Additional findings presented by both Russell (1982a) and others (De Frain, 1979; Lein, 1979), do suggest, however, that increased conflict is directly associated with fathers' increased participation in child care and household tasks. These studies report that conflicts arise because mothers are dissatisfied with the quality of fathers' task performance. Russell has suggested that these conflicts may be due in part to mothers feeling that their traditional domains of housework and child care are threatened when fathers take over these tasks. Much has been written about how men feel threatened by the feminist movement and the prospect of women moving into the paid work and public domains—traditionally the provinces of men; however, little has been written about the reverse process: women feeling threatened by men taking on more responsibility for housework, cooking, and child care. Perhaps this will only emerge as a major issue when indeed men do move into these traditional female domains at the same rate as women are moving into the traditional male domains. Nevertheless, this does appear to be an important issue for those fathers who have already made this move.

Although there was evidence of increased conflict when fathers became more highly participant, Russell (1982a) also reports that 30% of the families who said conflicts had increased also reported that this was primarily confined to the first few months of changing roles, during the adjustment period. How significant these conflicts are in the longer term is an open question and one that needs to be investigated in future studies.

What little data we have at present on the effects of increased paternal participation on the father-mother relationship, therefore, is equivocal. For some, the relationship appears to improve; for others there appears to be increased conflict and dissatisfaction; others still report that conflicts and dissatisfactions are limited to the early period of adjustment to their new parental roles. Data presented below also indicate that this early period of role change is important for the fathers' personal adjustment. It seems that emphasis will need to be placed on this period of adjustment in future studies and by those who might advocate changes in levels of paternal participation. Indeed, the success or otherwise of this process of adjustment and the level of support given by significant others might have important consequences for fathers' continued high levels of participation.

Father's Personal Development

Identity as a male.   Perhaps the most obvious issue for increased paternal participation concerns a father's identity as a male. Cultural stereotypes of masculinity do not usually include nurturant or care-giving behavior (Levine, 1976; Pleck & Sawyer, 1974; Russell, 1978). Males are expected to fulfill an instrumental role in the paid work force—to be the breadwinner—rather than fulfill an expressive role within the family. This is an integral part of male socialization in most Western societies, and indeed the majority of men define their father role in terms of their breadwinner responsibilities (Levine, 1976; Russell, 1982a). Moreover, as has been pointed out elsewhere, there are decidedly few cultural models of highly participant fathers (Rapoport, Rapoport, & Strelitz, 1977; Russell, 1982a). It may be then, that fathers will not feel comfortable being highly participant in child care, and will see this as a threat to their identity as males.

There has been little study of men's reactions to adopting behavior patterns that have traditionally been viewed as appropriate only for females. There is some evidence that suggests that males who are more likely to perform cross-sex behavior (e.g., interact with a baby, perform childcare tasks) are less likely to have self-concepts that are rigidly tied to traditional notions of masculinity (Bem & Lenney, 1976; Bem, Martyna, & Watson, 1976; Russell, 1978). Furthermore, responses obtained in interviews with highly participant fathers indicate that they view a father's concept of masculinity and his responses to the negative reactions of his male peer group as being critical both for the decision to become highly participant in the first place, and for the decision to continue (Russell, 1982a).

Highly participant fathers have been found to associate other fathers' reluctance to participate in child care with rather narrow views of masculinity and sex-appropriate behavior; in fact, highly participant fathers perceive their own behavior as being quite consistent with their identity as a male. In one study (Gronseth, 1978), only one out of 16 highly participant fathers expressed any difficulty with his identity as a male. In another study (Russell, 1982a), only five fathers (out of 37) who were both highly participant and unemployed expressed concern about their "failure" in one aspect of accepted male behavior—being the breadwinner. This was despite the fact that most fathers encountered negative reactions from their male peer group; only 27% of fathers said their male peer group was generally supportive of their heavy commitment to child care. It may be, however, that it is only those fathers who don't identify strongly with the cultural stereotype of masculinity who become highly participant in the first place. Indeed, there is some evidence, to be discussed below, that supports this hypothesis.

Negative reactions towards fathers, and possible threats to male identity, are not as likely to be as critical for increased paternal participation within a traditional family situation as they are when fathers share or have the major responsibility for care-giving as was the case in both the studies discussed above. Nevertheless, given the almost total absence of cultural models of fathers being fulltime childrearers, some fathers are likely to experience doubts and difficulties. Perhaps the experience and resolution of these problems might ultimately have important consequences for the personal development of fathers. This possibility is considered next.

Self-Esteem and Satisfaction.   Five recent studies report that fathers who are more highly participant report either enhanced self-esteem, self-confidence, or satisfaction with their parental role (Gronseth, 1978; Lamb et al., 1982; Lein, 1979; Russell, 1982a; Sagi, 1982). In one study, for example, enhanced self-esteem and satisfaction was found to be related to fathers' feelings of achievement and satisfaction with having mastered the care-giving role (Russell, 1982a). In another study (Sagi, 1982) of highly participant Israeli fathers, high correlations were reported between measures of paternal participation, but more especially participation in physical child care and nurturance, and fathers' satisfactions with their role. Moreover, of the fathers in this study who said they were dissatisfied, only one reported this to be because he was *too* involved with his children. In contrast, no relationship was found between amount of satisfaction with the father's role and amount of paternal involvement in child care in a study conducted in the U.S. (Radin & Sagi, 1982). Perhaps this lack of association was due to the self-selected nature of the American sample. All of the parents were at least moderately pleased with their childcare arrangement, whether the father had a major role or a minor role. It is also possible that a cultural variable might be operative, for it was in Australia and Israel that satisfaction and degree of involvement were positively linked and in the U.S. That they were not. Further cross-cultural research is clearly needed, particularly investigations in which the sample of nontraditional families is not confined to those who volunteer to be subjects.

Although findings lend support to the hypothesis that becoming highly participant results in enhanced self-esteem and satisfaction, it is plausible, of course, that it *only* fathers who are confident and high on self-esteem who take on nontraditional roles. Additional longitudinal research is required to explore this issue further to isolate what are causes and what are effects of high paternal participation.

Attitudes and Beliefs.   Fathers' attitudes to social issues, child rearing, and the role of women might also be expected to be influenced by increased partici-

pation. In support of this hypothesis, both mothers and fathers, (but more especially mothers) in one study (Russell, 1982a) reported that the experience of
caring for children had led to major shifts in fathers' attitudes towards children
(e.g., they now placed more value on children and on their welfare), child care
(they were more likely to argue for the need for childcare support systems for the
family), and the role of women (they were much more likely to be egalitarian in
their views about male/female roles, and to display an understanding and concern
for a person having to care for children fulltime). Furthermore, these changes
were as evident in the responses of fathers and mothers interviewed at the time
fathers were highly participant as they were in the responses of parents who were
interviewed after they had returned to a traditional lifestyle. Again, however, a
word of caution must be added about these findings. Data on attitudes and beliefs
were not collected before the fathers became highly participant, and so it may be
that, like other findings already noted, these beliefs and attitudes are not consequences, but causes of fathers' participation in child care.

Participation in Paid Work

If paternal participation in child rearing is to increase by any significant degree,
then a reduction in a fathers' participation in paid work, either in terms of time
spent, or in terms of psychological investment, will almost certainly be necessary. This is likely to present difficulties for some fathers for, as was pointed out
earlier, most fathers define their family role in terms of their paid work and the
status and income this brings to the family. Even so, there are pressures associated with breadwinning responsibilities, and it may be that some fathers would
also welcome a reduction in these pressures and responsibilities, and that a better
balance between time spent on paid work and family would be viewed as a positive change. Too often it is assumed that all fathers want and enjoy their jobs and
breadwinning status. Both of these responses from fathers—the difficulties and
relief experienced when they reduce their commitment to paid work—have been
reported in the literature.

Data presented by Pleck (1981) might lead us to expect that a change in relative commitments between family and paid work should be an easy transition.
Pleck's findings show that the majority of fathers already have a greater commitment to their family and derive more satisfaction from this than from their paid
work. It is an entirely different proposition, however, to actually reduce commitment to paid employment. Studies of the unemployed, together with research
into unemployed and employed care-giving fathers suggest that the complete loss
of work status, or the loss of status at work, and the increase in conflicts between
family and work, present difficulties for many fathers (Russell, 1982a).

Findings from the Australian study by Russell (1982a, 1982b) indicate that
fathers who were both unemployed and at home caring for children experience
difficulties in adjusting to their unemployed role and were subjected to criticisms
from their male peers because they were not employed. Moreover, 28% of the

fathers in this study reported, in response to an open-ended question, that the major disadvantage with their lifestyle was their loss of status associated with paid employment. Despite the difficulties experienced by many fathers with their reduction in commitment to paid work, a significant minority (approximately 10%) were highly satisfied. For these fathers the major advantage of their lifestyle was that they were relieved from career pressures and the strain associated with the breadwinner role.

In a study conducted in the U.S. of middle-class, primarily Caucasian fathers who were caregivers of their preschoolers, the major disadvantage reported by the men, although by a minority of the sample, was also job-related (Radin, 1982). However, here the disadvantage was seen as interference with success in the jobs that they held. (Only one man was unemployed and this was by choice.) For example, one father stated there was not enough time for career expansion; others referred to the difficulty in putting energy into professional work or in being competitive while caring for children. In contrast to the Australian fathers, none of the U.S. fathers expressed relief from career pressures as an advantage of the childcare arrangement. Additional support for the hypothesis that caring for children interferes with career advancement of middle-class fathers emerged in the Radin study when the disadvantages cited by the 19 fathers who cared for their preschoolers approximately 40% of the day (the moderately involved fathers) were compared with the disadvantages mentioned by the 20 fathers who were responsible for 57% of their children's care (the primary care-giving fathers.) In the former group, only 11% of the fathers felt their career was impeded; in the latter group the figure was 40%. Thus, men who maintain some level of employment while caring for children appear to experience different problems from those who are not employed at all.

The difficulties that emerge for men when work and family roles conflict have been amply detailed in the literature; most of the research, however, has been concerned with the ways in which the demands of work impinge on the family (Bailyn, 1978; Kanter, 1977; Pleck, 1981). Considerably less has been written about the difficulties that might arise when family commitments impinge on paid work. This is the issue that is more important for highly participant fathers. For example, problems are likely to arise if a father repeatedly leaves work early because of his responsibilities, e.g., to collect his children from school or take them to the doctor. Fathers' inability to meet extra demands placed on them in busy periods might also be a source of friction with other staff members. These conflicts, together with the reactions of employers who expect males to be totally committed to a company and to relationships with fellow workers, might also lead to a loss of status at work, and consequently hinder advancement. Indeed, Russell (1982a) reports that a group of fathers in his sample were particularly concerned that their reduction in commitment to work and concomitant loss in status meant they weren't promoted when they would normally have been expected to. And studies in both the U.S. (Radin, 1978, 1982) and Israel (Radin &

Sagi, 1982) of middle-class fathers of preschoolers found that amount of paternal involvement in child rearing was negatively related to the father's socioeconomic status, suggesting that job advancement may have been delayed for these caregiving men as well.

The difficulties and conflicts experienced by fathers who reduced their commitments to work, of course, resemble those experienced by mothers who are employed and still retain the major responsibility for children. Further consideration of this issue might therefore be better placed within the general context of the conflicts between family and work for parents regardless of gender. Unfortunately, none of the studies to date on highly participant fathers has systematically examined fathers' and mothers' satisfactions with their paid work roles. Future studies will need to include this variable, together with measures of satisfaction with the parental role, and assessments of the strategies used by these parents to resolve their work-family conflicts.

Summary

Increased paternal participation has been reported to have both positive and negative effects on fathers. Reports of positive effects have included: fathers feeling closer to and more sensitive towards their children; greater satisfaction and equality in husband-wife relationships; fathers expressing more satisfaction with their parental role and feeling more effective as parents; changes in fathers' attitudes and beliefs about child care and parental roles; and finally, a very small number of fathers reported that their associated reduction in commitment to paid work had a positive effect. On the negative side, increased conflicts and tensions were reported particularly with: parent-child and marital relationships; relationships with male peers; fathers' identities as males (a minor response); and relative commitments to family and paid work. There were also indications of costs in terms of job advancement and success for fathers with a major role in child rearing.

As was pointed out at the beginning of the section, however, data are limited and most have come from interview studies of fathers who either shared or had the primary responsibility for child care, and who had also reduced their commitments to paid work. Findings presented here, therefore, might not be expected to apply equally to the less radical increase in paternal participation within the context of the more traditional nuclear family. Moreover, none of the studies conducted to date has been designed to enable clear statements about cause and effect to be made. A longitudinal study would be needed to clarify the direction of causality, one that started before the men and women had children and continued throughout the childcare years. When such studies are performed, the findings reported here, rather than being consequences of increased paternal participation, may be shown to be causes of increased participation.

FACTORS THAT MAY INFLUENCE PATERNAL
PARTICIPATION

The present discussion of factors that may influence or constrain paternal participation is based on current knowledge about the antecedents of paternal participation. From the small amount of research that has been carried out, four areas
have emerged as being more obviously significant: beliefs held about parental
roles—both by individuals and those sanctioned by society; fathers' own experiences, and the socialization practices they have been subjected to; the experiences of mothers—several recent studies show that if we are to understand the
reasons why fathers do or don't participate in child rearing then we need to take
account of the experiences and attitudes/beliefs of mothers as well as fathers; and
finally, the amount of time fathers have available, and the constraints placed on
their time by paid work and career structures (Pleck, 1981; Radin, 1978; Russell,
1982a, 1982b; Sagi, 1982).

Beliefs about Parental Roles

When asked questions about their roles and responsibilities, fathers tend to emphasize their employment role, decision making within the family, their child's
career and education, and their involvement in play (Russell, 1982a). Furthermore, they are more likely to say their role is critical later in a child's life, and
that it is mothers who are especially important during the early years (Russell,
1979b). Much more critically, however, fathers in one study have been found to
be more likely to believe that these differences in roles are based on fundamental
differences between mothers and fathers (Russell, 1982a). Fathers, more than
mothers believe: There is a maternal instinct—that women are biologically pre-
disposed to parenting; fathers do not have the same capacity or ability to care for
children; and that it is better if children are cared for by their mothers (Russell,
1982a). Furthermore, the rejection of these beliefs by fathers has been found to
be associated with higher levels of paternal participation (Russell, 1981, 1982a).

   The way in which fathers define their roles, together with the beliefs that are
held and socially sanctioned, therefore, are likely to be critical factors in the
process of role adoption. A father who holds strong views that mothers have a
maternal instinct and that children need their mothers, for example, would most
likely be difficult to persuade that he take care of his 6-week-old child for an
entire day. Although it is clear from recent research that many fathers (and
mothers too) hold fairly rigid views about parental roles, research also indicates
that the evidence to support these stereotyped views is very scarce indeed.

   Clear support cannot be found for the belief that fathers do not have the same
sensitivity as mothers do, nor for the belief that fathers do not have the capacity
to assume the day-to-day responsibility for child care. On the contrary, studies
show that fathers can be just as sensitive and competent in care-giving as

mothers. In one group of studies, researchers have compared the psychological and physiological responses of mothers and fathers to infant smiles and cries (Frodi & Lamb, 1978; see also Berman, 1980). Findings show that when given this opportunity and encouragement, fathers are just as sensitive and responsive to infants as mothers are. In another group of studies (See Parke, 1979) mothers and fathers were observed interacting with their newborn babies in the first few days after birth. During this observational session, fathers were found to be just as involved with and nurturant towards their infants (e.g., in touching, looking at, kissing, talking to). Also, fathers were found to be just as competent at feeding. They were equally likely to be able to detect infant cues, e.g., sucking, burping, and coughing, and were just as successful, as measured by the amount of milk consumed by the infant.

Although the research has not been done, there seems little reason to expect that fathers would not display similar sensitivity and competence in day-to-day interactions with their children and in performing other childcare tasks. Some support is given to this by studies of highly participant fathers. In one study of families in which fathers were highly participant, mothers and fathers were asked whether they thought fathers had the ability to care for children. Not one of the mothers, and only 10% of the fathers in this sample replied in the negative (Russell, 1982a). Thus, although current beliefs that emphasize the importance of mothers might be seen as a constraining factor for increased paternal participation, particularly for participation in the day-to-day care of children, the research evidence does not support these beliefs.

Socialization and Experiences of Fathers

A father's socialization experiences and the models portrayed by his own parents are possible influencing factors for paternal participation in child rearing. Radin (1981) and Sagi (1982) have summarized possible predictions about paternal participation and the influences of parental models. One possibility is that fathers who adopt a nontraditional, highly participant role, will be more likely to have had fathers who were relatively unavailable, unloving, and powerless. Although there was some evidence for such a relationship in two other studies (De Frain, 1979; Eiduson & Alexander, 1978) the more recent findings of Radin (1981) do not support this hypothesis. The most important factor found in that study was that husbands and wives had both grown up in families in which mothers were employed. Additionally, Radin found a link between high paternal participation and the *mother's* relationship with her father. (The implications of this latter finding are discussed below.)

A second possibility is that the present highly participant fathers have modeled their own fathers who were also highly participant. Sagi (1982), using the same methodology as Radin but with an Israeli sample, has found support for this modeling hypothesis. Sagi reports high correlations between a father's report of his father's participation and his own participation on all six measures employed.

Before leaving these findings it should be pointed out that data about the family background in all of the studies mentioned above were obtained retrospectively, from the current generation of highly participant fathers. Perhaps other studies in which data are obtained from both generations of families might reveal entirely different patterns. Also, the studies listed here have not taken into account either: the reasons that a family pattern was adopted in which fathers were highly participant; or, which parent had more influence over the decision to change roles. The link between the present and the previous generation of men, for example, might be stronger when fathers rather than mothers have been more influential in the decision to change roles, and when the change has been a matter of choice rather than an economic necessity.

Other socialization variables that may influence paternal participation may be manifested in the psychological characteristics of fathers who are highly participant. Of the small number of relevant studies that have been reported, two variables have dominated: beliefs and attitudes towards sex roles (sex-role ideology), and the sex-role orientations of parents. Both groups of studies are based on the one general hypothesis: that it is the less stereotyped masculine father who is more likely to become involved in the very rigidly defined female role of child care. As a recent review by Pleck (1981) shows, data are generally consistent with this hypothesis, but the relationshp between sex-role attitudes and male involvement in family work is small in absolute terms.

Findings from studies that have attempted to link sex-role variables and paternal participation are by no means consistent. DeFrain (1979) has failed to find any differences between shared-role and traditional fathers; however, he did find that shared-role mothers described themselves in a less traditionally feminine way than traditional mothers. In contrast, Radin (1982) did not find any differences in mothers' sex-role self-descriptions as a function of paternal participation except within the group of mothers whose husbands were primary caregivers of their chidren, but she did find some differences in fathers' self-descriptions. Although fathers who were primary caregivers of preschoolers, performing approximately 57% of the childcare tasks, did not differ from traditional fathers who performed 22% of those activities, the intermediate group of men who performed 41% of childcare were more likely than traditional fathers to include traditionally feminine characteristics in their self-descriptions. Russell (1982a), in his Australian study, also reports a similar pattern of endorsement of traditional feminine characteristics by fathers who are highly participant. Nevertheless, in a more recent study of only traditional families (Russell, 1981), levels of paternal participation were found to be only very weakly related to fathers' endorsement of feminine characteristics, and in a study of highly participant Swedish fathers (Lamb et al., 1982), no relationship was found between sex-role scores and levels of participation. Similarly, in a study of middle-class preschool fathers, two-thirds of whom also appeared in the Radin study, shared care-giving men were not found to be more androgynous than the fathers in families where the mothers were the primary caregivers regardless of whether the women had careers or not (Carlson, 1980).

Thus, although the hypothesis that socialization into traditional male and female roles influences paternal participation seems an eminently reasonable one, the data to support it are equivocal. It may be, however, that the problem lies in the measuring instrument. The assumption being made in all of these studies is that a self-report inventory designed to measure traditional masculinity and femininity is a valid measure of a person's identification or incorporation of characteristics and behavior we have come to see as being most appropriate for one sex or the other. This might not be the case at all (Spence & Helmreich, 1980).

Rather than the degree of endorsement of traditional masculine and feminine personality characteristics being the most critical indicators of the relevance of male socialization, what fathers have been precluded from in their socialization might be more important. Possibilities include preclusion from performing nurturing roles in the early years (e.g., playing with dolls), during adolescence and early adulthood (e.g., it is rare for boys to care for young children), to the preclusion from the acquisition of skills around the time of having a child (e.g., it is rare for fathers to be encouraged by hospitals or other professional groups to learn basic childcare skills). An important differentiating variable for for fathers, therefore, could be the extent of their previous childcare experiences, and paternal participation therefore might be related to fathers': attendance at prenatal classes; attendance at the birth; being taught basic care-giving skills in the hospital immediately after the birth; and reading books or magazines on child care and child rearing. Recent studies lend some support to this recent-experience hypothesis.

Studies in both Australia and the U.K. have found a relationship between a father's attendance at birth and his later participation in child care (Russell, 1982a). Additionally, relationships have been found between father participation and whether or not fathers have read books on child care and have attended childbirth classes (Russell, 1981, 1982a). Moreover, all of these variables have been found to be associated with paternal participation in traditional families, and with the very high levels of participation in nontraditional families. All of these studies however, have been correlational in nature, and it could be, of course, that it is only the already highly committed father who attends the birth, participates in parent education classes, or reads books on child care. Nevertheless, the hypothesis that these experiences do have an effect on father participation, is given some support by the intervention study of Parke, Hymel, Power, & Tinsley (1979). These researchers provided new fathers in hospital with information about child development and demonstrated child care tasks to them, and found that this did have an effect on levels of reported father participation in the first three months of the child's life.

Socialization and Experiences of Mothers

The socialization and experience of mothers might also have an influence on the degree of paternal participation. When fathers are highly participant, the roles of mothers usually do not conform to traditional patterns either. Mothers in these families not only spend less time on child care, but, under most circumstances, they are employed outside the home too (Radin, 1982; Russell, 1982a; Sagi, 1982). It is possible, therefore, that mothers contribute as much as or more than fathers to the adoption of a nontraditional care-giving pattern. One study (Russell, 1982b) reports that, overall, mothers were more influential in the decision to adopt a lifestyle in which fathers are highly participant. Thirty-nine percent of families in that study agreed the mother had had more influence over the decision; 39% agreed it had been a joint decision; and in only 27% of families were fathers reported to be more influential.

Radin (1981; 1982) has examined the relationship between paternal participation and various aspects of the mothers' family experiences and has found support for such a relationship. Specifically, father participation was found to be higher: when mothers found their own father's participation gratifying and simultaneously experienced little of it; and when both husbands and wives had grown up in families in which the mother was employed. Thus, in contrast to the findings of Sagi, which were discussed earlier, Radin has found that the link with the mother's socialization experiences is stronger than it is with the father's.

There are additional factors related to mothers' experiences that may influence the degree of participation of fathers. Two recent studies, for example, show that paternal participation is higher when mothers' education levels are higher (Ericksen, Yancy, & Ericksen, 1979; Russell, 1981). One possible explanation for this finding is that more highly educated mothers are more likely to have read recent literature on child care and fathers, literature that has tended to place more emphasis both on fathers and on the absence of negative effects if children are cared for by people other than their mothers (Russell, 1982a). Ericksen et al. (1979), on the other hand, offers an explanation in terms of power relationships within the family. They argue that more highly educated mothers are more likely to have higher status and better earning capacities relative to their husbands, and therefore, they are in a better bargaining position with regard to the distribution of family work, work that is usually regarded as being of lower status relative to work outside the home. Alternatively, it may be that a mother being highly educated is more likely to be associated with a nontraditional sex-role socialization. These mothers, it could be argued, are also less likely to identify strongly with the maternal role, and less likely to feel threatened by fathers participating in their traditional domain.

Time Constraints and the Work/Employment Structure

One of the most obvious hypotheses is that the demands of a father's job place constraints on his available time, and therefore fathers who spend less time on paid work might be expected to be more involved in child care and play. Pleck (1981), in his recent review of U.S. studies, reports that the weight of evidence supports this hypothesis; there is a small, but nevertheless significant negative correlation between time spent in paid work and time spent in child care. Russell (1981), using measures of both time spent in paid work and the time a father is at home and available to his children, has also found support for the this hypothesis in an Australian sample. The time a father was at home and available for child care, rather than time spent on paid employment, however, was found to be the most critical variable. Furthermore, this relationship was much stronger for involvement in play than it was for involvement in childcare tasks such as feeding, dressing, and changing diapers. Thus it appears that the particular hours a father works is more predictive of paternal involvement in child rearing than the total number of hours. This conclusion is also supported by a study in the United States in which it was shown that men who were allowed to change the hours they worked, without reducing the total number, increased the time they spent with their children and spouses by 18% (Winett & Neale, 1978). Further, the men who were allowed to vary the time worked from day to day were significantly more involved in childcare tasks than other fathers who worked on flexitime jobs but were not allowed daily fluctuations.

Although time spent outside the home clearly influences paternal participation, data presented earlier show that it does not provide a *sufficient* explanation for levels of participation. Even so, time spent in paid employment is a critical factor that is central to any proposal for increased participation either within traditional families or nontraditional families. Possibilities for change, however, are also related to more general attitudes and social policies regarding work hours and career structures. These issues are discussed in detail in Chapter 7.

Summary

A multitude of factors appear to influence and constrain the degree to which a father participates in child care; e.g., fathers' and mothers' beliefs about parental roles; the degree of participation of fathers' and mothers' socialization experiences associated with sex roles and childcare skills; and the amount of time fathers are at home and available to their children. Research into the possible antecedents of paternal participation, however, is still very much in its infancy and questions of cause and effect are very much open to speculation.

One factor that has been overlooked in the above analysis and in most studies to date, but which might nevertheless be highly significant for paternal participation, is the family financial situation. Russell, in his Australian study, for example, found that nearly half of his families had adopted a lifestyle in which fathers were highly participant either because the father could not obtain employement and the mother could or because they felt both incomes were needed, and the best (and indeed sometimes, the only) solution to the "childcare problem" was for fathers to care for the children while the mother was at work (Russell, 1982a).

Thus, it is possible that changing economic and employment conditions could in fact facilitate increased paternal participation. This is a factor that is related to the more general structure of society and prevailing economic conditions, and again, is discussed in more detail in Chapter 7.

SUMMARY AND CONCLUSIONS

The present chapter has focused on three broad questions: What are the current levels of paternal participation? What are the likely effects on fathers themselves if they increase their levels of participation? And, what factors influence the degree to which fathers participate in child rearing?

Despite differences in samples and methods of data collection, a consistent pattern of paternal participation was evident across several different cultures. Relative to mothers' levels of participation in child rearing, fathers' were found to be much lower, and it is rare indeed for fathers to have significant responsibilities for the day-to-day care of their children. In contrast, several recent studies indicate that there is a small group of fathers who are highly participant in the day-to-day care of children. Furthermore, highly participant fathers were found in both traditional families, in which the father was employed and the mother wasn't, and in a nontraditional family form in which either childcare and employment roles were shared, or the mother had the responsibility for paid work and the father had the major responsibility for child care.

Studies of the likely effects of increased paternal participation on fathers themselves have been few in number and have focused mainly on families in which fathers shared or had the major responsibility or day-to-day child care. These studies revealed several possible positive consequences for fathers: closer and better relationships with their children and spouses; greater satisfaction with the parental role; and enhanced self-esteem. On the negative side, fathers who were highly participant also reported: problems in the initial stages of adjusting to their new role; increased tension and conflicts with children, spouse, and male peers; personal difficulties and conflicts with their identity as a male; tension generated by conflicts between the demands of work and family; and costs in terms of career advancement.

Thus, although it was a consistent finding that fathers who were highly participant felt they had gained considerably, especially in their relationships with their children, and that they were satisfied with their highly participant role, there were problems too. It is difficult to know at this early stage of the research just how much emphasis to place on the possible positive and negative consequences. Furthermore, there is considerable uncertainty about the status of many of the variables discussed, and whether of not they are effects or causes of paternal participation. If increased paternal participation is to be seriously considered, however, it is important that full discussion be given to both the possible positive and negative aspects.

The final question examined in this chapter was: What factors influence paternal participation? Paternal participation was found to be related to: fathers' and mother's beliefs about parental roles; mothers' and fathers' socialization experiences; fathers' knowledge and skills about child care; and the amount of time fathers are at home and available to their children. Again, however, it was difficult to decide which factors were antecedents and which were consequences of paternal participation. Further research is particularly needed to examine more systematically both the possible antecedents and possible consequences.

The emphasis in this chapter has been on fathers themselves. As was pointed out at the beginning, however, if we are to evaluate the full impact of increased paternal participation, then a broader perspective will need to be adopted. Moreover, the impact increased participation has on fathers might have important consequences for others. For example, increased participation might result in a change in fathers' self-esteem and his understanding of children and it might be these changes rather than simply increased participation that mediate observed changes in either mothers' marital satisfaction or child development outcomes. These are among the issues to be discussed in the next two chapters, which examine the possible consequences of increased paternal participation for mothers and children.

REFERENCES

Alwyn J. *Husband participation in childbirth*. Unpublished master's thesis, Australian National University, Canberra, 1977.

Bailyn, L. Accommodation of work to family. In R. Rapoport & R. N. Rapoport (Eds.), *Working couples*, St. Lucia, Queensland: University of Queensland Press, 1978.

Bem, S. L., & Lenney, E. Sex typing and the avoidance of cross-sex behavior. *Journal of Personality and Social Psychology*, 1976, *33*, 48–54.

Bem, S. L., Martyna, W., & Watson, C. Sex typing and androgyny: Further explorations of the expressive domain. *Journal of Personality and Social Psychology*, 1976, *34*, 1016–1023.

Berman, P. W. Are women more responsive than men to the young? A review of developmental and situational variables. *Psychological Bulletin*, 1980, *88*, 668–695.

Block, R. Personal communication, July 21, 1981.

Carlson, B. E. *Shared versus primarily maternal childrearing: Effects of dual careers on families with young children*. Unpublished doctoral dissertation, University of Michigan, 1980.

De Frain, J. Androgynous parents tell who they are and what they need. *The Family Co-ordinator*, 1979, *28*, 237–243.

Eiduson, B. T., & Alexander, J. W. The role of children in alternative family styes. *Journal of Social Issues*, 1978, *34*, 149–167.

Epstein, A., & Radin, N. Motivational components related to father behavior and cognitive functioning in preschoolers. *Child Development*, 1975, *46*, 831–839.

Ericksen, J. A., Yancey, W. L., & Ericksen, E. P. The division of family roles. *Jouranl of Marriage and the Family*, 1979, May, 301–313.

Field, T. Interaction behaviors of primary versus secondary caretaker fathers. *Developmental Psychology*, 1978, *14*, 183–184.

Frodi, A., & Lamb, M. E. Sex differences in responsiveness to infants: A developmental study of psychophysiological and behavioral responses. *Child Development*, 1978, *49*, 1182–1188.

Gronseth, E. Work sharing: A Norwegian example. In R. Rapoport & R. N. Rapoport, (Eds.), *Working couples*. St. Lucia, Queensland: University of Queensland Press, 1978.

Haire, D. *The cultural warping of childbirth*. Seattle, Washington: International Childbirth Education Association Supplies Center, 1975.

Harper, J. *Fathers at home*. Melbourne: Penguin, 1980.

Hood, J., & Golden, S. Beating time/making time: The impact of work scheduling on men's family roles. *The Family Co-ordinator*, 1979, *28*, 575–582.

Jackson, B. *Towards a sketch of the CHES father*. Unpublished paper. May, 1980.

Kanter, R. M. *Work and family in the United States: A critical review and agenda for research and policy*. New York: Russell Sage Foundation, 1977.

Kelley, S. *Changing parent-child relationships: An outcome of mother returning to college*. Unpublished paper, 1981.

Kotelchuck, M. The infant's relationship to the father: Experimental evidence. In M. E. Lamb (Ed.), *The role of the father in child development*. New York: Wiley, 1976.

Lamb, M. E. Interactions between 8-month-old children and their fathers and mothers. in M. E. Lamb (Ed.), *The role of the father in child development*. New York: Wiley, 1976.

Lamb, M. E. Fathers and child development. In M. E. Lamb (Ed.), *The role of the father in child development*. New York: Wiley, 1981.

Lamb, M. E., & Easterbrooks, M. A. Individual differences in parental sensitivity: Origins, components, and consequences. In M. E. Lamb & L. R. Sherrod (Eds.), *Infant social cognition: Empirical and theoretical considerations*. Hillsdale, N. J.: Lawrence Erlbaum Associates, 1981.

Lamb, M. E., Frodi, A. M., Hwang, P., Frodi, M., & Steinberg, J. Attitudes and behavior of traditional and nontraditional parents in Sweden. In R. Emde & R. Harmon (Eds.), *Attachment and affiliative systems: Neurobiological and psychobiological aspects*. New York: Plenum, 1982.

Lamb, M. E., Frodi, A. M. Hwang, C. P., Frodi, M., & Steinberg, J. Mother- and father-infant interaction involving play and holding in traditional and non-traditional Swedish families. *Developmental Psychology*, in 1982, *17*, xxx-xxx.

Lein, L. Male participation in home life: Impact of social supports and breadwinner responsibility on the allocation of tasks. *The Family Co-ordinator*, 1979, *29*, 489–496.

Levine, J. A. *Who will raise the children? New options for fathers (and mothers)*. New York: Bantam, 1976.

Newland, K. *Women, men and the division of labour*. Worldwatch Paper 37, May, 1980.

Newman, B. M., & Newman, P. R. *Infancy and childhood*. New York: John Wiley & Sons, 1978.

Parke, R. D. Perspectives on father-infant interaction, In J. D. Osofsky (Ed.), *The handbook of infant development*. New York: Wiley, 1979.

Parke, R. D., Hymel, S., Power, T. G., & Tinsley, B. R. Fathers and risk: A hospital based model of intervention. In. D. B. Sawin, R. C. Hawkins, L. O. Walker, & J. H. Penticuff (Eds.), *Psychosocial risks in infant-environment transactions*, 1979.

Pedersen, F. A., & Robson, K. S. Father participation in infancy. *American Journal of Orthopsychiatry*, 1969, *39*, 466–472.

Phillips, C. R., & Anzalone, J. T. *Fathering: Participation in labor and birth*. St. Louis: C. V. Mosby, Co., 1978.

Pleck, J. Husbands' paid work and family roles: Current research issues. In H. Z. Lopata (Ed.), *Research on the interweave of social roles: Women and men (Vol. 3)*. Greenwich, Conn.: JAI Press, 1981.

Pleck, J., & Rustad, M. *Husbands' and wives' time in family work and paid work in the 1975–76 study of time use*. Unpublished manuscript, 1980.

Pleck, J., & Sawyer, J. (Eds.) *Men and masculinity*. Englewood Cliffs, New Jersey: Prentice Hall/Spectrum, 1974.

Radin, N. *Childrearing fathers in intact families with preschoolers*. Paper presented to the American Psychological Association, Toronto, Canada, August, 1978. (ERIC Document Reproduction Service No. ED 194 850).

Radin, N. Childrearing fathers in intact families: An exploration of some antecedents and consequences. Merrill-Palmer Quarterly, 1981, 27, 489–514.

Radin, N. Primary caregiving and role-sharing fathers of preschoolers. In M. Lamb (Ed.). Nontraditional families: Parenting and child development. Hillsdale, N. J.: Lawrence Erlbaum Associates, 1982.

Radin, N., & Epstein, A. S. Observed paternal behavior with preschool children: Final report. Ann Arbor, Mich.: The University of Michigan, School of Social Work, 1975.

Radin, N. & Sagi, A. Childrearing fathers in intact families in Israel and the U.S.A. Merrill-Palmer Quarterly, 1982. 28, 111–136.

Rapoport, R., Rapoport, R., & Strelitz, Z. Fathers, mothers and others. St. Lucia, Queensland: University of Queensland Press, 1977.

Richards, M. Husbands becoming fathers. Unpublished paper, 1981.

Robinson, J. Changes in American's use of time, 1965–75. Cleveland, Ohio: Communications Research Center, Cleveland State University, 1977.

Russell, G. The father role and its relation to masculinity, femininity and androgyny. Child Development, 1978, 49, 1174–1181.

Russell, G. The roles of fathers in child development—An Australian perspective. Paper presented to the 15th National Conference of the Australian PreSchool Association. Sydney, 1979.(b)

Russell, G. A multivarate analysis of fathers' participation in child care and play. Unpublished paper, 1981.

Russell, G. The changing role of fathers. St. Lucia, Queensland: University of Queensland Press, 1982(a).

Russell, G. Shared-caregiving families: An Australian study. In M. E. Lamb (Ed.), Nontraditional Families: Parenting and Child Development. New Jersey: Lawrence Erlbaum Associates, 1982 (b).,

Sagi, A. Antecedents and consequences of various degrees of parental involvement in childrearing: The Israeli project. In M. E. Lamb (Ed.), Nontraditional families: Parenting and child development. New Jersey: Lawrence Erlbaum Associates, 1982.

Spence, J. T., & Helmreich, R. L. Androgyny vs. gender schema: A comment on Bem's Gender Schema theory. Unpublished paper, 1980.

Walker, K., & Woods, M. Time use: A measure of household production of family goods and services. Washington: American Home Economics Association, 1976.

Winett, R. A., & Neale, M. S. Family life and the world of work: A preliminary report of the effects of flexitime. Paper presented at the American Psychological Association Meeting, Toronto, August, 1978.

Yarrow, L. Fathers who deliver. Parents, 1981, 56, 62–66.

10 Increased Fathering: Effects on the Mother

Lois Wladis Hoffman
University of Michigan

In this chapter, we are asking a question about the future, namely: What is the effect on the mother's life of increased parenting by the father? There is a general agreement among the various scholars that at present the father's participation is not high, that truly shared parenting is still rare, and that the mother's employment may increase the father's role somewhat but not very substantially. To begin this inquiry, then, it is necessary first to establish that it is reasonable to assume that fathers will become more actively involved in parenting.

WILL PATERNAL PARTICIPATION INCREASE?

The expectation that fathers will become more actively involved is related to the observation that there is a general converging of sex roles. The specific prediction about increased fathering is based on:

1. Extrapolation from trends that show "increase in men's family role performance between the mid-1960s and 1970s [Pleck, 1981, p. 3]," and/or individual cases of fathers who have assumed major parenting roles or sought child custody.
2. Inferences drawn from the new ideology that emphasizes equality between the sexes and devalues traditional sex-role assignments.
3. The fact that mothers are predominantly and increasingly employed—a shift in the family division of labor that in turn imposes a pressure for a complementary shift in parenting functions. This last reason is probably the most significant of the three.

Extrapolation From Trends and Unusual Cases

The increase in men's involvements in family roles including parenting has been reported by Pleck (1981), who bases this on research conducted by Sanik (1979) and Nickols (1976). However, Robinson (1980) reports that the apparent increase in men's family work over the years disappears when demographic differences are controlled. Since all of these investigators are using comparable data—time-use data in which the respondent reports how he spends his time on given days—these inconsistencies are discouraging. But even if the trend were solidly and consistently documented, it is still not an adequate basis for predicting that fathers will assume a notable increase in parenting. It is difficult to know when minor shifts constitute the precursors of real trends (Hoffman, 1982). The decrease in family size in the thirties convinced demographers that family size would continue in that direction—until the upward shift in the fifties; that shift, in turn, was interpreted by many as a clear indication that family size would continue to grow (Blake, 1969)—until the trend turned downward again. Accurate prediction depends on understanding the dynamic factors involved, not simply extrapolating from the statistical pattern of the preceding years.

Similarly, future predictions cannot be made from the fact that there are a few families that have reversed tradition. Fathers who assume the major care-taking role and who have custody of their children after divorce are much studied and described in the media, but they are statistically rare. Nontraditional, powerful, and independent women have been described by Davis (1973) in 16th century France, but they did not signal the advent of feminism or sex-role equality.

Ideological Change

The documentation for diminished traditionalism in sex-role ideology in the last two decades is more robust than the documentation for an actual increase in the father's role. The replication of a national sample study after 20 years (Veroff, Douvan, & Kulka, 1981), a reinterview after 15 years of a national panel (Thornton & Freedman, 1980), as well as data reanalyzed from several sources (Mason, Czajka, & Arber, 1976) clearly document that Americans have changed in their endorsement of the traditional sex-role division of labor. These data have not focused specifically on the father's participation in parenting and household tasks. Instead, they have concentrated more on the woman's right to employment. They do provide some evidence, however, that Americans are more flexible about the family division of labor, and the participation of fathers in childcare and traditionally female household tasks is more acceptable now to a larger proportion of the population.

Furthermore, data indicate that not only has there been a relaxation of the rigidity of traditionalism with respect to husbands and wives' family roles but there has also been a relaxation of traditionalism in the task assignments of boys and girls (Duncan, Schuman, & Duncan, 1973). For predicting the future, this is particularly important, but here again, the data supporting change must be modified by the data supporting no change. For example, in their replication study of the household tasks children were expected to perform, Duncan, Schuman, and Duncan (1973) found both change and a continuation of traditionalism over an interval of 18 years. Most of the changes were modest: In the 1950s, 65% of the mothers said only boys should shovel snow; in the 1970s, 50% said this; in the fifties, 66% said only girls should dust, 62% in the seventies. Car washing and bed making, on the other hand, had changed more—dropping from tasks seen as sex specific by over half the mothers in the fifties (65% and 52%, respectively) to about 30% in the seventies. The vitality of traditionalism is further evidenced by a recent national sample study in which married couples were interviewed about their attitudes toward children (Hoffman, 1977a). In describing their goals for their children, family roles and interpersonal qualities were stressed more for daughters whereas occupational achievement goals were stressed more for sons. Asked why they might want to have children of each sex, one of the more frequent reasons for wanting a daughter was that she could help and learn about housework and childcare. This was not given as a reason for wanting sons.

The data from many different studies are consistent in demonstrating a movement from the rigid sex-role stereotyping of previous years toward more diffusion in family roles, but the movement is more modest than might be assumed. It is more pronounced in women than in men, among more rather than less educated respondents, in certain geographical areas more than others, and among the young. There is less solid evidence for a liberalizing of attitudes about what men should do in the family than there is for an acceptance of female employment (Veroff, Douvan, & Kulka, 1981; Hoffman, 1982; Mason, Czajka, & Arber, 1976).

Nevertheless, even this qualified shift is important. In the followng section it will be argued that the major basis for predicting an increase in the father's participation is the increase in women's employment rates. There are data to suggest, however, that when the mother is employed and the family ideology is traditional, a special effort may be made to keep the mother's employment from interfering with the traditional sex roles within the family (Hoffman, 1963b; Lein, 1979). Thus, an unfavorable ideology might block the force toward less traditionalism in childcare and household tasks that is exerted by maternal employment. Furthermore, the father's role in the family has been shown to be affected by ideology with maternal employment controlled as well as by maternal employment with ideology controlled (Hoffman, 1963b). And although it can be argued that the high maternal employment rates that now prevail are a response to economic and demographic factors (Nye, 1974b; Oppenheimer, 1973), they are also augmented by a favorable ideology.

Increased Maternal Employment

Although the greater participation of fathers in childcare and household tasks and the increased endorsement of a supportive ideology have been modestly demonstrated, the rising rate of maternal employment can be established unquestionably. Table 10.1 shows labor force participation rates of mothers between 1940 and 1980. There has been a steady increase at each reading.

If we consider just the families with husbands present, 57% of those with school-aged children only and 43% of those with preschool children have employed mothers. For these groups, maternal employment rates have increased even more rapidly than illustrated in Table 10.1. For example, the current employment rate for married mothers of preschoolers—43%—is more than double the 1960 rate of 19%. The most rapid rate of increase has been for married mothers with children under three, which now stands at 39%.

Not only have maternal employment rates been steadily rising over the years, but an analysis of the factors underlying this trend lead one to expect this pattern to continue. Increased maternal employment rates are largely a product of industrialization, technological advance, and long-range economic developments

TABLE 10.1
Labor Force Participation Rates of Mothers With Children
Under 18, 1940–1980

Year	% of Mothers
1980	56.6
1978	53.0
1976	48.8
1974	45.7
1972	42.9
1970	42.0
1968	39.4
1966	35.8
1964	34.5
1962	32.9
1960	30.4
1958	29.5
1956	27.5
1954	25.6
1952	23.8
1950	21.6
1948	20.2
1946	18.2
1940	8.6

Source: U.S. Department of Labor, 1977;
        U.S. Department of Commerce, 1979;
        U.S. Department of Labor, 1981.

(Hoffman, in press). Thus, although it is not impossible that swings in the business cycle could *temporarily* reverse the general upward trend, there is every reason to assume that high maternal employment rates are permanent and will in fact continue to increase, though perhaps at a decreasing rate in coming years.

Maternal employment will probably increase the participation of fathers in childcare and household tasks; there is a large volume of data supporting this hypothesis. One of the earliest demonstrations of this pattern was, in some respects, the most powerful. A study conducted in the 1950s compared the families of employed and nonemployed mothers by pair-matching. All families in the sample were intact, Caucasian, urban, and had at least one child in the third through sixth grades. Each employed mother family was matched to a nonemployed mother family with respect to the following variables: the number of children under 13, the age of the oldest child, the occupation of the father, and two different attitude scales—the attitude toward traditional family sex roles and the attitude toward male dominance. The participation of fathers in various activities was ascertained through questionnaires with mothers, fathers, and children, asking who in the household performed each of several specific tasks and the degree to which such participation occurred. The husbands of employed women were more active in household tasks generally, tasks usually performed by the mothers, and in childcare activities than the husbands of the nonemployed women. (Hoffman, 1963b).

Almost three decades of subsequent research have substantiated this pattern—namely, that in reasonably matched or homogeneous samples, fathers in dual-wage families are more involved in housework and childcare than fathers in single-wage families—not more than mothers, just more than the other fathers (Baruch & Barnett, 1981; Gold & Andres, 1978c; Hall & Schroeder, 1970; Hill & Stafford, 1978; Holmstrom, 1972; Pleck & Lang, 1978; Robinson, 1978). This effect is more pronounced when the mother's employment is full time (Hoffman, 1963b), when there is more than one child (Walker & Woods, 1976), and when there are no older children in the household, particularly no older daughters.

An apparent exception to this pattern of findings has been the data based on time-use studies in which respondents are asked to keep diaries of how they spend time on selected days. Until recently, time-use studies often reported no differences between employed and nonemployed mothers in the father's role (Pleck & Rustad, 1980). One of the reasons for this failure to find employed/nonemployed differences in the time-use data is that these data were often collected on heterongeneous samples and the researchers sometimes failed to control for such variables as family size and age of children. Since employed mothers are likely to have older children and fewer children, comparisons of the number of hours put into housework and childcare can be misleading. Newer time-use studies more consistently show the difference between families with employed versus nonemployed mothers. It has been suggested that this indicates a change in the father's responsiveness to his wife's total work-load (Lamb, 1981). This interpretation may be valid because as traditional sex-role ideology declines, one source of resistance diminishes. Thus fathers may actually be helping more when their wives are employed than they used to. Is is also possible, however, that this effect is more apparent because: (a) the new time-use studies are more sensitive to the variables of family size and age of child; and (b) now that the two-child family is so prevalent in the United States, the obscuring effect of a wide range in family size is diminished.

Even so, there are additional limitations to the general pattern of increased participation of fathers in response to maternal employment. One interesting point is raised by Pleck (1981): Possibly the fathers are not putting in more hours so much as mothers are putting in less; that is, the increase may be relative rather than absolute. Data indicate that it is not *only* a relative increase, however. Mothers who have entered and left the labor force have reported specific changes in their husbands' roles, noting that the husbands engage in more household tasks and childcare responsibilities during periods of the mother's employment (Hoffman, 1963a); and employed-mother families report with greater frequency than matched nonemployed-mother families that fathers engage in a variety of specific childcare activities and tasks conventionally designated as "women's work" (Baruch & Barnett, 1981; Gold & Andres, 1978c; Hoffman, 1963b). Nevertheless, it is an interesting point that some of the convergence in parental roles may result from the decrease in the mother's in-the-home activity. The increased efficiency of modern homemaking combined with smaller family size have resulted in a reduction of the *necessary* hours for housework and childcare (Hoffman, in press) and even fewer actual hours for both employed and nonemployed women (Pleck, 1981). It is noteworthy for the topic of this chapter that the widest discrepancy in total work loads—including home-based and job-based—is now between the nonemployed mother and all other parents; employed mothers have a total work load more like employed fathers (Pleck, 1981).

Another limitation to the general pattern of the father's increased within-family role that accompanies maternal employment is suggested by a provocative exploratory study by Pedersen and his colleagues (Pedersen, Cain, Zaslow, & Anderson, in press). This research is one of several recent efforts to explore the effects of maternal employment on families with infants. The interaction patterns between parents and 5–month–old infants were observed during the early evening hours to compare dual-wage families with single-wage families. The employed mothers had more verbal interaction with their infants and higher rates of social play than their husbands or either parent in the single-wage family. The dual-wage fathers, on the other hand, showed the lowest amount of infant interaction. The investigators suggest that when both parents return from work, the father helps by handling various household demands while the mother uses this time as a period of intense mother-child interaction. This is mother's special time when she compensates for her absence during the day. In the single-wage family, on the other hand, this period is the father's time with the baby and the mother turns to other activities. Thus, what may be operating here, if the pattern is confirmed in subsequent research, is that the father's help is directed toward household tasks rather than childcare because of the prevailing belief that mother-infant interaction is particularly important—another example of how the interaction between ideology and the mother's employment status affects the father's role.

The evidence, then, that fathers will become more active in childcare is not definitive, but there is enough of a case for this prediction to warrant speculation about the effects of this pattern. There is a modest trend in that direction, an increase in the supportive ideology, and an increase in maternal employment rates which exert a pressure toward the father's more active involvement in household tasks and parenting functions.

EFFECTS ON THE MOTHER

In this chapter, only the effects on the mother will be considered. This analysis will be speculative rather than empirical because relevant data are scant. Not only have there been few studies on this topic, but what has been done is limited by the fact that the data were gathered under different social conditions; the correlates of high father participation obtained when that pattern was unusual cannot be assumed to prevail when that pattern is the mode (Hoffman, 1982).

Stress of Work Overload Eased for Employed Mothers

Perhaps the most readily predicted effect of the father's increased parenting role is that it would ease the workload of the employed mother. There are several recent social changes that have combined to decrease generally the workload of the housewife-mother role. Family size norms in the United States have diminished; the two-child family has become the overwhelming preference. Since the sixties, families of four or more have become less common. Technological advances and modern food processing techniques have cut down considerably the amount of necessary housework. Nevertheless, most research indicates that the combined roles of housewife, mother, and employee are more than a fulltime job, and there is little leeway for emergencies (such as, the illness of the child, mother, or babysitter) or special occasions (such as a no-school holiday). Childcare arrangements are frequently a problem—particularly for the preschooler but also for the school-aged child when employment hours and school hours do not overlap. Thus, although data indicate that the employed mother generally has higher morale than the fulltime homemaker-mother (Gold & Andres, 1978a; 1978b; Kessler & McRae, 1981), there is often stress from work overload, anxiety about adequate childcare and supervision, and a shortage of time for rest and leisure.

Since maternal employment is already the modal pattern in the United States and seems likely to be even more prevalent in the future, one clear advantage of the more active father will be alleviation of the overload and stress that befalls the employed mother. Although their husbands help more than the husbands of nonemployed mothers, the major burden and responsibility for childcare and household tasks have been the mother's. She carries out more of the regular routines; she is responsible for the childcare arrangements; she handles and readjusts her schedule when unexpected problems come up. The increased role of the father, then, would mean the mother's task would be lessened, the responsibilities and anxieties would diminish, and there would be more time for leisure.

Furthermore, diminished stress might be expected not only directly because the mother's workload would be lightened and her responsibilities shared but also indirectly through the effects on the child. One source of anxiety for employed mothers is concern about how well their children are faring. If the child will benefit from the father's more active parenting, stress on the mother may be expected to lessen when the father's participation increases. The effect of the father's role on the child is discussed more fully in Chapter 11. Particularly relevant here, however, is the effect on the child of high father participation when the mother is employed. Although the evidence is sparse, some data suggest that the father's involvement may be particularly valuable for the sons of employed mothers. This hypothesis has been most fully explored by Gold and her colleagues (1978a; 1978b; 1978c; 1979). Research has sometimes indicated that the middle-class sons of employed mothers, compared to middle-class sons of nonemployed mothers, show lower cognitive performance. Gold and her colleagues have explored the hypothesis that this effect can be ameliorated by greater paternal involvement. In a study of middle-class Canadian 4–year–olds, they found that the sons of employed women in an English-speaking sample had lower Stanford Binet IQ scores than the sons of the fulltime homemakers (Gold & Andres, 1978c). This was their only negative finding for the maternal employment group. This difference was not found, however, with their French-speaking sample (Gold, Andres, & Glorieux, 1979). The authors suggest that the difference is explained by the greater involvement of fathers among the French-speaking Canadians. This interpretation was supported by data that indicated that French-Canadian fathers were more active in parenting, but no direct relationship was found between father involvement and IQ in either group. In two additional studies, however, one with 10–year–olds and one with adolescents, father involvement was found to be positively related to several cognitive indices— particularly when the mother was employed (Gold & Andres, 1978a; 1978b). Thus, there is some evidence that father involvement has a positive effect on the son's academic performance when the mother is employed, and this is otherwise the one manifestation of a negative effect of maternal employment. Thus it is reasonable to suggest that higher father involvement might also alleviate anxiety for the employed mother because of the positive or ameliorative effects on the child. Data from a recent national sample study indicate that the advantages of employment for the mother's mental health are particularly enhanced when the husband shares childcare, and that childcare help is more important in this respect than help with housework (Kessler & McRae, 1981).

It has also been noted that positive effects of maternal employment on the child can be blocked if the situation involves particular strain, as when a childcare arrangements are inadequate or when there are six or more children (Woods, 1972; Cherry & Eaton, 1977). Here again the father's involvement can ease the mother's situation directly by lessening the pressure and indirectly through the positive effects on the child.

There is one other important advantage that would be gained by employed mothers through a more equal splitting of the tasks and responsibilities of parenting. The particular occupations that women have chosen and their subsequent career patterns have been enormously shaped by the assymetry in parental responsibilities. Greater parental involvement would make possible increased occupational commitment and thus enable them to appreciate more the benefits of employment. The occupational pursuits of women have shown two patterns:

1. Because the responsibilities of motherhood are particularly heavy when there are preschool children, the typical career pattern for women has involved a withdrawal from the labor force during this period and a resumption as the children become older.
2. Because mothers have primary responsibility for the child's daily care, jobs that offer schedules consistent with school hours, with summer months free, have been preferred.

It has been suggested that the sex-labeling of occupations reflects their fit to these patterns and also that the salaries associated with jobs reflect their sex-labeling (Oppenheimer, 1975; Rossi, 1965).

Periodic withdrawal from the labor force has been a handicap for women in a number of additional ways: Some employees are hesitant to hire them because of this pattern; seniority rights are lost; skills, special training, and education can become rusty and obsolete. Thus, across social class, this pattern has limited the range of occupational choice for women, often keeping them from the more challenging and higher status occupations and slowing their pace of advancement within other occupations.

The need to find jobs that fit their children's schedules has similarly limited women's occupational choice. Teaching is one of the few professions that fits and its popularity with women is related to this fact. In many cases, women have settled for parttime work, which is often difficult to find, underpaid, and devoid of employee benefits such as paid vacations, seniority, and insurance advantages. In addition, women's jobs are often chosen for extrinsic reasons that also reflect childcare responsibilities such as the distance from home or the child's school.

If the father shared the parenting role equally, it is quite likely that neither parent would be *forced* to withdraw from the labor force or take only jobs that fit the child's schedule, particularly in light of other facilitating social changes such as the now prevailing two-child family. And either parent might *choose* this route. Thus, women would be freer to choose their occupations and to give a fuller commitment to their work; the sex stereotyping of occupations would diminish; and women could reap more of the rewards of employment—material and psychological.

In summary then, if the focus is only on the father's more active parenting as a sharing of tasks and an easing of work overload, the effects can be seen as positive for the employed mother. She is under less strain and a source of her anxiety is diminished. Increased personal and leisure time would become available. Furthermore, women would be able to plan and pursue careers more freely without the restrictions they have experienced because of their having the primary responsibility for childcare. New job opportunities would become available and the job structure in the United States might itself shift.

Nonemployed Mothers

The situation for the nonemployed mother would appear to be quite different. The diminution in required homemaking time brought about by technological development, food processing advances, and smaller family size has changed the role of the fulltime housewife-mother. Recent time-use studies (Pleck, 1981) indicate that this role now involves relatively little work time. Furthermore, because so many women are employed, the current fulltime mother may feel defensive. Even creative, quality homemaking that is nonessential may not seem a valuable contribution when the woman knows that her time represents potential wages for the family. Thus, studies suggest that, particularly when the children are of school age, the nonemployed mother may feel a need to amplify her maternal role. She may feel threatened by the child's growing independence that signals the diminishment of the role that has been her major source of self-esteem (Hoffman, 1979). The modern nonemployed mother of two school-aged children is not likely to be suffering from work overload but rather from anxiety about how valuable her contribution to the family really is. For her, the greater participation of the father in parenting might exacerbate her anxiety insofar as it further undermines her feeling that she is a contributing member of the family who provides a unique service.

Time Spent Together

The father's increased participation in parenting would probably affect the amount of time he spends with his wife, but it could increase or decrease it. The new fathering style might mean that the father is with the family more than previously and also that he and his wife jointly participate in more activities. On the other hand, it could involve instead the two parents taking turns, and in that case less time might be spent together. Although it might seem that splitting equally the tasks of family life—economic functions, household tasks, and childrearing—should mean more time for shared *leisure,* this depends on whether these activities are carried out at the same or different times. It is possible that neither the leisure hours nor the parenting and work functions overlap. In research by Lein and her associates (1974) it was found that some dual-wage couples worked split shifts so that one parent would always be home with the chlidren. This pattern solved the problem of childcare, but it so diminished the husband-wife interaction that it was a strain on the marital relationship.

Similarly, the quality of the time the couple spends together could be affected in either direction. One might assume that the greater similarilty of roles would increase commonality, but it could also increase the spheres of potential conflict. This will be considered more fully in the following section where the similarlity of the parental roles is the focus.

Convergence of Roles

Sex Differences Diminished.   The increased participation of fathers implies a merging of parental functions. If fathers increase their participation in parenting and household tasks as women have already increased their participation in breadwinner functions, the traditional sex-based division of labor would be eroded. The ramifications of this shift might have far-ranging implications for childrearing patterns and personality development. It has been suggested elsewhere, for example, that sex differences in childrearing patterns reflect, in part, the expectation that boys will be as adults primarily involved in occupational pursuits, whereas girls will be involved in mothering. As the adult sex roles merge, the sex-based socialization differences should also diminish. Girls might be given more opportunities for independent exploration, less encouragement of dependency on others for coping, more push in academic-occupational pursuits. Boys might be given more encouragement in expressing tenderness and less push toward independence (Hoffman, 1977a). In turn, sex differences in personality would be expected to diminish since these are seen as reflecting sex-linked differences in socialization patterns.

There are also many psychological theories that hold that various facets of human personality are attributable to the fact that the early caretaker is a woman—for example, the theories of Dinnerstein (1976), Chodorow (1978), Hoffman (1972), Lynn (1969), and, of, course Freud and other psychoanalytically oriented writers. Thus, if the father's chldrearing role were equal to the mother's in infancy and early childhood, Dinnerstein and Chodorow would predict fewer conflicts in relationships between adult men and women; Hoffman and Lynn would predict new patterns of achievement and cognitive functioning; and psychoanalytic writers might expect shifts in patterns of moral internalization, identification, hostility, and love.

If the father's increased role involves a merging of parental functions and a diminishment of the sex-based division of labor then, one long-range effect on mothers is that they will be different in personality and outlook from present-day mothers because their own early childhood experiences will have diverged in ways that are significant in the socialization process. Furthermore, their husbands will be different also. As these changes develop, some of the more short-run effects of the father's new role may be altered.

Personality and attitudes may be affected also through adult experiences and a more immediate effect of this role change may come about because each parent will have a wider variety of experiences. Changes as a result of new roles have been empirically demonstrated—as a result of parenthood by Michaels (1981), Rosenthal and Keshet (1978), and Feldman and Nash (1978), and as a result of occupations by Kohn (1963), Hughes (1958), Steinmetz (1974), Gerstl (1961) and others. From these studies, it seems reasonable to predict that the experience of caring for children will foster greater nurturance in men, and the freeing of restrictions in occupational roles for women may bring about a more intense work commitment. Furthermore, the increased prevalence of like roles means also that specialization based on interests and talents rather than the ascribed status of sex could more easily occur. There would be more opportunity to examine a variety of activities and less social pressure against reversing tradition.

Increased Commonality of Interests. The convergence of parental roles, then, might be expected to diminish sex differences because the experiences of early childhood will become similar across sex and also because there will be fewer adult experiences that reinforce these differences. In addition, role similarlity may lead to more commonality of interests between spouses. In research on marital satisfaction, one pattern that has been described is a "growing apart" because of separation of functions (Dizard, 1968). Marital relationships have often been seen as moving from an early stage of companionship to one in which the husband becomes more involved in work, the wife in the home and children. Indeed, some researchers view the advent of children as dysfunctional for marriage because it moves the husband and wife into different spheres and, as a consequence, their interests and outlooks, their recreational preferences, and even their priorities for the family budget, diverge (Campbell, Converse, & Rodgers, 1976; Dyer, 1963; Hoffman & Manis, 1978; Rollins & Cannon, 1974; Spanier, Lewis, & Cole, 1975). Furthermore, although most respondents in a national sample study of married couples (Hoffman & Manis, 1978) thought that children brought couples closer together rather than further apart, a reason commonly cited for the latter view was that the wife became so absorbed in mothering that she no longer functioned adequately as a wife. This was mentioned most often by couples in the early stage of parenthood. This schism might be avoided if both parents were equally active in the parent role.

A convergence of roles would also mean that the stages of the life cycle would be more similar: Career involvements and parenting involvements would wax and wane at the same pace. For example, a particular pattern that often occurs at present, particularly in the middle class, is that women in their forties are in a relatively early stage in their career involvements, having been delayed by earlier childcare responsibilities, while men at that age are more established and even bored (Bardwick, 1974; Rubin, 1979). Retirement plans are sometimes complicated because women may be at the height of their career involvement when the man is psychologically nearer to the end. Whether or not a closer match in the life cycle represents a net gain, however, is complicated, for there may be some advantages of asymmetry.

Increased Conflict. As already stated, however, the greater similarity of roles could also lead to more conflict between couples. The advantages of the traditional sex-based division of labor in the family have been noted by Parsons (1955) and there is still some validity to this view. Complementarity of functions provides a tie of interdependence. Separation of spheres diminishes competition between spouses. It also cuts down the amount of negotiation that is necessary in carrying out family and household routines.

The pattern at present is a compromise between the traditional sex-based division of labor and the equal participation of husband and wife in occupational, parental, and housekeeping pursuits. Both parents are employed, but the husband's occupation is typically viewed as the more important (Garland, 1972; Hoffman, 1977b; Komorovsky, 1973; Rapoport & Rapoport, 1971), and the wife is the chief parent. Although there are many problems with this arrangement, as already mentioned in this chapter and others in this volume, it nevertheless has certain advantages. The wife may be less free to pursue occupational interests fully and she may be under stress because of the dual role, but she does have more control over the household and parenting role. The wife's autonomy in these areas is relinquished as the father increases his involvement; as responsibilities become shared, so does authority (Bahr, 1974).

This shift does not merely mean a loss of control in these spheres for the mother, it also means that there is a sizable increase in the number of activities and decisions that have to be negotiated. Trivial decisions about household routines, cooking procedures, and childrearing have to be worked out by two when two are carrying them out. It has always been difficult for couples to work through common operating procedures for joint domains because each has come from a different family where such patterns as spending priorities, for example, may have been different. The father's greater involvement means the number of such joint domains is increased. There are more opportunities for conflict.

Satisfactions of Motherhood Diminished.   For the woman then, shared parenting might mean a loss of autonomy and an increase in conflict. In addition, it may also mean the loss of a source of feeling competent, even indispensable, and the diminishment of a valued emotional tie. At the present time, motherhood is a very salient part of a woman's sense of self and an enormous source of gratification. In two recent national sample studies, parenthood far outstripped the job or any other role as a source of personal satisfaction for women (Hoffman & Manis, 1978; Veroff, Douvan, & Kulka, 1981). Among employed women, for example, 96% said that being a parent was a great deal of satisfaction, whereas fewer than half indicated such satisfaction from their jobs (Hoffman, 1982). Although men also ranked parenthood somewhat higher than the job, the pattern was less pronounced. Asked what they would like to overhear someone saying about them, the modal response for women was that they would like to overhear that they were "a good mother" (Veroff, Douvan, & Kulka, 1981). The data from these studies clearly indicate that, despite the stress and complaints, motherhood is a very major source of satisfaction and self-definition for women. The pattern was particularly marked for less educated women; motherhood came through strongly as their major gratification (Hoffman & Manis, 1978).

Would this satisfaction be diminished if fathers became more actively involved in parenting? Would mothers lose a sense of expertise? If the father also does what now only the mother does, would she lose a sense of special importance, of being an indispensable member of the family? Would mothers feel a loss because of the diminished intensity of the mother-child relationship? Is there a special pleasure from being the MOTHER in the family, in charge of the children, in charge of love, the major force shaping the children's lives? Some of the satisfactions of motherhood may come from its unique status in the family, from the fact that the role of mother conveys a treasured monopoly.

But how would the other changes accompanying increased father participation affect this pattern? Elsewhere we have suggested that some of the satisfactions from parenthood stems from the fact that there are no alternative sources of satisfaction for various needs (Hoffman, 1977a). If the increased fathering led to new sources of satisfaction, would the particular salience of motherhood for women be diminished? The answer to these questions would no doubt be different for different individuals and for different segments of society. For example, employment provides satisfaction for women in all social classes (Ferree, 1976;

Hoffman, 1979; Walshok, 1978), but the opportunity for a fuller commitment to work provided by the father's greater role in childcare would not yield the same increment of satisfaction to the less educated woman as to the more educated. On the other hand, if the father's involvement increased the areas of commonality between the spouses, the less educated women would have a great deal to gain (Hoffman & Hoffman, 1973; Hoffman & Manis, 1979; Rainwater, 1965).

Nevertheless, part of the satisfaction of mothering comes from the fact that it is one of the few jobs available which offers autonomy, authority, and a feeling of being irreplaceable. Many mothers feel that only they can provide the particular comfort, training, and satisfactions that their children need, and their families, as well as much of society, concur. Research points to the fact that mothers wish their husbands would help more (Lein, 1979; Veroff, Douvan & Kulka, 1981), but whether equal sharing of the role is desired is another question. Furthermore, as discussed above, family size has diminished and technological advances are continually streamlining household operations. Thus the gain of splitting the task equally may not be worth the price.

Power. Is it possible that although the more equal sharing of the parental role might diminish the mother's autonomy in childcare and other traditionally female household activities, it might increase her power in other areas of family life? Research on power relationships in the family suggests that economic decisions, often seen as the major decisions in the family, are affected by the economic contributions of the members. Thus if the shared role enabled her to increase her occupational commitment and her economic contribution, her power in these areas might increase. For example, a great deal of work has been done exploring how maternal employment affects the power relationship between the husband and wife. A crude summary of the prevailing view is that employed mothers have more power than nonemployed with respect to major family decisions, particularly economic decisions, and less with respect to household routines. This effect is modified by social class and ideology, and the results of individual studies differ somewhat, but several reviews draw this conclusion from the prevailing research (Bahr, 1974; Blood, 1963).

These studies do not investigate whether the degree of employment is important—whether the relationship is a linear one. It may be that the sheer fact of being employed is enough to have an effect, and the degree of occupational commitment makes no difference. If that is true, the increased participation of the father in childcare and housework would have no power advantage for the employed mother even if it did increase her occupational commitment. Thus, although these data support the theory that, when one parent becomes active in the area previously assigned to the other, there are corresponding shifts in decision making, they do not clearly indicate that an overall increase in power will result for women.

Nevertheless, this is a reasonable hypothesis. To the extent that the power differential between men and women is affected by function differences, the convergence of roles should diminish gender-based power differences. Just as women might be expected to lose control over household routines and childcare as men become involved in these activities, so they might be expected to gain in major decision making through their greater economic role. Furthermore, economic independence makes divorce less frightening for women. There is some evidence that the woman's perception of economic dependence on her husband leads her to tolerate an otherwise unacceptable marriage and a position of subordination (Sawhill, Peabody, Jones, & Caldwell, 1975).

Divorce

Any inventory of the changes that mark the emerging family form includes, along with increased maternal employment and decreased family size, the increased instability of marriage. It is important, then, to consider how an increase in the father's parenting role might relate to divorce. First, would it increase or decrease divorce rates, and, second, would it affect the consequences of divorce for women?

Divorce Rates.   As already indicated, to the extent that the father's increased parenting role resulted in the mother's greater occupational commitment, divorce would be easier for women. Divorce rates are higher for employed women, and data seem to indicate that this is not because employment diminishes marital satisfaction but rather that it facilitates divorce if the marriage is not satisfying (Sawhill, 1975; Nye, 1974a). In fact, employment is sometimes a planned route to obtaining a divorce (Sawhill, 1975).

In a similar vein, it might be argued that sex-role convergence means that a man is also less dependent on his wife, for he also would have the domestic skills now typically attributed to women. There is no evidence, however, that this particular symbiosis has been a deterrent to divorce. Accurate or not, it is widely believed that domestic skills are either unimportant or easily acquired.

Yet the assumption of diminished interdependence if roles were similar rather than complementary may not be accurate in the light of new socioeconomic conditions. American family life is becoming increasingly dependent on two incomes. In the lower socioeconomic class, it is frequently the second income that lifts the family from the poverty level (Cherry & Eaton, 1977; U.S Department of Labor, 1977). In the middle class, the second income is also seen as essential in maintaining an acceptable standard of living. Thus duplication of functions does not necessarily mean independence of functions. In a family where the economic level is maintained by two equal or nearly equal wages, establishing separate living quarters and splitting the family income may be an economic hardship for both partners. It may be less of an economic hardship for women than at present because women's earnings would be greater; but, for this same reason, it would be more of an economic hardship for men—their family income would be halved. For both the man and the woman, shifting to one income is a loss when one has become acclimated to living on two; for both, the dual-wage family involves economic interdependence. It seems likely, then, that the increased paternal role, with its presumed concomitant increased occupational role for women, would lead to greater equality with respect to the economic deterrents to divorce, but whether the new ratio would yield a higher or a lower total is unclear.

A major noneconomic deterrent to divorce has been the children, and here again a complex shift might be expected, with the final balance uncertain. From the father's standpoint, if increased fathering were to lead to a stronger attachment between the father and the children, as might be expected, the price of no longer living in the same house with them would be a very high one. On the other hand, increased fathering would also have implications for custody decisions and the father's chances for major custody[1] would be improved. From the mother's standpoint, increased fathering would mean that divorce entailed the loss of a partner in childcare. It would also mean that she would not necessarily have major custody of the children nor would she be socially expected to demand it. For some women, this would represent a lost privilege; for others, a gained freedom.

Thus, both economic and noneconomic deterrents to divorce would probably shift in response to increased involvement of the father in parenting, but no conclusion can be drawn as to whether the net result would tend to increase or decrease the divorce rate. If we look to the other side of the divorce rate, marital satisfaction, it is obvious from the discussion earlier that a very similar observation can be made—there will be change but the direction of the change is unclear. If fathers and mothers shared parenting and household functions more equally, many dimensions of the marital interaction would be affected. As already indicated, many aspects of personality would be changed and sex differences would be diminished. Chodorow (1978) and Dinnerstein (1976) would probably predict increased marital adjustment at least in subsequent generations, for both of these theorists see much of the conflict between men and women as stemming from the fact that the early nurturer is a woman. There would probably be more commonality of interests between the husband and wife, and their life stages would progress in a more parallel fashion, but they might also have more conflict as they increased the number of shared decisions and the potential competition. They might or might not spend more time together, depending on whether they took turns or acted jointly.

Because there is no single effect of increased fathering, predictions about marital adjustment per se are very difficult. Deterrents to divorce would be more

---

[1]Even in shared custody, it seems likely that the child would reside most of the time with one parent. In this chapter the term "major custody" is used to describe this inbalance: the parent with whom the child resides is said to have "major custody."

equalized between men and women, but the final balance cannot be predicted. The most that can be done about predicting divorce rates is to indicate, as we have, some of the relevant dimensions, for, in addition to everything else, the causes of divorce are complex, varied, and little understood. Furthermore, it is even possible that the occurrence of divorce is affected as much by the norms about divorce as by the dynamics of the marital relationship, and its increasing acceptability may assure an increased divorce rate quite apart from the family dynamics discussed here.

Divorce effects.   Turning now from the likelihood of divorce to its effects, it can be noted again that equality between the spouses is the safest prediction. If the father's parenting role were equal to the mother's, the effects of divorce on each would be closer to equal, or at least any inequality would not be based on gender. In theory, at least, each should have an equal right to custody; each should have an equal ability to rear the child alone, or by some joint arrangement, except in so far as individual, non-sex-based differences were involved. At present, remarriage opportunities are greater for men, and it is difficult to know if this would shift. What would not shift, however, is the longevity of fertility: Reproductive functions deteriorate in women at a younger age than in men. Thus the opportunity for women to form new families is more limited by biology.

Again, however, equality involves both gain and loss for women. The woman alone would be better able economically to handle single parenthood than she is at present. Furthermore, the closer attachment between the father and children might mean his help—both economic and noneconomic—would be more assured. On the other hand, bitter custody battles would be more frequent if each parent must prove him- or herself the more worthy, without any presumed advantage for motherhood. And mothers, like fathers, would be expected to contribute to the child's economic support even if they did not have custody. There would be some economic hardship for each since maintaining two households is more costly than maintaining one (Espanshade, 1979). The parent who obtains major custody would lose an *active* helper, and the parent who loses custody would, as now, lose the particular closeness of shared residence but gain some freedom.

Would the effect of the divorce be more or less severe for the child if parenting were equal? This is important to consider even though the focus here is only on the effects for the mother, because part of the problem of coping with divorce has to do with the child's response (Hetherington, 1979; Hetherington, Cox, & Cox, 1978). In Hetherington's study of divorce between parents of 4–year–old children, one of the important variables for the child was the extent to which routines were disrupted. The greater likelihood that the mother would be employed since the child's birth would be beneficial in this respect because Hetherington's results indicated that employment helped the mother cope with divorce—socially and economically—and, if it preceded the divorce, its effects were salutary. If, on the other hand, a previously nonemployed mother started employment at the time of the divorce—a common pattern—effects were negative because of the additional disruption in the child's routines. These data suggest that increased father involvement might minimize disruption for the child through its effects on women's career patterns, i.e., the increased likelihood of continual employment.

In the Hetherington research, however, families followed the currently typical pattern in which the child remains with the mother who is the primary caretaker. If parenting were shared, the separation of parents would involve for the child the loss of half his caretakers. Even though the absent parent remained very involved in the child's welfare, the shift might be considerable for the young child. For the older child, however, the greater involvement that shared parenting should produce could provide considerable compensation even though the parent were absent from the house.

If one looks to the studies of father-absent families (which have unfortunately often lumped together widows, divorcees, and unmarried mothers), one cannot but be impressed with the advantage that would accrue to the child from the mother's greater earning power that would likely result from the shared-parenting situation. In several reviews of these studies, particularly the one by Herzog and Sudia (1973), many of the apparent negative effects of rearing children in fatherless families seem to be primarily the result of the economic deprivation that at present accompanies father absence. If shared parenting improves the financial situation as it might because of the mother's own improved occupational status, as discussed earlier, and because of the father's continued financial and nonfinancial help, both the child and the mother should fare better than under the present circumstances.

On balance then, shared parenting would probably make divorce easier for mothers. Particularly important here is the greater opportunity for occupational commitment by mothers. Their wage-earning ability would be higher and their employment would be part of the family pattern, not just an emergency measure because of the divorce and an additional disruption for the child. Further, assuming that the father's more active involvement in parenting would increase his attachment, his continued support in childrearing as well as economics would be more likely. The loss for the mother would be that she would not be as assured of obtaining the major custody, but a gain would be that she would not be as socially pressured to seek it.

SUMMARY AND CONCLUSIONS

In this chapter we have considered what the effects of increased participation by fathers in childrearing and household tasks would be for mothers. Although the evidence is far from definitive, there are indications that this change in the father's role is a real possibility. Should it occur, however, it would be part of a complex of changes. In anticipating the effects, therefore, it is important to keep in mind that other aspects of the social situation will also be different.[2] Thus, it has been noted here that even the personalities of men and women will be different. As sex roles converge, sex differences in childrearing patterns will tend to diminish, thereby affecting the adult personalities of future generations. The enactment of new roles as adults, parenting roles and occupational roles in particular, may also bring about adult personality change. Thus, it is with considerable caution that the dynamics of this change must be analyzed.

In those instances where the mother is employed, increased participation in childcare by the father would lessen the stress on mothers—both directly, by reducing her workload at home, and indirectly, through beneficial effects accruing to the child. For the nonemployed mother, however, increased father participation might serve to undermine her position. Individual families might work out a pattern where one parent, mother or father, handled the major childcare functions while the other was the major breadwinner, but the equal sharing of childcare would make it psychologically very difficult for one parent to remain unemployed.

On the other hand, shared parenthood would make possible occupational equality and much of the impact of increased parental involvement would be mediated by this particular effect. Thus, for example, predictions regarding the wife's influence in major family decisions, and predictions about the aftermath of divorce, were based largely on the anticipated increased economic power of women resulting from shared childrearing.

Other more direct effects were also discussed. Converging parental roles would probably create more commonality of interests between spouses, though it would also increase the possible areas for conflict. It is easier to leave the trivial decisions to another when one is not oneself an active participant. Thus there would be more negotiation between spouses in the routine childrearing and household activities; women would lose much of the autonomy they now enjoy in these areas. They would also lose the opportunity to feel that they made a unique contribution to the family, and the impact of the emotional tie with the child, with its gratifying and oppressive qualities, would be diminished. As was pointed out, these effects would vary among individuals and according to social class.

Women, and men too, may be expected to benefit from an increased opportunity to work out a lifestyle based on individual preferences rather than on gender. The establishment of greater equality between the sexes, an outcome noted at several points in this chapter, is particularly likely to benefit women because they

---

[2]The very interesting work of Clarke-Stewart (1978) and others, which examines, by means of behavioral observations, the effects of the father's presence on the mother's interaction with the child, is not considered in this chapter because these effects might be quite different in a family where the father shared childrearing responsibilities more equally with the mother.

now have less status and power than men. And yet, there may be losses too, because the opportunity to assume the major parenting role offers satisfactions that may be difficult to replace.

ACKNOWLEDGMENT

The author wishes to thank Herbert Zimiles for his help in the preparation of this manuscript.

REFERENCES

Bahr, S.J. Effects on power and division of labor in the family. In L. W. Hoffman, & F. I. Nye (Eds.),*Working mothers*. San Francisco, Calif.: Jossey-Bass, 1974.

Bardwick, J. The dynamics of successful people. In D. G. McGuigan (Ed.), *New research on women*. Ann Arbor, Mich.: The University of Michigan, Center for Continuing Education of Women, 1974.

Baruch, G. K., & Barnett R. C. Father's participation in the care of their preschool children. *Sex Roles*, 1981, *10*, 173–193.

Blake, J. Population policy for Americans: Is the government being misled. *Science*, 1969, *164*, 52–529.

Blood, R. O., Jr. The husband-wife relationship. In F. I. Nye & L. W. Hoffman (Eds.), *The employed mother in America*. Chicago: Rand McNally, 1963.

Campbell, A., Converse, P., & Rodgers, W. *The quality of American life*. New York: Russell Sage Foundation, 1976.

Cherry, F. F., & Eaton, E. L. Physical and cognitive development in children of low-income mothers working in the child's early years. *Child Development*, 1977, *48*, 158–166.

Chodorow, N. *The reproduction of mothering: Psychoanalysis and the sociology of gender*. Berkeley, Calif.: University of California Press, 1978.

Clarke-Stewart, A. And daddy makes three: The father's impact on mother and young child. *Child Development*, 1978, *49*, 466–478.

Davis, N. Z. City women and religious change in Sixteenth-Century France. In D. G. McGuigan (Ed.),*A sampler of women's studies*. Ann Arbor, Mich.: The University of Michigan Center for the Continuing Education of Women, 1973, 17–46.

Dinnerstein, D. *The mermaid and the minotaur*. New York: Harper and Row, 1976.

Dizard, J. *Social change in the family*. Chicago: Community and Family Study Center, University of Chicago, 1968.

Duncan, D., Schuman, H., & Duncan, B. *Social change in a metropolitan community*. New York: Russell Sage Foundation, 1973.

Dyer, E. D. Parenthood as crisis: A restudy. *Marriage and Family Living*, 1963, *25*, 196–201.

Espanshade, T. J. The economic consequences of divorce. In G. McDonald & F. I. Nye (Eds.), *Family policy*. Minneapolis, Minn.: National Council on Family Relations, 1979.

Feldman, S. S., & Nash, S. C. *Antecedents of interest in babies among males and females*. Unpublished manuscript, Stanford University, 1978.

Ferree, M. Working class jobs: Housework and paid work as sources of satisfaction. *Social Problems*, 1976, *23*, 431–441.

Garland, T. N. The better half? The male in the dual professional family. In C. Safilios Rothschild (Ed.), *Towards a sociology of women*. Lexington, Mass.: Xerox College Publishing, 1972.

Gerstl, J. E. Leisure, taste, and occupational milieu. *Social Problems*, 1961, *9*, 56–68.

Gold, D., & Andres, D. Developmental comparisons between adolescent children with employed and nonemployed mothers. *Merrill-Palmer Quarterly*, 1978, *24*, 243–254. (a)

Gold, D., & Andres, D. Developmental comparisons between 10–year–old children with employed and nonemployed mothers. *Child Development*, 1978, *49*, 75–84. (b)

Gold, D., & Andres, D. Relations between maternal employment and development of nursery school children. *Canadian Journal of Behavioral Science*, 1978, *10*, 116–129.(c)

Gold, D., Andres, D., & Glorieux, J. The development of Francophone nurseryschool children with employed and nonemployed mothers. *Canadian Journal of Behavioral Science*, 1979, *11*, 169–173.

Hall, F. T., & Schroeder, M. P. Time spent on household tasks. *Journal of Home Economics*, 1970, *62*, 22–37.

Herzog, E., & Sudia, C. Children in fatherless families. In B. M. Caldwell & H. N. Ricciuti (Eds.), *Review of child development research* (Vol. 3). 1973 Chicago: University of Chicago Press.

Hetherington, E. M. Divorce: A child's perspective. *American Psychologist*, 1979, *34*, 851–858.

Hetherington, E. M., Cox, M., & Cox, R. The aftermath of divorce. In J. H. Stevens, Jr. & M. Mathews (Eds.), *Mother-child, father-child relationships*. Washington, D.C.: National Association for the Education of Young Children, NAEYC, 1978.

Hill, C. R., & Stafford, F. P. Parental care of children: *Time diary estimates of quantity predictability and variety*. Working paper series, Institute for Social Research, University of Michigan, Ann Arbor, 1978.

Hoffman, L. W. The decision to work. In F. I. Nye & L. W. Hoffman (Eds.), *The employed mother in America*. Chicago: Rand McNally, 1963. (a)

Hoffman, L. W. Parental power relations and the division of household tasks. In F. I. Nye & L. W. Hoffman (Eds.), *The employed mother in America*, Chicago: Rand McNally, 1963. (b)

Hoffman, L. W. Early childhood experiences and women's achievement motives. *Journal of Social Issues*, 1972, *28*, 129–156.

Hoffman, L. W. Changes in family roles, socialization, and sex differences. *American Psychologist*, 1977, *32*, 644–657. (a)

Hoffman, L. W. Fear of success in 1965 and 1974, a reinterview study. *Journal of Consulting and Clinical Psychology*, 1977, *45*, 310–321. (b)

Hoffman, L. W. Maternal employment: 1979. *American Psychologist*, 1979, *34*, 859–865.

Hoffman, L. W. Social change and its effects on parents and children: Limitations to knowledge. In P. W. Berman & E. R. Ramey (Ed.), *Women: A developmental perspective*. Washington, D.C.: U.S. Government Printing Office, 1982.

Hoffman, L. W. Work, family, and the socialization of the child. In R. D. Parke (Ed.), *The review of child development research* (Vol. 7). Chicago: University of Chicago Press, in press.

Hoffman, L. W., & Hoffman, M. L. The value of children to parents. In J. T. Fawcett (Ed.), *Psychological perspectives on fertility*. New York: Basic Books, 1973.

Hoffman, L. W., & Manis, J. D. Influences of children on marital interaction and parental satisfactions and dissatisfactions. In R. Lerner & G. Spanier (Eds.), *Child influences on marital and family interaction: A life-span perspective*. New York: Academic Press, 1978.

Hoffman, L. W., & Manis, J. D. The value of children in the United States: A new approach to the study of fertility. *Marriage and the Family*, 1979, *41*, 3, 583–596.

Holmstrom, L. *The two-career family*. Cambridge, Mass.: Schenkman, 1972.

Hughes, E. *Men and their work*. Glencoe, Ill.: Free Press, 1958.

Kessler, R. C., & McRae, J. A. Jr. The effect of wives' employment on the mental health of married men and women, Unpublished manuscript, Institute for Social Research, University of Michigan, 1981.

Kohn, L. Social class and parent-child relationships: An interpretation. *American Journal of Sociology,* 1963, *68,* 471–480.

Komorovsky, M. Cultural contradictions and sex roles: The masculine case. *American Journal of Sociology,* 1973, 873–884.

Lamb, M. E. Fathers and child development: An integrative overview. In M. E. Lamb (Ed.), *The role of the father in child development* (Rev. ed.), New York: Wiley, 1981.

Lein, L. Male participation in home life: Impact of social supports and breadwinner responsibility on the allocation of tasks. *Family Coordinator,* 1979, *26,* 489–495.

Lein, L., et al. *Work and family Life.* Final Report to the National Institute of Education, 1974. Cambridge, Mass: Center for the Study of Public Policy, 1974.

Lynn, D. B. *Parental and sex-role identification: A theoretical formulation.* Berkeley, Calif.: McCutchan, 1969.

Mason, K. O., Czajka, J. L., & Arber, S. Change in women's sex role attitudes, 1964–1974. *American Sociological Review,* 1976, *41,* 573–596.

Michaels, G. Y. *Transition to parenthood: Impact on moral-personal values, attitudes and life goals.* Unpublished doctoral dissertation, University of Michigan, 1981.

Nickols, S. *Work and housework: Family roles in productive activity.* Paper presented at the National Council on Family Relations, New York, October 1976.

Nye, F. I. Husband-wife relationship. In L. W. Hoffman & F. I. Nye (Eds.), *Working mothers.* San Francisco: Jossey-Bass, 1974. (a)

Nye, F. I. Socio-cultural context. In L. W. Hoffman & F. I. Nye (Eds.), *Working mothers.* San Francisco: Jossey-Bass, 1974. (b)

Oppenheimer, V. K. Demographic influence on female employment and the status of women. *American Journal of Sociology,* 1973, *78,* 1, 20–54.

Oppenheimer, V. K. The sex labeling of jobs. In M. T. S. Mednick, S. S. Tangri, & L. W. Hoffman (Eds.), *Women and achievement.* Washington: Hemisphere Publishing, 1975.

Parsons, T. The American family: It's relation to personality and the social structure. I. T. Parsons & R. F. Bales (Eds.), *Family, socialization and interaction process.* New York: Free Press, 1955.

Pederson, F. A., Cain, R., Zaslow, M., & Anderson, B. Variation in infant experience associated with alternative family role organization. In L. Laosa & I. Sigel (Eds.), *Families as learning environment for children.* New York: Plenum, in press.

Pleck, J. H. *Changing patterns of work and family roles.* Paper presented at the American Psychological Association, Los Angeles, August 1981.

Pleck, J., Lang, L., & Rustad, M. *Men's family work, involvement, and satisfaction.* Unpublished manuscript, Wellesley College Center for Research on Women, 1978.

Pleck, J. H., & Rustad, M. Husbands' and wives' time. In *Family work and paid work in the 1975–76 study of time use.* Unpublished manuscript, Wellesley College Center for Research on Women, 1980.

Rapoport, R., & Rapoport, R. *Dual career families.* Baltimore: Penguin, 1971.

Rainwater, L. *Family design: Marital sexuality, family size, and contraception.* Chicago: Aldine, 1965.

Robinson, J. P. *Changes in Americans' use of time: 1965–1975—a progress report.* Cleveland, Ohio: Communications Research Center, Cleveland State University, 1977.

Robinson, J. P. *How Americans use time: A sociological perspective.* New York: Praeger, 1978.

Robinson, J. P. Housework technology and household work. In S. F. Berk (Ed.), *Women and Household Labor.* Beverly Hills, CA: Sage, 1980.

Rollins, B. C., & Cannon, K. L. Marital satisfaction over the family life cycle: A re-evaluation. *Journal of Marriage and the Family,* 1974, *36,* 271–283.

Rosenthal, K. M., & Keshet, H. F. The impact of childcare responsibilities on part-time or single fathers. *Alternative Life Styles.* 1978, *1,* 465–491.

Rossi, A. S. Equality between the sexes: An immodest proposal. In R. J. Lifton (Ed.), *The woman in America.* Boston: Houghton Mifflin, 1965.

Rubin, L. *Women of a certain age: The midlife search for self.* New York: Harper & Row, 1979.

Sanik, M. A twofold comparison of time spent in household work in two-parent, two-child households: Urban New York State in 1967–68 and 1977. Unpublished doctoral Dissertation, Cornell University, 1979. (University Microfilms No. 7910832).

Sawhill, I. V., Peabody, G. E., Jones, C. A., & Caldwell, S. B. *Income transfers and family structure.* The Urban Institute Working Paper 979–03, Washington, D.C. 1975.

Spanier, G. B., Lewis, R. H., & Cole, C. L. Marital adjustment over the family cycle: The issue of curvilinearity. *Journal of Marriage and the Family,* 1975, *37,* 263–275.

Steinmetz, S. K. Occupational environment in relation to physical punishment and dogmatism. In S. Steinmetz and M. Strauss (Eds.), *Violence in the Family.* New York: Dodd, Mead, 1974.

Thornton, A., & Freedman, D. Changes in the sex role attitudes of women 1962–1977: Evidence from a panel study. D. McGuigan (Ed.), *Changing family, changing work place—new research.* Ann Arbor: University of Michigan, Center for the Continuing Education of Women, 1980.

U.S. Department of Labor, Bureau of Labor Statistics. *Marital and family characteristics of workers, March, 1980.* ASI 6748–58 (News release on microfish) 1981.

U.S. Department of Labor, Women's Bureau. *Working mothers and their children.* Washington, D.C.: U.S. Government Printing Office, 1977.

U.S. Department of Commerce. *Bureau of the Census Population profile of the United States: 1978, population characteristics* (Current Population Reports, Series P–20, No. 336). Washington, D.C.: U.S. Government Printing Office, April, 1979.

Veroff, J., Douvan, E., & Kulka, R. *The inner American.* New York: Basic Books, 1981.

Walker, K., & Woods, M. *Time use: A measure of household production of family goods and services.* Washington, D.C.: American Home Economics Association, 1976.

Walshok, M. L. Occupational values and family roles: A descriptive study of women working in blue-collar and service occupations. *The Urban & Social Change Review,* 1978, *11,* 12–20.

Woods, M. B. The supervised child of the working mother. *Developmental Psychology,* 1972, *6,* 14–25.

11 Increased Father Participation and Child Development Outcomes

Norma Radin
University of Michigan

Graeme Russell
Macquarie University

Studies demonstrating the influence that fathers exert on children have burgeoned in the past decade after years of neglect (Belsky, 1979; Blanchard & Biller, 1971; Lamb, 1977; Lynn, 1974; Parke & Sawin, 1976; Radin, 1972; Reis & Gold, 1977; Spelke, Zelazo, Kagan, & Kotelchuck, 1973). Concurrently, in the past half decade, there has been a growth of interest by researchers in nontraditional families, stimulated in part by new family forms that emerged in the late 1960s and early 1970s (Carlson, 1980; Eiduson & Alexander, 1978; Smith, 1980). A small number of these investigations have focused on a unique type of nontraditional family: that in which men take a great responsibility for the care of young children (Field, 1978; Gersick, 1979; Lamb, Frodi, Hwang, & Frodi, 1982; Mendes, 1976; Radin, 1978; Russell, 1978; Sagi, 1982; Santrock & Warshak, 1979). The discussion to follow will focus on the point at which these two research trends converge and will examine the influence care-giving fathers have on children. Possible effects will be examined following a review of what is known about father influence on children in more traditional families. Special emphasis will be placed on the extent to which developmental outcomes are altered when parental roles are partially reversed or when there is no mother in the family.

Before reaching the substantive issues, a brief summary will be presented of the major research strategies that have been employed in the field of child development. Some conceptualizations concerning the processes by which paternal influence may be exerted will follow. Specific aspects of child development that have been found to be influenced by fathers will then be described, along with research findings on families with fathers highly involved in child care. A comparison of the data concerning paternal influences in traditional and father-involved families will ensue. Finally, the gaps in knowledge about the impact that involved fathers have on children will be considered, and suggestions offered for future invesigations.

RESEARCH STRATEGIES EMPLOYED IN THE STUDY OF PATERNAL INFLUENCES

Several techniques, each of which has strengths and weaknesses, have been used to study the influence fathers exert on children. (Lytton, 1971, 1973; Sears, 1965; Yarrow, 1963). Brief comments will be made on each of these methods in order that findings subsequently discussed can be better evaluated.

Mothers and fathers are sometimes asked to complete questionnaires about the child-rearing practices of the father or about his personal characteristics. These responses are then related to data concerning the children collected by researchers who administer tasks, tests, or questionnaires to the youngsters. At times information about the children is obtained from parents or teachers. In other studies, mothers and fathers are interviewed separately, or together, and asked questions about paternal child-rearing practices and paternal characteristics. In some investigations, only one parent is interviewed, but in either situation the responses are related to measures of the children.

In other studies, fathers are observed interacting with their child in a laboratory setting, and the child is given some specific tasks to complete, e.g., a jigsaw puzzle. Father behaviors are then related to the observed child behaviors, and/or to other data collected about the child. Such studies can also be conducted in the child's home. Mothers, fathers, and children are also observed as a triad in a laboratory or home, often with the participants being given tasks to complete. Occasionally fathers are observed with children when no assignment is given, for example, while they are awaiting someone's arrival, and their interactions are then observed in this unstructured context. In contrast, the situation in which the families are observed can be highly structured. For example, the father can be asked to leave the room and then return at a specified time so that his child's responses to his departure and arrival can be assessed. In some laboratory investigations, one-way mirrors are used so that observers not in the room can watch and record with pencil and paper, or with audio or video equipment, what is occurring. In the home observations, one researcher is sometimes assigned the task of recording what is taking place, by hand or with some mechanical or electronic device. At other times, a single individual records on audiotape the interactions in the room as the interview is conducted.

In general, the more structured and controlled the situation, the easier it is to collect reliable data and to isolate one or two variables to be studied. For example, in a laboratory investigation, it is possible to control all variables except the single one to be studied, such as the effect on the child of the entrance of a stranger after the father leaves the room. However, the validity of the information obtained can be questioned because of its highly controlled nature. Would the parent or child react in the same way in the familiar home environment? How typical of natural behavior is the interaction recorded? In contrast, the less structured the situation, the more natural the setting, and the less obtrusive the recording devices, the more valid or representative the behavior is likely to be. Under these conditions, however, it is difficult to obtain accurate and reliable records of what has occurred. Many different events can take place that would affect the data and contaminate the variables the researcher is trying to study. Furthermore, although the use of video equipment ensures reliable coding of interactions between father and child, whether anyone can relax in the presence of bulky electronic equipment (and bright lights) is open to question. Even with the use of the best equipment and techniques, however, many aspects of family life are necessarily neglected ion observational studies. The entire family, including other children, friends, grandparents, and relatives, is virtually never present.

Questionnaires and interviews avoid these problems, but we cannot be certain that respondents give honest replies or merely provide socially desirable answers. There are even questions about the ability of individuals to describe what they do with accuracy for they are often unaware of their own behaviors. Questions about the accuracy of self-reports are particularly salient when respondents are asked to recall past events. Nevertheless, responses to questionnaires or interviewers' questions are reflections of individuals' attitudes, beliefs, and perceptions of what is currently taking place or what ocurred in the past. To this extent, they do have validity. Behavior may not be congruent with attitudes, beliefs, or perceptions, but this does not invalidate either set of measures. Thus interview, questionnaire, and observational strategies all have limitations but they also contribute valuable information to researchers.

PROCESSES BY WHICH PATERNAL INFLUENCE MAY BE EXERTED

It has been noted by numerous theorists and researchers that fathers influence their children both directly and indirectly (Clarke-Stewart, 1978; Lamb, Frodi, Chase-Lansdale, & Owen, 1978; Lewis & Weinraub, 1976; Parke, Power, & Fisher, 1980; Pedersen, 1976; Radin, in press). Direct influence is exerted when the father does something that has an impact on the child, for example, when fathers serve as models for their children or use reward or punishment to increase or decrease their behavior. Both of these means of influence, modeling and reinforcement, have been discussed and researched at length by social learning theorists (Bandura & Walters, 1963; Gewirtz & Stingle, 1968; Patterson & Guillon, 1968). Fathers also influence their children directly by establishing rules and by expressing expectations for their behavior. Such expectations can be expressed overtly, or covertly as is the case when fathers take on roles that are reciprocal to those they wish their children to play. Appropriate reciprocal behavior is then typically elicited from the children. For example, fathers who play the role of "buddy," "master," or "flirt" vis à vis their children elicit very different types of responses from them. In more general role theory terminology (see Feld & Radin, 1982), the above interactions can be called altercasting for they involve casting the other person (alter) in a certain role and then responding to that individual as a reciprocal role partner.

Fathers also influence their children directly by providing direct instruction or explicit training. This form of influence is seen most frequently in the academic realm. Finally, through the use of cognitive modification strategies, a term popularized by Meichenbaum (1977), fathers bring about change in their children. One example of such strategies is the use of reasoning and rational persuasion. Highlighting discrepancies between the behavior and the values a child holds, and labeling the child are two other cognitive modification techniques (Feld & Radin, 1982).

Fathers influence their children indirectly through at least four difference processes. One involves the mothers serving as a mediator of father influence; that is, the father does something that influences his spouse, who, as a consequence, treats the child in a different way. For example, it has been suggested that fathers who have little power in the occupational sphere tend to assert power over their wives at home, who in turn use power-assertive strategies in interactions with their children. The frequent use of power assertion by mothers is associated with "weak moral development" in children according to M.L. Hoffman (1970). A second type of indirect influence has been labeled second order effects (Belsky, 1979; Bronfenbrenner, 1973; Lamb, 1976a; Lytton, 1979). Here the father by his mere presence influences the mother's behavior with the child. For example, it has been shown that mothers interact less with their infants when the child's father is present (Clarke-Stewart, 1978; Lamb, 1976a) and also that they appear to be spurred on to do what is expected of them with the child in the presence of their husband (Lytton, 1979).

A third form of indirect influence—the influence of social networks—has been conceptualized by Cochran and Brassard (1979). One example of this form of influence is fathers putting their children in contact with members of their own social network, that is, individuals outside the household who engage in activities with the fathers. These network members can introduce children to new modes of interaction; serve as models for behaviors not exhibited by parents; and provide children with opportunities for vicarious learning.

A fourth form of indirect paternal influence can result when fathers provide physical materials and settings that can affect their children's development (Rheingold & Cook, 1975). An obvious example is a father's purchase of a television set for the home. Numerous studies have demonstrated that children's behaviors, both prosocial and antisocial, are affected by the programs they watch

(Ball & Bogartz, 1977, Coates, Pusser, & Goodman, 1976; Davidson, Yasuna, & Tower, 1979; Friedrich-Cofer, Huston-Stein, Kiphis, Susman, & Clewett, 1979; Lieberts, 1972; Thomas & Drabman, 1975).

Before leaving the topic of paternal influence, it should be noted that there is unanimity among researchers studying the socialization process that influence is not exerted in one direction only (Bell, 1968, 1974; Buss, 1981; Osofsky & O'Connell, 1972). Furthermore, it is not merely bidirectional, from child to father or from father to child; rather it is circular or transactional to use Sameroff's (1977) terminology. Thus a parent can influence a child who in turn influences the same parent or the second parent and this individual then influences the child, etc. Clarke-Stewart (1978) demonstrated that such circular influence patterns may exist among mothers, fathers, and infants. Any discussion of paternal influence on children is therefore readily acknowledged to be a focus on one small aspect of a very complex process.

FATHER-INFLUENCES ON CHILD DEVELOPMENT

Conceptualizations Based on Research on Traditional Families

Sex-Role Development   Sex-role development of both boys and girls has been shown to be influenced by fathers' behaviors and attitudes. The process appears to be different for the two sexes, however. Fathers who are nurturant, powerful, and available have been found to be frequently modeled or imitated by their sons, who in turn develop a masculine gender role (Hetherington & Frankie, 1967; Kagan, 1958; Mussen & Distler, 1960; Mussen & Rutherford, 1963; Payne & Mussen, 1965; Sears, 1953). It has also been found that fathers reinforce appropriate sex-typed behavior in their sons (Fagot, 1978; Goodenough, 1957; Radin, 1981c) and punish inappropriate behavior (Langlois & Downs, 1980), thus further fostering the expected gender role. Although fathers also differentially reinforce appropriate sex-typed behavior in girls, the father's responding to his daughter as an interested male responds to a female appears to have the greater impact (Johnson, 1977). By playing the male role, or reciprocal role to the female role, fathers teach daughters the female role and female sex-typed behavior. In Johnson's (1977) words, the father's behavior towards his daughter is in direct response to her sexuality, and he affirms her heterosexuality. (Johnson argues, however, that mothers do not respond to boys in a corresponding way to affirm their heterosexuality). Johnson links paternal fostering of daughters' heterosexuality to the fact that the male role involves dealing with external relations and suggests that this relationship would change if societal roles changed and there were no longer differences in the expectations held for women and men.

Cognitive Development.   Cognitive development is another domain that appears to be sensitive to father influence. In the case of boys, findings suggest that the more nurturant the father, the more the young boy models him and internalizes his modes of thinking and problem solving (Radin, 1981c). Further, father-contact has been found to be positively related to a boy's intellectual development (Radin, 1972, 1981c). The father's interest in the boy's academic success may also exert a positive influence (Aberle & Naegele, 1952). On the other hand, authoritarian paternal control, or hostility and restrictiveness (Harrington, Block, & Block, 1978; Radin, 1972, 1981c) have been found to be negatively related to boys' cognitive development. Negative relationships have also been found with feelings of inadequacy and powerlessness on the part of the father, possibly because powerless models are not as readily imitated (Bowerman & Elder, 1964; Grunebaum, Hurwitz, Prentice, & Sperry 1962).

The cognitive style of the young male has also been found to be related to the amount of time fathers are available. Lynn (1969) has postulated and supplied support for the thesis that when fathers are moderately available, boys develop an analytic or field independent style of thinking (Dyk & Witkin, 1965). That is, they tend to disembed details of a problem from its context and ignore irrelevant cues in the environment. The development of an analytic cognitive style has been attributed to the need of boys to abstract the dimensions of masculinity, for example, initiative and independence, from limited information in the environment (Lynn, 1969). According to Lynn's hypothesis, if fathers are frequently present, boys will tend to rely on imitation to develop masculine sex-typed behavior, and their analytic skills will not be fully developed. In this case, or if the father is virtually never present, the boy will tend to develop a global or field dependent cognitive style typically seen in females. In the typical female style, details of a problem are not disembedded from the context. An analytic cognitive style is particularly relevant to intellectual competence, for it has been shown to be related to mathematical and spatial ability (Bing, 1963; Carlsmith, 1964; Maccoby & Jacklin, 1974). In sum, for boys there appears to be a curvilinear relationship between father availability and field independence and, by extrapolation, one can say that father availability appers to be curvilinearly related to mathematical ability in boys.

The influence that fathers exert on girls' cognitive development is far more complex and ambiguous than the pattern for boys. There is virtually no evidence from studies of traditional families that nurturance or quantity of contact between fathers and daughters is positively related to girls' intellectual growth (Epstein & Radin, 1975; Pedersen, Rubenstein, & Yarrow; 1979; Radin & Epstein, 1975). Rather, it appears that paternal strictness in the context of warmth and moderate distance between fathers and daughters, as well as autonomy from fathers, are related to daughters' intellectual functioning (Jordan, Radin, & Epstein, 1975; Radin, 1981c), but even this evidence is tenuous. One reason that has been offered for the weak link between father behavior and daughters' mental ability is that fathers are not as concerned with academic achievement for daughters as they are for sons. Instead, there appears to be greater interest in the girls' interpersonal relationships and her future as a wife and mother (Aberle & Naegele, 1952; Block, Block, & Harrington, 1974; Hoffman, 1977).

The one clear relationship that has been found with girls concerns mathematical skills. Father's presence especially when his daughter is between one and nine appears to be related to the girl's competence in mathematics (Landy, Rosenberg, & Sutton-Smith, 1969; Radin, 1981c). No clear reason has ever been offered for the relationship, nor has the process by which paternal presence influences girls' mathematical skills been explicated. (See Radin [(1976, 1981c)] for a fuller discussion of these issues and the more general issue of the difficulty of establishing cause and effect in these studies).

For both boys and girls, it appears that extensive father participation in their children's mastery or problem-solving efforts does not facilitate the child's cognitive development (Boerger, 1971; Crandall, Dewey, Katkovsky, & Preston, 1964; Radin, 1981c; Radin & Epstein, 1975; Solomon, Houlihan, Busse, & Parelius, 1971). Instead, when fathers remove themselves from the task and allow the children to solve the problem themselves, intellectual growth appears to be fostered. There are indications that is is as true for black fathers as white (Busse, 1969; Dill, 1975). Also common to both sons and daughters is the mother-as-mediator form of indirect influence. For example, it has been found that when mother-father relationships are good, mothers spend more time with their preschool sons, and the more time spent with them, the better their problem-solving ability (Gold & Andres, 1978). Another study reported evidence that a father's future expectations of his daughter's academic achievement were related to the girl's cognitive functioning, although his behavior was not (Radin, 1981c, Radin & Epstein, 1975). It was the mother's academically stimulating behaviors that were related to the intellectual competence of girls. The data suggested that the father's expectations may have influenced the mother's stimulating behavior and therefore indirectly fostered the girl's cognitive development.

Finally, there is evidence that the father's education is predictive of his child's educational attainment as an adult, and that father's educational and occupational levels are linked with his child's intellectual competence (Honzik, 1963; Jencks, Smith, Acland, Bane, Cohen, Gintis, Heyns, & Michelson, 1972; McCall, 1977; Radin, 1981c). There are many possible reasons for these relationships. For example, the educated father may provide a model of someone who is scholarly and interested in reading; or provide material resources such as books; or reinforce his children for achievement in school; or offer direct instruction when the child is having problems with school work; or he might bring educated adults into the home from his social network. Thus, both direct and indirect influence processes may be operative in the connection between the educational status of fathers and the intellectual ability of sons and daughters.

Social Competence.   Social competence, or competence in interactions with others, is another domain for which there is suggestive evidence of paternal influences, and once again, sex differences have been reported. Boys whose fathers are involved and nurturant have been found to be better adjsted and more socially competent (Biller, 1976). For example, it was found that adolescent boys with unaffectionate relationships with their fathers were likely to feel rejected and unhappy (Mussen, Young, Gaddini, & Morante, 1963). College males who obtained high scores on a personal adjustment scale perceived their fathers as highly available and at least moderately nurturant, or highly nurturant and at least moderately available (Reuter & Biller, 1973). It has also been found that males who were assessed as having achieved successful emotional and interpersonal adjustment in adulthood were likely to have had highly involved fathers (Block 1971). Adult males who were relatively low in social skills, e.g., in making friends, were likely to have grown up in a home where fathers were either uninvolved or weak and neurotic (Block, von der Lippe, & Block, 1973).There is some evidence as well that the relationship between deliquent sons and their fathers is marked by rejection and hostility (Bandura & Walters, 1959). In addition, it has been shown that authoritative childrearing by fathers as well as by mothers (that is, high warmth associated with rule setting or control) fosters social competence in boys; warmth and permissiveness do not (Baumrind, 1967, 1970, Baumrind & Black, 1967).

The picture is not nearly as clear-cut for girls, and there are data that suggest that fathers who are demanding, challenging, and somewhat abrasive, to use Baumrind's (1977, 1978) term, raise the most socially competent, independent and agentic or intrinsically motivated daughters. In general, Baumrind found that assertive, independent behavior in daughters is associated with firmness and maturity demands by both mothers and fathers, and negatively associated with high acceptance. For example, in a five-year follow-up of her observational study of preschoolers in their homes, Baumrind found a positive relationship between independent behavior on the part of the girls and abrasiveness in parents particularly fathers. This linkage was seen as congruent with Bronfenbrenner's (1961) observation that among educationally advantaged subgroups, too much warmth and support was associated with passivity in girls. Baumrind (1977) concluded that exposure to vigorous, abrasive interaction with parents by girls, along with the receipt of rewards for acts of independence and achievement, may save them from the compassion trap in which girls become conforming and lacking in self-determination. Further, she argues, provocative parental behavior is needed, for biology and society "conspire" to create passivity in girls. This is not true for boys, for whom biology and society "conspire" to create independence (Baumrind, 1977).

Other researchers have collected evidence supportive of Baumrind's view. For example, in a study of preschool children it was found that children's perceptions of fathers as punitive were associated with internality for girls only (Carlson,

1980). Sex-of-child differences also emerged in an observational laboratory investigation of 9-year-old children. The data showed that fathers tended to reduce support to girs who played actively and it was the sedentary girls, not the active ones, who were given paternal support (Tauber, 1979). In another observational study in a laboratory, the speech of mothers and fathers was analyzed as children played with a complex toy that could be taken apart (Masur & Gleason, 1980). Fathers' interactions with girls seemed to be testing and displaying the daughter's knowledge of the parts of the toy. In contrast, mothers supplied vocabulary information only when the daughter did not know the term. The effectiveness of the father's approach was demonstrated by the higher levels of linguistic production used by the children in their interactions with fathers. The investigators cocluded that their results were consistent with those of Baumrind who found that the demandingness of parents, especially fathers, facilitated independence and intellectual achievement, particularly in girls.

There are suggestions that the conclusions drawn about social competence in the previous discussion do not apply to minority children (Baumrind, 1972). More will be said about this issue at a later point.

Child Development and Extensive Father Involvement

Several studies have been performed in the past few years that have focused on fathers with a major role in child-rearing. These investigations include two that compared the behavior of primary care giving and traditional fathers as they interacted with their infants (Field, 1978; Lamb, Frodi, Hwang, & Frodi, 1982); five that focused on interviews with single fathers raising children (Gersick, 1979; Katz, 1979; Mendes, 1976; Smith & Smith, 1981; Watson, 1981); and three involving interviews with couples, together or separately, where fathers assumed a major responsibility for child care (De Frain, 1979; Russell, 1978; 1979a, 1979b, 1980, 1982; Smith, 1980; Smith & Reid, 1980). None of these studies except for that by Lamb et al. included child development measures, but in several cases the parents reported that the children were doing well. For example, in the Russell (1982) study of 50 families in which fathers had a major role in rearing their children, 76% of the fathers and 64% of the mothers said that their children had not experienced any major problems with their change in lifestyle. Katz (1979), who studied single fathers raising children, reviewed the literature in the field and concluded that overall the studies suggested that fathers are doing a relatively good job of raising children by themselves. Smith and Smith (1981), who interviewed 27 single fathers, reached a similar conclusion. Indicative of the competence displayed by the single fathers were their responses to a question about whether they felt capable of caring for the emotional needs of their children. Over 75% believed they could handle most problems. Finally, in a study of six men who had sole custody of their children, Watson (1981) found that all of them felt strongly that they were effective parents. They saw themselves as child-oriented and were closely involved with their offspring beginning from the time of the children's birth. Thus, although no specific type of paternal influence was described in these studies, at a minimum, the findings suggest that children do not develop serious mental or emotional problems when fathers are highly participant in child care.

Four studies have been conducted in the past decade that did provide extensive data about children raised in homes where fathers were highly involved in child rearing. These will be reviewed in detail, for they offer an opportunity to examine the possible influence such men have on their children. The studies were conducted by Santrock and Warshak (1979), Carlson (1980, 1981), and Radin (1978, 1981a, 1981b, 1982) in the United States, and by Sagi (Sagi, 1982; Sagi & Reshef, 1981) in Israel.

In the Santrock-Warshak study, boys and girls raised by single fathers were compared, and these children were also compared with their same-sex peers raised in intact families and single-mother families. Several methods of data collection were employed. The children were observed and videotaped while interacting with their parents in a laboratory situation; structured interviews were conducted with the parents; the parents and children were asked to assess themselves on rating scales; and both completed projective tests. The sample consisted of 64 white middle-class families with children aged 6 to 11 years old. Approximately one-third of the children were in father custody, one-third in mother custody, and one-third in intact families. The children in single father homes were obtained first through visits to various community agencies and by following leads given by students and faculty members. A mother-custody family was then matched individually to a father-custody family with respect to age of child, family size, family socioeconomic status, and age of child when parents separated. Finally, intact families were matched to the two custody groups on all of these variables except the last one.

Compared to boys in two-parent families, boys in father-custody families were rated to be: more socially competent; warmer; higher on self-esteem; and more mature and independent. In contrast, girls in father-custody homes were less warm, less mature, had lower self-esteem, and were less independent than girls from intact families. When boys and girls from single-father families were compared, the boys were uniformly found to be more socially competent and mature than the girls. These results cannot be interpreted as suggesting better adjustment of boys residing with one parent, for when boys and girls in mother-custody homes were compared, the girls were found to be more competent.

In addition to the comparisons across sex and family, the style of parenting employed by the fathers was examined using Baumrind's (1967) classification of authoritative (warm with clear limit-setting and extensive verbal give-and-take), authoritarian, and laissez-faire. It was found that regardless of custodial arrangement, the use of authoritative parenting was positively associated with social competence in children, with their maturity, sociability, warmth, and self-esteem. On the other hand, a positive correlation was obtained between an authoritarian paternal child rearing style in fathers with custody and anger and lack of independence in children.

The results of the Santrock-Warshak study appear to be consistent with the earlier reported research on traditional families indicating that adjustment and social competence in boys are associated with fathers being highly involved and warm, and the more contact boys have with their fathers, the more competent they are. Further, the Santrock-Warshak findings are consistent with other data on traditional families suggesting that authoritarian paternal behavior involving restrictiveness and punitiveness does not facilitate the cognitive growth of sons.

The data obtained for daughters raised by fathers agree with findings obtained in mother-primary-caregiver families that suggested that girls do better when there is moderate distance between fathers and daughters. Perhaps the lack of independence in daughters raised by fathers is related to their failing to make sufficient demands on the girls and to be sufficiently challenging. Santrock and Warshak (1979) indicated that authoritative paternal parenting fostered maturity and social competence regardless of sex or custodial arrangement, but did not indicate how many single-parent fathers rasing girls were authoritative. Since these girls were generally found to be immature and lacking in social competence, one can infer that single fathers were less likely to be authoritative in their behavior with their daughters, that is, the least likely to combine warmth with demands for mature performance.

Although the Santrock-Warshak study represents an advancement over many other studies on this topic, especially through its use of a multi-method approach, it still has several limitations. For example, given the method of recruitment, these samples may not be representative of single-parent families. In addition, data have not been provided on how these families differed before adopting a single-parent lifestyle; the observed differences may have been present before the separation. Thus the findings should be treated with caution at this time.

The three studies of two-parent families in which fathers were highly participant and in which data were obtained about children will be discussed together because they employed the same basic methodology. The design was developed by Radin (1978) and a group of students who worked with her at The University of Michigan in 1975–1979. One of those students was Carlson, who subsequently completed a dissertation using the same general approach and many of the subjects in the Radin study. The methodology was also utilized by Sagi (1982), of the University of Haifa, using an Israeli sample. The specific procedures and samples of the three studies will be described in some detail, but in summarizing the results less will be said about the Carlson findings because two-thirds of her subjects overlapped with Radin's.

In all of the investigations, fathers were interviewed in their homes using the same semi-structured instrument that contained, among other things, questions concerning their involvement in child care and the quality of their interactions with their children. All three investigations also included a session in which the preschool-aged child was asked to complete a series of tasks. In all of the studies, the following instruments, with slight modifications in some cases, were used with the children: The Stanford Internal-External Scale (Mischel, Zeiss, & Zeiss, 1974), which assesses the child's locus of control; the It Scale (Brown, 1956), which primarily assesses the child's gender role; and a test developed by Kagan and Lemkin (1960), that provides information on personality traits (specifically punitiveness and nurturance that children ascribe to mothers and fathers. In addition, Sagi and Radin administered the Borke (1971, 1973) Empathy Scale, which assesses the child's ability to empathize. Carlson and Radin also used the Peabody Picture Vocabulary Test, a verbal intelligence test, and the Parent Role Perception Test (an instrument developed by the staff of the Radin project that is similar in format to the It Scale). The Parent Role Perception Test measures children's perceptions of the activities typically performed by each parent at home.

The samples in the three studies differed considerably. In the Radin study there were 59 families, all middle class and predominantly white. All had a child 3 to 6 years of age and had maintained the current childcare arrangement for at least six months. The sample was obtained by advertisements in local papers, notices posted in childcare facilities, radio announcements, etc. The sample was clearly self-selected and consisted of individuals who responded to requests for fathers in two-parent families who had a major role in child care. Traditional families with the same demographic characteristics were obtained by word-of-mouth. Based on assessment of the responses to the lengthly questionnaire of both fathers and mothers who were interviewed separately in their home, the families were classified as father primary caregiver, mother primary caregiver, and intermediate. Five indices of father involvement were employed: (1) his activities involving the physical care of the child; (2) his involvement in the socialization of the child (e.g., setting limits for the child's behavior); (3) his power, vis-á-vis his wife, in decision making about the child; (4) his availability to the child; and (5) an overall estimate of his involvement in rearing his preschooler. A total score of the five indices of paternal involvement was obtained for each parent and then the two totals added for a grand total score of father involvement for each family. These grand totals were rank ordered and the top third of the sample was labeled father primary caregiver group, the bottom third, mother primary caregiver group, and the middle third, the intermediate group. The groups so labeled were closely associated with both mothers' and fathers' global estimates of the relative time the father had prime responsibility for the child. For the father primary caregiver group, the mean of the percentages cited by the fathers was 58% and the mean of the percentages cited the mothers, 56%. For the intermediate group, the mean of the percentages cited by fathers was 40% and by the mothers, 41%. For the mother primary caregiver group the figures were 22% and

23%. Although the study required that all participant families had maintained the present childcare arrangement for at least six months, in fact, the average length of time the arrangement had been in place was 35 months—most of the children's lives. (The average age of the children was 54 months.)

The Sagi sample of 60 middle class, white Jewish fathers also contained one-third father primary caregiver families, one-third with intermediate sharing of childcare. (Sagi also included a measure of paternal nurturance in his total score for father involvement.) These families were recruited in a different fashion; they were not self-selected. All of the families had a child 3 to 6 years of age attending a school in a suburb of Haifa. Parents completed a brief questionnaire distributed at the school, asking about the distribution of childcare responsibilities in the family. Families qualified for participation in the study if both parents agreed on the extent of the father's involvement with the child. Of the 150 families who met this criterion, 15 agreed that the father was more involved than the mother, and 20 agreed that both parents took equal responsibility. These 35 families were included in the sample, along with 25 traditional families selected at random from the remaining 115 families who concurred that the mother was the primary caretaker. Although the sample was selected on the basis of both parents' views of the father's role in child rearing, the final assessment of the levels of paternal involvement was derived from father responses to the questionnaire used by Radin, admininstered in the father's home. As in the Radin investigation, the instruments described above were later completed by the children, with no one present but the teacher.

The Carlson study also consisted of 60 white middle-class families with a child between the ages of 3 and 6; however, in this case, one-third of the sample consisted of dual career families in which the father had at least an equal share in childcare, one-thrd were families in which the mother did not work and was the primary caregiver, and one-third were dual-career families in which the mother was also the primary caregiver. Approximately 40 of the families used in the Radin study fitted into the first two categories and thus their data were incorporated into the dissertation study. Carlson recruited 20 additional families to complete her sample. These 20 new families were obtained in the same manner that the nontraditional families were recruited by Radin. With the new subjects, as with the old, the father's involvement in child-rearing was determined by administering the ''common'' questionnaire to each mother and father separately in their home. As in the Sagi and Radin projects, the children later completed the tasks described above.

Overall, findings for relationships between father participation and child development variables were much stronger in Sagi's Israeli study than in either of the U.S. studies. What follows is a discussion of the similarities and differences between Sagi's and Radin's studies, and then a brief comparison between Radin's and Carlson's U.S. studies.

Two important findings emerged in the Radin and Sagi investigations. In both studies, father involvement was positively associated with an internal locus of control in boys as well as girls; that is, the children were more likely to assume responsibility for the consequences they experienced, positive and negative, when fathers were major caregivers (or, the children were more likely to perceive themselves as masters of their fate). Internality has been found to be associated with academic achievement, especially in white children, in the United States (Bridge, Moock, & Judd, 1979; Coleman, Campbell, Hobson, McPartland, Mood, Weinfeld, & York, 1966); thus the results are suggestive of future achievement in school. In addition, in both studies, the gender role of boys was unrelated to father participation in childcare, and the scores for boys were significantly greater than the girls' scores in all groups in both countries, indicating that the boys' gender role was more masculine than the girls.

Although the finding concerning the son's gender role suggests that paternal modeling has relatively little influence on boys' sex-typed behavior, one cannot discount that process completely at this stage. In the Radin study, the Bem Sex Role Inventory (Bem, 1974; Bem & Watson, 1976), which assesses an adult's gender role, was administered, and there were no differences in masculinity or femininity scores between traditional fathers and those who were primary caregivers. Nor were there differences in the children's perceptions of fathers' nurturance across groups. Thus childrearing fathers appeared to be as masculine as their more traditional peers.

Further evidence of this fact was found in the same study in the self-report and spouse scores for paternal nurturance; they were unrelated to the degree of paternal involvement in childcare. Audio tapes had been made of father interactions with their preschooler during the interview and data from this source also supported the view that the primary caregivers did not differ from traditional fathers in warmth. (The children had been asked to be present during the interview so that paternal behavior could be assessed). The tapes were coded using categories and procedures employed in previous Radin studies of paternal behavior (Radin, 1970, 1972; Radin & Epstein, 1975). No differences were found in paternal nurturance or restrictiveness between fathers who were primary caregivers and those whose wife assumed that role. Perhaps the most persuasive finding suggesting that modeling was operative was the significant positive correlation obtained between one of the father's Bem scores reflecting masculinity and the It Scale score of their sons in the Radin (1978) investigation. In sum, the men who were caring for their preschoolers appeared to be traditionally masculine in their traits if not in their activities, and the boys may have been modeling these qualities rather than what the father did in the home. Hence the sons appeared to develop a masculine gender role.

In numerous areas, the Sagi and Radin data differed. The most obvious discrepancy was that in the American study the children's perception of fathers as punitive was positively related to the amount of paternal participation in childcare; the more the men were involved, the more children perceived their fathers as punitive. This relationship is congruent with the finding that caregiving men were stereotypically masculine, as described above. Perhaps when assertive, powerful, aggressive individuals are present for long periods of time, their assertiveness becomes more salient and they are perceived, on the whole, as more punitive. In contrast, in Israel, father involvement was negatively associated with children's perceptions of fathers as punitive. These findings are in agreement with other data collected by Sagi for example, the children of involved fathers in Israel perceived fathers as more nurturant, and the more involved men perceived themselves as more nurturant than did children and fathers in traditional homes.

Radin and Sagi (1982) suggested that this difference in their findings may have been related to the fact that in the United States all of the wives of the primary care-giving men were working or involved in an educational program on a fulltime basis and were unavailable to their children most of the day. In Israel, however, 55% of the wives of primary care-giving men were neither working, involved in educational programs, nor participating in voluntary activities. Thus most of the care-giving fathers in the Israeli study undertook major childcare responsibilities in spite of the physical availability of their wives. They may indeed have been highly child-oriented and child-loving.

The second major difference between the Sagi and Radin studies concerned the gender role of girls. In the United States, there were no differences between It Scale scores of daughters raised in father-primary-caregiver and mother-primary-caregiver homes. In Israel, however, daughters of primary care-giving fathers were less effeminate in their toy preferences than daughters of traditional fathers. The explanation for the discrepancy in findings may be attributable to the discrepancy observed in the men's nurturance. In keeping with the reciprocal role theory of sex role development (Johnson, 1977), the Israeli men who were primary caregivers and also less traditionally masculine, may have been less likely to treat their daughters as traditional females than men who were not highly involved in childcare; as a result, the girls may have developed less traditionally feminine gender roles, or may have been less sex-role stereotyped. Thus the daughters of primary care-giving fathers in Israel and the United States may have reflected in their gender roles the differences in paternal behavior to which they were exposed.

Finally, congruent with the above discrepancies was the finding that empathy in Israeli children was positively associated with degree of paternal involvement in childcare; in the American study, the relationship was insignificant. Perhaps as has been suggested for mothers (Barnett, King, Howard, & Dino, 1980) highly nurturant fathers are also highly empathetic, and their children have the same quality because they model their fathers and are differentially reinforced for displaying empathetic behavior. Primary care-giving fathers who are not particularly nurturant, as was the case in the United States, may not be particularly empathetic, and their children may reflect this fact as well.

The two instruments used by Carlson and Radin but not Sagi shed some additional light on the nature of paternal influence when fathers have an important role in childrearing. In both investigations, the PPVT mental age of the children was positively associated with degree of father involvement in childrearing. This was true for both boys and girls. Further, in both studies, the scores on the Parent Role Perception Test, reflective of stereotypes of father activities performed in the home, were negatively associated with high paternal involvement in childrearing. These data suggest that some of the perceptions held by children about paternal behavior are affected by the models they observe in their families. It was evident from the Radin data that children are able to distinguish paternal characteristics from paternal activities: They can conceive of assertive or powerful fathers performing domestic chores.

One other type of analysis performed only in the Radin study is relevant to the literature on traditional families. The children's mental ages on the PPVT were correlated with measures of the quality of paternal involvement. Significant findings emerged only for boys. Boys' verbal intelligence scores were associated with the quality of involvement, specifically with self-reports and spouse reports of paternal nurturance. For girls, none of the responses concerning how loving the father was correlated significantly with girls' verbal intelligence.

As with the Santrock and Warshak (1979) study, the studies by Radin, Sagi, and Carlson have the positive feature of employing several different data collection methods (observational techniques, task performance by children, questionnaires completed by parents). However, some caution must be expressed about making cause and effect statements in relation to these studies too. Little data have been provided about the antecedents of the adoption of a highly-participant-father family pattern, and it is possible that the relationships reported here are mediated by other, antecedent, variables (e.g., the reasons for adopting a nontraditional lifestyle; paternal sensitivity and commitment to parenting).

One other study that attempted to investigate the influence of high paternal participation is that conducted by Lamb and his colleagues in Sweden (Lamb, Frodi, Hwang, & Frodi, 1982; Lamb, Frodi, Hwang, Frodi, & Steinberg, 1982; Lamb, Hwang, Frodi, & Frodi, 1982). This is a short-term longitudinal observational and interview study comparing families in which fathers had been the primary caretakers of their infants for at least one month (the average for the sample was 2.8 months), with families in which fathers adopted traditional roles. Family observations were carried out at 3, 8, 12, and 16 months. Findings from this study indicate that there are few differences between the two family types in the security of a child's attachment to his/her father or mother (assessed at 12 months) as measured by a standardized technique (Ainsworth, Blehar, Waters, & Wall, 1978). Thus, it appears that high father involvement does not have a negative effect on the quality of infants' attachment to their parents. Unfortunately, few of the fathers in this study maintained a high level of involvement in childcare throughout the course of data collection, and therefore, findings for 12 and 16 months perhaps should be treated with more caution. Additional limitations of this and other studies of highly participant fathers are discussed in a following section.

SIMILARITIES AND DIFFERENCES IN FINDINGS FOR PATERNAL INFLUENCE IN TRADITIONAL AND HIGH-FATHER-INVOLVED FAMILIES

Sex-Role Development.   Contrary to the modeling theory of the development of gender role, it appears that for boys, their adoption of a traditional male sex role is not influenced by fathers performing traditionally female functions in the home. Findings also suggest that the male gender role is adopted even in preschoolers whose care-giving fathers have traditional female or expressive traits. One could attribute this stability to a number of factors including the influence of peers, preschool curricula, television, and books (Maccoby, 1980). Cognitive factors may also have been influential, as Kohlberg (1966) has argued. With the attainment of gender constancy, the boys own self-categorization as males may have organized their choices of activities and the adoption of a traditional masculine gender role.

Regarding girls, there appears to be support for Johnson's theory that fathers are influential in their daughter's gender role adoption. Further, it appears that father influence in this regard is not solely dependent upon the activities he undertakes but is also dependent upon his personal characteristics. Thus, the father who is not traditionally masculine in either behavior or traits may well raise androgynous daughters, but the father who is involved in nonmasculine activities but traditionally masculine in disposition may rear a typically female daughter.

Cognitive Development.   Findings from traditional families suggesting that the amount of father contact with young boys is positively associated with their intellectual development is congruent with the findings from the Radin, Carlson and Santrock studies of care-giving fathers. The literature linking paternal nurturance and cognitive competence of boys also agrees with the data collected in families in which fathers are highly involved. For girls, the picture is more complex. There are indications that fathers who are highly involved with daughters both facilitate and hinder their cognitive development. The Santrock and Warshak (1979) study of father custody homes suggested that there may be some hindrance, although they discussed social competence and maturity rather than cognitive competence. The constructs are not unrelated however, for Baumrind's (1967, 1978) term competence has been defined by Belsky, Robins, and Gamble

(1982) as including the ability to be instrumentally resourceful and achievement striving, and Baumrind (1970) reported that correlations between IQ and measures of achievement orientation and independence are very high.

The findings linking high father involvement with cognitive ability in girls in two-parent families appear to differ from findings for traditional families where no such relationship was found. Some insight into a possible explanation for this discrepancy is given by an analysis of responses to the Cognitive Home Environment Scale (Radin & Sonquist, 1968) that was incorporated into the lengthy "common" questionnaire. The Cognitive Home Environment Scale (CHES) assesses the cognitive stimulation in the home, for example, the respondent's efforts to teach the child colors or correct grammar, and the educational materials in the home. The questionnaire was administered by both Sagi and Radin and both found the total score significantly higher for primary care-giving fathers than for traditional fathers. Further, in the Radin study, an interaction effect was found between sex of child and paternal involvement. Highly involved fathers of girls were found to have the highest total score on the CHES; fathers with a low level of involvement had the lowest. Radin also correlated the degree of paternal involvement with 3 of the 4 factors of the instrument: direct teaching; educational material in the home; and future expectations for the child. She found that for girls, there were more educational materials in the home but no indication of more direct teaching by fathers. Perhaps the father is stimulating the girls' intellectual growth through more indirect means, possibly through informal interaction around the considerable amount of educational material in the home, e.g., crayons, paper, small scissors. The provocative question of specifically how involved fathers promote their daughter's cognitive development will have to remain unanswered until more data become available.

Social Competence.   It appears that high father involvement in the context of a two-parent family does nothing to impair the child's adjustment or ability to function well. For example, Carlson concluded that the children in all three family groups she studied were remarkably similar on the indices of social development employed. These included measures of gender role, cognitive development, internality, and perceptions of parents. Sagi found the children of highly involved fathers to be more empathetic, and Radin found the children of caregiving fathers were no less empathetic than those of traditional fathers. There were certainly no indications that the children in two-parent families where fathers played an important role in childrearing were less competent than their peers raised in homes where mothers were the primary caretakers. There were indications from Radin's study that children of child-rearing men perceived fathers as more punitive, but this is not an indication of social incompetence and may be a very realistic assessment, given the other data collected about the fathers in the study and their salience for the children. Further, Russell's (1980) father-involved families reported that the men were indeed stricter and had higher standards for children's performance than their spouses.

The situation for middle-class single fathers raising daughters appears to be quite different. According to Santrock and Warshak's (1979) findings, these girls are less socially competent at 6 to 11 years of age than matched girls raised in two-parent families or middle-class boys raised by single men. Although the Santrock-Warshak results appear to conflict with the positive outcomes obtained on numerous studies of single fathers, none of these investigations collected measures of the children themselves; they merely reported what the men said.

Although there were no prior indications in the literature that high paternal involvement in childcare fostered internality in children, it must be acknowledged that no previous study assessed children's locus of control in these nontraditional families. Thus it appears reasonable to suggest that fathers foster internality in children when they themselves exhibit internality by taking on the quintessential female role-caregiver of young children—especially when the men value internality and reinforce it in their children. It also appears that under the conditions of primary or shared care-giving by fathers, children can overcome stereotypes about the family activities fathers undertake. In the past, there have not been any studies that provided data on children's perception of specific parental domestic activities when there was a conflict between societal and family norms. The tentative conclusion that can be drawn from studies of child-rearing men is that children can maintain their own traditional gender role and traditional stereotypes about paternal traits while overcoming stereotypes about parental functions in the home.

GAPS IN OUR KNOWLEDGE ABOUT THE INFLUENCES OF HIGHLY PARTICIPANT FATHERS

The gaps in our knowledge of child-rearing men's influence on children are considerable. All of the studies that have been conducted to date that collected data on both fathers and children have been confined to white middle-class families. It is readily acknowledged by researchers that one cannot generalize data from one social class to other stratifications. In addition, a number of recent articles have argued persuasively that one cannot generalize data from one race to another, or one ethnic group to another, even with social class controlled (Beckett, 1978; Buriel, 1981; Cazenave, 1979; Landry & Jendrek, 1978; Ogbu, 1981; Staples & Mirande, 1980; Velasquez & Velasquez 1980). For example, Ogbu (1981) asserted that parents socialize their children for instrumental competency within their environment and the characteristics associated with competence in one context or subculture may not be linked with competence in another. Thus one must study the context with its own "cultural imperatives" before evaluating parental child-rearing competency or making intergroup comparisons in child-rearing effectiveness. Similarly, other researchers have argued that future research on minority families must focus on the minority family unit as an autonomous system with its own norms and standards (Staples & Mirande, 1980).

There is also a growing body of literature demonstrating that culture and race can interact with parental behaviors to produce different effects on children. For example, it was found that for Mexican-American lower-class fathers, paternal demandingness was positively associated with internal control in their children 9 to 11 years of age but the same relationship did not hold for a matched group of Anglo fathers and their children (Buriel, 1981). Similarly, Baumrind (1972), using a small sample of middle-class black families, found that authoritarianism on the part of fathers and mothers was linked to social competence and independence in black girls, but this was not true in white families.

Including the father's social class, ethnicity, and race as important variables in studies of the influence on children of child-rearing men is only the tip of the iceberg of what has been called the ecological approach. Numerous researchers such as Bronfenbrenner (1977), Lamb and Bronson (1980), Belsky (1981), and Ogbu (1981), to name a few, have stressed the fact that the entire environment in which the father and child are enveloped must be taken into consideration to understand parental influence. Bronfenbrenner (1977) conceptualized the ecological environment of the child as consisting of the microsystem of the family, including all the interpersonal relationships of the members; the mesosystem or other systems in which the child functions, such as the school or peer group; the exosystem or setting that does not itself contain the child but in which events occur that affect the setting containing the child, for example, the workplace of the father; and the macrosystem, which encompasses the patterns of belief systems, lifestyles, and social organizations of the culture or subculture in which the child is functioning. Thus, to comprehend children's development, one must understand all of the systems that are operative in their lives: the micro, meso, exo and macrosystems.

Illustrations of the importance of the macrosystem in child development have been offered above in the discussion of the interaction effects between race or ethnicity and paternal behavior. An example of the influence of microsystem factors on the child was seen in an observational study of fathers interacting with preschool boys and girls who were either only children or middle children with a same-sex older sibling (Bell, Johnson, McGillicuddy–Delisi, & Sigel, 1981). It was found that fathers of only children showed nearly twice as many approval behaviors when the child was a male but, in three child families, daughters received more approval than sons from their fathers. The researchers concluded that unless the effect of family constellation are taken into account in research investigations, the results may be artificial. Kohn's (1969) study of the linkage between father's job and parental child-rearing values also highlighted the importance of the exosystem on the child's development.

The above illustrations suggest that considerable research needs to be done before an adequate understanding is attained of the influence exerted by involved fathers on children. For example, data must be collected about the employment setting of the father and pressures he receives from peers and superiors. On the microlevel, not only must marital relationships be considered as has been suggested (Belsky, 1981) but sibling relationships, and grandparent-grandchild relationships as well. The child's birth order, the family size, and the crowding in the home are also relevant factors. The impact of the father's social network on both father and child must be considered, as well as the mesosystem in which the child functions, for example, the childcare facility. Further, the cultural milieu of the family must be taken into account—its values, standards, and norms. Particularly important are the policies established by the governments at various levels affecting fathers who care for children. For example, are flexible hours of work encouraged? Are paternity leaves assured? To complicate matters even further, researchers must engage in long-term longitudinal investigations to determine more precisely the nature and stability of the influence patterns, to detect if there are any sleeper effects operative such as those found in other domains of child development (Hetherington, 1972; Kagan & Moss, 1962), and to establish the direction of influence within father-caregiver families (Clarke-Stewart, 1973).

Clearly no single researcher can tackle all of the tasks that must be performed. However, if investigators maintain an ecological perspective, they will be more sensitive to the limitations of their data and will attempt to fill the lacunae in our knowledge one brick at a time, if necessary. Not only must family sociologists and developmental psychologists become aware of one another's literature, as has recently been suggested (Belsky, 1981), but the pool of shared knowledge must include relevant literature from the fields of obstetrical medicine (Yarrow, 1981), cultural anthropology (Campbell & Naroll, 1972), social psychology (Kahn, Wolfe, Quinn, Snoer, & Rosenthal, 1964), and public health (Cobbs, Broks, Kasl, & Connelly, 1966) as well, to name but a few disciplines that can contribute to an understanding of paternal influence on child development. It is hoped that interdisciplinary investigations will become commonplace in the future so that many aspects of the child's ecological environment can be studied simultaneously.

To conclude, the data that have been collected to date suggest that fathers who have a major role in raising their children in two-parent families influence the development of both sons and daughters. Some of the findings for intensive paternal involvement could have been predicted from a knowledge of the research literature on father influence on children in traditional families. However, it appears that some unique relationships between father-involvement and child development also emerge when fathers make caring for children one of the most important and time consuming activities in their lives.

REFERENCES

Aberle, D. F., & Naegele, K. D. Middle-class fathers' occupational role and attitudes toward children. *American Journal of Orthopsychiatry,* 1952, *22,* 366–378.

Ainsworth, M. D. S., Blehar, M., Waters, E., & Wall, S. (Eds.), *Patterns of Attachment.* Hillsdale, N.J.: Lawrence Erlbaum Associates, 1978.

Ball, S., & Bogartz, G. A. Research on Sesame Street: Some implications for compensatory education. In E. M. Hetherington, and R. D. Parke (Eds.), *Contemporary readings in child psychology.* New York: McGraw-Hill, 1977.

Bandura, A., & Walters, R. H. *Adolescent aggression.* New York: Ronald Press, 1959.

Bandura, A., & Walters, R. H. *Social learning and personality development.* New York: Holt, Rinehart, & Winston, 1963.

Barnett, M. A., King, L. M., Howard, J. A., & Dino, G. A. Empathy in young children: Relation to parents' empathy, affection and emphasis on feelings of others. *Developmental Psychology,* 1980, *16,* 243–244.

Baumrind, D. Child care practices anteceding three patterns of pre-school behavior. *Genetic Psychology Monographs,* 1967, *75* 43–88.

Baumrind, D. Socialization and instrumental competence in young children. *Young Children,* 1970, *26,* 104–119.

Baumrind, D. An exploratory study of socialization effects on black children: Some black-white comparisons. *Child Development,* 1972, *43,* 261–267.

Baumrind, D. *Social determinants of personal agency..* Paper presented at biennial meeting of the Society for Research on Child Development, New Orleans: March, 1977.

Baumrind, D. Reciprocal rights and responsibilities in parent-child relations. *Journal of Social Issues,* 1978, *34,* 179-189.

Baumrind, D., & Black, A. E. Socialization practices associated with dimensions of competence in pre-school boys and girls. *Child Development,* 1967, *38,* 291–327.

Beckett, J. L. Racial differences in why women work. In S. Golden (Ed.) *Work, family roles, and support systems.,* Ann Arbor, Mich.: The University of Michigan Center for the Continuing Education of Women, 1978.

Bell, C. S., Johnson, J. E., McGillicuddy-Delisi, A. V., & Sigel, I. E. The effects of family constellation and child gender on parental use of evaluative feedback. *Child Development,* 1981, *52,* 701–704.

Bell, R. Q. A reinterpretation of the direction of effects in studies of socialization. *Psychological Review,* 1968, *75,* 81–95.

Bell, R. Q. Contributions of human infants to caregiving and social interaction. In M. Lewis & L. A. Rosenblum (Eds.), *The effect of the infant on its care-giver.* New York: Wiley, 1974.

Belsky, J. Mother-father-infant interaction: A naturalistic observational study. *Developmental Psychology,* 1979, *15,* 601–607.

Belsky, J. Early human experiences: A family perspective. *Developmental Psychology,* 1981, *17,* 3–23.

Belsky, J., Robins, E., & Gamble, W. Characteristics, consequences and determinants of parental competence: Toward a contextual theory. In M. Lewis, & L. Rosenblum (Eds.), *Social connections—beyond the dyad.* New York: Plenum, 1982.

Bem, S. L. The measurement of psychological androgyny. *Journal of Consulting and Clinical Psychology,* 1974, *42,* 155–162.

Bem, S. L., & Watson, C. *Scoring packet; Bem Sex-Role Inventory*, Unpublished paper, Stanford University, Stanford, Calif., 1976.

Biller, H. B. The father and personality development: Paternal deprivation and sex-role development. In M. E. Lamb (Ed.), *The role of the father in child development*. New York: Wiley, 1976.

Bing, E. The effect of childrearing practices on development of differential cognitive abilities. *Child Development*, 1963, *34*, 631–648.

Blanchard, R. W., & Biller, H. B. Father availability and academic performance among third-grade boys. *Developmental Psychology*, 1971, *4*, 301–305.

Block, J. *Lives through time*. Berkeley, Calif.: Bancraft Books, 1971.

Block, J., von der Lippe, A., & Block, J. H. Sex-role and socialization: Some personality concomitants and environmental antecedents. *Journal of Consulting and Clinical Psychology*, 1973, *41*, 321–341.

Block, J. H., Block, J., & Harrington, D. M. *The relationship of parental teaching strategies to ego-resiliency in preschool children*. Paper presented at the meeting of the Western Psychological Asociation, San Francisco, 1974.

Boerger, P. H. The relationship of boys' intellectual achievement behavior to parental involvement, aspirations, and accuracy of IQ estimate. *Dissertation Abstracts International*, 1971, *31*, 5191.

Borke, H. Interpersonal perception of young children. *Developmental Psychology*, 1971, *5*, 263–269.

Borke, H. The development of empathy in Chinese and American children between three and six years of age: A cross-culture study. *Developmental Psychology*, 1973, *9*, 102–108.

Bowerman, C. E., & Elder, G. H., Jr. Variations in adolescent perception of family power structure. *American Sociological Review*, 1964, *29*, 551–567.

Bridge, R. G., Moock, P. R., & Judd, C. M. *The determinants of educational outcomes: The impact of families, peers, teachers and schools*. New York: Ballinger, 1979.

Bronfenbrenner, U. Some familial antecedents of responsibility and leadership in adolescents. In L. Petrillo & B. M. Bass (Eds.), *Leadership and interpersonal behavior*, New York: Holt, Rinehart, & Winston, 1961.

Bronfenbrenner, U. *Interactions among theory, research, and application in child development*. Paper presented at the meeting of the Society for Research in Child Development, Philadelphia, March, 1973.

Bronfenbrenner, U. Lewinian space and ecological substance. *Journal of Social Issues*, 1977, *33*, 199–212.

Brown, D. G. Sex-role preference in children. *Psychological Monographs*, 1956, *70*, (14, Serial No. 287).

Buriel, R. The relation of Anglo- and Mexican-American children's locus of control beliefs to parents' and teachers' socialization practices. *Child Development*, 1981, *52*, 104–113.

Buss, D. M. Predicting parent-child interactions from children's activity level. *Developmental Psychology*, 1981, *17*, 59–65.

Busse, T. V. Child rearing antecedents of flexible thinking. *Developmental Psychology*, 1969, *1*, 585–591.

Campbell, D. T., & Naroll, R. T. The mutual methodological relevance of anthropology and psychology. In F. L. K. Hsu (Ed.), *Psychological Anthropology*. Cambridge, Mass.: Schenkman, 1972.

Carlsmith, L. Effect of early father absence on scholastic aptitude: *Harvard Educational Review*, 1964, *34*, 3–21.

Carlson, B. E. *Shared vs primarily maternal child-rearing: Effects of dual careers on families with young children*. Unpublished doctoral dissertation, University of Michigan, 1980.

Carlson, B. E. Preschoolers' sex-role identify, father-role perceptions, and paternal family participation. *Journal of Family Issues*, 1981, *2*, 238–255.

Cazenave, N. A. Middle-income black fathers. An analysis of the provider role. *The Family Coordinator*, 1979, *27*, 583–593.

Clarke-Stewart, K. A. Interactions between mothers and their young children: Characteristics and consequences. *Monographs of the Society for Research in Child Development*, 1973, *38*, (Serial No. 153).

Clarke-Stewart, K. A. And daddy makes three: The father's impact on mother and young child. *Child Development*, 1978, *49*, 466–478.

Coates, B., Pusser, H. E. & Goodman, I. The influence of "Sesame Street" and "Mister Rogers' Neighborhood" on children's social behavior in the preschool. *Child Development*, 1976, *47*, 138–144.

Cobbs, S., Brooks, G. W., Kasl, S. V., & Connelly, W. E. The health of people changing jobs: A description of a longitudinal study. *American Journal of Public Health*, 1966, *56*, 1476–1481.

Cochran, M. M., & Brassard, J. A. Child development and personal social networks. *Child Development*, 1979, *50*, 601–616.

Coleman, J. S., Campbell, E. O., Hobson, C. J., McPartland, J., Mood, A. M., Weinfeld, F. D., & York, R. L. *Equality of educational opportunity*. Washington, D.C.: Department of Health, Education, and Welfare, Office of Education, 1966.

Crandall, V., Dewey, R., Katkovsky, W., & Preston, A. Parents' attitudes and behaviors and grade-school children's academic achievements. *The Journal of Genetic Psychology*, 1964, *104*, 53–66.

Davidson, E. S., Yasuna, A., & Tower, A. The effects of television cartoons on sex-role stereotyping in young girls. *Child Development*, 1979, *50*, 597–600.

DeFrain, J. Androgynous parents tell who they are and what they need. *The Family Coordinator*, 1979, *28*, 237–243.

Dill, J. R. *Indices of socialization: Black father-son interaction (a preliminary report).*, Paper presented at the Society for Research in Child Development Biennial Conference, Denver, April, 1975.

Dyk, R. B., & Witkin, H. A. Family experiences related to the development of differentiation in children. *Child Development*, 1965, *36*, 21–55.

Eiduson, B. T., & Alexander, J. W. The role of children in alternative family styles. *Journal of Social Issues*, 1978, *34*, 149–167.

Epstein, A., & Radin, N. Motivational components related to father behavior and cognitive functioning. *Child Development*, 1975, *46*, 831–839.

Fagot, B. J. The influence of sex of child on parental reactions to toddler children. *Child Development*, 1978, *49*, 459–465.

Feld, S., & Radin, N. *Social psychology for social work*. New York: Columbia University Press, 1982.

Field, T. Interaction behaviors of primary versus secondary caretaker fathers. *Developmental Psychology*, 1978, *14*, 183–184.

Friedrich–Cofer, L. K., Huston-Stein, A., Kiphis, D. M., Susman, E. J., & Clewett, A. S. Environmental enhancement of prosocial television content: Effects on interpersonal behavior, imaginative play, and self-regulation in a natural setting. *Developmental Psychology*, 1979, *15*, 637–646.

Gersick, K. E. Fathers by choice: Divorced men who receive custody of their children. In G. Levinger & O. C. Moles (Eds.), *Divorce and separation*, New York: Basic Books, 1979.

Gewirtz, J. L., & Stingle, K. G. Learning of generalized imitation as the basis for identification. *Psychological Review*, 1968, *75*, 374–397.

Gold, D., & Andres, D. Comparisons of adolescent children with employed and non-employed mothers. *Merrill-Palmer Quarterly*, 1978, *24*, 243–254.

Goodenough, E. W. Interest in persons as an aspect of sex difference in the early years. *Genetic Psychology Monographs*, 1957, *55*, 287–323.

Grunebaum, M. G., Hurwitz, I., Prentice, N. M., & Sperry, B. M. Fathers of sons with primary neurotic learning inhibition. *American Journal of Orthopsychiatry*, 1962, *32*, 462–473.

Harrington, D. M., Block J. H., & Block, J. Intolerance of ambiguity in preschool children: Psychometric considerations, behavioral manifestations and parental correlates. *Developmental Psychology*, 1978, *14*, 242–256.

Hetherington, E. M. Effects of father absence on personality development in adolescent daughters. *Developmental Psychology*, 1972, *7*, 313–326.

Hetherington, E. M., & Frankie, G. Effects of parental dominance, warmth, and conflict on imitation in children. *Journal of Personality and Social Psychology*, 1967, *6*, 119–125.

Hoffman, L. W. Changes in family roles, socialization, and sex differences. *American Psychologist*, 1977, *32*, 644–657.

Hoffman, M. L. Moral development. In P. H. Mussen (Ed.), *Carmichael's manual of child psychology (Vol. 2, 3rd ed.)*, New York: Wiley, 1970.

Honzik, M. P. A sex difference in the age of onset of the parent-child resemblance in intelligence. *Journal of Educational Psychology*, 1963, *53*, 231–237.

Jencks, C., Smith, M., Acland, H., Bane, M. J., Cohen, D., Gintis, H., Heyns, B., & Michelson, S. *Inequality*. New York: Basic Books, 1972.

Johnson, M. M. Fathers, mothers and sex typing. In E.M. Hetherington and R. D. Parke (Eds.), *Contemporary readings in child psychology*. New York: Mc-Graw-Hill, 1977.

Jordan, B., Radin, N., & Epstein, A. S. Paternal behavior and intellectual functioning in preschool boys and girls. *Developmental Psychology*, 1975, *11*, 407–408.

Kagan, J. The concept of identification. *Psychological Review*, 1958, *65*, 296–305.

Kagan, J., & Lemkin, J. The child's differential perception of parental attributes. *Journal of Abnormal Social Psychology*, 1960, *61*, 440–447.

Kagan, J., & Moss, H. A. *Birth to maturity: A study in psychological development*. New York: Wiley, 1962.

Kahn, R. L., Wolfe, D. M., Quinn, R. P., Snoer, J. D., & Rosenthal, R. A. *Organizational stress: Studies in role conflict and ambiguity*. New York: Wiley, 1964.

Katz, A. J. Lone fathers: Perspectives and implications for family policy. *The Family Coordinator*, 1979, *28*, 521–528.

Kohlberg, L. A cognitive-developmental analysis of children's sex-role attitudes. In E. Maccoby (Ed.), *The development of sex differences*. Stanford, Calif.: Stanford University Press, 1966.

Kohn, M. L. *Class and conformity*. Homewood, Ill.: The Dorsey Press, 1969.

Lamb, M. E. Effects of stress and cohort on mother-and father-infant interaction. *Developmental Psychology*, 1976, *12*, 435–443. (a)

Lamb, M. E. (Ed.), *The role of the father in child development*. New York: Wiley, 1976. (b)

Lamb, M. E. Father-infant and mother-infant interaction in the first year of life. *Child Development*, 1977, *48*, 167–181.

Lamb, M. E., & Bronson, S. K. Fathers in the context of family influences: Past, present and future. *School Psychology Review*, 1980, *9*, 336–353.

Lamb, M. E., Frodi, A. M., Chase-Lansdale, L., & Owen, M. T. *The father's role in nontraditional family contexts: Direct and indirect effects*. Paper presented at the American Psychological Association Convention, Toronto, Sept. 1978.

Lamb, M. E., Frodi, A. M., Hwang, C–P., & Frodi, M. Varying degrees of paternal involvement in infant care: Attitudinal and behavioral correlates. In M. E. Lamb (Ed.), *Nontraditional families: Parenting and childcare*. Hillsdale, N.J.: Lawrence Erlbaum Associates, 1982.

Lamb, M. E., Frodi, A. M., Hwang, C-P., Frodi, M., & Steinberg, J. Mother-and father-infant interaction involving play and holding in traditional and non-traditional Swedish families. *Developmental Psychology*, 1982, *17*, xxx xxx.

Lamb, M. E., Hwang, C-P., Frodi, A. M., & Frodi, M. Security of mother-and father-infant attachment and its relation to sociability with strangers in traditional and non-traditional Swedish families. *Infant Behavior and Development*, 1982, *5*, in press.

Landry, B., & Jendrek, M. P. The employment of wives in middle-class black families. *Journal of Marriage and the Family,* 1978 *40,* 787–797.

Landy, F., Rosenberg, B.G., & Sutton–Smith, B. The effect of limited father absence on cognitive development. *Child Development,* 1969, *40,* 941–944.

Langlois, J.H., & Downs, A.C. Mothers, fathers, and peers as socialization agents of sex-typed play behaviors in young children. *Child Development,* 1980, *51,* 1217–1247.

Lewis, M., & Weintraub, M. The father's role in the child's social network. In M.E. Lamb (Ed.), *The role of the father in child development.* N.Y.: Wiley, 1976.

Lieberts, R.M. Some immediate effects of televised violence on children's behavior. *Developmental Psychology,* 1972, *6,* 469–475.

Lynn, D.B. Curvilinear relation between cognitive functioning and distances of child from parent of the same sex. *Psychological Review,* 1969, *76,* 236–240.

Lynn, D. The father: *His role in development.* Monterey, Calif.: Brooks/Cole, 1974.

Lytton, H. Observation studies of parent-child interaction: A methodological review. *Child Development,* 1971, *42,* 651–684.

Lytton, H. Three approaches to the study of parent-child interaction: Ethological, interview, and experimental. *Journal of Child Psychology and Psychiatry,* 1973, *14,* 1–17.

Lytton, H. Disciplinary encounters between young boys and their mothers and fathers. Is there a contingency system? *Developmental Psychology,* 1979, *15,* 256–268.

Maccoby, E. *Social development, psychological growth, and parent-child relations.* New York: Harcourt Brace Jovanovich, 1980.

Maccoby, E.E., & Jacklin, C.N. *The psychology of sex differences.* Stanford, Calif.: Stanford University Press, 1974.

Masur, E.F., & Gleason, J.B. Parent-child interaction and the acquisition of lexical information during play. *Developmental psychology,* 1980, *16,* 404–409.

McCall, R.B. Childhood IQ's as predictors of adult educational and occupational status. *Science,* 1977, *197,* 482–483.

Meichenbaum, D. *Cognitive-behavior modification. New York: Plenum Press, 1977.*

Mendes, H.A. Single fatherhood. *Social Work,* 1976, *21,* 308–312.

Mischel, W., Zeiss, R., & Zeiss, A. Internal-external control and persistence: Validation and implications of the Stanford Preschool Internal-External Scale. *Journal of Personality and Social Psychology,* 1974, *29,* 265–278.

Mussen, P., & Distler, L. Child-rearing antecedents of masculine identification in kindergarten boys. *Child Development,* 1960, *31,* 89–100.

Mussen, P., & Rutherford, E. Parent-child relations and parental personality in relation to young children's sex-role preferences. *Child Development,* 1963, *34,* 589–607.

Mussen, P.H., Young, H.B., Gaddini, P., & Morante, L. The influence of father-son relationships on adolescent personality and attitudes. *Journal of Child Psychology and Psychiatry,* 1963, *4,* 3–16.

Ogbu, J.U. Origins of human competence: A cultural ecological perspective. *Child Development,* 1981, *52,*413–429.

Osofsky, J.D., & O'Connell, E.J. Parent-child interaction: Daughters' effects upon mothers' and fathers' behaviors. *Developmental Psychology,* 1972, *7,* 157–168.

Parke, R.D., Power, T.G., & Fisher, T. The adolescent father's impact on the mother and child. *Journal of Social Issues,* 1980, *36,* 88–106.

Parke, R.D., & Sawin, D.B. The father's role in infancy; A re-evaluation. *The Family Coordinator,* 1976, *25,* 365–371.

Patterson, G.R., & Guillon, E.M. *Living with children.* Champaign, Ill.: Research Press, 1968.

Payne, D.E., & Mussen, P.H. Parent-child relations and father identification among adolescent boys. *Journal of Abnormal and Social Psychology,* 1965, *52,* 358–362.

Pedersen, F.A. Does research on children reared in father-absent families yield information on father influences? *The Family Coordinator,* 1976, *25,* 459–464.

Pedersen, F.A., Rubenstein, O.L., & Yarrow, L.J. Infant development in father-absent families. *Journal of Genetic Psychology,* 1979, *135,* 51–61.

Radin, N. Childrearing antecedents of cognitive development in lower-class preschool children. (Doctoral dissertation, University of Michigan, 1969). *Dissertation Abstracts International,* 1970, *30,* 4364B. (University Microfilms No. 70–4170).

Radin, N. Father-child interaction and the intellectual functioning of 4–year–old boys. *Developmental Psychology,* 1972, *6,* 353–361.

Radin, N. The role of the father in cognitive/academic and intellectual development. In M.E. Lamb (Ed.), *The role of the father in child development.* New York: Wiley, 1976.

Radin, N. *Childrearing fathers in intact families with preschoolers.* Paper presented at the annual meeting of the American Psychological Association, Toronto, September 1978. (ERIC Document Reproduction Service No. Ed 194 850)

Radin, N. *Childrearing fathers in intact families: Some antecedents and consequences.* Merril-Palmer Quarterly, 1981, *27,* 489–514. (a)

Radin, N. *Wives of childrearing men.* Paper presented at the biennial meeting of the Society for Research in Child Development, Boston, April 1981.(b)

Radin, N. The role of the father in cognitive/academic intellectual development. In M.E. Lamb (Ed.), *The role of the father in child development.* Second Edition. New York: Wiley, 1981. (c)

Radin, N. Primary caregiving and role sharing fathers of preschoolers. In M.E. Lamb (Ed.), *Nontraditional families: Parenting and child development.* Hillsdale, N.J.: Lawrence Erlbaum Associates, 1982.

Radin, N. The unique contribution of the family to childrearing during the preschool and early years. S.G. Moore & C. Cooper (Eds.), *The young child: Reviews of research.* Washington, D.C.: National Association for the Education of Young Children, in press.

Radin, N., & Epstein, A. *Observed paternal behavior with preschool children: Final report.* Ann Arbor, Mich.: The University of Michigan, School of Social Work, 1975. (ERIC Document Reproduction Service No. ED 174 656)

Radin, N., & Sagi, A. Childrearing fathers in intact families in Israel and the U.S.A. *Merrill-Palmer Quarterly,* 1982, *28,* 111–136.

Radin, N., & Sonquist, H. *The Gale preschool program: Final report.* Ypsilanti, Mich.: Ypsilanti Public Schools, 1968.

Reis, M., & Gold, D. Relation of paternal availability to problem solving and sex-role orientation in young boys. *Psychological Reports,* 1977, *40,* 823–829.

Reuter, M.W., & Biller, H.B. Perceived paternal nurturance-availability and personality adjustment among college males. *Journal of Consulting and Clinical Psychology,* 1973, *40,* 339–342.

Rheingold, H.L., & Cook, K.U. The contents of boys' and girls' rooms as an index of parents' behavior. *Child Development,* 1975, *46,* 459–463.

Russell, G. The father role and its relation to masculinity, femininity and androgyny. *Child Development,* 1978, *49,* 1174–1181.

Russell, G. *Father as caregivers: (The could . . . if they had to'')* Paper presented at 49th Congress of ANZLAS, Aukland, New Zealand, January 1979. (a)

Russell, G. *The role of fathers in child development: An Australian perspective.* Paper presented at the National Conference of the Pre-School Association, Sydney, May 1979. (b)

Russell, G. *Fathers as caregivers: Possible antecedents and consequences.* Paper presented to the study group on "Fathers and Social Policy," University of Haifa, Haifa, Israel, July 1980.

Russell, G. Shared caregiving families: An Australian study. In M.E. Lamb (Ed.), *Nontraditional families: Parenting and childrearing.* Hillsdale, N.J.: Lawrence Erlbaum Associates, 1982.

Sagi, A. Antecedents and consequences of various degrees of paternal involvement in child-rearing: The Israeli project. In M.E. Lamb (Ed.), *Nontraditional families: Parenting and child development.* Hillsdale, N.J.: Lawrence Erlbaum Associates, 1982.

Sagi, A., & Reshef, R. *Degree of paternal involvement in childrearing in intact families in Israel: Antecedents and effects.* Paper presented at the biennial meeting of the Society for Research in Child Development, Boston, April 1981.

Sameroff, A.J. Early influences on development: Fact or fancy? In E.M. Hetherington & R.D. Parke (Eds.), *Contemporary readings in child psychology.* New York: McGraw-Hill, 1977.

Santrock, J.W., & Warshak, R.A. Father custody and social development in boys and girls. *Journal of Social Issues,* 1979, *35,* 112–125.

Sears, P.S. Child rearing factors related to the playing of sex-typed roles. *American Psychologist,* 1953, *8,* 431. (Abstract)

Sears, R. Comparison of interviews with questionnaires for measuring mothers' attitudes toward sex and aggression. *Journal of Personality and Social Psychology,* 1965, *2,* 37–44.

Smith, A.D. Egalitarian marriages: Implications for practice and policy. *Social Casework,* 1980, *61,* 288–295.

Smith, A.D., & Reid, W.J. *The family role revolution.* Paper presented at the Annual Program Meeting of the Council on Social Work Education, Los Angeles, March 1980.

Smith, R.M., & Smith, C.W. Childrearing and single-parent fathers. *Family Relations,* 1981, *30,* 411–417.

Solomon, D., Houlihan, K.A., Busse, T.V., & Parelius, R.J. Parent behavior and child academic achievement, achievement striving, and related personality characteristics. *Genetic Psychology Monographs,* 1971, *83,* 173–273.

Spelke, E., Zelazo, P., Kagan, J., & Kotelchuck, M. Father interaction and separation protest. *Developmental Psychology,* 1973, *9,* 83–90.

Staples, R., & Mirande, A. Racial and cultural variations among American families: A decennial review of the literature on minority families, *Journal of Marriage and the Family,* 1980, *42,* 887–904.

Tauber, M.A. Sex differences in parent-child interaction styles during a free-play session. *Child Development,* 1979, *50,* 981–988.

Thomas, M.H., & Drabman, R.S. Toleration of real life aggression as a function of exposure to televised violence and age of subject. *Merrill-Palmer Quarterly,* 1975, *21,* 227–232.

Velasquez, J.S., & Velasquez, C.P. Application of a bicultural assessment framework to social work practice with Hispanics. *Family Relations,* 1980, *29,* 598–603.

Watson, M.A. Custody alternatives: Defining the best interests of the child. *Family Relations,* 1981, *30,* 474–479.

Yarrow, L. Fathers who deliver. *Parents,* 1981, *56,* 62–66.

Yarrow, M.R. Problems of methods in parent-child research. *Child Development,* 1963, *34,* 215–226.

12 Costs and Benefits of Increased Paternal Involvement in Childrearing: The Societal Perspective

Abraham Sagi

Nachman Sharon
University of Haifa

In recent years, scholars have paid considerable attention to the role of the father, providing evidence for potentially significant paternal contributions to child development and family life (Lamb, 1981; Yogman, 1981). Wolins (see Chapter 7), going beyond the usual micro level analysis of parent-child interaction and its effects, provides a broader perspective in which the father is viewed as an asset to the psychological, physical, and economic situation of the family. Others have studied father-absent families in order to assess the father's significance (e.g., Hetherington and Deur, 1972). There is also a growing body of knowledge showing that increased paternal involvement in child rearing contributes to the well being of both father and family (Heath, 1978; Radin, 1982; Russell, 1982; Sagi, 1982).

The problem, however, is that paternal participation in child rearing is not sufficiently established in our society. Previous chapters in this book emphasized the costs and benefits of increased paternal involvement for men, women, and children; the present one takes a broader view by examining costs and benefits for families and for society at large. Most of the analyses in this chapter are on the macro level, and because data are scarce and controversial many of the ideas presented are speculative.

Our discussion begins with a brief survey of the literature demonstrating that most people seem to prefer the nuclear family arrangement. We then note the changes in role division between males and females in nuclear families that have made females more active in the work force, while men have not become significantly more active in child care and household duties. Next we speculate that the differences in the pace of role changes among men and women constitute one of several factors accounting for some of our current social and demographic problems, such as increasing rates of divorce and abandonment and decreasing birthrates. Subsequent sections suggest that increased paternal involvement should be encouraged by creating an environment that allows mothers and fathers to combine work and family activities more flexibly, depending on their own preferences. The analysis that follows is aimed at identifying the variables preventing significant change toward more paternal involvement. Finally, we analyze the financial costs of attempting to increase paternal involvement and the possible benefits for individuals as well as for society at large.

PREFERENCES FOR THE NUCLEAR FAMILY ARRANGEMENT

There are various indications that the nuclear family is a very robust institution. Scanzoni and Scanzoni (1976) and Bane (1977) have pointed out that significant increases in the divorce rate do not mean that adults prefer not to be involved in families, since concurrent increases in the rates of remarriage show the tendency to enter into new nuclear, family arrangements. In other words, current male and female roles may be such that the likelihood of divorce is increased; but the family institution is not on its way out.

In their large national (United States) survey, Campbell, Converse, and Rodgers (1976) reported that married men and women were more satisfied with their lives than singles, divorcees, and widows were. Moreover, Hoffman and Hoffman (1973) showed that more people prefer to have children than not. At the same time, unusual "familial" arrangements such as families in communes, unwed motherhood, and group marriages may only constitute short-range solutions. Recent reports (Berger, Hackett, & Millar, 1972; Bowman & Spanier, 1978; Kanter, 1973) show that most communes tend to be short lived; most of the persons who entered communes in the late 1960s and early 1970s have since left them; many have married and today live in more traditional arrangements. Kilgo (1972) suggests that the problems encountered by group marriages are probably too great for most people to overcome; it is thus not surprising that group marriages tend to be short lived and unstable (Bowman & Spanier, 1978).

The changing role of families in Israeli kibbutzim provides another example of the tendency toward the nuclear family arrangement. When first founded, all kibbutzim had their children cared for by metaplot (caregivers), with children sleeping in children's houses rather than in their parents' apartments. In recent years, however, the centrality of the family has been reinforced, and the most significant change has involved a shift toward a more conventional sleeping arrangement, with the children staying overnight in their parents' homes. In 1981, for example, about 42% of the kibbutzim maintained what Tiger and Shepher (1975) refer to as the familistic arrangement, and a further 5% are in the process of shifting to this arrangement.

In sum, we can see that the nuclear family is still the most popular arrangement for childrearing, and that whenever deviations from it are attempted, corrective mechanisms seem to draw families back toward the nuclear family arrangement.

CHANGING FAMILY ROLES

According to the functionalist approach (Parsons & Bales, 1955), equality in the division of responsibilites between males and females is not viable because stability and equilibrium require each partner to specialize in one major domain, for example, with men specializing in instrumental tasks and women in expressive tasks. In her sociological analysis however, Bernard (1981) has shown that the traditional family structure, in which the wife-mother is the housewife and husband-father is the provider, has changed substantially in recent years. Scanzoni and Scanzoni's (1976) sociological-historical analysis shows that a gradual change has occurred. Prior to the 20th century, the family was characterized by the owner-property arrangement, with men being owners and women their property. Then followed a transition to the head-complement arrangement: Women's feelings were taken into consideration and they were granted some rights. Fathers, however, remained the heads of the family, enjoying more rights than their wives. By moving into the labor force in the 1960s and 1970s, women began to acquire more rights and privileges of their own, and men gradually became senior partners rather than heads. The status of women thus increased from that of complement to that of junior partner. This is the characteristic arrangement in Western society today.

Scanzoni and Scanzoni's analysis is very useful because it suggests a clear and persistent trend toward a state of equilibrium in family roles. Recent data confirm the existence of these trends. For example, Ramey (1977) showed that few people now perceive ''the ideal family'' as one consisting of an employed father and a mother at home caring for two children. This finding is supported by statistics (Newland, 1980) showing that in the mid 1970s only 7% of American households conformed to such a description. There is an increasing number of families whose members share at least some family responsibilites.

As Hoffman (1979) argues, women's participation in the labor force has increased regardless of economic conditions. This again is supported by recent multinational statistics (Newland, 1980) showing that in the last two decades, more women and mothers have sought employment, and that the difference between the numbers of employed males and females has decreased. Changes in role allocation and in the privileges and rights of men and women are also reflected in contemporary social policies and legislation concerning the status of men and women. Kamerman (1980) has shown that in a number of countries a growing number of laws dealing with sexual equality, maternal benefits, and childcare arrangements have been introduced.

The growing tendency for more sexual equality is particularly evident in the increased numbers of women participating in the labor force (Newland, 1980), while changes in paternal involvement seem minimal. In developed or developing, capitalist or socialist, agricultural or industrial societies, women's contributions to the family are multifaceted (paid work, housework and child rearing), whereas males are mainly involved in paid work. This suggests that the total workload of women is greater than that of men.

When comparing the total workload of men and women, however, it is important to distinguish between full time and part time working mothers. Time-use analyses show that only in the case of full time working mothers is the total workload of women greater than that of men (Pleck & Rustad, 1980). Consequently, it is particularly this group of women that enjoys less leisure time. There is no evidence that the total work load of part time working mothers is higher than that of men who are employed full time. This may lead one to suggest that, because mothers who are employed part time invest about as much time in paid and family work combined as do fathers who are employed full time, these women are not disadvantaged. However, one of the reasons for holding part time positions may be the women's knowledge that a full time position would make their total workload too onerous. By taking part time employment, however, these women may be limiting their professional opportunities. Further, although many employed mothers today are part time employees, a growing number of women are employed full time (Glick & Norton, 1979) because of economic problems and the insufficient availability of satisfactory part time positions. Thus, although mothers who are employed full and part time face different problems, sexual inequality places both under stress. The following sections examine the possible consequences of these role asymmetries on the family.

CONSEQUENCES

In this chapter, we focus on two important social phenomena: increasing divorce rates and declining birthrates. Although these topics do not represent the entire spectrum of issues that might be discussed in this context, they are sufficient to demonstrate the implication of role asymmetries within the family for society at large.

Disharmony in the Family

Kamerman and Kahn (1978) and Scanzoni and Scanzoni (1976) both show that however divorce rates are computed, rates have been increasing recently in most industrialized countries. Some scholars contend that these trends may be attributed largely to women's increasing demands for self-actualization, independence, rights, and benefits (Goode, 1963; Scanzoni & Scanzoni, 1976). Although increasing numbers of women have been able to improve their status outside the family (for example, in the labor force), motherhood often conflicts with the individual goals of the parent. Most societies have not yet reached a level compatible with what Rapoport, Rapoport, and Strelitz (1977) call the "conception of balance" between the husband's and wife's involvement in the areas of paid work, housework, child rearing, and social involvement with persons outside the family. The larger workload of women in such families may constitute one reason for the increasing number of divorces occurring today.

Further, according to Scanzoni and Scanzoni (1976), women are likely in the future to demand improvements in their status from that of junior partners in the family. These demands may exceed the ability of most men to accomodate such changes even in developed societies, and as a result, divorce rates may rise even higher. Men's inability to respond appropriately to women's desires for greater self-actualization may also affect divorce rates among couples in middle and late adulthood. For example, the "empty nest" phenomenon (Duvall, 1977) manifests itself in heightened self-awareness and self-actualization needs among many women whose children have grown up. Many men are ill-prepared to deal with these. The fact that divorced men are more likely to remarry than are divorced women (Census Bureau, 1980) supports our claim that women, rather than men, are frustrated by marriages and thus hesitant to remarry.

In those countries where the legal and cultural system does not permit formal divorce, some women (and of course some men) choose to abandon their families. Although there may be many causes for this (personality, love affairs, etc.), one major cause may be women's discomfort with their situation and their feelings of insufficient self-actualization in the face of their husbands' inability to empathize and to react appropriately (Scanzoni & Scanzoni, 1976; Todres, 1978). Todres, nothing the increasing numbers of runaway wives in Canada and the U.S., suggested that running away is usually a planned rather than an impulsive act. Many of the women tried to signal to their husbands before resorting to such a drastic solution, but their cues were inappropriately perceived. This interpretation is supported by qualitative material presented by Friedan (1963).

In summary, divorce and runaway rates are rising in many countries, regardless of their political or economic structure, and across all age groups. Role asymmetry and sexual inequality, whereby the joint work-family load of women is higher than that of men, may be one of the causes for this.

Birth Rate

Another widespread phenomenon among the developed countries is the declining birthrate, and also a decreasing number of women who expect to have three or more children, and an increasing number who expect to remain childless or to have only one child (Census Bureau, 1980; Scanzoni & Scanzoni, 1976). Among possible explanations for this decline are economic circumstances and aspirations, the desire for a freer life style, and women's heightened motivation for self-actualization and personal growth. Many women choose to participate in the labor force rather than to have children.

Some scholars have claimed that decreasing birthrates may be partly the result of a process whereby childlessness has come to be a legitimate family arrangement (Veevers, 1974). Discussing whether childless career women are pursuing a freely chosen lifestyle, or whether their decision not to have children is a result of situational barriers, Hoffman and Hoffman (1973) noted that if the former is true, then little can or should be done, whereas if the latter is true, society could change the situation, should such a change be desired. Veever (1973) found that about two–thirds of the childless women he studied wanted children but were waiting to have them sometime in the future. Other data show that there are more people who want children than who do not (Hoffman & Hoffman, 1973). Far from being a voluntary way of life, therefore, it seems that childlessness may often be the result of society's failure to take into consideration the aspiration and needs of women. Many women may choose to postpone having children, to have fewer children, or not have children at all, knowing that children would make their overall workload heavier than that of their husbands. This too may contribute to the decline in birthrate.

Summary

Many scholars today believe that the family is still the primary transmitter of societal values. According to Kamerman and Kahn (1978), people from many countries share a view of "the family as the central institution for the economic support, nurturance, care and socialization of children . . . The family is uniquely qualified for the production of children. No institution is viewed as a replacement for the family (p. 10)." Congruent with this are the findings that most Americans place a high value on family life, (Campbell et al, 1976) and that a declining proportion of adults believe that divorce should remain as easily obtainable as it is today (Census Bureau, 1980). Moreover, while divorce rates increase, so too do the number of remarriages. These facts all indicate that the family remains an important social institution. This raises an interesting paradox: On the one hand, increasing rates of divorce, family violence, and abandonment seem to indicate a weakening of the family institution; on the other hand, we find expressions of support for marriage and the family manifested in both attitudes and behavior. Society's failure to resolve this paradox, Kamerman (1980) suggests, may lead to intense pressures on the family and a possible "loss in the quality and quantity of future generations (p. 38)."

We have attempted to show that some of the social and demographic problems confronting modern societies may be attributed in part to role asymmetry within the family. An increasing number of women invest more time than males in the combination of paid work and family work. To alleviate this, families should perhaps be allowed to choose for themselves how to divide responsibilites for breadwinning, housework, and child care. In some families, this will probably require increased paternal participation in household duties and child care. We must then find ways to facilitate increased paternal involvement.

TOWARD INCREASED PATERNAL INVOLVEMENT

Previous sections of this chapter emphasized the importance of the nuclear family and identified the need to encourage greater paternal participation in the family. This suggestion is far from revolutionary; as far back as the Renaissance (Fasteau, 1975), men have been considered capable of integrating instrumental and expressive skills. This integration of skills can prove to be very rewarding, as demonstrated by the high level of development of the arts, architecture, and literature. Crites and Fitzgerald (1978), in their historical-literary analysis, have shown that the distinction between instrumental male roles and expressive female roles was artificially induced, creating the myth of the competent male.

Levine (1980) has suggested that in the next decade we should not only change the image of the father, but also form a new image of the family that reflects a more equitable partnership between mothers and fathers. Unfortunately, while some factors are currently advancing this process, others, both on the micro and macro levels, are hindering or preventing change. In the following sections, we analyze the forces that both facilitate and block change. We then compare the costs to society of asymmetric role division in the family, with the costs of increasing the options available to families and parents.

DETERMINANTS OF PATERNAL INVOLVEMENT

In this section, we examine the simultaneous impact of various forces restraining change toward increased paternal participation. Then we discuss those forces that push men toward greater paternal involvement.

The norms and attitudes governing individuals in their parenting roles act as restraints on the micro level. According to Levine (1980), for example, it is difficult for most men to be highly involved in both family work and paid work. Lamb and Levine (Chapter 4) report that, even in a society like Sweden, with its advanced family policy and legislation, employers have a negative attitude toward men who take paternal leave. The fact that the current value system is incompatible with the advanced legislation may explain why a relatively small number of men decide to take paternal leave, even though they are entitled to it. Moreover, social reinforcements for fathers who decide to eschew their traditional role are still lacking (Scanzoni & Scanzoni, 1976). Women too are often not helpful in the pursuit of change: They themselves do not easily give up their responsibilities in the family, because they wish to maintain their status (Lein, 1979; Levine, 1980).

Forces on the macro level restricting paternal involvement include the current structure of the labor force, opportunities for family activities during leisure time, and existing social services and policy. Of these, the structure of the labor force is perhaps most important, with factors such as type of work, flexibility in workload and worktime, seniority and status, level of income, and the like being especially consequential. The difficulties may thus be even greater for lower class citizens (DeFrain, 1975), for people with more specialized occupations, and for the self-employed (Lamb & Levine, Chapter 4).

Ramey (1977) has pointed out that most social legislation was designed with the traditional family in mind, although an increasing number of countries have recently introduced family policies designed to facilitate women's access to the labor force. The result is that while attempting to eliminate long-standing discrimination against women, legislators have failed to develop more global family policies. Although the intent of the legislation designed to protect women is positive, legislators have not considered mobilization of fathers as a means of promoting the development of families in general and of women in particular. Thus, despite improving conditions for women, the system still impedes increased paternal involvement in family life.

Childcare arrangements are also oriented to mothers, and thus are not satisfactory for parents who wish to share parenting and breadwinning responsibilities (DeFrain, 1979). Moreover, social service professionals are generally not equipped either conceptually or practically to facilitate the process that leads to increased paternal involvement (see Jaffe, Chapter 8).

To summarize, most men are not sufficiently prepared, either psychologically or practically, for more participation in child care. Furthermore, the entire social structure is not oriented toward more equal role division.

The forces driving toward increased paternal involvement are of two major types: (a) maternal desire for self-enhancement and personal growth; and (b) paternal desire for more involvement in child care. It seems that the first is more pronounced, because of economic and attitudinal pressures on women. Mothers' desire for personal growth promotes change in their husbands, however, because, as more women join the labor force, more husbands should be drawn into child-rearing and household responsibilities (Hoffman, 1977).

Although the paternal desire for increased participation in child rearing has been widely touted in recent years, it still seems to have a relatively weak impact, mainly because of current attitudes and norms. It thus appears that the maternal desire for self-enhancement and the paternal desire for greater participation in child-rearing are not synchronized, and that women's needs and desires are more pronounced and receive more recognition. Many factions of the feminist movement concentrated heavily on women, while overlooking the need for change in both male and female roles. This may account for the "psychological lag'' suggested by Rapoport et al. (1977). The gains that women in many countries have achieved, particularly in terms of equal rights and better employment opportunities (Newland, 1980) are not part of a concerted movement to establish a new image of the family.

Because structural pressures toward and male desires for increased paternal involvement are either small or latent, there have been no major attempts on the macro level to facilitate paternal involvement in child care. In fact, the reduction of discrimination against women may paradoxically reinforce the forces restraining paternal involvement. In some countries, for example, revision of tax codes are maternally–oriented rather than family-oriented. Although such revisions may encourage more women to participate in the labor force, they do not significantly affect paternal roles. Therefore, such legislation may end up preventing a more equitable role allocation.

Structural and attitudinal restraints intersecting with those forces promoting change have created a state of quasi-equilibrium in which there remain substantial inequities between males and females. Females are still predominantly responsible for child rearing and housekeeping despite their increased participation in the labor force; males remain the primary breadwinners, with limited involvement in child care.

STRENGTHS AND PROBABILITIES

Any attempt to alter the state of quasi-equilibrium, in which paternal involvement in child care is limited, should assess: (a) the relative *strength* of the driving and restraining forces maintaining the status quo; and (b) *the probability* of successfully changing these forces. For example, we have shown that current social and cultural norms do not provide appropriate conditions for more egalitarian roles, and maintain low paternal involvement in child care. The fundamental nature of norms and attitudes is such that the probability of changing them in the short run is low. On the other hand, fathers' lack of preparation for child care may be remedied by training, which can be accomplished with a fairly high probability of success. However, the lack of skill probably has less effect on the existing organization of roles than norms and values have. Thus the overall effect could be limited. It seems therefore, that in the short run any attempt to produce change will result in small gains. More significant gains are possible only with long-range, carefully planned efforts. Some sociologists believe that slow but significant gains are already taking place. Scanzoni and Scanzoni's (1976) historical-sociological analysis indicates a gradual trend towards more equal role division, and they expect this process to continue in the future. Their analysis raises an interesting question: If this process indeed exists, planned intervention focusing on new social policies may be unnecessary, and perhaps undesirable, because massive interventions are very expensive. However, the social and demographic problems created by the current situation already involve costs to society. The question is whether it is possible to expedite the slow process toward a more equitable role division, without substantial additional costs. An analysis of the likely costs follows.

COST ANALYSIS

We present here an assessment of the costs and benefits of: (a) the current situation; and (b) a society that provides more opportunities for men and women to define their own roles and responsibilities.

The costs associated with each system may be divided into two classes: (1) transitional costs; and (2) ongoing costs.

Transitional Costs

Transition is change, and every change can be costly. The move from one state of affairs to another is often accompanied by confusion, resistance, the need to adjust, and similar effects that cost time, energy and other tangible resources. Any move toward options for increased paternal involvement would thus be costly, although it is difficult to calculate accurately all the transitional costs. For one thing, it is difficult to assess how long the transition would take, and for another, transitional costs often depend on the specific strategies selected to bring about change.

Conceptually, transitional costs fall into two general categories: *program costs,* and costs related to *program effects* during transition. Transitional program costs refer to the research and development stages, and to costs of setting up new programs. The costs of initial implementation, evaluation, and modifications are also included. Thus the initial costs of developing new legislation concerning various aspects of maternal employment are calculated as transitional program costs, as are the costs of developing programs in child care for fathers. Legal costs involved in test cases brought to court during implementation are another example. On the other hand, the costs of ongoing training and the maintenance of programs for fathers, beyond the research and development stage, are usually considered as ongoing rather than transitional costs.

With regard to program effects, many programs do not show the desired effects during the initial stages of implementation (Greenberg, 1977), probably because of resistance to change, and the dislocation and disorientation that often accompany social intervention. The introduction of flexible work hours, for example, may initially cause problems because foremen and supervisors are confused or may have difficulty organizing workers. This may affect productivity adversely until employers adjust. Other transitional effects are much more serious. It is probable, for example, that initial stages of transition will be accompanied by stress and tension in the family as well as on the societal level, so that costs to society may increase, rather then decrease, in the short run.

Ongoing Costs

Beyond the stage of transition, it is assumed that every developed country has some system of social welfare services, whether explicit or implicit. The nature and extent of these services are obviously determined by the political ideologies and economic capabilities of each society.

Many of the forces that restrain paternal involvement have become institutionalized and are reinforced by expensive government-sponsored social programs. In Israel, for example, working women are entitled to three months paid postnatal leave, and in addition nine months unpaid leave of absence. This constitutes a powerful restraint of paternal involvement, because the national insurance benefit is granted to mothers but not fathers. Some may argue that policies such as this are necessary and that the costs are thus acceptable. Similar attitudes apply to child allowances, tax reductions for employed mothers, subsidized fees or priority in admission to public daycare centers for children of employed mothers, job security for employed mothers, security of rights and seniority for women on maternity leave, flextime, sick leave during the child's illness and the like. Should a society decide to make sexual equality attainable, it must be prepared to pay for the new arrangements designed to make it possible, for example, paternal benefits similar to those enjoyed by mothers.

In order to prepare men and women for greater paternal participation in child care and the family, parent education and childcare programs must be designed, hospitals must adjust to paternal involvement beyond mere participation in childbirth and delivery, new programs and centers for family leisure activities must be developed, etc. Not all such programs would involve an immediate increase in actual costs. Since the existing programs in many societies are costly, it may be possible to cover some of the additional expenses by reallocating resources. For example, sex education is provided in many countries; by redesigning these programs, one could move toward the desired goal without substantial additional costs. However, even with efficient resource reallocation, a more explicit family policy designed to encourage paternal involvement in child care may involve additional ongoing costs. These costs should be justified by anticipated benefits such as increases in total family income and standard of living for many families and reduced expenditures on child care because of the increased involvement of fathers. Moreover, as we argued previously, redefined sex roles, which entail, among other things, increased paternal involvement in child-rearing and household responsibilities, could be beneficial to both children and parents.

In previous sections we suggested that some social and demographic problems, such as increases in divorce rates and decreases in birthrates may in time be mitigated by more flexible family policies. Of course these problems are not completely accounted for by the present imbalance in role division, but this certainly seems to be involved. Since divorce and marital disharmony are problems that necessitate costly professional intervention on a number of different levels, anything that reduces these social problems would reduce the costs of these social interventions, and thus permit the reallocation of existing personnel, services, and resources. For example, family counselors may have to spend less time providing divorce mediation and thus would more actively assist families in allocating roles and responsibilities optimally.

Another problem follows from the decreasing birthrates, which are expected to decline further during the 21st century (Kamerman, 1980) while life expectancy rises as a result of improved medical technology. The decreasing birthrate and increasing numbers of old people create major economic problems, especially in the developed countries. Should current trends continue, even with liberalized retirement restrictions, a shrinking number of workers will have to produce the goods and services required to maintain an increasing proportion of nonworking people. This makes it necessary to maximize the productivity of women as well as men. More flexibility in sex roles could significantly enhance a couple's capability to allocate responsibilities so as to increase the family's income. Such flexibility could also improve the quality of other aspects of personal and family life.

In sum, a redefinition of sex roles and an increase in the number of options available to families may ultimately create sufficient economic, psychological, and social benefits to justify any increase in ongoing costs.

Summary

Unfortunately, the current state of research does not allow us to assign precise numerical coefficients of strength and probability to the various forces that restrain or impel increased paternal involvement. This makes it difficult to calculate the exact costs of the measures needed to bring about change. On the whole, however, ongoing and transitional costs seem likely to be high if a change in role division is to occur, but because short-run transitional costs will tend to decrease, and ongoing costs can be reduced by reallocating resources, it seems that in the long run, overall costs will gradually decrease.

GENERAL SUMMARY

In this chapter we have attempted to examine from the societal perspective the costs and benefits associated with increased paternal involvement in child rearing. Our analysis stemmed from the assumption that paternal involvement in child care and housework may contribute to the functioning of the family, to child development, and to society at large.

Our analysis of costs and benefits is based on three premises:

1. The nuclear family was shown to be the most important context in which adults fulfill their primary needs and develop optimally.
2. Family structures were described as continuously changing.
    In time women have acquired more rights and power outside the family, and in recent years there have been some signs of a shift to the equal-partner arrangement between husbands and wives. However, current family roles are still more or less at the level of the senior-junior partnership.
3. It was suggested that for many working mothers, participation in the labor force means an increase in total workload. We submitted that the imbalance in family roles could be attributed in part to insufficient paternal participation in family work, and that this may contribute to marital disharmony.

These conclusions suggest that our major concern should be the nuclear family, and that more opportunities for balance in sex roles should be provided in four major areas (Rapoport et al., 1977): occupation, income, child rearing and household work, and the integration of the family into the social environment.

So far, however, attempts to improve women's rights and status have concentrated on women's roles outside the family, but men have not yet increased their participation at home. At present, the resources used to assist women to enter the labor force itself restrain possible change toward a more balanced role division. In order to initiate a change toward increased balance it may be necessary to reallocate resources.

Kamerman (1980) has proposed that there are two universal needs in our society: the need and desire to work and the need and desire for parenthood. The inability to satisfy either may be detrimental to productivity, to the economy, and possibly also to the quantity and quality of future generations. In the current state of quasi-equilibrium, a successful combination of work and parenthood for both men and women cannot take place. Lamb and Levine (see Chapter 4) point out that a comprehensive family policy like the one accepted in Sweden, where fathers and workers are treated equally, has not yet had the desired impact on paternal involvement, for reasons that are not yet understood. Nevertheless, despite forces that restrict paternal involvement, more Swedish fathers are involved with their children today than were before 1974, when the new laws came into effect.

We contend that in order to achieve significant change, the problem should be dealt with comprehensively and on a variety of levels. Policy makers and legislators must decide on the reallocation of resources and if they accept either Kamerman's proposal that comprehensive family policy may have an impact on family size, on children's health and development, and on the economy, or the assumption that greater equality in role division is likely to occur in the future, then they should design programs, services, and laws to promote these trends.

Social planners and policy makers must be flexible enough with regard to individual and cultural differences so that they permit individual families, whether more or less traditional, to divide responsibilities according to their own preferences. In the long run, the availability of a greater number of options may enhance the quality of family life and benefit society at large.

REFERENCES

Bane, M. J. *Here to stay*. New York: Harper & Row, 1977.

Berger, B., Hackett, B., & Millar, R. M. The communal family. *The Family Coordinator*, 1972, *21*, 419–417.

Bernard J. The good-provider role: Its rise and fall. *American Psychologist*, 1981, *36*, 1–12.

Bowman, H. & Spanier, G. B. *Modern marriage*. New York: McGraw-Hill, 1978.

Campbell, A., Converse, P. E., & Rodgers, W. L. *The quality of American life: Perceptions, evaluations, and satisfactions*. New York: Sage, 1976.

Census Bureau, U.S. Department of Commerce. *American families and living arrangements*. (Prepared for the White House Conference on Families). Washington, D.C.: Government Printing Office, 1980.

Crites, J. O. & Fitzgerald, L. F. The competent male. *The Counseling Psychologist*, 1978, *7*, 10–14.

DeFrain, J. D. *Socioeconomic and personal influences on androgynous an conventional parenting modes*. Paper presented at the Biennial Meeting of the International Society for the Study of Behavioral Development, Guildford, England, 1975.

DeFrain, J. Androgynous parents tell who they are and what they need. *The Family Coordinator*, 1979, *28*, 237–243.

Duvall, E. *Marriage and family development*. Philadelphia: Lippincott, 1977.

Fasteau, M. F. *The male machine*. New York: Dell, 1975.

Friedan, B. *The feminine mystique*. New York: W. W. Norton & Company, 1963.

Glick, P. C., & Norton, A. T. Marrying, divorcing and living together in the U.S. Today. *Population Bulletin*, 1979, *32*, 5.

Goode, W. J. *World revolution and family patterns*. New York: Free Press, 1963.

Greenberg, B. G. The evaluation of social programs. In F. G. Caro (Ed.), *Readings in evaluation research*. New York: Sage, 1977

Heath, D. H. What meaning and effects does fatherhood have for the maturing of professional men? *Merrill-Palmer Quarterly*, 1978, *24*, 165–278.

Hetherington, E. M. & Deur, J. L. The effects of father absence on child development. *Young Children*, 1972, *26*, 233–248.

Hoffman, L. W. Changes in family roles, socialization and sex differences. *American Psychologist*, 1977, *32*, 644–658.

Hoffman, L. W. Maternal employment: 1979. *American Psychologist*, 1979, *34*, 859–865.

Hoffman, L. W. & Hoffman, M. L. The values of children to parents. In J. T. Fawcett (Ed.), *Psychological perspectives on fertility*. New York: Basic Books, 1973.

Kamerman, S. B. Child care and family benefits: Policies of six industrialized countries. *Monthly Labor Review*, November, 1980, 31–43.

Kamerman, S. B. & Kahn, A. J. *Family policy: Government and families in fourteen countries*. New York: Columbia University Press, 1978.

Kanter, R. M. *Communes: Creating and managing the collective life*. New York: Harper and Row, 1973.

Kilgo, R. D. Can group marriage work? *Sexual Behavior*, 1972, *2*, 8–14.

Lamb, M. E. Fathers and child development: An integrative overview. in M. E. Lamb (Ed.), *The role of the father in child development*. (Rev. ed.). New York: Wiley, 1981.

Lein, L. Male participation in home life: Impact of social supports and breadwinner responsibility on the allocation of tasks. *The Family Coordinator*, 1979, *28*, 489–495.

Levine, J. *Images of the new fatherhood*. Paper presented at a study group on "The role of the father in child development: Theory, social policy and the law," sponsored by the Society for Research in Child Development, Haifa, Israel, July, 1980.

Newland, K. Women, men and the division of labor. *Worldwatch Institute Report*, 1980, (Whole No. 37).

Parsons, T., & Bales, R. F. *Family, socialization, and interaction process*. Glencoe, Ill.: Free Press, 1955.

Pleck, J. & Rustad, M. *Husbands' and wives' time use in paidwork and the family, in the 1975–76 study of time use*. Unpublished manuscript, Center for Research in Women, Wellesley College, Wellesley, Mass., 1980.

Radin, N. Role sharing fathers and preschoolers. In M. E. Lamb (Ed.), *Nontraditional families: Parenting and child development*. Hillsdale, N.J.: Lawrence Erlbaum Associates, 1982.

Ramey, J. W. Legal regulation of personal and family life styles. *The Family Coordinator*, 1977, *26*, 349–355.

Rapoport, R., Rapoport, R. N., & Strelitz, Z. *Fathers, mothers, and others: Toward new alliances*. London: Routledge & Kegan Paul, 1977.

Russell, G. Shared caregiving families: An Australian study. In M. E. Lamb (Ed.), *Nontraditional families: Parenting and child development*.Hillsdale, N.J.: Lawrence Erlbaum Associates, 1982.

Sagi, A. Antecedents and consequences of various degrees of paternal involvement in child rearing: The Israeli project. In M. E. Lamb (Ed.), *Nontraditional families: Parenting and child development*. Hillsdale, N.J.: Lawrence Erlbaum Associates, 1982.

Scanzoni, L., & Scanzoni, J. *Men, women, and change: A sociology of marriage and family*. New York: McGraw-Hill, 1976.

Tiger, L., & Shepher, J. *Women in the kibbutz*. New York: Harcourt Brace Jovanovich, 1975.

Todres, R. Runaway wives: An increasing North-American phenomenon. *The Family Coordinator*, 1978, *27*, 17–21.

Veevers, J. E. Voluntary childless wives: An exploratory study. *Sociology and Social Research*, 1973, *57*, 356–366.

Veevers, J. E. The life style of voluntary childless couples: In L. Larson (Ed.), *The Canadian family in comparative perspective*. Toronto: Prentice-Hall, 1974.

Yogman, M. W. Development of the father-infant relationship. In H. E. Fitzgerald, B. M. Lester & M. W. Yogman (Eds.), *Theory and research in behavioral pediatrics*. New York: Plenum, 1981.

13 Cross-Cultural Uses of Research on Fathering

Rivka Eisikovits
University of Haifa
Martin Wolins
University of California, Berkeley

A famous temperance song by Henry Clay Work may well reflect the state of research on fathering:

Father, dear father, come home with me now; The clock in the steeple strikes one,
Our fire has gone out, our house is all dark, and mother's been watching since tea,
With poor brother Benny so sick in her arms And no one to help her but me.

Gradually, over the past several decades, fathers have been coming home, particularly in industrial and postindustrial societies. They return before one, stoke up the fires, light up the house, and increasingly tend to brother Benny. They do so out of necessity—in the single-parent households, in families with two employed parents—or out of desire and conviction. The scenarios across the landscape and eras are multitude, even though the father as childcare taker seems to have been— and in some measure still is—a relatively rare phenomenon. Information about him in this role is rarer yet.

New patterns of fathering—fathering that extends beyond the procreative act itself—are nevertheless evolving. Inevitably, they will become a factor in social policy as evidence accumulates about the virtues and flaws in various arrangements of work, housing, child care, income support, and other issues related to substantial paternal sharing in child rearing. As policy is being made, one point will rapidly become clear: The clock has struck one for this type of research and little cross-cultural data are available. If such information is to be assembled, a few guidelines may be helpful for a start. Inquiry about the father's child-caring role and its correlates in the extra-familial world is likely to be most fruitful if it encompasses the largest range of human experience. This implies the assembly of data on fathering experiences in social circumstances of various types. Societies open and closed, rural and urban, agricultural and industrial are bound to be of equal interest. Each is capable of revealing correlates of particular paternal roles, as well as the effectiveness and benefits such roles entail for both father and family.

Evolution of an individual role within an existing cultural matrix is always a source of tension. Social systems are inherently conservative and readily sacrifice individual growth for systemic security. It is therefore not surprising that parental roles are more rigidly fixed in self-doubting systems or in those under external threat than in open, secure societies. The Soviets, The Oneida Community, the Amish, and other strongly normative societies, doubtful of parental allegiance and consequent behavior, place considerable emphasis on extrafamilial control. Open societies are more accepting of variation, but even in them social controls over parenting, derived from tradition and present convenience, tend to perpetuate the status quo. Only major upheavals appear to modify drastically the parent-parent and parent-child juxtaposition. Such modifications occur in immigrants and, in certain instances of prolonged unemployment, in those whose identities are work related.

In both of the above conditions of role adjustment, a considerable shift occurs in fathering patterns, permitting a cautious conclusion that fathering roles can, will, and possibly should, change. But the evidence, though provocative, is still quite meager, surely insufficient to guide the formulation of national policies. Only a sustained and coordinated effort for gathering data of this kind is likely to produce a viable basis for policy making, which can in turn specifically affect the fathering role in a desired direction. The present chapter is a very modest attempt to chart something of the known information and suggest some of what is needed in future research.

WHY CROSS-CULTURAL RESEARCH/INFORMATION ON FATHERING?

All Western industrial societies are undergoing rapid changes in their economic, social, and ideational spheres. Traditional family structures are influenced by massive changes in women's rights, education, and labor market participation. All of the above render the phenomenon of paternal child care of cross-national interest.

Furthermore, in the era of the "global village" and telecommunication, developments in one society affect social behavior elsewhere. Thus, cross-cultural information on patterns of fathering can serve as a heuristic device for generating flexible scenarios of paternal involvement to suit various cultural needs. As has been pointed out in Chapter 2, one of the major obstacles to culturally valid alterations in parenting styles is the unavailability of models for intensive participation of fathers in child care. The collection of more cross-cultural information on the topic can serve as an important avenue for broadening our imagination.

For that to happen, it is necessary to understand the various contexts of parenting. In most writing on society and the family, the latter is treated as the dependent variable on which larger cultural systems such as the economy, sociopolitical structures, and religion all make their imprints (Kenkel, 1973; Nimkoff, 1965). The current trend toward self-development and self-actualization has raised the family to the position of an independent variable. This is likely to have repercussions on the macro systemic level. Hence the rationale underlying a call for more active paternal participation further affirms the right of all primary groups, including the family, to claim the allegiance of their members because of the mutual benefits derived.

The accommodation of various societies to this trend is a function of their ideological climates and political systems. Totalitarian societies with both revolutionary and reactionary regimes regard the family as a suspect institution—a haven in which individual identity can be anchored. To them, such a self-serving claim as the intrinsic needs of individual family members is usually unacceptable. The Russian revolution, for example, wanted to do away with the family, but only succeeded in "nationalizing" it (Valsiner, 1981). This radical intent—forcefully represented by Lenin's leading feminist comrade, Alexandra Kollontai—was abandoned only upon realizing that it would have meant taking over all familial social functions. Nevertheless, in theory at least, the revolutionary ideas of Kollontai were still propounded in the 1960s by a leading Soviet academician. For example, Strumilin (1960) states: "Children's collectives are incomparably better suited to giving the most thorough inculcation of the best social habits in a child than the most loving or attentive mother [p. 206]." The father's role in the child-rearing enterprise is obviously so inconsequential in this perception of sexual equality as to merit no mention whatever. Both parents should be replaced by well-prepared professionals so that "public forms of upbringing . . . will expand . . . at such a rate that within fifteen to twenty years they will be general for the whole population, from the cradle to the graduation certificate [p. 208]."

Simultaneously, another and more powerful trend was evident in the Soviet Union. Spurred by greater abundance, increased leisure, and the inordinate costs of "public upbringing," there developed a wary accommodation between family and state. Following Strumilin in a later issue of the same journal (*Novyi Mir*), academician Kolbanovski (1961) introduced the notion of parental responsibility and competence as suggested earlier by A. S. Makarenko (no date). Kolbanovski states: "If one takes into consideration a significant increase in freedom from productive and domestic work, one can see that the family will have more opportunity to bring up their children. . . . Parents in the future will joyfully give their attention to children and their development . . . [and to assure that it will be done] a body of knowledge on childrearing must be included in the general education of each citizen and family man [p. 282]." As a result, the Soviet regime considers itself the senior partner in the child-rearing enterprise, usually guiding but, if necessary substituting for the family. Thus, in addition to parent education, a system of elaborate all day daycare centers and schools was created, matching the working days for both parents. In this arrangement, the primary obligation of all Soviet parents is to cooperate with the State in order to bring up loyal and useful citizens.

In the Oneida Community of 19th century America, communal rather than state control was exercised to assure cultural continuity of a rather divergent social order. "Infants, when weaned, went to the Children's House. They stayed there during the day. From the age of three, they stayed overnight. Selected members took shifts with the children [Lawson, 1972, p. 61]." Among the Amish (Hostetler & Huntington, 1971), another highly normative society, parenting is also viewed as a socially mandated activity, this time by a religious community rather than the state. Whereas the Soviet system mistrusts both parents and would really like to keep the child under strict state surveillance, the Amish, living in a small tightly knit community, regard both parents as equal guardians of the child who, as a team, should bring up the child to become a loyal member of the community. With the Amish, the community boundaries serve as an efficient mechanism for social control, so that the entire responsibility for the process of socialization can be safely entrusted to the parents.

On the other hand, in liberal societies, the family, despite its diversity, is considered a reliable ally and considerable variation in family styles is tolerated. In this framework, the claim that more active paternal participation in child rearing is in the child's and family's best interest (therefore, in society's interest) more acceptable (Wallace, 1961).

More intensive paternal involvement in child care can be viewed as an adaptive style of family life for both parents in their quest for the achievement of full potential in both the work *and* the family domains. There is increasing evidence that men are no longer turning toward work as their sole source of meaning because that world is often alienating, harsh, and depersonalizing. Instead, they are, more than ever before, anchoring their personal as well as social identity in the family (Fein, 1978; Heath, 1978; Hoffman, 1977). In *Culture Against Man,* analyzing the American scene of the 1950s, Jules Henry (1963) shows how in spite of the prevailing Parsonian stereotype of the emotionally remote father, men were turning towards their children and family for warmth and affection. Alienation from the world of work due to unemployment of fathers also led to considerable restructuring of familial roles, often to the point of full role reversal. However, during the period of the Great Depression of the 1930s, this phenomenon of housekeeping, child-rearing fathers, compelled into this role by their own unemployment and the wife's extradomestic employment, led to the husband's loss of status within the family (Angell, 1936).

In the 1930s or even 1950s, however, most wives in reality and by virtue of social expectations, were still fulltime homemakers. This state of affairs has changed dramatically, with more than 50% of women now holding dual roles as housewives and workers. With both parents employed, neither full role reversal nor occasional parenting are tenable alternatives for fathers. If they opt to have their family as a major source of gratification, they must make a substantial investment to the point of an egalitarian division of labor in the household.

The observations about different parenting styles in several cultures are not, however, grounded in systematic empirical research. This is not because there is a dearth of research about child development and parenting in various societies, but rather because of the narrow disciplinary paradigm within which much of this research was originally conceptualized. As Bronfenbrenner (1979) has pointed out:

> The capacity of psychology, both as a discipline and as a profession, to deal with problems arising in the contexts of child rearing confronts a gap in scientific knowledge. Our science is peculiarly one-sided. We know much more about children than about the environments in which they live or the process through which these environments affect the course of development. As a result, our ability to address public policy concerns regarding contexts of child rearing is correspondingly limited [p. 844].

To fulfill the heuristic promise whereby cross-cultural research carries the potential of increasing our repertoire of fathering models, we should heed Bronfenbrenner's admonition to make our inquiries as thoroughly context specific as possible.

THE CASE OF IMMIGRATION

Various forms of voluntary or coerced migration are a byproduct of rapid social change and also a further cause of it. In such a forced rearrangement, familial roles often undergo surprising shifts. There is a widespread belief that the experience of immigration shatters the family unit, and the father is often the member of the family who is hardest hit. This is so because he derives status in the family from his occupational and social role in the larger community. When he forfeits these roles by migrating to a new community, the family disintegrates and the father often deserts because he cannot fulfill the various traditional functions. Official policy, as embodied, for example, in the American Aid to Families of Dependent Children, often exacerbates this trend. Ironically, fathers find themselves having to abandon their family, thereby providing for their children, who then become eligible for welfare assistance. Abandoned by their paternal members, such families, many of them Black, tend to be basically matriarchal systems, possibly as a result of two factors: migration; and scapegoating of the Black father (Snyder, 1979) by a lack of a coherent profamily policy (Kamerman & Kahn, 1978). The American Indian family has not fared much better throughout the process of urbanization (King, 1967; Wolcott, 1967).

The case of Greek, Italian, Spanish, Turkish, and Yugoslav guestworkers in highly industrialized countries such as Germany and Sweden is another unfortunate story. Although the host societies have advanced social legislation for their own citizens (Kamerman & Kahn, 1978), these progressive laws and services have seldom been extended to include guestworkers (Öberg, 1974). Such results as high rates of school dropouts and delinquency among the children, and isolation and alienation of the women, who do not speak the local language, weigh heavily on both these families and their receiving communities. Again, the father takes the brunt of the blame from both sides: from the community, which has to handle the negative consequences of maladaptation, and from the members of his own family, who hold him accountable because his employment problems caused the dislocation.

In Israel, a country that prides itself on its supportive immigrant absorption policies, a considerable rate of family disintegration occurred during the mass immigration waves of the 1950s. (Weintraub & Shapira, 1971; Weintraub & Parness, 1971). In this case, it took the form of intergenerational struggle within the families of North African and Asian Sephardi Jews. This again was an interplay between the weakening of paternal authority in these originally patriarchal extended families, and the encouragement of a differential pace in the integration of the younger and older generations of the immigrant population. These families, collateral in basic value orientation (Kluckhohn & Stodtbeck, 1961), clashed with the largely individualistic, socialistic, and Zionist ethos of the Ashkenazi (European) Jews, who founded and were largely governing the State at that point. Prevailing philosophies of immigrant absorption in the newly created Jewish State, rooted in the melting pot model, favored the mixing of various cultural groups and the removal of talented youngsters to residential schools, where they could be socialized to the norms of their new homeland more efficiently than in their original family settings (Frankenstein, 1951; Frankenstein, 1961; Rottenschtreich, 1951).

At the heart of this problem may well have been yet another diminution of paternal authority. Most of the Sephardi Jews were religiously observant in their original North African and Asian environments. Because of substantial isolation from local civil authority, due to religious discrimination, law for these families was derived from God, interpreted by the rabbi, transmitted and enforced by the father in each family. The secularist Israeli State (or at least its dominant leadership at the time of the great migration of 1948-1960) was basically antireligious. Combined with the geographic and social dislocation the migration then left the family—unaccustomed to civil authority—without any authority whatsoever as God, rabbi *and* father had lost their traditional position.

The melting pot ideology proved not to be the answer. In its name, a variety of interventions, with the best of intentions but with little awareness of cultural differences, inadvertently hastened the dissolution of immigrant families. For example, various women's voluntary organizations, in their desire to improve the position of female immigrants, made wives more aware of their lowly position in the family, which often led to more turmoil, such as husbands deserting, wife-battering, and other forms of family violence. Confusion about the value base of Israeli society was thus inevitable. Conflict was not far behind. Intergenerational tension, alienation, and uprootedness of both the young and the old caused a massive social problem for both the new immigrant groups and the absorbing communities. In due course of a democratic society, the interethnic tensions became politicized and exploded in full force by the 1970s and 1980s. A pluralistic approach is gradually replacing the previous absorption model. It is based on recognition of the various newcomers' home cultures, their original family support systems, decision-making processes, parenting styles, division of labor in the home, and intergenerational relations that may be active in their self-monitored process.

Anthropological research conducted among recent immigrants from Russian Georgia (Eilam, 1980) and the Caucasus (Eisikovits & Adam, 1981) demonstrate that these groups have a strong commitment to safeguarding their traditional family structure as well as their ethnic identity throughout the immigration process. To be sure, family roles changed. Contrary to tradition, women went out to work in menial service jobs and children served as translators and mediators between their parents and the authorities—both radical departures from the patriarchial family patterns. These were indeed essential changes that brought about a new intrafamilial balance of power, giving the women and children more influence in decision-making. Nevertheless, these families went to great lengths to preserve the outward appearance of a paternally dominated unit as a symbol of family integrity (Eisikovits & Adam, 1981). Similar adaptive changes that preserve paternal roles following cultural change due to migration are reported in studies from Canada, Australia, and Brazil.

There is other empirical evidence showing that families in the course of migration are open to change and tend toward a more egalitarian distribution of labor in the home, thus improving their internal dynamics and enhancing their ability to cope. A study of Indian and Pakistani immigrants in Canada demonstrates that both husband and wife began to share parenting and household duties, although they never did in their home country (Siddque, 1977). Cut off from their extended family, their primary source of support, they had to become self-sufficient in all their family responsibilities. Another study reports that rural Italian immigrants in a farming area of Australia exhibited the same trend. These immigrants have been found to practice a more egalitarian family style and adopt more democratic decision-making in the home than did the original Australian Anglo-Saxon inhabitants of the area (Phillips, 1975). A similar pattern has been found in the intranational migration of Brazilian peasants moving to Sao-Paulo (Rosen, 1973). In none of these cases were the immigrants highly educated, so that their openness to change cannot be attributed to educational level. It should also be noted that these adaptations in family style occurred irrespective of the availability of local absorption policies and/or services.

As Eaton (1971), points out, gloomy scenarios are not inevitable. The problems faced by immigrants, often dealt with successfully by themselves, could be further ameliorated by more relevant welfare planning based on substantive information about the immigrants' customs, values, and needs. Not only could the integration be handled more smoothly from the point of view of the immigrant, but it could also prove to be an asset to the absorbing community, where it would help break down class distinctions, sustain democracy, and even provide viable models for coping with family crises. The Eilam and Eisikovits examples serve as a dramatic illustration of how important it is for the representatives of officialdom to understand and respect the traditional family structure, or at least the image thereof, that these groups are so determined to project.

THE KNOWLEDGE WE HAVE: THE KNOWLEDGE WE NEED

Direct cross-cultural knowledge about fathering that is context-specific (Bronfenbrenner, 1979) is scarce. The next closest sources of information are to be found in the literatures on family policy (Fein, 1978; Giele, 1978; Kamerman & Kahn, 1978) and early child development (Robinson & Robinson, 1972, 1973, 1974, 1976, 1978, and 1979).

In reviewing these works, two points stand out:

1. Although Kamerman and Kahn state that family policy needs to be sensitive to and take into account cultural and ethnic differences in family styles, all chapters (with the exception of the one on Canada, which touches on the French-Canadian and Eskimo subgroups) treat the family institution monolithically. The International Monograph Series on Early Child Development and Care (Robinson & Robinson) also seems to orient toward the modal or the "approved" family. The series describes institutional childcare systems and the training of their personnel in great detail for all countries. The omission of references and data about cultural minority groups—often of substantial size—may be inevitable due to several constraints. First, government bodies collecting and sharing data are not always eager to emphasize diversity, particularly when it may also show inequality of services. Second, in highly diverse open societies, such as the United States, Israel, or Canada, any attempt at description of subcultural variations vitiates the effort at producing a comprehensible national image. The forest is lost in the trees, so to speak. Third, in a world where emphasis

on diversity as a common goal is in the ascendancy, no government is prepared to admit that it pursues *unity* even at the expense of *diversity* while claiming to hold to unity *in* diversity slogans.

2. With the exception of Sweden (Liljestrom, 1978) and, to a very small extent Norway (Heniksen, 1978), the father as a meaningful participant in a family policy context is not mentioned in Kamerman & Kahn's book. Hence we can learn about his potential role only by inference from the missing data. In Germany (Neidhart, 1978), for example, it is clearly stated that fathers have never been seriously expected to become actively involved in child care. The same holds true for Austria (Krebs, 1978), where a recent public opinion poll revealed that although it is considered acceptable for married women to work outside the home, it is absolutely against social norms for mothers of children under 18 to hold paid jobs. In the socialist countries such as Hungary (Ferge, 1978), Czechoslovakia (Vergeiner, 1978), and Poland (Sokolowska, 1978), that are interested in women's intensive participation in the labor force, the favored option involves out-of-home daycare arrangements for the child. This is contrary to the direction suggested by Russell (1979), who sees the solution lying in the introduction of flexible work schedules that would allow both parents to share the child-tending role.

In the International Monograph Series (begun in the 1960s and completed in the 1970s), there is not even one subheading devoted to the father as the child caretaker in either Western or socialist societies. Intensive paternal involvement in child care has only recently become a social phenomenon with some visibility.

In other large-scale cross-cultural studies, such as Whiting and Whiting's *Children of Six Cultures* (1975), there is only cursory reference to males in the parenting role. Stephen's (1963) study of the family in a cross-cultural perspective, based on 220 ethnographic examples, contains one subheading devoted to the father-child relationship. Not unexpectedly, the dimension singled out is father-child power and deference relations. The responsibilities of the father are not dealt with at all.

Another tangentially related area is that of cross-cultural developmental psychology. Much of this work tends to rely on experimental designs and emphasizes the cross-cultural validation of various instruments. The policy applicability of such studies is limited by their predominant interest in the nomothetic, universal aspects of human development, rather than in the ideographic or culturally specific.

Hardly any systematic comparative data exist on the role of fathers as childtenders. What kind of information is needed? Studies can be designed that would provide policy makers and service providers with the systematic information required to inform their decisions.

How this information should be collected, interpreted, and conceptualized to be of such relevance? We suggest the following:

1. To be applicable, comparisons need to be made among nations, societies, and groups facing similar issues and problems. Such material as is offered by West and Konner (1976) on fathering behavior among the Bushmen, along with a cross-phylogenetic analysis of the phenomenon, are clearly of little practical value.
2. The studies need to be broadly conceptualized and prefaced with rich ethnographic detail collected by naturalistic observation and open-ended interview methods. The analysis of the material should be on a deeper cultural level rather than relating to such value-neutral entities as the modal family used in demographically oriented discussions. Statistics need to be used cautiously, to avoid reducing the complexity of local realities to meaningless numbers.
3. Team research seems to be a good way of organizing such studies. However, they should not be overly coordinated in order to avoid confining the independence and flexibility of individual field workers and researchers. Such restrictions would render them less sensitive to absorbing the uniqueness and intricacies of the various cultural scenes. Such team efforts as mounted by Kamerman and Kahn (1978) or by the International Study Group on Early Child Development and Care (Robinson & Robinson, various dates) are examples of fruitful collaboration that produced considerable amounts of policy-relevant cross-national data.
4. In cross-cultural research, special attention should be paid to a variety of subcategories that engender differences in parenting styles. Particularly salient variables seem to be the following:
   (a) urban versus rural locus of residence;
   (b) class and ethnic distinctions;
   (c) parent caretaker extrafamilial obligations such as employment, studies, caring for others outside the household;
   (d) extent of adult help available in household due to three-generation living arrangements, partial employment of spouse(s), adult children;
   (e) views of relevant members of parents' social networks on the "proper" parenting role of each gender;
   (f) actual paternal involvement in parenting with particular reference to the specific activities performed by fathers; the time allotted to such tasks and the children's reactions.

CONCLUSION

The primary task of cross-cultural research on fathering should be, as has been noted in the introduction, helping father, dear father to come home . . . now. To do so, the research should reveal the cultural roots of active fathering. Such research should allow for the separation of trends in fathering from developments in feminism—both apparently significant, but possibly independent phenomena of the second half of the 20th century. It should also permit some conclusions about the generalizability of paternal child care as a viable phenomenon of contemporary industrial and postindustrial society. Such research could test the contention that men increasingly seek identity in familial roles and outside of the work world. Cross-cultural knowledge generated in this way will have policy relevance and will lead to a better understanding of more general academic questions about the nature of fathering in the familial matrix.

REFERENCES

Angell, R. C. *The family encounters the depression*. New York: Scribner's, 1936.

Bronfenbrenner, U. Contexts of child rearing: problems and prospects. *American Psychologist*, 1979, *34*, 844–850.

Eaton, J. W. (Ed.). *Migration and social welfare*. New York: National Association of Social Workers, 1971.

Eilam, Y. *The Georgians in Israel: anthropological perspectives*. Jerusalem Hebrew University, 1980.

Eisikovits, R., & Adam, V. The social integration of new immigrant children from the Caucasus in Israeli schools. *Studies in Education*, 1981, *31*, 77–84.

Fein, R. A. Research on fathering: Social policy and an emergent perspective. *Journal of Social Issues*, 1978, *34*, 122–135.

Ferge, Z. Hungary. In S. B. Kamerman, & A. J. Kahn (Eds.), *Family policy: Government and families in fourteen countries*. New York: Columbia University Press, 1978.

Frankenstein, K. To the problem of ethnic differences. *Megamot*, 1951, 2 261–276.

Frankenstein, K. The school without parents. *Megamot*, 1961, *12*, 3–23.

Giele, J. Z. Social policy and the family. *Annual Review of Sociology*, 1978, *5*, 275–302.

Heath, D. H. What meaning and effects does fatherhood have for the maturing of professional men. *Merrill-Palmer Quarterly*, 1978, *24*, 265–277.

Heniksen, H. U., Holter, H. Norway. In S. B. Kamerman & A. J. Kahn (Eds.), *Family policy: Government and families in fourteen countries*. New York: Columbia University Press, 1978.

Henry, J. *Culture against man*. New York: Random House, 1963.

Hoffman, L. W. Changes in family roles, socialization and sex differences. *American Psychologisst*, 1977, *34*, 644–657.

Hostetler, J., & Huntington, G. *Children in Amish Society*. New York. Holt, Rinehart & Winston, 1971.

Kamerman, S., & Kahn, A. J. (Eds.). *Family policy: Government and families in fourteen countries*. New York: Columbia University Press, 1978.

Kenkel, W. F. *The family in perspective* (3rd ed.). New York: Appleton-Century-Crofts, 1973.

King, A. R. *The school at Mopass: a problem of identity*. New York: Holt, Rinehart, & Winston, 1967.

Kluckhohn, F. R., & Strodtbeck, F. L. *Variations in value orientations*. Evanston, Ill: Row Peterson, 1961.

Kolbanovski, V. N. Readers' comments: working life and communism. *Novyi Mir* 1961, *37*, 276–282.

Krebs, E., & Schwarz, M. Austria. In S. B. Kamerman & A. J. Kahn (Eds.), *Family policy: Government and families in fourteen countries*. New York: Columbia University Press, 1978.

Lawson, D. *Brothers and sisters all over this land: America's first communes* New York: Praeger, 1972.

Liljestrom, R. Sweden. In S. B. Kamerman & A. J. Kahn (Eds.), *Family policy: Government and families in fourteen countries.* New York: Columbia University Press, 1978.

Makarenko, A. S. *A book for parents.* Moscow: Foreign Language Printing House, no date.

Neidhart, F. Germany. In S. B. Kamerman, & A. J. Kahn (Eds.), *Family policy: Government and families in fourteen countries.* New York: Columbia University Press, 1978.

Nimkoff, M. F. *Comparative family systems.* Boston: Houghton Mifflin, 1965.

Öberg, Kjell. Treatment of immigrant workers in Sweden. *International Labor Review,* 1974, *110,* 1–16.

Phillips, D. The effects of immigration on the family: The case of Italians in rural Australia. *The British Journal of Sociology,* 1975, *26,* 218–226.

Robinson, H. B. & Robinson, N. M. International monograph series on early child care in *Early Child Development and Care,* London: Gordon and Breach. Volumes on France 1974, *4*(1), 1–148, Great Britain 1974, *3*(4) 299–473, Hungary 1972, *1*(4) 337–454, India, 1979, *5*(3,4) 149–360, Israel 1976, *4*(2,3) 149–345, Poland 1978, *5*(1,2) 1–148, Sweden 1973, 2(2) 97–248, Switzerland 1973, *3*(2) 89–210, and the United States 1973, *2*(4), 359–581.

Rosen, B. C. Social change, migration and family interaction in Brazil. *American Sociological Review,* 1973, *38,* 198–212.

Rottenschtreich, N. Absolute measures. *Megamot,* 1951, *2,* 327–338.

Russell, G. *Fathers as caregivers: They could if they had to.* Paper presented at the Australia and New Zealand Association for the Advancement of Science Congress, Auckland, January, 1979.

Siddque, C. M. On migrating to Canada: The first generation Indian and Pakistani families in the process of change. *Sociological Bulletin,* 1977, *26,* 203–226.

Snyder, L. M. The deserting, nonsupporting father: Scapegoat of family nonpolicy. *The Family Coordinator,* 1979, 594–598.

Sokolowska, M. Poland. In S. B. Kamerman & A. J. Kahn (Eds.), *Family policy: Government and families in fourteen countries.* New York: Columbia University Press, 1978.

Stephens, W. N. *The family in cross-cultural perspective.* New York: Holt, Rinehart, & Winston, 1963.

Strumilin, S. G. Working life and communism. *Novyi Mir,* 1960, *36,* 203–220.

Valsiner, J. The father's role in the social network of a Soviet child: The nationalization of the family. In M. E. Lamb (Ed.), *The role of the father in child development* (2nd ed.). New York: Wiley, 1981.

Vergeiner, W. Czechoslovakia. In S. B. Kamerman & A. J. Kahn (Eds.), *Family policy: Government and families in fourteen countries.* New York: Columbia University Press, 1978.

Wallace, A. F. C. Schools in revoluntionary and conservative societies. In F. C. Gruber (Ed.), *Anthropology and education.* Philadelphia: University of Pennsylvania Press, 1961.

Weintraub, D., & Shapira, M. The family in the process of change: Crisis and continuity. In D. Weintraub (Ed.), *Immigration and social change.* Manchester: Manchester University Press, 1971.

Weintraub, D., & Parness, T. The younger generation—Commitment to the moshav, orientation to change and modernization. In D. Weintraub (Ed.), *Immigration and social change.* Manchester: Manchester University Press, 1971.

West, H. M., & Konner, M. J. The role of the father: An anthropological perspective. In M. E. Lamb (Ed.), *The role of the father in child development.* New York: Wiley, 1976.

Whiting, B. B., & Whiting, J. W. M.Children of six cultures: A psycho-cultural analysis. Cambridge Massachusetts: Harvard University Press, 1975.

Wolcott, H. F. *A Kwakiutl village and school.* New York: Holt, Rinehart, & Winston, 1967.

Work, H. K. *Songs.* New York: Da Capo Press, 1974.

14 Summary and Recommendations for Public Policy

Michael E. Lamb
University of Utah
Graeme Russell
Macquarie University
Abraham Sagi
University of Haifa

Our goal in this volume has been to assess the influence of contemporary social and legal practices on paternal participation in child care; to appraise and evaluate the consequences of increased involvement on mothers, fathers, children, and society at large; and to suggest ways in which societies could move toward providing a greater range of options for fathers. Our aim has been to conduct an analysis that is sensitive to individual and cultural differences in the aspirations and values of parents; consequently, we have striven to avoid value judgments wherever possible, and to identify them as such when discussion is unavoidable. In addition, we have emphasized the need to make increased paternal participation possible for those who want it, rather than prescribing high father involvement as a universal goal or panacea.

Two general conclusions emerge from the analyses included in this volume. First, it is the consensus of the contributors that in many, though probably not all, families, increased paternal participation could have beneficial consequences for mothers, fathers, and/or children. Most of the contributors agree that increased paternal participation can have negative consequences as well, but these seem likely to be less extensive than the positive effects, yielding a net benefit for many families. Unfortunately, we do not at present know just how many families would benefit from increased paternal involvement. Changing political and socioeconomic circumstances throughout the Western world seem likely to increase their numbers. Thus the time is ripe for economic, legal, and public policies that increase the opportunity for paternal participation in child care.

A second general conclusion is that contemporary legal and social policies in most Western societies do not facilitate paternal participation; indeed, existing practices more commonly restrict and limit the opportunities for male involvement in the family. Interestingly, furthermore, one of the clearest attempts to increase male involvement—the Swedish parental insurance program—has not had as clear an effect on paternal participation as anticipated, for reasons that are not at all clear (see Chapter 4). This suggests that, if we are correct in concluding that many families might benefit from increased male participation, a broader array of options must be offered.

Our goal in this concluding chapter is to suggest changes in family and public policy that would increase the opportunities for men to become more involved in child care if they wished to do so. For analytic purposes, we have organized these suggestions in terms of the arenas or institutional sectors to which they pertain. Most of the sectors distinguished here are among those on which Levine, Pleck, and Lamb's Fatherhood Project (see Chapter 6) is focused.

EMPLOYMENT

It is widely argued that the attitudes of employers and related practices in the employment sector constitute the major restrictions on male participation in the family (e.g., Pleck & Rustad, 1980). In most Western countries, many employers assume that men are more dependable and committed employees than women are, and it seems reasonable to argue that these assumptions help preserve sex discrimination in employment practices and thus limit male participation in the family in a number of ways. First, employers are much more tolerant of work-family conflicts in women than in men; consequently, a man who takes off time to care for a sick child or to attend parent-teacher conferences is likely to be perceived as a less committed and thus less desirable employee than one whose family responsibilities never affect his performance at work. Second, pervasive sex discrimination helps ensure that men generally earn much more than women and thus preserves the status and importance of men as primary breadwinners in most two-parent families. This may serve to inhibit any action (such as increased family involvement) that would jeopardize the individual's occupational reputation. Third, despite recent changes, men remain more concerned about their achievement in the workplace than women are, although it is not easy to determine whether this is a cause, or an effect, or simply a correlate of greater female participation in family work. This also serves to limit male participation in the family when this participation is likely to affect others' perceptions of the employee's commitment to his work.

These circumstances suggest a number of changes that are necessary if one wishes to reduce or eliminate the inhibiting effects of employment practices on male participation in childcare. Most important and most difficult are changes in the assumption that increased family participation necessarily occurs at the expense of performance and productivity at work. In fact, a father's inability or reluctance to attend to family needs (e.g., having a sick child at home alone) because of actual or perceived work demands might create pressures that adversely affect performance at work. Because employers' attitudes are likely to change only when their experiences confirm the inappropriateness of their assumptions, efforts could be made to eliminate barriers that increase the likelihood of work-family conflicts. One such barrier is posed by rigid working hours that are not synchronized with the equally rigid schedules of schools, substitute caretakers, etc. Although employers have generally viewed flextime as a practice likely to improve the job satisfaction (and thus performance) of female employees, the practice could be beneficial to some employed fathers as well. Most employers have found that flexible time-scheduling does not have an adverse effect on productivity, and may have a positive effect on absenteeism. Job-sharing and permanent parttime work are two other options that reduce work-family conflict by limiting the extent of work demands on the individual.

Another practice that would reduce work-family conflicts would be to permit either parent to take parental leave for the care of young children. In most countries today, "maternity" leave is by definition available only to new mothers: In fact, Israeli mothers are *required* to take paid maternity leave after delivery. Although the Swedish national insurance has been utilized by relatively few men (10% of those who were eligible), it has permitted those Swedish men who desired increased involvement to obtain it. Similar opportunities may be welcomed by some men in other industrialized countries. In these economically and politically conservative times, of course, it is unlikely that many countries would opt for a publically–financed system like that instituted by the Swedes. The current conservative government in Australia, for example, recently abolished a paternity leave scheme for federal employees that had been instituted by a previous labor government. One of the arguments used against the scheme was that is was too costly. Nevertheless, the notion of *parental* rather than *maternity* leave— whether paid or unpaid—could and should have wider application. The net increase in the cost of offering leave to new parents rather than just new mothers would probably be very small, both because many of the expenses are administrative costs that are constant regardless of the sex of the beneficiary, and because, in the aggregate sense, each time a male requested parental leave, one less mother would need it. In highly competitive fields, companies may at little cost obtain a recruitment advantage over other firms simply by permitting couples to choose for themselves which parent would take parental leave. Another argument against restrictive maternity leave schemes is that, while overtly discriminating against men, they also may limit the employment or promotion of women who are, in their employers' eyes, at risk for taking maternity leave.

In any event, for both economic and psychological reasons, a declining number of mothers and fathers today want to quit work for any length of time. For dual-breadwinner families, a long parental leave to care for new children (especially if the leave is largely unpaid) is perhaps less desirable than the opportunity for a brief leave after delivery, a gradual return to work, and permission to use additional leave on later occasions to take care of the child in times of need. Flexible working hours would also be helpful for such parents. (A system of this sort has been successfully introduced for mothers on Israeli kibbutzim.)

Because the total amount of paid leave involved may well be less, it may be cheaper for employers to offer flexibility and reduced working hours to both male and female employees than to institute and support a sex-neutral parental leave policy. Furthermore, because they are concerned about the loss of income, or the loss of visibility, status, and indispensability, men may prefer the greater flexibility to lengthy period of parental leave, so the effect on paternal involvement may well be greater in the former case also. In this regard, it is interesting that whereas few men have taken even a month or more of leave under the Swedish parental insurance policy (see Chapter 4), many more have taken some of the childcare sick leave to which parents are entitled during the early years of their children's lives.

Finally, a commitment to broadening the options available to fathers who wish to participate more extensively in child care may also require reevaluation of the policies of some employers (for example, the armed forces; mining and exploration companies) who require men to spend extended periods of time away from their families. Perhaps recognizing this need, one Australian company has changed its practices so as to limit the length of time men are sent on assignments away from their homes and to ensure that—when longer assignments are necessary—families may accompany, visit, or be visited by them.

LEGAL PRACTICES

In the legal arena, Thompson (Chapter 5) concludes his analysis of guidelines concerning child custody decisions by suggesting that we should introduce a set of decision rules that are neutral with respect to the parent's sex. This recommendation is consistent with recent legislation in various countries, including the United States, Sweden, and Israel. As Thompson points out, the key issue is the psychological relationship between parent and child, with courts striving wherever possible to cause as little emotional trauma to children as possible. If we adopt this as our goal, then custody should usually be awarded to the parent who has played a primary role in the care and nurturance of the child, because that person is likely to have assumed psychological primacy in the child's life. Although involvement in physical caretaking becomes less and less important as the child grows older, the parent who devotes the most time to organization and facilitation of the child's activities probably remains most psychologically important to the child. In addition, the child's preference (whether assessed verbally or by an examination of the child's and the parents' behavior) becomes increasingly important with age. Notice that appplication of these rules would award custody to mothers in most contested custody cases today, but would do so on the basis of decision rules that are not biased to ensure this simply because of the parents' sex rather than because of their responsibilities and roles. The rules that Thompson advocates would also offer a fair chance to highly involved fathers.

Because it imposes major restrictions on the parents after divorce, may require extensive cooperation between estranged former spouses, and may be difficult for children to adapt to, joint custody may be a satisfactory arrangement only for relatively few divorcing couples. Nevertheless, this option should at least be considered by divorcing families, especially those in which both parents have been highly involved, have close relationships to their children, and wish to avoid having either parent cut out of the children's lives. In other words, joint custody is probably most relevant as an option in cases where the primary caretaker rule does not yield clear recommendations. Because various types of joint custody arrangements are possible, the arrangements made in particular cases could be designed to fit the job conditions of the parents and any geographic constraints imposed by their new living arrangements.

Even when fathers are not awarded either complete or joint custody, attempts could be made to maximize the opportunity for continued involvement in the lives of their children, especially when the children are young. Hess and Camara's (1979) findings are important in this regard: These researchers found that the postdivorce adjustment of children was strongly influenced by the quality of pre- and postdivorce relationships with both custodial and noncustodial parents. In addition, it seems likely that fathers will make child support payments more regularly if they are able to maintain relationships with their children, thus obviating the need for expensive and often marginally successful legal enforcement procedures (Chambers, 1979). In some jurisdictions, it is still rare for fathers to be allowed overnight or extended access to preschool-aged children on the grounds that fathers are not competent to care for them and that the children would experience severe separation anxiety if separated from their mothers. Both beliefs are probably indefensible in many cases.

Regardless of the final custodial disposition of the children, an increasing number of custody decisions in the United States are now being made by mutual agreement, facilitated by an impartial mediator, rather than by hostile adversarial procedures that frequently worsen the relationship between the parents and reduce the likelihood of continued cooperation in the interests of the children. Divorce and custody mediation may be especially important to fathers, who often feel that they have no real chance of a fair hearing in traditional legal proceedings. Most industrialized countries have introduced 'no fault' divorce as a means of eliminating adversarial procedures that benefited only the attorneys, but this has yet to be followed by widespread changes in the way decisions about custody and child support are reached. Divorce mediation represents a step in the right direction.

HEALTH PRACTICES

Particularly with respect to pre- and perinatal health care practices, there has been a dramatic increase in the opportunities for paternal participation in the last decade. As Russell and Radin (Chapter 9) point out, for example, an increasing number of hospitals throughout the Western world now permit, and some even encourage, fathers to attend the delivery of their children, although there are no good recent statistics on the proportion of eligible fathers who are present in the delivery room. Contrary to the alarmist warnings of hospital administrators and conservative obstetricians, furthermore, no adverse medical complications have resulted. Indeed, although good empirical documentation is lacking, most fathers apparently feel profoundly moved by the experience and feel that it helps them establish closer relationships to their children. Further, recent reports suggest that the presence of a support person may substantially reduce the length of labor and the occurrence of obstetrical complications (Sosa, Kennell, Klaus, Robertson, & Urrutia, 1980). The more recent trend in the U.S. toward allowing fathers into surgery for cesarean section deliveries has also been well received by both mothers and fathers. Overall, the humanization of birthing practices has permitted parents and children to share a profound emotional experience, with both medically and psychologically positive consequences.

However, paternal participation in childbirth and delivery is usually not followed by the encouragement of or education of fathers for postnatal child care. Most hospitals, for example, show new *mothers* how to bathe, dress, change, carry, and feed their newborns; these skills are seldom taught to fathers, even though they have probably had less experience with infants and thus have a greater need for training. Parke and his colleagues (1980) have shown that brief training in newborn care indeed increases paternal participation in child care and has a beneficial impact on fathers' attitudes toward their children. This suggests that, at minimal cost, the same support and parent education now provided for mothers could be provided to new fathers. Even if most of the fathers do not intend to become primary caretakers or to be highly involved in child care, many fathers would benefit from training in child care and parenting skills that are traditionally denied to them because this would improve their familiarity with and understanding of their children, while enhancing the fathers' sense of effectance and competence as parents. Like childcare classes, postnatal support groups usually limit membership to new mothers, often on the grounds that the presence of men would inhibit discussion and embarrass those who wished to nurse during group meetings. The net impact of these omissions is to inhibit male participation in child care, even though they may seem rather trivial in themselves. In addition, we also need discussion groups in which fathers' attitudes, feelings, aspirations, and fears can be openly and freely discussed.

Just as the humanization of birthing practices has not led to less discriminatory postnatal practices, so the inclusion of fathers at delivery has not led to changes in policies regarding the hospitalization of children. For example, although many hospitals in the U.S. now permit parents to remain overnight to comfort frightened and sick young children, most hospitals still limit this opportunity to mothers. Again, the message to young fathers is rather clear. In the absence of any obvious reason for this proscription, it would be more equitable for hospitals to permit ''parents'' to sleep over and let parents themselves decide which one should stay. Even if most couples decide that it would be better for mothers rather than fathers to stay over, the option should be available to couples who might choose differently, as well as to single fathers.

The same open-mindedness could be beneficial in regard to regular health maintenance. Many clinics have extended their hours so as to accommodate working parents, and this may eliminate one of the barriers to paternal involvement in their children's health care. However, pediatric clinics continue to focus attention on mothers. They send reminders of appointments to mothers, circulate brochures that are aimed primarily at mothers, and even furnish their waiting rooms with women's magazines. At no real cost, clinics could clearly signal their acceptance of participation by fathers—not as curiosities or exceptions, but as full participants in the health care of their children.

EDUCATION

In the educational arena, discrimination is evident both in regard to expectations concerning parents as well as in the curriculum offered to pupils. On the first score, we can point to practices like: scheduling parent-teacher conferences during working hours, often at short notice (a practice that discriminates against employed parents of both sexes); sending notes to, and communicating with, mothers in cases of problematic behavior; and implicitly assuming that highly involved or primary caretaking fathers necessarily provide care and supervision of inferior quality. In Israel, for example, the assumption that mothers alone are involved in their children's education is so strong that in an ironic quirk it is mothers rather than fathers who usually take turns protecting schools against attacks by terrorists. Even in the traditionally organized families, which still constitute the vast majority, greater efforts could be made to include fathers in school-related activities in which their talents and skills could be useful: coaching of sports; maintenance of grounds, equipment, and buildings; and presentations to classes about the type of work they do. In addition, fathers' presentations on their work would help eliminate one of the factors which, according to Bronfenbrenner (1970), has increased parent-child (especially father-child) alienation within the family. Such efforts would have substantive as well as symbolic value to the extent that they implicitly recognize that many children do have two parents and that both may be eager to participate in the child's education if given the opportunity. It is interesting that several programs for severely

handicapped children have recently decided that parental intervention is more effective and parental participation easier to maintain when fathers as well as
mothers are involved in the program.

As far as the curriculum is concerned, we are impressed by recent attempts in a
few 'avant garde' schools to provide courses in child care and child development
to preadolescents of both sexes. Ideally, such courses would begin during the
years when norms about the inappropriateness of male involvement in child care
have yet to be internalized. The point is not to transmit the message that boys
should be caretakers, but that baby care can actually be fun and is an option boys
might like to have open to them. Such remedial efforts are especially necessary
because boys are often excluded from the activities (doll care; babysitting; horse
and pet care) in which girls learn and practice nurturant skills that facilitate their
later adoption of parenting roles. Finally, efforts should be made to increase the
number of men employed as volunteers, caretakers, aides, and teachers in
daycare programs, preschools, and regular schools by raising salary levels and
the status of teaching positions as well as by curricular changes that suggest child
care or teaching as desirable occupations for men. The availability of salient
models of male nurturance may do as much to increase the likelihood that boys
will consider adopting such roles themselves as will didactic courses designed to
transmit childcare skills, especially if the latter are taught by women.

There are two significant problems that may inhibit the elimination of sex discrimination in the educational arena. The first is the widespread fear about men
in childcare roles, particularly when their charges are not their own children. The
folk belief that men are more likely to molest, abuse, or neglect children helps
maintain popular fears about the undesirability of male teachers and caretakers in
many parts of the world. Remarkably, similar concerns are sometimes voiced
even today about highly involved fathers. The second problem is the likelihood
of home versus school conflict if the egalitarian attitudes taught at school contrast
with the more traditional attitudes, values, and behaviors of the parents. Up to
now, this problem has been avoided by ensuring that schools remain, by and
large, bastions of conservative values—a practice that counteracts the efforts of
"modern" parents. The school system, in other words, is unlikely to change unless and until there is widespread, popular, pressure for change.

Parent education is another arena in which efforts could be made to include
fathers, either with their partners or in special classes focused on fathers. Here it
is not sufficient simply to permit men to attend; it may be necessary to focus
recruitment efforts specifically on men if substantial enrollment is to be
achieved. Again, it is important that the instructors of such courses remain sensitive to the fact that there are many ways in which fathers may express their involvement in the family, and that all of these—however traditional or
nontraditional—are legitimate and worthy of encouragement.

SOCIAL SERVICES

As Wolins suggests in Chapter 7, human service professionals tend to consider fathers as problematic or irrelevant components of families rather than as assets. Jaffe (Chapter 8) too notes that fathers are the "forgotten clients" of social service agencies. Although professionals in social service agencies emphasize the centrality of "the family," intervention is usually aimed at women and children rather than families. "Enrichment" programs for "disadvantaged" families, for example, are usually designed for, and serve, mothers and their children. In their absence, however, fathers and husbands are often labeled as irresponsible, uncooperative troublemakers by professionals eager to explain or understand their female clients' circumstances. Both diagnosis and intervention would surely be easier if social services were made accessible to men, women, and families.

Unfortunately, social service professionals, like those in the health, education, legal, and employment sectors, reflect the values and norms of society—values and norms that tend to ignore the needs and importance of fathers. However, to the extent that human service professionals provide advocacy assistance and social mediation while serving as "social monitors" and social change agents, they may play an especially important role in the design of new programs and emphases. Thus their reeducation may be critical.

In order to make social service facilities more family-focused and more flexibly responsive to the needs of men as well as women, changes may be needed in the recruitment, training, development, and behavior of social service professionals. First, more men should be recruited into the helping professions, especially those like social work, which are now predominantly female occupations. Regardless of their gender, furthermore, the flexibility and tolerance of those being admitted for training should be assessed. Second, training programs need to emphasize not only the potential importance (for good or ill) of fathers and husbands, but also the need for sensitive adaptation to either different or changing values and norms. Social service professionals have an unfortunate tendency to regard deviation from middle-class norms as indices of ill health, and to be quite rigid in their beliefs about who should be served and in what ways. They need to recognize that many legitimate family forms exist and may need their professional assistance. Third, the value of community outreach programs should be underscored, because such efforts are not only more sensitive to the needs of families but are also more likely to encounter fathers. This gives the outreach professional the opportunity to understand the family constellation as a whole. Greater flexibility in working hours would, of course, also be important in this regard. Finally, if the goal is to encourage equal opportunities for men and women, agencies themselves should aim to set an example by employing more women in those settings (e.g., correctional institutions) that are currently dominated by men, more men in those settings (e.g., community social service agencies) currently dominated by women, and individuals of both sexes at all levels of the professional and bureaucratic hierarchies.

PUBLIC POLICY

The elimination of discrimination in the public sector is of immense importance, given that the number of people dependent on this sector ranges from about a third in capitalist countries like the United States to more than one-half in socialist or mixed economies like the United Kingdom and Sweden. The private sector is unlikely to heed antidiscrimination legislation if the government itself pays only lip service to these regulations. Further, because so much of the private sector is dependent on government grants and contracts, a requirement that sex discrimination be eliminated before contracts can be awarded might have a dramatic impact on recruitment, on-the-job training opportunities, basic pay scales, college admissions, etc.

Among the most destructive public policy practices is the well-known administrative edict of the U.S. welfare system requiring that benefits to mothers and children be *reduced* when there is a male in the home, whether or not he is employed. Although designed to encourage men to seek employment rather than remain on welfare, the clearest effect has been to encourage desertion. Practices such as these, which inhibit paternal involvement, need to be eliminated. At no additional cost, furthermore, welfare support could be offered to any parent (regardless of sex) who needs to stay home with young children. Such a sex-neutral policy would allow the most employable partner to seek work. Surely, families will become self-supporting more rapidly if the most employable of the parents, regardless of sex, can seek employment without jeopardizing access to essential social services and payments.

Regulatory authorities apparently forget fairly often that equal opportunity legislation is designed to prohibit discrimination against either men or women. Although discrimination against women is more widespread and pervasive, discrimination against men is just as inequitable, and its existence may facilitate the continuation of discrimination against women. For example, the denial of parental leave to fathers forces mothers to take it, thus contributing to the notion that women are less reliable as employees and hence should be paid and trained less. If more fathers took childcare leave, it would eliminate one of the more pervasive rationalizations for discriminatory pay practices. Along with other changes of the sort described in this chapter, it would also make the application of antidiscrimination legislation consistent with the ostensible intent of the law. To our knowledge, only in Sweden has a serious and thoroughgoing attempt been made to eliminate the various forms of sex discrimination by requiring that all public and private benefits and pay scales be neutral with respect to sex. As a result, the sex-related pay differentials in Sweden today are accounted for largely by differences in seniority, education, and training rather than by sex per se (Gustafsson, 1979). Few other countries have approached this level.

CONCLUSION

In this brief chapter, we have reviewed the sorts of changes that could be made in several social and institutional sectors in order to increase the opportunity for male participation in child care and the family. Most of the suggestions we have made are not original, as they have already been implemented by employers, educators, health care providers, and legislators who are committed to the goals of equal opportunity and the elimination of discrimination on the basis of sex. Indeed one goal of the Fatherhood Project, which was described by Levine and his colleagues in Chapter 6, is to identify innovative practices designed to facilitate paternal involvement in child care and to determine the circumstances in which each of these practices appears to be more or less successful. Obviously, any organization must consider the specific needs of its clientele or work force before changing its operating procedures; our goal here has simply been to describe some of the changes that could be considered. Each of the changes we have mentioned seems likely to have an immediate and direct effect on paternal participation or is known to have been at least somewhat successful in past applications. Equally important, each of the innovations we have discussed could be implemented at minimal cost to the organization, government, or employer. This is probably of special importance today since economic conditions throughout the world militate against costly innovations and expensive social engineering.

We should emphasize once again that our appeal is for an increase in the opportunities for male involvement in child care and the family; we would not recommend or mandate this as a universally desirable goal. So long as a significant number—no matter how small a minority—of men might take advantage of the opportunity to become more involved in their families, and thus enhance their own satisfaction, the general welfare is enhanced, because changes that increase the opportunities available to all men should not reduce the life satisfaction of those who choose not to take advantage of these opportunities. Policies and practices that implicitly or explicitly restrict male involvement in child care significantly limit the freedom of choice that is the goal of any democratic society.

REFERENCES

Bronfenbrenner, U. *Two worlds of childhood*. New York: Russell Sage Foundation, 1970.

Chambers, D. *Making fathers pay: The enforcement of child support*. Chicago: University of Chicago Press, 1979.

Gustafsson, S. Women and work in Sweden. *Working Life in Sweden*, 1979, (Whole No. 15).

Hess, R. D., & Camara, K. A. Post-divorce family relationships as mediating factors in the consequences of divorce for children. *Journal of Social Issues*, 1979, *35*, 79–96.

Parke, R. D., Hymel, S., Power, T., & Tinsley, B. Fathers and risk: A hospital-based model of intervention. In D. Sawin & R. C. Hawkins (Eds.), *Psychosocial risks during pregnancy and early infancy*. New York: Brunner/Mazel, 1980.

Pleck, J. H., & Rustad, M. *Husbands' and wives' time in family work and paid work in the 1975–76 study of time use*. Unpublished manuscript, Wellesley College, 1980.

Sosa, R., Kennell, J., Klaus, M., Robertson, S., & Urrutia, J. The effect of a supportive companion on perinatal problems, length of labor, and mother-infant interaction. *New England Journal of Medicine*, 1980, *303*, 597–600.

Author Index

Snyder, L. M., 240, *246*
Sokolowska, M., 243, *246*
Solnit, A. J., 57, *96*
Solomon, D., 197, *218*
Sonquist, H., 208, *217*
S.O.S., 132, *137*
Sosa, R., 252, *258*
Spanier, G. B., 179, *190,* 220, *232*
Spelke, E., 68, 77, *98, 99,* 191, *218*
Spence, J. T., 159, *165*
Spencer, J., 129, *137*
Sperry, B. M., 196, *214*
Spindler, G. D., 15, *22*
Spinetta, J. J., 120, *128*
Spradley, J. P., 15, *22*
Stafford, F. P., 171, *188*
Stafford, L. M., 18, *22*
Stephens, W. N., 243, *246*
Staples, R., 102, *111,* 209, 210, *218*
Statens Offentliga Ufredningar, 45, 47, *51*
Steinmetz, S. K., 178, *190*
Steinberg, J., 75, *97,* 145, 152, 158, *164,* 206, *215*
Stevenson, N., 118, *127*
Stone, P. J., 65, *99*
Strelitz, Z., 151, *165,* 223, 227, 231, *233*
Strodtbeck, F. L., 240, *245*
Strumilin, S. G., 237, *246*
Sudia, C., 119, *127,* 184, *188*
Sudia, C. E., 61, *96*
Susman, E. J., 195, *214*
Sutton-Smith, B., 197, *216*
Svenska Arbetsgivare Föreningen, 43, *51*
Swedish Institute, 41, *51*
Szalai, A., 65, *99*

T

Tasch, R. J., 73, *99*
Tauber, M. A., 199, *218*
Taylor, C. M., 83, *96*
Thoman, E. B., 71, *97*
Thomas, M. H., 195, *218*
Thompson, R. A., 67, *99*
Thornton, A., 168, *190*
Tiger, L., 220, *233*
Tinsley, B., 252, *258*
Tinsley, B. R., 66, 67, *98,* 159, *164*
Todres, R., 83, *99,* 130, *137,* 223, *233*
Tower, A., 195, *214*

Tronick, E., 65, 68, *100*
Turner, J. B., 134, *137*

U

Unit for Judicial and Social Welfare Statistics, 42, *51*
Urrutia, 252, *258*
U.S. Bureau of the Census, 115, 124, *128*
U.S. Congress House Committee on the Judiciary, 119, *128*
U.S. Department of Commerce, Bureau of the Census, 125, *128,* 170, *190*
U.S. Department of HEW, 115, 116, 119, 120, *128*
U.S. Department of Labor, Bureau of Labor Statistics, 170, *190*
U.S. Department of Labor, Women's Bureau, 170, 182, *190*

V

Valsiner, J., 237, *246*
Veevers, J. E., 224, *233*
Velasquez, C. P., 209, *218*
Velasquez, J. S., 209, *218*
Vergeiner, W., 243, *246*
Veroff, J., 168, 169, 180, 181, *190*
von der Lippe, A., 198, *213*

W

Wald, M., 57, *99*
Walker, K., 65, *99,* 142, *165,* 171, *190*
Wall, S., 68, 71, *95,* 206, *212*
Wallace, A. F. C., 238, *246*
Wallerstein, J., 78, 80, 81, 82, *97, 99*
Walshok, M. L., 180, *190*
Walters, R. H., 193, 198, *212*
Warshak, R. A., 82, 83, 87, 88, 89, 90, *99,* 191, 200, 201, 206, 207, 209, *218*
Waters, E., 68, 71, *95,* 206, *212*
Watson, C., 151, *163,* 204, *213*
Watson, M. A., 199, *218*
Weinfeld, F. D., 204, *214*
Weintraub, D., 240, *246*
Weintraub, M., 72, *100,* 193, *216*
Weitzman, L. J., 55, 56, 57, *100*

Subject Index

Marital relationship, 133, 139–140, 149, 155, 171–172, 177, 178–179, 183, 184, 211, 225

Marital satisfaction, 163, 182, 183

Marriage, 28, 84

Marriage, attitudes towards, 53

Masculinity, 114–115, 117, 151, 152, 158, 159, 195, 196, 204, 204–205, 207 (*see also* Sex roles; Male roles)

Maternal

custody, 54, 61

earning power, 185

education, 45–46

employment, 4, 65, 75, 139, 169, 170–173, 174, 174–175, 176, 181, 182, 184–185, 185, 223, 228, 229, 243 (*see also* Female employment)

instinct, 156

nurturance, 53, 56, 63–64, 86 (*see also* Nurturance)

role, 20, 74, 160, 176 (*see also* Parenting; Child care; Childrearing; Sex roles; Traditional families; Nontraditional families)

Maternity benefits, 40–41

Maternity leave, 3, 29, 32, 34, 229, 249 (*see also* Parental leave)

Mathematical ability, 196, 197 (*see also* Academic achievement)

Mental health, 174–175

Middle class families, 49, 154–155, 174, 179, 200, 202, 203, 208–209, 209–210, 210, 222, 255–256 (*see also* Social class differences; Economic conditions)

Military service, 61

Minorities, 105, 106, 107, 107–108, 108, 109, 209–210 (*see also* Ethnic differences; Social class differences)

Modeling, 16, 157–158, 195, 205–206, 207, 239, 242

Models, traditional, 16–17 (*see also* Traditional families)

Models, unavailability of, 236–237

Moral development, 16, 80–81, 102, 178

Mother surrogate role, 132

Mother-child conflict, 79

Mother-child interaction, 74, 77, 80, 172–173 (*see also* Parenting; Caretaking; Childrearing; Traditional families; Nontraditional families)

Mother-child relationship, 3–4, 32–33, 63–64, 64–65, 68, 74, 79, 84, 114–115, 146, 180

Mother-custody families, 64, 79–80, 83, 84, 88, 200 (*see also* Divorce)

Mother-father relationships, 197

Mother-infant interaction, 65, 67, 69, 70, 74, 75, 172–173

Mother-infant relationship, 68–69, 71

Mother-son relationship, 79–80, 92

Motherhood, satisfaction of, 180–181

N

Noncustodial father, 61

Noncustodial parent, loss of, 78–79

Noncustodial parent-child relationship, 88

Noncustody seekers, 84, 85

Nonfamilial environments, 123

Nontraditional families, 15, 61, 74–77, 160, 203, 206, 209

Nontraditional male roles, 4–5

Nurturance, Parental, 23–24, 29, 33–34, 35, 55–56, 86, 110, 123, 124, 125, 151, 152, 156–157, 159, 178, 183, 195, 196, 196–197, 198, 200–201, 201–202, 203, 204, 205, 224, 250–251, 254

O

Occupational

commitment, 10, 182, 185

responsibilities, 78–79

roles, 79, 178, (*see also* Female employment; Maternal employment; Family income)

P

Parent education, 107, 159, 229, 237–238, 254

Parent-child alienation, 253–254

Parent-child interaction, 76–77, 82, 86–87, 88–89, 219

Parent-child relationship, 58, 83, 88, 93–94, 148–149, 155 (*see also* Mother-child relationship; Father-child relationship)

Parental Insurance System (Sweden), 8–9, 39–52, 104, 108–109, 248

Parental

attitudes, 155

behavior, 75, 76, 198 (*see also* Parenting; Child care; Child rearing; Caretaking)